Central Asia

Also by Hafeez Malik

Central Asia

◉ ◉ ◉

Its Strategic Importance and Future Prospects

Edited by Hafeez Malik

ST. MARTIN'S PRESS
NEW YORK

© Hafeez Malik 1994

First published in the United States of America 1994

Printed in the United States of America

ISBN 0-312-10370-0

Library of Congress Cataloging-in-Publication Data

Central Asia : its strategic importance and future prospects / edited
    by Hafeez Malik.
        p. cm.
    Includes bibliographical references and index.
    ISBN 0-312-10370-0
    1. Asia, Central—Politics and government. 2. Asia, Central—
Foreign relations. 3. Asia, Central—Strategic aspects.
4. Geopolitics—Asia, Central. I. Malik, Hafeez.
DK859.5.C46 1993
327.58—dc20   93-9083
                                                         CIP

Interior design by Digital Type & Design

C·O·N·T·E·N·T·S

P·R·E·F·A·C·E

In 1989, after one of my research visits to the Soviet Union, and especially to the Central Asian republics, I concluded in a preface to *Domestic Determinants of Soviet Foreign Policy Towards South Asia and the Middle East* (1990) that "Muslim nationalities in the Soviet Union have entered a new phase of self-assertion which is not only religious and cultural, but also has a degree of political significance. This new Muslim self-assertion, it is hypothesized, would call for the restructuring of their relations with Moscow, and the Muslim world." I estimated privately that the Central Asian republics would attain full freedom and sovereignty by the end of the twentieth century. Their unexpected freedom as a consequence of the Soviet Union's disintegration by the end of 1991 was the biggest surprise of the century to all specialists.

Three centuries of Russian expansion were undone in a few months, from August to December 1991. Suddenly, Central Asia burst upon the political consciousness of the West and the Islamic East. In the wake of this development, the British geographer Sir Halford Mackinder's theory of geopolitics (1904), which had projected Central Asia as the core region of Eurasia, acquired new importance in international politics. Also, the political dynamics within both Russia and Central Asia called for a serious analysis.

Consequently, I organized an international seminar on October 30-31, 1992, at Villanova University to examine three dimensions: (1) the Russian conquest of Central Asia and its impact on the Turkic Muslim populations, which are indigenous to this region; (2) ethnic conflicts spawned by the collapse of the Soviet state, and (3) the emergence of new interactions among the Central Asian states, Russia, the United States, and the Southwest Asian states of Iran, Afghanistan, and Pakistan. The Soviet war (1979-1989) in Afghanistan had a profound impact on the Russians' psyche, and precipitated the collapse of their morale. To help us fully grasp this phenomenon, Professor Yuri V. Gankovsky, a well-known Russian scholar, and his colleague at the Institute of Oriental Studies in Moscow—a former major general of the KGB—Victor Spolnikov, made valuable contributions. Two Central Asian scholars, one from Uzbekistan, Abdujabbar A. Abduvakhitov, and the other from Tajikistan, Mavlon Makhamov, presented equally insightful analyses of the current conflicts in Central Asia. The addition of indigenous perspectives to this collective endeavor is the significant aspect of this volume.

The political dynamics in Russia and in Central Asia are seeking new directions as the options of foreign and security policies are hammered out. The Central Asian republics have begun to really feel like independent states. They are in the process of developing their own currencies, custom posts, armies and embassies, and borders. Finally, would these states jettison economic and security links with Russia, which were forged during the Soviet/Russian rule? Would they build new relations with the southwest Asian states, and/or with Turkey? These issues are also having a profound impact on Russia, where the government and private thinking are reacting to the environmental imperatives. Some emerging foreign policy orientations are discernable in Russia and in the Central Asian states.

In Russia, extensive debates have continued among the Atlanticists, who perceive Russia's future with the West. This also implies a free and open market economy, freedom of assembly, speech, and conscience, and guaranteed civil rights—the hallmarks of western liberal democracy. Rightly, the Atlanticists believe that this new foreign policy direction would attract substantial economic aid from the West. Of course, the price is the abandoning of independent foreign policy that might conflict with American leadership. Against the Atlanticists are arrayed the conservatives—former Communists turned nationalists to arch conservatives.

To them, the loss of the Soviet empire is most painful. The arch conservatives project Eurasia as a catalyst to revive Russia. They define Eurasia as lands occupied by Russia and other states that have replaced the Soviet Union. Culturally, they perceive Russia neither in Europe nor in Asia, but as "a distinctive Eurasian cosmos" in symbiosis of one combination or another: (1) Slavic-Turkic; (2) Irano-Turanian; and (3) Ugro-Mongol. These conservatives deride the Atlanticists for their current foreign policy, which consigns Russians "to another bout of suffering from an inferiority complex," not only in relations with the West, but also with respect to Japan and China. Also, they see danger to Russia from the independent Central Asian states because, through the latter, politicized Islam has penetrated "the lower and middle Volga regions" including Bashkirtostan and Tatarstan.

Looking at Russia's problems pragmatically rather than ideologically, the Yeltsin administration pressed ahead with an economic and customs union with Ukraine and Belarus in July 1993. The three Slavic states account for more than 70 percent of the old Soviet Union's population and even more of its industrial wealth and sophisticated technology. The prime ministers of Russia, Ukraine, and Belarus stated that other states of the former Soviet Union may also join, but on the terms the Slavic states have laid down. Ukraine, however, perceived the "union" as more of a European community than a new Russian Federation or empire.

Which way would Central Asian states gravitate: to southwest Asia and/or Turkey or back to Moscow? Despite a degree of economic collaboration with Russia, the Central Asian states are unlikely to move back to the Russian empire. Two trends are visible among the Central Asians' relations: (1) the revival and consolidation of the Central Asian states, and (2) Pan-Turkism, which also embraces Turkey, Tatars, Bashkirs, and various Turkic collectivities in the caucuses.

In January 1993 the presidents of the Central Asian states held a summit meeting in Tashkent and then announced that all necessary conditions had been met for the formation of a commonwealth of Central Asian states. Interestingly enough, the agreement to hold the Tashkent summit was reached in October 1992 in Ankara, where the Turkic presidents of the Central Asian states had held a meeting.

Encouraged by the United States and Turkey, the Central Asian republics decided in January 1993 to establish an intergovernmental coalition to be known as the Central Asian Regional Union (CARU). Clearly, the CARU was formed on the basis of their common ethnicity, Turkism. The founders also expressed a commitment to the concept of creating a greater Turkistan and the so-called Turkic belt, which would encompass a vast geopolitical expanse extending from the Mediterranean Sea to Eastern Siberia, including the Turkic Muslim autonomous entities and territories of Russia, namely, Tatarstan, Bashkirtostan, the Volga region, and northern caucuses.

The CARU not only rang alarm bells in Iran, but also alerted the Kremlin in Moscow. The Russians complained that the newly established alliance violated a prior agreement on a single strategic defense space within the Commonwealth of Independent States (CIS) and called into question the possibility of implementing the Collective Security Treaty of May 15, 1992, in Asia under the aegis of Russia. The CARU was applauded by the United States, Turkey, and according to Russians, by Saudi Arabia and even by Israel. Russia thought that China and India were not pleased.

The CARU appeared to follow these objectives: (1) to demarcate Turkic ethno-cultural space from the Slavik components of the CIS; (2) to provide the Turkic community of nations a firm geostrategic position in Central Asia between Russia and China, for greater political maneuverability; (3) to implement regional economic integration. Provisions were also made for the CARU members to eventually leave the ruble zone;

(4) to integrate the CARU members into a Turkic common market under the aegis of Turkey and within the framework of the Economic Cooperation Organization (ECO), linking the Central Asian states with Pakistan, Iran, and Turkey; and (5) to create a single strategic defense space with military and technical assistance from Russia, Turkey, and Pakistan.

The economic role of Central Asia and Turkey is ideologically explained in cultural terms as well. The president of the Assembly of the Turkic Peoples, Rafael Ferdivich Mohammetdinov, who lives in Kazan, Tatarstan, presented the Turkic belt between the East and the West as a middle ground. The West, according to him, includes the United States, Europe, and even Japan; the East encompassed Arab countries, Iran, Afghanistan, and Pakistan. In his perception, the Turkic world is in the middle, linking the East and the West.

Much the same kind of formulations were expressed by Prime Minister Suleyman Demirel of Turkey when he visited Pakistan in 1992. He emphasized Turkey's efforts in establishing world peace as building a bridge between the 200 million people of Europe and 300 million people of ECO and the Middle East countries.

Is Pan-Turkism a genuine yearning of the Turkic people for political unity or is it simply a new grand strategy of the United States in which Turkey is playing the role of an ideological surrogate? Only time will tell.

One strand of U.S. foreign policy is already discernable—its desire to isolate Iran and Afghanistan and to discourage the Central Asian states from getting heavily involved with these two states. This policy is unlikely to succeed for two obvious reasons: First, geography and history are in the favor of Iran and Afghanistan; second, Turkey's economic and industrial resources are inadequate for the Central Asian states, which are desperately in need of vast help to restructure their economies and to cope with the Soviet-created ecological disasters in their territories.

Moreover, Turkey is unlikely to entangle itself in the morass of ethnic conflicts in Central Asia, which are likely to spread in the foreseeable future. Despite its Islamic rhetoric, Iran has been reluctant to involve itself in the war between Armenia and Azerbaijan over Nagorno-Karabagh. In fact, Iran has followed an even-handed policy between these two states. Yet, in the face of U.S. opposition Iran, Afghanistan, and to a certain degree, Pakistan are likely to reinforce and expand their relations with the Central Asian states. Consequently, the ECO is likely to play a fairly dynamic role in this strategically important region.

Finally, it might be of some interest to note that the collapse of the Soviet Union has inspired a powerful quest in the United States for the identity of a new enemy. From now on, it is projected, "the clash of civilizations will dominate global politics." Recently, an American scholar who has worked in foreign policy matters for the U.S. Department of State and the National Security Council eloquently speculated on this theme. Interaction between Islam and the West is seen by him as "a clash of civilizations" that has been "going on for 1,300 years." Central Asia, consequently, is another Islamic region that theoretically becomes "another enemy." If this trend of "strategic thinking" and the need to protect the Judeo-Christian world against the "Islamic world's onslaught" continues, the relation between the two worlds and their civilizations would revert back to the period of the Crusades. What a tragic development that would be!

The seminar on Central Asia on October 30-31, 1992, was held in honor of Villanova University's sesquicentennial celebration. Also, it was sponsored by the Pakistan-American Foundation. Villanova University has not only been an intellectual haven for me, but it has generously supported over the last 18 years the *Journal of South Asian and Middle Eastern Studies*, the Pakistan-American Foundation, and the American Institute of Pakistan Studies, which have also received generous support from the Ministry of Education of the Government of Pakistan.

I am equally indebted to Edmund J. Dobbin (president), Lawrence Gallen (Vice President of Academic Affairs), and Kail C. Ellis (Dean of Arts and Sciences, and Director of the Center for Contemporary Arab and Islamic Studies of Villanova University). Fr. Ellis also presided over one of the sessions of the seminar, and Dr. Javid Iqbal, former Justice of the Supreme Court of Pakistan, presided over another session and managed to keep the level of discourse very high between hotly contested political views about Russia's role in the former Soviet Central Asian republics. Secretary-General of the Ministry of Foreign Affairs of Pakistan, Akram Zaki, delivered a keynote address highlighting Pakistan's foreign policy initiatives in Central Asia.

Among my friends, I single out Nadia Barsoum, who helped me in many ways to make this seminar a successful enterprise. Some of my friends, both in the United States and abroad, have always been a source of encouragement and support: Yuri V. Gankovsky, Riaz Malik, Afaq Haydar, Jack Schrems, Naim Rathore, Lori Kephart, Syed Abid Ali, Zaheer Chaudhry, M. Imtiaz Ali, Riaz Ahmad, Stanley Wolpert, Muhammad Ali Chaudhry, Igor V. Khalevinski, and (Akhuna) Khalil Ilyas. I value their friendship and cherish their affection. My administrative assistant, Susan K. Hausman, handled the details of the seminar with her usual efficiency and her imaginative skills.

Hafeez Malik
VILLANOVA UNIVERSITY

Central Asia

▲ ▽ ▲

1

Central Asia's Geopolitical Significance and Problems of Independence: An Introduction

◆

Hafeez Malik

With the disintegration of the Soviet Union in 1991, a new chapter opened in the struggle for power between the Central Asians and their former overlords, the Russians. At the core of their relations lurks a psychological dimension, which, at the risk of oversimplification, can be spotlighted in the Russians' ingrained sense of inferiority toward the West and their obvious feeling of superiority over the Central Asians and their cultural and religious heritage.

The Eurasian steppe, which in 1904 Sir Halford Mackinder called the "heartland of the world," has undergone political and cultural transformation since time immemorial as a result of the interaction between the Russians and various Turkic ethnic groups that originated in Central Asia. In the eighth century the Turkic tribes of Khazars settled about the mouth of the Volga and farther west. Some of them adopted the Jewish faith, some became Muslim, and some were converted to Christianity.[1] The Khazars' expansion was halted by the Slavs, whose descendants now inhabit Russia. Eventually these Slavs split into three groups: (1) the Great Russians (in present-day European Russia); (2) the Little Russians (in the Ukraine); and (3) the White Russians (in contemporary Belarus). In 1992 Ukraine played the leading role in hastening the Soviet Union's demise, thus lowering the Russians' international power. There is obviously not much love lost among the three Slavic cousins.

Historically, the Russian state began to grow when the Great Russians emigrated toward the region of the upper course of the Volga and its tributaries, where Suzdal became the first capital. Vladimir near the Volga was the second capital in 1157, and finally, Moscow. Within the twelfth and the thirteenth centuries the armies of Chinggis Khan (1162?-1227) and his immediate descendants, hailing from Mongolia, conquered most of Eurasia, especially Russia, in addition to smashing the Muslim Abbasid Baghdad and Iran. By 1400 Russia comprised no more than the land within a radius of roughly 250 miles around Suzdel.[2] The Mongol general Batu Khan, who conquered the Russian lands from 1238 to 1240, was the grandson of Chinggis Khan. Neither he nor his grandfather was a Tatar or a Muslim, yet according to Russian historiography, during their 250 years of domination Russia was under the "Tatar yoke," a term understood now as synonymous with Muslim rule. The Tatar people were the traditional enemy of the Mongols; and in revenge Chinggis Khan slaughtered them wholesale.[3]

The only extant history of Chinggis Khan's life and rule, the *Tobechbian*, gives a detailed account of this grisly slaughter. Certainly, the Tatars were soldiers in Batu Khan's army, because Mongols always augmented their ethnic Mongol army by drafting the youth of conquered people. When the Mongols in "Russia" converted to Islam cannot be stated definitively; it is known, however, that Batu's son, Berke Khan (ruled 1256-1266), had adopted Islam. Moreover, for the Bulgars (or the Volga Tatars), Islam was the center "around which the spiritual life of the Bulgar State [around Kazen] developed after the tenth century."[4] Evidently, with the passage of time, Mongols and other Turkic populations came to acquire the ethnonym of Tatar.

What had set the Mongols apart was their invention of cavalry: "fast-moving men on horseback using compound bows to direct a withering passage of arrows at their enemies from a distance."[5] Their power became invincible in the thirteenth century under Chinggis Khan and his three descendants: Ogodei (reigned 1228 to 1241), Mongke (1251 to 1259), and Batu (d. 1255). According to Nicholas Riassonovsky, this phase was the first traumatic historical experience for Russia in its encounter with Central Asia and especially Mongolia. However, by the middle of the eighteenth century, "revolutions in technology and transportation had shifted the military balance of power"[6] in the favor of Russia, and then Central Asia was in retreat. In 1980 Russia celebrated the 600th anniversary of its victory over the Tatars in 1480. This was the second epoch in the historical struggle for power between Russians and Tatars. The third one got under way with the dissolution of the Soviet Union in 1991.

A word of explanation about the Russians' feeling of superiority over the Central Asians and their sense of inferiority toward the West is in order.

During the process of the Russian conquest of Central Asia in the nineteenth century, Russian ideologues, historians, geographers, and proponents of the Eurasianist view of Russia's manifest destiny evolved a distinctly civilizing role for Russia in Central Asia. This role, they believed, would also lessen the burden of Russian inferiority in relation to the West. Fyodor M. Dostoyevski articulated this *weltanschauung* par excellence:

> What is the need of the future seizure of Asia? What is our business there? This is necessary because Russia is not only in Europe, but also in Asia; because the Russian is not only a European, but also an Asiatic. Not only that; in our coming destiny, perhaps it is precisely Asia that represents our main way out. . . .
>
> In Europe, we were hangers-on and slaves, whereas to Asia we shall go as masters. In Europe, we were Asiatics, whereas in Asia we, too, are Europeans. Our civilizing mission in Asia will bribe our spirit and drive us thither. It is only necessary that the movement should start. Build two railroads: begin with the one to Siberia, and then to Central Asia, and at once you will see the consequences.[7]

Today the Russian sense of inferiority in relation to the West reflects itself in the ongoing debates on foreign policy between the so-called Atlanticists and the Eurasianists, which I observed in 1992 in Moscow. The Atlanticists or westernizers believed that Russia must join western civilization and cut its losses in the East. In order to restore growth of production, Russian goods must gain access to western markets, and conditions must be created within Russia for foreign aid and private investment. This economic imperative, the Atlanticists argued, determined Russia's foreign policy strategy, the essence of which is the decisive rejection of Russia's opposition to the world community. The argument, shorn of its niceties, implied Russia's subordinate role to the West at the global level.

Evidently, the Eurasianists are most vocal in Vice-President Aleksandr V. Rutskoi's Free Russia Peoples Party. They have argued that the United States, Japan, Germany, and other western states would help Russia only "to remain afloat, but hardly to embark on any lengthy autonomous voyage." They urged Russian leadership to turn to Saudi Arabia and the Persian Gulf states and to join the Organization of Petroleum Exporting Countries (OPEC). Finally, almost in Dostoyevski's language, they appealed to the Russian national pride: "Wouldn't it be better to be a leader of the Third World than an outsider in the First World?"

In reacting to these Russian national dilemmas and the failures of the Commonwealth of Independent States (CIS), the Communist-turned-nationalist leaders of the Central Asian states launched in 1993 the idea of a Turkistan, which in reality existed before the Bolshevik reconquest of Central Asia. Meeting on January 4 in Tashkent, the capital of Uzbekistan, they declared a set of policies that, if implemented earnestly, would establish a five-state Commonwealth of Central Asia. The Tashkent conference emphasized: (1) closer economic interaction, such as Kazakhstan's intention to send a significant portion of its crude oil to refineries in Uzbekistan and Turkmenistan and the plan to construct a railroad to Iran, giving access to the Persian Gulf and Turkey; (2) regularly monitoring the implementing of interstate treaties and agreements (to this end a council of experts was created to commence work in Alma-Ata, the capital of Kazakhstan, on January 15, 1993); (3) exchange of ambassadors by February 1, 1993; (4) an international fund to save the Aral and Caspian seas.

Finally, the so-called integrationist leader, President Nursultan Nazarbayev of Kazakhstan, stated that the CIS's ineffectual existence might lead the Central Asian states to join their own independent military political alliance.[8]

Most significantly, the catalytic force for the Tashkent conference was provided by the Turkic states' meeting of October 1992 at Ankara. Uzbekistan's president Islam Karimov objected to the unilateral postponements of the summit meetings of the CIS. Again invoking the repulsive nature of Russia's superiority syndrome over Central Asia, Karimov decried "the new elder brother" behavior and then remarked: "But we joined the CIS as equals."[9]

The seminar at Villanova University that was held on October 30-31, 1993, dealt with Russian conquest of Central Russia and the Bolshevik reconquest, the problems spawned by the Soviet Union's disintegration, and the emerging relationships between the Central Asian states, the states in Southwest Asia, and the Middle East. Last, but not least, the American dimension was highlighted, since the United States, as the sole superpower, will inevitably play a significant role in affecting the economic and security policies of the Central Asian states. The wealth of scholarship and personal insights that were brought to bear on these problems are truly impressive. Nevertheless, let it be stated once again that when dealing with Russian-Central Asian relations, Central Asian, Russian, and other non-Russian scholars, wittingly or unwittingly, brought out in their analyses the perennial theme of this superiority versus inferiority syndrome.

RUSSIAN CONQUEST AND THE BOLSHEVIK RECONQUEST OF CENTRAL ASIA AND THE ISLAMIC-NATIONAL RESPONSE

In this present volume, Seymour Becker, Stephen Blank, and Abdujabbar A. Abduvakhitov exhaustively discuss the Russian conquest, the Bolshevik reconquest of Central Asia, and the manner and style in which the Central Asian Muslims responded to the thrust of westernized Russia.

Seymour Becker, a well-known historian of Russia's expansion in Central Asia, divides his analysis into two parts. The first highlights the process of conquest in the nineteenth century, when the local military commanders often violated St. Petersburg's instructions and kept pushing forward the frontiers of the Russian empire. The second part dwells at length on the social, economic, and political policies followed by the Russian administration. By 1898 a unified Turkistan, divided into four *oblasti* (Sir Darya, Samarkand, Fergana, and Semirech'e) under the Russian imperial rule, had become a political reality. Legally classified as *inorodtsy* (aborigines), Muslims "had neither the full rights nor the same obligations as the tsars' other subjects." Justice, taxation and irrigation became the primary responsibilities of the native self-government institutions.

Attempts were also made to disrupt what Becker calls "traditional Muslim society." (Muslim traditionalism is also the central theme of Victor Spolnikov's analysis). Among the sedentary population, formal elections, instead of consensus, created local leaders and *kazis* (judges). Consequently, the buying of elections and bribing of Russian officials became a standard practice. General Von Kaufman, the first governor-general of Turkistan, however, asserted that "the obvious superiority of Russian culture over Islamic" would convince the Muslims "to abandon their barbarous customs." The foundations for the cotton monoculture, which became the bane of Uzbek economy under the Bolsheviks, was laid down; cotton occupied 36 to 38 percent of the sown area on the eve of the 1917 revolution. Already by 1911, Central Asian cotton supplied half the total needs of Russia's textile industry.

Russian immigration started to change the demographic picture of Turkistan. "Net Russian immigration was 206,000 in the decade from 1896 to 1905 and 834,000 in the period from 1906 to 1916; some 300,000 to 500,000 settlers had arrived by 1896." By the end of World War II, this trend resulted in the Kazakhs becoming a minority of 36 percent in their own state, while the Russians, Ukrainians, Volga Germans, and other European nationalities constituted the majority of population. After 1992 Russia turned the Russian settlers' question into that of human rights issues and the acme of international law and morality. The western powers are now being wooed to support the Russian contention.

These colonial policies, and especially the June 25, 1916, decree ordering the mobilization of almost half a million Muslim men for military service behind the front lines, "touched off a chain reaction of rebellion," but it was suppressed. Becker's verdict is that the Russian government was "neither honest nor efficient," and the Russians' superior attitude toward the Central Asians compounded its failures.

Stephen Blank has elaborated in his excellent analysis the theme of the Russian superiority syndrome over Central Asia and Islam. In many ways the Bolshevik policies were similar to that of tsarist administration. Blank says: ". . . Islamophobia and ambivalence to Asia are constant but dynamic factors of the Soviet period." Zinoviev, an outstanding collaborator of Lenin, who was later executed by Stalin, succinctly stated in 1920 what Blank thinks reflects the true heart of the Bolshevik orientation toward Central Asia: "We cannot do without the petroleum of Azerbaijan or the cotton of Turkistan. We take those products not as former exploiters, but as older brothers bearing the torch of civilization."

Since the advent of their rule in Turkistan, Blank feels the Bolsheviks perceived "Muslim ethnocentrism and its religious based identification" as a threat. The Pan-Islamic or Pan-Turkic trends in Turkistan raised the possibility of "a culturally homogeneous nationalist or religious bloc collaborating in the anti-Soviet uprisings that began in 1920." These developments convinced Lenin and Stalin to speed up the fragmentation of Muslim unity. This motivation led them to carve up Central Asia into six republics and to gerrymander boundaries to place diverse ethnic and linguistic groups within each republic. Subsequently, in order to create the new Soviet man, antireligious propaganda campaigns and Latinization (and then Russification) of the Turkic and Persian languages were attempted. In particular, the language policy paved the way to shattering Muslim unity.

In the last section of his analysis, Blank briefly outlines the current dynamics: (1) republican nationalism; (2) a visible Islamic resurgence, whose "implications are as yet unrevealed both culturally and politically"; (3) massive socioeconomic crisis; (4) some revival of Pan-Turkicism; and (5) a form of post-Soviet association. Finally, what is a lesson of Central Asia's Soviet experience? Blank sums it up: "The Bolshevik *folie de grandeur*."

The Muslim responses to the Russian-Soviet policies were not only periodic revolts and violent and passive resistance. The Central Asian Muslims (like their co-religionists in the India-Pakistan subcontinent and the Middle East) also recognized that while westernized Russia knew no democracy, it possessed the arsenal of modern sciences and technology and had succeeded in establishing an overwhelming political-military power over them. This phenomenon called for some degree of mutual acceptance and intellectual accommodation. This recognition spawned the Jadid (modernist) movement, which originated during tsarist rule under the leadership of Ismail Bey Gaspirali (1851-1914).

An outstanding Uzbek scholar, Abdujabbar A. Abduvakhitov (who was until recently a senior scholar at Uzbekistan's Institute of Oriental Studies at Tashkent and is currently director of the Miros [Heritage] Foundation) demonstrates that despite the physical destruction of the Jadid institutions and its intellectual leaders during the Stalinist period, the impact of the Jadid movement in Central Asia, especially in Uzbekistan, is currently visible. Gaspirali believed, Abduvakhitov rightly points out, that "modern life and capabilities were not secrets reserved for Europe and its offshoots, but were available to all societies willing to face the challenge of change, and willing to sacrifice worthless tradition for progress."

Despite 70 years of Soviet repression, Abduvakhitov believes that the Jadid ideas have acquired a new direction: the Jadid Party of Uzbekistan has come into existence; Jadid books and pamphlets are being reprinted; and Islamic revival is under way. Pointing to the existence of a very large Muslim population within the Russian Federation, he sees Islamic revival in Uzbekistan as a catalytic force for the "Russian" Muslims. "The comparative study of the two communities may provide us an opportunity to make prognoses for the future." It is sound advice in scholarship.

RUSSIAN POLICIES: PERESTROIKA, AFGHANISTAN AND RELATIONS WITH CENTRAL ASIAN STATES

Three eminent American and Russian scholars—Melvin Goodman, Victor N. Spolnikov, and Yuri V. Gankovsky—who specialize in different aspects of the Soviet relations with the United States and the regional states, zero in on Mikhail Gorbachev's domestic policies; *perestroika*, which profoundly transformed Central Asia and Soviet foreign relations; the Soviet Union's war in Afghanistan and its collateral political damage in Central Asia; and finally, Russia's emerging relations with the newly independent states in the region.

A well-known Soviet foreign policy specialist at the U.S. National Defense University, Melvin Goodman identifies Gorbachev's *perestroika* as the ultimate factor in the collapse of the Soviet Union. Wittingly or unwittingly, Gorbachev hastened the Soviet demise in a number of ways: Depoliticizing the Communist Party of the Soviet Union (CPSU) had a role. The policy of *glasnost* transformed suppressed nationalism in the empire into a revolutionary struggle for self-determination. Moves against the CPSU organs ended the legitimacy of the centralized government. And discussion of autonomy encouraged the republics to assert their sovereignty. No one would really disagree with this analysis.

Goodman points out that the four pillars of *perestroika* (democracy, *glasnost*, political renewal, and economic modernization) gave birth in Central Asia to new civil rights organizations and political movements such as Birlik (unity) in Uzbekistan, which challenged Moscow's domination. While independence was attained in 1992 rather unexpectedly the Central Asian states emerged to engage in the process of nation-building and national identity. They are, Goodman believes, "wary of Turkish and Persian influence," and Tajikistan particularly fears "Turkish encroachment." Kazakhstan and Kyrgyzstan, with significant Russian populations, favor short-term cooperation with Russia in order to build their economies and to build their militaries.

Goodman believes that the Central Asian states would have "more independence and flexibility if they would count on western economic and security guarantees." If, however, the United States did not lead the effort to assist them, "they ultimately will have to negotiate with the Kremlin." This remains to be seen.

A former Major General of the Soviet KGB and currently a senior scholar and associate at the Russian Institute of Oriental Studies in Moscow, Victor N. Spolnikov presents a fairly developed thesis about the impact on Central Asia of the Soviet war in Afghanistan. Spolnikov focuses primarily on the Central Asian Society, which he describes as traditional. Traditionalism, according to Spolnikov, means "rejection, negation of new elements into customary and traditional way of life." If one asks any Central Asian what defines his life and what laws or code of behavior govern his daily conduct, invariably the answer would be, first, the "Muslim way"; second, tradition. Selectively, successive generations of Muslim parents transmitted Islamic and traditional values to their children, blocking out all contrary values or information. Within the framework of "Islamic traditionalism," Central Asians adapted to the Soviet rule.

How did this adaptation work out? Spolnikov's explanation is elaborate: (1) the Central Asian intellectuals believed "all which is ours is good"; (2) pre-Islamic culture is ignored; (3) Arab conquest is presented as an "advanced state system and culture"; (4) Amir Timur's (1336-1405) rule is eulogized; and (5) Central Asian history is fictionalized, when Chinggis Khan is presented as a Muslim. Spolnikov then singles out the blemishes of the traditional Islamic culture, which hide corruption, and makes a blatantly false charge that "in Islamic theory and practice there is no juridical concept of bribe." In order to refute Spolnikov's charge, one can cite five major compendiums of the prophetic traditions (*ahadith*), including *Sahiy al-Bukhari,* containing the Prophet Muhammad's condemnation of bribe: *al-Rashiy wa-almartashiy fil nar* (one who bribes and the one who receives bribe are condemned to hell.)[10]

Fatawa-i Alamgiri, an internationally known digest of Islamic law, has provided a variety of punishments for bribery. So how could there be no juridical concept of bribe in Islamic law? A military and political strategist, Spolnikov is not a specialist of Islam; therefore, one can easily ignore such misstatements and focus on the main kernel of his theory. (Incidentally, bribery and stealing of state property was common during Leonid Brezhnev's rule in the Soviet Union; these vices did not exist just in Central Asia's Islamic culture.) Otherwise, Spolnikov's views on the existence of strong family, clan and tribal relations, and respect for the elders, reflecting their impact even in residential districts (thwarting the CPSU's reach), are on the mark.

That Islam defeated Russian Marxism and the CPSU's ideology is an appropriate admission. A dyarchy of structures in the Central Asian administration had developed long before the Soviet invasion of Afghanistan in 1979. This conclusion is based on the KGB's analysis to which Spolnikov had access. In other words, "official structures [Party Committee, Kolkhozs, courts, etc.] were functioning on the surface, but in reality, all of them are no more than outward forms of traditional Islamic structures." In 1980 Yuri Andropov, the CPSU's Secretary-General and former KGB chief, admitted to Spolnikov that in some regions of the Caucasus, Soviet power did not exist at all. Very candidly, Spolnikov admits: "Even if the well-known events in Afghanistan did not take place, the Islamic idea in the USSR was bound to turn into an important political factor." This factor, in his eyes, is Islamic fundamentalism, which has broken into Central Asia through Tajikistan. He blames the Russian leadership for thoughtlessly dealing with the Afghan fundamentalists.

An internationally known scholar at the Russian Institute of Oriental Studies in Moscow, Professor Yuri V. Gankovsky, takes issue with Victor Spolnikov on the significance of Islamic fundamentalism and then projects the view that "the fate of the Commonwealth of Independent States," and especially the Central Asian states, will be determined by Russian political dynamics. Islamic fundamentalism is not necessarily dangerous to Russia's state interests; as a political phenomenon it has existed for a thousand years, first appearing at the end of the thirteenth century in the activities of Fakhar-ud-Din Zarradi (d. 1326). Some leaders of Islamic fundamentalism, Gankovsky asserts, deserve respect; what is noteworthy is their political orientation and objectives, and the methods they might use to achieve their goals. In this regard, Gankovsky approvingly cites academician Vasili Vladimirovich Barthold (1869-1930): "Islamic slogans are always used as a doctrine and not as a religious one, but as a political doctrine and mostly as means of achieving quite definite political aims."

In Gankovsky's analysis, Russia has only two political options: either a return to the Stalinist model of totalitarianism or a move to an authoritarian order with some element of democracy. He bemoans some unnamed foreign leaders' "reckless" statements on limiting Russia's territorial extent to the 1552 borders, which lend support to the fascist forces within the Russian Federation. The current phase of privatization in Russia has corrupted the upper strata of bureaucracy and created "kings" of the "black market." These developments, Gankovsky implies, do not necessarily lead to democracy. Similar economic difficulties have created social tensions in Central Asia. Despite these problems, the leaders of Central Asian states have taken steps in 1992 that tend to politically institutionalize cooperation between these states.

Finally, Gankovsky highlights the presence of Russians in the Central Asian states—they comprise 23 percent of the population and frequently become the ethno-national factor in the struggle for power among the ruling strata. The exogenous powers could best help the situation by not interfering in the internal affairs of the CIS and especially the Central Asian states. As the CIS commander-in-chief has stated, such an interference could ignite World War III. Russians, Gankovsky points out, want Russia to remain a great power, even if doing so sours their relations with the rest of the world. Revealing his injured national pride, he concludes: "Those in the West who are glad that the bells toll for the USSR are to be told: Ask not for whom the bell tolls, it tolls for thee." Clearly, sometimes national injuries can be as painful as the personal ones!

U.S. INTERESTS IN CENTRAL ASIA

A senior political scientist at the RAND Corporation and a former vice chairman of the National Intelligence Council at the Central Intelligence

Agency, Graham E. Fuller is uniquely qualified to articulate U.S. interests in Central Asia. Despite his background in long-range forecasting of political developments, he confesses to the need for "a lot of new thinking" on the subject of this "fabled and obscure" land. American national interests, he believes, are quite limited and primarily "negative" in character. He reduces them to six basic areas: (1) to prevent the reemergence of "Russian radical or ideological expansionism," which could re-create global nuclear confrontation; (2) to cause civil war or breakup of nations; (3) to avoid nuclear proliferation; (4) to avoid the development of radical antiwestern forms of political Islam; (5) to support the spread of democracy and human rights; and (6) to enable the United States to have a role in the economic development of the region, especially its raw materials.

Fuller then presents a detailed exposition of these interests in regard to Russia and Central Asia. Some kernels need to be singled out. The future in Central Asia of 25 million expatriate Russians could be a serious international problem. The West could help solve "the problems of this decolonization process." In Kazakhstan, where Russians and others outnumber the Kazakhs, "pleasant talk about a binational state simply will not wash." Turkey has moved swiftly to cement relations with five Turkic states, while "Iran considers Central Asia historically part of the Great Iranian cultural continuum, and a natural extension of its interests." A "small multinational Pashtun empire" of Afghanistan is threatened by the political developments in Central Asia, and if Afghanistan breaks up it will lead to major complications in multiethnic Pakistan.

Against the landscape of problem-ridden Central and Southwest Asia, Fuller's articulation of the American role in the region makes abundant sense. Yet U.S. private investments in potentially oil-rich states, such as the Chevron Oil Company's $10 billion investment for oil exploration in Kazakhstan, will in the long run turn this region into the U.S. strategic zone. Also, Central Asia is likely to emerge as an alternative source of oil supply, lessening the U.S. reliance on the Middle East oil. Competition between the two major producers of oil would certainly make oil cheaper on the international market, while both regions will have much less political clout in the West. While future developments alone will demonstrate the validity of these arguments, their thrust is noteworthy.

CENTRAL ASIA'S PROBLEMS: TERRITORIAL, ENVIRONMENTAL, AND NATIONAL

Seven respected and well-published American, Tajik, and Russian scholars, including Tadeusz Swietochowski, Michael Glantz, Alvin Z. Rubinstein,

Igor Zonn, Mevlon Makhamov, Muriel Atkin, and James Critchlow, explore in depth the problems of irredentism, environmental degradation, and explosive nationalism, which derives nourishment from the reassertion of Islam in the states of Central Asia.

There are at least a dozen major territorial problems, which have the potential of turning Central Asia into a hotbed of ethnic and religious antagonism and violence. Nogorno-Karabagh in Transcaucasia was the first to explode, tearing apart a tenuous modus vivendi between the Azerbaijani Turks and Armenians, and the end is not in sight yet. Swietochowski demonstrates that the foundations of this conflict were laid in the nineteenth century, when Russia defeated Iran and captured these territories by virtue of the treaties of Gulistan (1813) and Turkmanchai (1828). Russia then carved out Armenia and Azerbaijan, which contains the Armenian enclave of Nogorno-Karabagh. Subsequently, Armenian immigrants came from Iran and Ottoman Turkey, gradually altering the demographic balance. By 1905 relations between the Azerbaijanis and Armenians had degenerated into intercommunal massacres. In 1917, when the tsardom was toppled, Nogorno-Karabagh passed several times from Russian to Turkish control. In 1920 Armenia, Azerbaijan, and Nogorno-Karabagh were safely under Bolshevik control. The ethnic conflict remained "in hibernation" until 1988 when the Armenian SSR revived its claims to Nogorno-Karabagh.

After the Soviet Union disintegrated, the conflict between the Armenians and Azeris degenerated from interethnic conflict to war. Armenia seized Azerbaijan's territory in the summer of 1992 and opened a secure overland route linking Nogorno-Karabagh with Armenia.

While Armenia has made substantial territorial gains, it has been brought to its knees by an economic blockade, first imposed by Azerbaijan as a strategic step in the war, and now (February 1993) aggravated by fighting in neighboring Georgia, that cut off Armenia's critical rail links to Russia. This crisis turned into a catastrophe when the last remaining gas pipeline, which runs through Georgia, was ripped by an explosion in January 1993. In order to help Armenia survive, Russia released 20 billion rubles in credits in December 1992 and promised 50 billion rubles in credits during 1993. Finally, in utter desperation, Armenian President Levon Ter-Petrosyan, who was largely responsible for starting the Nogorno-Karabagh conflict in 1988, sued for unconditional cease-fire with Azerbaijan in February 1993.[11]

Two American scholars, Michael H. Glantz and Alvin Z. Rubinstein, and a Russian, Igor Zonn, collaborate to produce a definitive report on the

Soviet tragedy of environmental pollution in the Aral Sea, which was, in the 1950s, the fourth largest inland body of water in the world and stretched from Uzbekistan into Karakalpakistan and Kazakhstan. This tragedy started with Nikita Khrushchev's scheme of "virgin lands," which aimed at growing wheat on the arid and semiarid steppes of Kazakhstan. At the same time, the cultivation of cotton in Uzbekistan became a Soviet priority. By the mid-1960s "about half the sown area in Uzbekistan was in cotton"; however, "by 1990 cotton was sown on about two-thirds of the agricultural lands." The cotton was shipped, in a typical colonial style of economy, to the textile plants around Moscow and to other large Russian cities.

Prior to the early 1960s, the two river systems, the Amuedarya and Syrdarya, had sustained a stable Aral Sea level. However, a huge amount of water was diverted for cotton cultivation, altering the ecological balance. It was estimated that "as a result of poor land use planning and inefficient water resource management practices, the Aral Sea was drying up and, at the existing rate of desiccation, would likely disappear by the year 2010." Moreover, upsetting the ecological balance in the Aral Sea basin has had a devastating impact on human health: high infant mortality and morbidity rates, a sharp increase in esophageal cancers directly attributable to "poisoned" water resources, gastrointestinal problems, typhoid, and high rates of congenital deformation. When the Soviet government finally recognized the problem in the 1980s, it was already in the middle of serious economic crises and could undertake no remedial action.

Leaders of independent Central Asian states have proposed water diversions from north-flowing Siberian rivers as the only key source of new water for maintaining the level of the sea and human activities in the basin. This is not acceptable to Russia. Glantz, Rubinstein, and Zonn believe that outside assistance is needed, especially from the World Bank, the United States, and even the United Nations, to bring together leaders from all the affected states to save the Aral Sea basin.

When it comes to problems of nationalism and the accompanying role of Islam, Tajikistan has been in the forefront of Central Asian states. A Tajik scholar, Mavlon Makhamov, examines the interaction of nationalism with Islam as an insider, and a well-known American scholar, Muriel Atkin, analyzes the same phenomenon as an outsider. Both examine the same political movements, old and new political parties, and leaders' orientations, but they come to different conclusions. Despite this welcome divergence, both authors shed light on Tajikistan's political developments.

Makhamov analyzes the interaction of nationalism and Islam in the context of Tajikistan's prevailing economic conditions, the impact of regionalism and tribalism, and the intrusive influence of some neighboring states, especially Afghanistan, Pakistan, and Iran. He also studies the effects of the collapse of the Soviet Union and the rise of Islam-oriented political parties, which are endeavoring to grab state power. Potentially quite rich in natural resources, Tajikistan was plunged into recession because its economic ties with the former Soviet states were fractured. Into this economic chaos moved highly politicized Islamic parties to further their chances for power. These parties exploited the educated classes, who were already dissatisfied with their living standards and the general quality of academic life. They flocked to these parties immediately. Widespread unemployment, lack of housing, and exceptionally poor medical care swelled the ranks of the opposition parties, who put "Islam" to work for them. Consequently, the Democratic Party of Tajikistan (DPT), the nationalist Rostokhez party, and the Islamic Renaissance Party (IRP) became quite influential, in addition to several minor organizations that marginally influenced the political processes. To the IRP the inspiration for activism came from the Russian Federation, when the IRP of the Muslims of the Soviet Union was inaugurated in Astrakhan in June 1990.

Makhamov believes that Iran's influence is spreading widely in Tajikistan. Tajik intellectuals believe that Tajikistan's national revival cannot be achieved without Iran's help. Cultural ties with Afghanistan have expanded because of the large Tajik population in Afghanistan. However, both Iran and Afghanistan have supported the IRP and Rostokhez. Relations with Pakistan have progressed smoothly because the focus is on trade, economic cooperation, and Pakistan's desire to purchase electric power from Tajikistan. Finally, Makhamov addresses the issue of what political model is most suitable for Tajikistan's economic and political conditions. Neither the Iranian nor the Turkish model is appropriate; the most suitable one, asserts Makhamov, is the Chinese model, where there is political stability and discipline and abundant economic liberalism assuring the growth of a market economy.

Muriel Atkin sees Tajikistan's drama in terms of a struggle for power and privilege between the Communist old guard, led by the veteran Communist leader Rahman Nabiev, and the opposition parties, including the DPT, IRP, Rostokhez, and a newer reformist group, Loli Badakhshan. In the fall 1992 presidential campaign, most of the opposition joined together to support the candidacy of filmmaker Davlat Khudanazarov against Nabiev, but Nabiev won the election. Atkin questions the legitimacy of this election, because the Communist old guard prevented the opposition from operating openly. In other Soviet republics the non-

Communist parties acquired legal status, but "the regime in Tajikistan blocked that from happening," and 95 percent of the seats in Tajikistan's Supreme Soviet were held by Communists. Tajikistan's first direct presidential election on November 24, 1991, provided scarcely more legitimacy than the legislative relations. "Khudanazarov charged ballot stuffing and voter intimidation." Atkin also points out that while hard-liners at the Soviet center failed in their attempt to seize power in August 1991, the hard-line Communists in Dushanbe overthrew those fellow Communists who were willing to compromise with the opposition. When the CPSU was banned after the August coup, in Tajikistan the party retained its name and property.

When the opposition parties took to demonstrations in the streets, scores of their leaders were arrested in the first few months of 1992. Nabiev then created a private army—composed of the national guard and the local militias—to crush the opposition. "Much of the political violence in the country during 1992 took place in the southern province of Qurghonteppa, where support for the reformers was strong." Then on October 24, 1992, the Kulyab militia attacked Dushanbe in order to restore Nabiev to power. In the spring of 1992 many of opposition's representatives were to meet to sign an agreement to establish a coalition government; Nabiev failed to attend the meeting, and he and his colleagues repeatedly demonstrated bad faith in the implementation of their agreements with the opposition. Finally, at gunpoint the opposition demonstrators obtained his resignation on September 7, 1992. Now it is well known that Uzbekistan's president, Islam Karimov, another hard-line "former" Communist, alarmed by the success of opposition in Tajikistan, quietly supported Nabiev's followers in recapturing Dushanbe at the end of 1992.

Atkin's conclusion is that Nabiev by his obstinacy and double dealing strengthened the small camp of "Islamicizing radicals": They were called Islamic fundamentalists in order to win sympathy in the West and especially in Russia. While it is obvious that insider Makhamov and outsider Atkin perceive the Tajikistani crisis from diametrically opposed perspectives, I suspect that there are large grains of truth in both analyses.

James Critchlow, an internationally known specialist on Uzbekistan, analyzes the interaction between nationalism and Islam in Uzbekistan, which is the most populous state and in many ways the heart of Central Asia. Since the Timurid period the people of Uzbekistan have played a pivotal role in regional politics and still retain the vivid memories of their imperial grandeur, which made Uzbekistan the bright star of the Islamic world in medieval times. Imam Ismail al-Bukhari (194-256 A.H.), the compiler of the Prophet Muhammad's Traditions, *Sahiyh al-Bukhari* (a source of Islamic religion second only to the Qur'an), died in Samarkand, and so did Abu'l-Laith Samarqandi (d. 373), who wrote the celebrated commentary *Bahr al-ulum* on the Qur'an. Also, such luminaries of philosophy, science, and medicine as Abu-Nasr Al-Farabi (d. 950) and Ibn Sina (d. 1037), whose two major works, *Kitab al-Shifa* (Book of Healing) and *Al-Qanun Fi Al-Tibb* (Laws of Medical Science) served as principal texts in medical instruction in the West from the twelfth to the seventeenth centuries, hailed from the lands of Uzbekistan.

Ulug Beg, the grandson of Timur, was patron of the science of astronomy. His astronomical laboratory's remains are extant in Samarkand and still attract foreign and proud local Central Asian visitors. This area was once the cradle of Islamic civilization.

No wonder that Critchlow finds Uzbeks resisting the Soviet efforts "to create a homogenous Soviet man"; in Uzbek eyes "an important ethnic difference was Islamic tradition." With the dawn of freedom, Critchlow maintains "the glory days of the Great Silk Road and the Islamic Renaissance, when 'Uzbek' regions such as Bukhara, Samarkand, and Khorizm were at the pinnacle of world trade and civilization, replaced Marxist-Leninist ideology as a source of inspiration." These interpretations are the undercurrents of Critchlow's thematic analysis. Anyone who knows anything about Central Asia immediately recognizes the accuracy of his perceptions. Uzbekistan moved swiftly to establish diplomatic and cultural ties with Muslim countries of the Middle East and South Asia and joined the Economic Cooperation Organization (ECO) sponsored by Turkey, Iran, and Pakistan.

Islam is in vogue. At his inauguration on January 4, 1992, President Islam Karimov, a longtime Communist, "swore an oath on the Qur'an." Soon, however, the urgency of economic and ethnic problems replaced the initial atmosphere of euphoria, and the president resorted to repression, unleashing the brutal methods of local KGBs. Fear of "Islamic fundamentalism" advancing from Iran, Afghanistan, and Saudi Arabia via Tajikistan further hardened the Uzbek governments' repressive policies toward its own citizens. Yet Critchlow believes that "there are reasons to discount the likelihood of an Iranian 'takeover' of Central Asia." He sees Afghanistan's influence in Central Asia as disruptive and destabilizing, because a large number of Tajiks and Uzbeks live in Afghanistan. Consequently, the Central Asian elites have begun to look hopefully toward Turkey "as a model of a secular Islamic [meaning Muslim] state."

Actually, President Karimov, asserts Critchlow, has offered a new approach to economic problems by "promising to lead Uzbekistan in the transition to a market economy," while he has opposed privatization of land and water resources and provided incentives to small enterprises. Despite Uzbekistan's serious economic problems and unemployment, Critchlow sees "definite signs of progress," compared to what the conditions were under Soviet rule.

NEW RELATIONSHIPS BETWEEN CENTRAL ASIAN STATES AND POLICIES OF SOUTHWEST ASIAN AND ARAB STATES

Three well-published scholars specializing in Russian-Soviet and Southwest Asian states' interstate relations have analyzed in depth the emerging pattern of relations between these states.

Hafeez Malik examines the government of Pakistan's vigorous initiatives in Central Asia. He asserts that the guiding spirits behind the present (1992-93) Nawaz Sharif government are the strategic planning of private think tanks (especially the Central Asia-Pakistan Friendship Society, which was headed by the late Khalid Wahid) and Pakistan's military. Malik analyzes the history of regional cooperative activities in Southwest Asia under the leadership of Turkey, Iran, and Pakistan in the 1950s and 1960s, which had U.S. backing. Based on the past regional cooperation, these three states could build a larger infrastructure of economic and cultural commonwealth, linking Southwest Asian states with Central Asia. Malik highlights positive trends in this direction.

Because of the collapse of the Soviet Union, Malik projects his analysis to include the Muslim-Turkic autonomous states of the Russian Federation in the emerging commonwealth. Five of these 13 Russian Federation states are located in the Volga-Ural basin: Tatarstan, Bashkirtostan, Udmurtia, Moria, and Chuvasia; the remaining states are in the Caucasus: Daghistan, Ingushtia, the Republic of Checheniya, Kabardino-Balker, Abkhazia, Adzharia, Karachaya-Cherkessia, and Kalmykia. The fact that the Volga-Ural basin is not contiguous to the Caucasian region would prove a formidable obstacle to any of these autonomous states to achieving independence from the Russian Federation and forging unity. Despite this territorial anomaly, Tatarstan and the Republic of Chechniya have steadfastly refused to join the Russian Federation. In light of the "impossible," which has happened within the Soviet Union, the future of these two regions could not be frozen in the previous pattern of Russian domination. This is indeed Malik's futuristic speculation.

Malik suggests that, despite obvious U.S. backing of the Turkish model of secularism, Iran, and to a comparatively lesser degree, Pakistan and

Afghanistan will play their natural geopolitical role in Central Asia. Obviously, Turkey, Iran, and Afghanistan have the advantage of geography. Geography is an obstacle to Pakistan, but it can be mitigated if Pakistan retains cooperative fraternal relations with Afghanistan. Malik sees the potential of almost unlimited mutual benefits for Pakistan's security and economic well-being in its association with Central Asian states, if only Pakistan manages to shed its "Indian liability" of ongoing antagonism.

Among the Southwest Asian states, Turkey and Iran have a special significance to U.S. diplomacy—Turkey is a North Atlantic Treaty Organization (NATO) ally; Iran is an Islamic Republic turned antagonist to the United States when the loyal shah was toppled from power in 1979. Oles M. Smolansky offers a thorough analysis of the rapidly growing relations of Iran and Turkey with the Central Asian states.

Landlocked Central Asian states also realize that their access to the sea can be attained through Iran (and to a lesser degree through Pakistan via Afghanistan). The Iranian leadership is keenly aware of this geographic imperative. Consequently, Iran has proposed to the Central Asian leaders "the revival of the silk route." Practically, this strategy includes the building of road links and land routes of the Central Asian states to Iran. Agreements were reached initially to build a 200-kilometer (km) railroad line from Mashhad to Sarakhs, linking Iran with Turkmenistan, and an additional 300 km of line in Kazakhstan, connecting Iran to China and the Pacific. Smolansky concludes that Turkmenistan and Kazakhstan, being contiguous to Iran, are central to its geostrategic planning.

In addition to establishing bilateral diplomatic relations with all Central Asian states, Iran embarked on a number of regional initiatives, including especially the ECO, and organizing the states bordering on the Caspian Sea. The latter initiative brought together Iran, Azerbaijan, Turkmenistan, Kazakhstan, and Russia. This opened up for the Central Asian states the possibility of transferring exportable goods to international waters in the south, to Caspian littoral states in the north, to the Middle East in the southwest, and to Turkey and Europe in the west. These states signed a protocol on protection of the Caspian environment, navigation, and passenger traffic. In addition to ties to these Turkish states, Iran's linguistic and cultural links with Tajikistan will enable it to forge a special relationship with Tajikistan.

In the developing competition with Iran, Smolansky believes that Turkey has valuable assets of its own. In addition to geography, Turkey has historic, ethnic, religious (Sunni Islam), and linguistic affinity with the Turkic-speaking Central Asian states, except Tajikistan, which is a cultural continuation of Iran. Moreover, Turkey has given large credits to Uzbekistan ($500 million), Kazakhstan ($200 million), Turkmenistan ($75 million), and Kyrgyzstan ($75 million), in addition to establishing television links, cultural exchanges and Turkish-language training programs. Smolansky concludes that in its economic competition in Central Asia, "Turkey seems to come out ahead," and "the Turkish model of political and socioeconomic development is found more attractive in the Muslim republics than its Iranian counterpart."

Finally, Carol R. Saivetz focuses on the emerging relations among the Central Asian states, the Arab states of the Middle East, and Israel. She indicates that in Central Asia, the role of Southwest Asian states has been more vigorous and socioeconomically more productive than the thrust of the Arab states. Of all the Arab states, only Saudi Arabia, Egypt, Kuwait, and Oman became active in Central Asia in the early part of 1992. Some moved because of economic opportunities that appeared, while some "reacted out of fear that Iran could succeed in creating some sort of pro-Iranian alliance in the region." All Arab states expected "Central Asia's entry into the Middle East state system."

Israel was motivated to establish relations with the Central Asian states by a strong desire "to prevent these new Muslim states from siding with anti-Israel Iran." Israel also "hopes to encourage or gain neutrality" from these states "with regard to the Arab-Israeli dispute." Moreover, Israeli private business saw Central Asia as a potentially vast export market and "projected up to $100 million a year business in the future." Israeli firms have already established direct-dial links with Kazakhstan and helped Uzbekistan with irrigation techniques, and the Israeli government "has worked to open embassies in the Central Asian capitals."

Saivetz's conclusions are intriguing: First, "Whether intended or not, there seems to be a community of interests among Russia, Turkey, the Arabs, Israel, and the current secular Central Asian leaders." However, she is apprehensive of Islamization in Central Asia, which leads to her second conclusion that it "could well portend significant shifts in foreign policies" of the Central Asian states. Third, she concludes that all these Central Asian and Arab states, Russia and Israel, have a common interest in "preventing Islamization and radicalization" in Central Asia. Fourth, she has suggested that "if Turkey, the oil-rich Gulf states, and Israel can assist in the economic stabilization of the region, that would be to Russia's advantage."

How these conclusions will play out in Central Asia remains to be seen.

N·O·T·E·S

1. Walter Kirchner, *History of Russia* (New York: Barnes and Noble, 1976), p. 3.

2. Ibid., pp. 25-26.

3. *The History and the Life of Chinggis Khan*, trans. Urgunge Onon (Leiden: E. J. Brill, 1990), pp. 52-53, 68-69.

4. On the issue of the ethnonym Tatar, see Azade-Ayse Rorlich, *The Volga Tatars: A Profile in National Resilience* (Stanford, CA: Hoover Institution Press, 1986), pp. 1-15.

5. Thomas J. Barfield, *The Perilous Frontier: Nomadic Empires and China* (Cambridge: Basil Blackwell, 1989), pp. 1-2.

6. Ibid.

7. F. M. Dostoyevski, *Polnoe Sobranie Sochineniy* (St. Petersburg, 1896), vol. 21, pp. 513-23, and *The Diary of a Writer*, trans. Boris Brasol (New York: Charles Scribner, 1949), vol. 2, pp. 1043-52; also Milan Hauner, *What Is Russia to Us? Russia's Asian Heartland, Yesterday and Today* (Boston: Unwin Hyman, 1990), pp. 1-2.

8. "Uzbekistan: Closer Interaction Among the Region's Countries Is Discussed," *Nezavisimaya Gazeta,* January 5, 1993; *Current Digest of the Soviet Press* (*CDSP*), vol. 45, no. 1, February 3, 1993.

9. Semyon Novoprudsky, "Alliance: A New Turkistan," *Nezavisimaya Gazeta,* January 6, 1993; *CDSP,* vol. 45, no. 1, February 3, 1993.

10. See also A. J. Wensinck, *Concordance et Indices de la Tradition Musalmane* (Leiden: E. J. Brill, 1992), p. 262.

11. Celestine Bohlen, "Amid War for Enclave, Armenia Sees Little Hope," *New York Times,* February 7 and 12, 1993.

▲ ▽ ▲

2

The Russian Conquest of Central Asia and Kazakhstan: Motives, Methods, Consequences

◆

Seymour Becker

The incorporation of the Kazakh Steppe and western Turkistan into the Russian Empire during the six decades ending in 1885 was the last chapter in Russian state-building before the 1917 Revolution. As such, it was the culmination of a centuries-old process whereby a Muscovite/ Russian state growing in strength expanded its territory at the expense of neighboring societies that were at a much lower level of technological and organizational development or that had lost their former capacity to deal with Russia as equals or superiors.

Muscovite state-building in the Far East was suspended in the seventeenth century when it reached the limits of the Eurasian landmass and the frontiers of the young and vigorous Manchu Empire; in the mid-nineteenth century the radically changed power relationship between a westernized Russia and a China in an advanced stage of decline was reflected in a substantial alteration of the border in the Amur region in Russia's favor. In the century and a quarter ending in 1829, Russia's boundaries in Europe and the Caucasus were pushed far to the west and south at the expense of three formerly threatening neighbors (Sweden, Poland, and the Ottoman Empire), which were no longer a match for Russia. In 1878 additional territory was acquired from Turkey in western Transcaucasia.

Only between the Caspian Sea and China's western borders did there remain a situation of major disequilibrium along Russia's frontiers at the end of the 1820s. Lines of fortified outposts had been established along the upper Irtysh River in the second decade of the eighteenth century to delimit Russian western Siberia, and along the Ural River in the 1730s to reduce the Bashkirs. After a century passed, Russia's frontier along the northern periphery of the Kazakh Steppe no longer demarcated two societies with roughly equal abilities to bring power to bear locally. The advance of Russian Cossack and peasant colonization southward into the steppe and the Kazakhs' frequent raiding of Russian settlements had created a very volatile situation. In the reign of Nicholas I the nomadic Kazakhs were gradually brought under Russian control by enveloping them in lines of fortifications. By the beginning of the Crimean War two lines had been established, one from the Aral Sea up the Sir-Darya as far as Ak-Masdjid (renamed Fort Perovsk, now Kizil-Orda) and another from the Siberian line at Semipalatinsk southward to Vernyi (now Alma-Ata).

Russia's advance across the Kazakh Steppe brought it into direct contact with the khanates of Khiva and Kokand—sedentary societies better equipped to compete with Russia than were the nomads. In fact, Khiva had recently inflicted a crushing defeat upon a Russian expeditionary force sent to conquer it in 1839-40, thereby repeating its success against an earlier Russian attempt in 1717. With Russia now firmly established on the threshold of the oasis societies of Turkistan, as it had not been in 1839, no longer was the question its ability to bring a preponderance of power to bear on those societies, but its will to do so.

On that score the policymakers in St. Petersburg were divided in the decade after the Crimean War.[1] Preoccupied with the enormous tasks of internal reconstruction that bore fruit in the Great Reforms of the 1860s and '70s, the ministries of finance and foreign affairs, especially, were anxious to avoid taking on unnecessary responsibilities that would further strain the government's budget and its relations with Great Britain. The latter power was, as ever, anxious to keep Russia at a healthy remove from the northwestern marches of India.

The view from Orenburg, to whose governor-general the Sir-Darya line was subordinate, was quite different. The 600-mile gap between forts Perovsk and Vernyi that existed from 1854 was a constant reminder of the lack of a secure frontier in Central Asia. When in 1861-1863 the new governor-general of Orenburg, General A. P. Bezak, urged the immediate unification of the Sir-Darya and New Siberian lines, together with the occupation of the towns of Turkistan and Tashkent, he received support from the new minister of war, D. A. Miliutin, and the new director of the foreign ministry's Asiatic Department, General N. P. Ignat'ev. As a result of strong opposition from Minister of Finance M. Kh. Reutern and Foreign Minister A. M. Gorchakov, Bezak received permission only for reconnoitering expeditions to explore the region between Perovsk and Vernyi.

At this point the ambitions of local commanders in the field, typified by Colonel M. G. Cherniaev, began to shape Russian policy in Central Asia at least as much as did the cautious approach of the emperor and his finance and foreign ministers. Cherniaev, Bezak's chief of staff and commander of one of the reconnaissance missions, exceeded his instructions by occupying the Kokandian fortress of Suzak, northeast of the town of Turkistan, and declaring it under Russia's protection in June 1863. Miliutin seized this opportunity to raise again the question of establishing a continuous line of fortifications, and this time Gorchakov was persuaded by what he termed "Colonel Cherniaev's successful activities without special expenditures."[2]

With Gorchakov's and the emperor's approval, the unification of the frontier lines was effected in 1864 with the capture of Turkistan, Aulie-Ata, and Chimkent. Cherniaev, who had led the advance from Vernyi, was promoted to major general and given command of the newly formed New Kokand line, under the governor-general of Orenburg. As far as Gorchakov was concerned, Russia's goals in Central Asia had now been achieved, and he was opposed to any further advance, such as Cherniaev's unauthorized and unsuccessful attack on Tashkent, which came only five days after the fall of Chimkent. In his November 1864 circular dispatch to Russian diplomatic representatives abroad, the foreign minister articulated the principles of Russia's policy in the area, principles never completely abandoned down to 1917.[3]

In his circular, Gorchakov distinguished between two types of neighbors of civilized (read "European") states such as Russia — nomadic tribes and sedentary societies organized into "more regularly constituted states." Faced with nomadic neighbors — by definition half-savage brigands — a civilized state has no choice but to subjugate them, as Russia had just finished doing with the Kazakhs, "in the interest of the security of its frontier and its commercial relations." This accomplished, and with a stable frontier established in a region fertile enough to ensure supplies for the garrison and support for Russian colonization, argued Gorchakov, Russia had no interest in further expansion. The "more regularly constituted states" that were now Russia's immediate neighbors in Central Asia, although culturally backward and not as politically stable as might be wished, offered "every chance" of peaceful relations. The annexation of these khanates, on the other hand, "would entail considerable exertions," greater than those required to reduce the nomads, and would draw Russia into "unforeseen complications" (presumably with Great Britain as well as locally). As the British ambassador, Lord Augustus Loftus, correctly defined it in 1872, St. Petersburg's policy was "to abstain from extending Russian territory in Central Asia, whilst at the same time . . . obtaining a complete control over the small States of which Central Asia is composed. . . by conciliatory means through the existing Rulers."[4]

Gorchakov's formulation of Russia's aims in Central Asia proved much too optimistic on two points—the ease of making good neighbors of Khiva, Bukhara, and Kokand, and Russia's ability to restrain its own ambitious commanders in the region. In early 1865 Gorchakov was still warning against "any interference in the internal affairs" of Russia's new neighbors, as well as against "the acquisition of new territory,"[5] and yet over the next three and a half years Russia acquired Tashkent and Khodjent from Kokand and the upper and middle Zarafshan valley, including Samarkand, from Bukhara before peace was finally concluded. On the one hand ambitious commanders in the field regularly interpreted their instructions in the broadest possible manner or even, like Cherniaev, clearly violated them, in the conviction that they were in a better position than their superiors in St. Petersburg to judge what measures were necessary.

On the other hand, those very instructions continually delivered mixed signals. Warnings against unnecessarily adding to the burdens of empire alternated with admonitions not to show weakness or indecision in the face of obdurate Asiatics. Typical were the joint instructions from the war and foreign ministries to Major General D. I. Romanovskii upon his appointment as successor to Cherniaev in early 1865 as governor of the new Turkistan *oblast'*. Romanovskii was instructed, "while steadfastly striving not to extend our direct possessions in Central Asia, not to reject, however, for the sake of that goal, such actions and orders as may be necessary for us, and in general to keep in mind, above all, Russia's true interests." He was further reminded that "the Asiatic respects only armed force, that the slightest vacillation and indecisiveness, and especially concession, in response to any kind of inappropriate declarations or actions on their [*sic*] part, will be taken by them for weakness and thus not only will not attain its aims but may have a disastrous effect on the regions newly taken by us as well as on our steppes and on our former lines."[6]

Bukhara's all-too-obvious reluctance to accept Russia's southward advance from Chimkent into a region it regarded as its own sphere of influence gave Cherniaev and Romanovskii, and the latter's successor, General K. P. von Kaufman, appointed in 1867 to the new post of governor-general of Turkistan, ample opportunity to demonstrate Russian decisiveness through the use of armed force, leading to new territorial acquisitions and finally, in 1868, to peace.

Nor was that the end. Khiva, occupying a strong natural defensive position as an island in a sea of deserts and undoubtedly encouraged by Russia's two previous failures to subdue it, failed to draw the proper conclusions from the fate of Kokand and Bukhara. The khan's chief minister rejected Russia's demands to halt Khiva's traditional practices of raiding Russian frontier posts along the Sir-Darya, plundering caravans engaged in trade with Russia, and inciting Russia's Kazakh subjects against it. The foreign ministry's hopes that the establishment of a fortified trading post at Krasnovodsk in 1869 would suffice for "the reduction of Khiva to the same denominator as Kokand and Bukhara"[7] proved as overly optimistic as its earlier hopes that the Russian advance could be halted at Chimkent. Kaufman's insistence, supported by Minister of War Miliutin, on teaching Khiva the same kind of lesson as had proved effective in Bukhara's case finally won the day; even the foreign ministry was convinced by Khiva's refusal to play the role assigned to it. In December 1872 the emperor authorized an armed campaign against the khanate to reduce it to the same degree of political dependency as Bukhara and Kokand, but Kaufman was expressly warned against "an extension of the empire's borders."[8] Eight months later, however, after the successful conclusion of a five-pronged attack on Khiva, Kaufman persuaded St. Petersburg that the khanate's future good behavior could best be guaranteed by the annexation of the east coast of the Caspian Sea, the Ust-Urt Plateau, and most important, the Kizil Kum Desert from the lower Sir-Darya up to and including the fertile right bank of the lower Amu-Darya.

With the reduction of Khiva in 1873 and the conclusion of a formal understanding with Britain in the same year setting the Amu-Darya as the line of demarcation between Russia's and Britain's spheres of influence, St. Petersburg had apparently achieved its goals in Central Asia. Defensible borders had been established with relatively well-organized sedentary societies that had been taught the futility of resisting Russia's demands; Britain's expansion had been forestalled in the political near vacuum between the Caspian Sea and China; and the added responsibilities and costs of empire had been limited, albeit not so strictly as the emperor and the foreign ministry had hoped. The khanates retained full responsibility for their own internal affairs while relinquishing to Russia de facto control of their foreign relations.

Once again the policymakers in St. Petersburg proved to have underestimated the difficulty of achieving their aims while avoiding unwanted

responsibilities. In 1875-76 Kokand ceased to satisfy Russia's requirements for internal stability, dissolving instead in internal strife and thereby
forcing a reluctant Russia to approve its local commanders' plans for
annexation. A somewhat different case was the pacification and annexation between 1877 and 1884 of the Kara Kum Desert and the oases along
its southern periphery—ostensibly Khivan territory, but the home of tur-
bulent Turkoman nomadic tribes who in fact recognized no external
authority. The latter instance of territorial expansion led in 1885 to St.
Petersburg's negotiation with London of the Russo-Afghan boundary, by
which the line demarcating the Russian and British spheres of influence
was extended westward from the middle Amu-Darya to the Persian frontier. Unlike Kokand, Bukhara and Khiva performed their roles as obedi-
ent and stable neighbors well enough to ward off repeated suggestions,
from Russian officials and from private observers, for their annexation.
Their autonomy was preserved, however, only at the cost of periodic
armed intervention in support of the native regimes against their domestic
opponents—in Bukhara in 1868, 1910, and 1913, and in Khiva in 1874,
1875, 1877, 1915, and 1916.[9]

The territories that had been incorporated directly into the empire,
often against St. Petersburg's better judgment, were governed in a manner
that suggests that the government had not altered its definition of Russia's
interests in the region since the preconquest era.[10] Security continued to
be the uppermost concern, and a military establishment was maintained in
Central Asia that was, proportionate to population, much larger than that
the British maintained in India. Administration was in the hands of military commanders at the government-general, *oblast'*, and *uezd* levels. The
territorial jurisdiction of the Turkistan governors-general waned and
waxed with St. Petersburg's desire to provide suitable satrapies for its
favorites. Turkistan consisted of four *oblasti*—Sir-Darya, Samarkand,
Fergana, and Semirech'e—from the annexation of Kokand until 1882,
when Semirech'e was transferred to the newly created Steppe government-general. Semirech'e was reattached to Turkistan in 1898, at the same
time the Transcaspian *oblast'* was added, although the actual transfer of
the latter province to Tashkent's jurisdiction took place only in 1904. To
the north of Turkistan lay the four steppe *oblasti*—Ural'sk, Turgai,
Akmolinsk, and Semipalatinsk—the latter two included in the government-general of the Steppe.

RUSSIAN POLICIES IN TURKISTAN

Apart from police functions, administration at the sub-*uezd* level was dele-
gated to popularly elected institutions and officials. In districts colonized
by Russians (primarily in the northern *uezdy* of the steppe *oblasti* and in
Semirech'e), these institutions were the ones created for the peasant estate
in Russia after 1861: a two-tiered structure of communes and *volosti*
(townships). The Muslim natives, legally classified as *inorodtsy* (aborigines), had neither the full rights nor the same obligations as the tsar's other
subjects, but were nevertheless given self-government institutions mod-
eled on those created for the Russian peasantry. Among the sedentary
population several neighboring *kishlaks* (villages) constituted a *volost'*,
while among the nomads a *volost'* was composed of several neighboring
auls (encampments). *Kishlak* and *aul* elders, deputies to the *volost'* assembly, *volost'* heads, and judges of the native courts were all elected—by
assemblies of heads of households at the *kishlak* and *aul* levels or by the
volost' assembly. *Volost'* heads and judges had to be confirmed in office and
could be dismissed, by the *oblast'* governor, as could *kishlak* and *aul* officials by the *uezd* commandant. Native towns were divided into quarters
and given a similar two-tiered administration.

Justice, taxation, and irrigation were the primary responsibilities of the
native self-government institutions. These institutions were no more
intended to prepare the population for a greater measure of autonomy in
the future than were the institutions of peasant self-government in
European Russia. In each case St. Petersburg was simply delegating
responsibility for local matters to suit its own convenience, since it lacked
both the personnel and the funds to assume those burdens itself.

Nor was the intent to preserve traditional Muslim society from the disruptive impact of alien rule. Among the sedentary population formal elections replaced the choosing of leaders by consensus, and elected *kazis*
(judges), each with exclusive jurisdiction over a given district, replaced
those appointed by the khans for their knowledge of the written law and
available to any litigants who sought their services. Thus did the imposition of a Russian sense of order and administrative regularity violate traditional conceptions and practices. Among the nomads clan and tribal elders
had always served as leaders and as interpreters of the unwritten customary law, but now headmen and judges were elected by *volost'* assemblies
that normally, and deliberately, included representatives of at least two
different kinship groups—so as to weaken traditional loyalties and diminish potential resistance to Russian rule. The native population adjusted to

the unfamiliar ways of their conquerors in an understandable if not always admirable manner. The buying of elections and bribing of the Russian officials who supervised the working of the self-government institutions became all-too-regular features of the system.

St. Petersburg took little responsibility for the welfare or development of the region, or even the basic human needs of its population. This is not surprising, given the level of services and development prevailing in even the ethnically Russian core provinces of the empire. Kaufman, the first governor-general of Turkistan, set the tone with his belief that the obvious superiority of Russian over Islamic culture would in time, and without any particular effort on Russia's part, convince the natives to abandon their barbarous customs. In the meantime Russia's civilizing mission was confined to the suppression of slavery and the slave trade, of torture, and of corporal and capital punishment. But the colonial administration was hardly an effective advertisement for the superiority of Russian culture. Russian officials were too few in number, overworked, poorly paid, and often of low quality. They were prone to accept bribes and extort money from the native population, and sometimes even from the rulers of the vassal khanates.

The policy of neglect established by Kaufman and followed by his successors applied to religion and education in particular. Russification was not to be pressed upon the natives lest they be provoked into rebellion, but at the same time their culture had to be deprived of external sources of support. Kaufman prevented both the Russian Orthodox Church from establishing a new diocese in Tashkent and from carrying on missionary activity in Turkistan, and the Muslim Religious Administration in Ufa from extending its jurisdiction to the government-general. Few Russian schools were established for the native population (and those few were meant to train clerks and interpreters for the civil service) — only 157 by 1913 for a Muslim population of 3.3 million in the four steppe *oblasti* and Semirech'e, and 89 by 1911 for 5.1 million natives in the Turkistan government-general minus Semirech'e.[11] Before the conquest there had been no schools among the nomads, but the sedentary population had an extensive system of traditional *maktabs* (grammar schools) and *madrasas* (seminaries). Even so, literacy rates in the early twentieth century were only 2 to 3 percent for the adult sedentary Muslim population and 1 percent for the nomads. In the entire empire only the natives of Siberia had lower rates.

Under the impact of Russia's neglect and less-than-shining example, the Muslim community underwent minimal cultural change down to 1917 and showed little sign of recognizing the superiority of Russian ways. The rule of infidel conquerors did, however, serve to undermine the authority of the *kazis* and *mullahs* (learned men) and of the traditional values they represented.

Improvements to Central Asia's transportation infrastructure were of concern to official Russia only insofar as they were required by military considerations. Telegraph lines, post roads, and railroads were planned to serve Russia's security and administrative needs. The Transcaspian Railroad began as a short line, built in 1880-81 during the campaign against the Teke Turkomans, extending from the Caspian coast halfway to Askhabad. Only after the clash between Russian and Afghan troops at Penjdeh, south of the Merv oasis, did St. Petersburg authorize the railroad's extension via Bukhara to Samarkand in 1885, and a decade later to Tashkent. Like the Orenburg-Tashkent Railroad, completed in 1906, the Transcaspian line was built and operated by the war ministry with primarily strategic considerations in mind.

Ironically, the building of the Transcaspian Railroad proved to have far greater economic than military significance. Despite some pressure from Russian merchants interested in Turkistan as a market and as a source of raw cotton, economic considerations had exercised little or no influence over the decisions that resulted in the Russian conquest. Nor did the advent of Russian rule have much immediate impact on Russia's trade relations with the region or on the latter's economy. It was not until 1881 that the establishment of customs posts on Turkistan's frontiers with Bukhara and Khiva gave some protection to Russian trade in the government-general against competition from British and Indian imports. Trade with Bukhara received the same protection only in 1894 when the Russian customs frontier was advanced to the Bukharo-Afghan border. It was the coming of the railroad that bound the Central Asian economy firmly to that of the metropole and produced significant change in the region.

The substantial lowering of transportation costs produced by the railroad encouraged the cultivation of American upland cotton, superior in quality to the local variety, for the Russian market. St. Petersburg stimulated this development in 1887 by placing a protective tariff on foreign cotton. In the period from 1888 to 1907 cotton shipments from the Turkistan government-general to European Russia increased by over 1100 percent; by 1911 Central Asian cotton was supplying half the total needs of Russia's textile industry. While cotton culture remained of secondary importance to grain in the protected khanates, in Turkistan (minus Semirech'e) by 1913 almost 20 percent of the irrigated acreage was planted in cotton; in Fergana *oblast'*, which alone contained two-thirds of the total cotton acreage in the government-general, cotton occupied 36 to 38 percent of the sown area on the eve of the 1917 revolution.[12]

To encourage the trend toward monoculture, St. Petersburg in 1893 lowered the freight rate on grain shipped to Turkistan, where Fergana and

some other districts had become grain-deficit areas. The inauguration of
the Orenburg-Tashkent Railroad, by shortening the rail distance between
the latter city and Moscow by over one-quarter, and the travel time by
more than one-third, further facilitated the delivery of inexpensive grain
to Turkistan. The government-general shipped not only cotton but fresh
fruit to the metropole, while the steppe *oblasti* supplied cattle and grain.
The growth of local industry was quite limited; the ginning and pressing
of cotton fiber and extraction of oil from cotton seed accounted for 85 percent of Turkistan's total industrial production in 1914. Natives constituted
the great bulk of the un- and semi-skilled workers, while Russians held
most of the skilled jobs and all of the managerial positions.[13]

Russian rule in Central Asia had a very mixed economic impact on the
native population. In an attempt to drive a wedge between the peasantry
and the privileged elite, Governor-General von Kaufman effected a radical
land reform, transferring title from the former khans and the landowning
aristocracy to those who actually worked the land; only lands held by
Muslim ecclesiastical institutions were left untouched. By the 1890s, however, with Turkistan specializing increasingly in production for export to
the metropole and becoming ever more dependent on food imports, the
peasantry found their situation worsening. Cotton and grain prices were
set by world market conditions over which the peasants had no control. A
bumper cotton harvest in the United States, the world's largest exporter,
for instance, depressed the price of cotton even if Turkistan's crop was
smaller than usual. A poor harvest, low cotton prices, high grain prices, or
any combination could throw a peasant hopelessly into debt to the native
merchant-broker who advanced him money, seed, and consumer goods
such as tea at exorbitant rates of interest against the purchase of his cotton. Many peasants lost their recently acquired land and reverted to the
status of sharecroppers, as land once again became concentrated in the
hands of the wealthy.

Some natives prospered as merchant-brokers, often borrowing their
working capital from the branches of Russian banks that opened in
Turkistan after the coming of the railroad. A few even became processors
of cotton fiber and seed or distillers and vintners supplying the wherewithal to quench the thirst of the Russian community. Native craftsmen,
on the other hand, experienced more loss than profit from the development of closer economic links with the metropole. The railroad brought a
flood of Russian manufactures—especially textiles and metalwork, but
also pottery and leather and wooden goods—that were often cheaper
than, and sometimes superior to, local wares.

As significant as it was for Turkistan, the economic and social impact of Russian rule was even more disruptive in the steppe *oblasti* and in Semirech'e because of Russian colonization. In the three core *oblasti* of Turkistan and in Transcaspia, Russians accounted for less than 4 percent of the total population in 1911. Two thirds of them were urban—soldiers, civil servants, merchants, managers, technicians, skilled workers—inhabiting the European-style Russian settlements laid out alongside established native towns such as Tashkent, Samarkand, and Kokand. In Semirech'e by contrast, in the same year Russians accounted for 17 percent of the total population; and in the four steppe *oblasti*, 40 percent. These five *oblasti* towns were entirely Russian in aspect and predominantly Russian in population, but four out of five Russians were not urbanites but agricultural colonists.[14]

Russian peasant colonization in Central Asia began slowly and hesitantly, gained real momentum only after a generation, and then turned into a flood that transformed the demographic and economic characteristics of large parts of the region.[15] After the conquest, St. Petersburg, as the heir to the previous rulers, claimed title to all uncultivated land. Nomads were given rights of usage, but the state retained the implicit right to determine the acreage needed by the nomads. Russian peasant colonization beyond the line of Cossack settlements began in Semirech'e in 1868, in Akmolinsk and Semipalatinsk in 1875, and in Turgai and Ural'sk in the 1880s. The movement was kept to a minimum, however, by St. Petersburg's opposition to the resettlement of peasants from the metropole out of concern for the potentially destabilizing effect on the peasantry and rural economy of European Russia.

As rural overpopulation in the metropole came to be recognized as a problem, the government's attitude began to change. In the Resettlement Act of 1889 the state offered land allotments, tax exemptions, and interest-free loans to peasant colonists, while still requiring them to go through a lengthy bureaucratic procedure to obtain legal permission to migrate. During the following years the government also began expanding the pool of land available for Russian settlement by reducing the acreage reserved for the use of Kazakh nomads. The opening in 1894 of the West Siberian sector of the Transsiberian Railroad between the Ural Mountains and Omsk, with special rates for peasant colonists, provided convenient and affordable transportation to the very threshold of the fertile grasslands of the northern Kazakh Steppe. In 1896 the Resettlement Administration was established to promote colonization in Siberia and the Kazakh Steppe, and Russian squatters were given protection against the claims of natives. In 1904 the requirement of special permission for removal to Asiatic Russia was abolished, and in the wake of the peasant uprisings of 1905 to 1907 in the metropole, the pool of land available for colonization was enlarged by 70 percent by once again lowering the norms defining the land needs of the nomads.

Net Russian immigration to Central Asia was 206,000 in the decade from 1896 to 1905 and 834,000 in the period from 1906 to 1916; some 300,000 to 500,000 settlers had arrived before 1896. Of the total net immigration between 1896 and 1916, 56 percent settled in Akmolinsk *oblast'* (primarily in its northern half), 24 percent in Turgai and Ural'sk (largely along their northern peripheries), 19 percent in Semipalatinsk (again along the northern periphery) and Semirech'e (primarily in the east and south), and only 1 percent in Syr-Darya (mostly in the southeast).[16]

Russian colonization had a dramatic impact on the traditional economy of the steppe. Between 1906 and 1916 the sown area in the four steppe *oblasti* increased by almost four times, with 95 percent of the increase the result of Russian colonization. In 1916 Russians farmed from 64 percent to 96 percent of the cultivated land in the Steppe *oblasti* and 36 percent in Semirech'e.[17] The expansion of the sown area took place at the expense of the nomads' pastures. The Cossack settlements established along the northern rim of the steppe beginning in the eighteenth century had already blocked the traditional seasonal migration routes of some of the nomads and expropriated much of the best winter pastures. Large-scale peasant colonization from the 1890s cut additional migration routes and severely reduced grazing lands.

Nomads were forced to find other pastures, often on marginal land in the more arid southern reaches of the steppe. Herds and incomes consequently declined just as Russian and Tatar traders became regular visitors among the nomads, creating new consumer wants and increasing the nomads' dependence upon the traders' wares. The more impoverished nomads were susceptible to Russia's offer of tax exemptions for the first five years and reductions for the next five to nomads who took up agriculture. By 1916 roughly 30 percent of the Kazakhs had settled down as agriculturists, but many had little or no land or land of marginal value; many were agricultural laborers. Some nomads shifted to a semisedentary grain and livestock economy.[18]

The settlement in only two decades of over a million Russian colonists in the northern and eastern districts of the Kazakh Steppe was the result of St. Petersburg's efforts to solve the problems of rural overpopulation in the metropole and security against China on the frontier—but with scant thought for the interests of the native population of the region. The disruption caused in the latter's traditional way of life and economy fostered grievances that contributed in a major way to the 1916 revolt that would dramatically reveal the shortcomings of Russian rule in Central Asia.

After the end of the era of conquest, Russia remained very sensitive to any threat to its control of Central Asia. For purposes both of defense and internal policing, it maintained up to 45,000 troops in the region. Lest the native population receive training in arms, St. Petersburg both exempted them from conscription into the Russian army and rejected the idea of organizing native auxiliaries. The pitifully trained and poorly armed troops of the emir of Bukhara posed no danger. Even the more serious of the infrequent native revolts before 1916 were suppressed in a matter of days.

Such revolts were often led by *mullahs* — defenders of the traditional culture and ardent opponents of the rule of the infidel — and were frequently provoked by some offense to local sensibilities committed by Russian officialdom in its ignorance of and contempt for native mores. Public health measures that to the Russian mind were clearly necessary were perceived by the natives as violating custom and the supernatural order. A case in point was Russia's efforts to combat cholera in Tashkent in 1892, which led to serious riots. Of a different character was the Andijan uprising of 1898, planned over many months by conservative *mullahs* and members of the former Kokandian ruling elite, aimed at the restoration of Kokand's independence and the expulsion of the infidel from Central Asia, and supported by peasants suffering from a one-third decline in cotton prices over the preceding several years. Various reforms were considered in the wake of the revolt, but the only action taken was the stationing of additional troops in Turkistan and the arming of Russian colonists.

Muslims remained aloof from the 1905 revolution in Central Asia, which was confined to the Russian population. However, the revolutionary events of 1905 to 1907, not only in Russia but also in the Muslim world from Morocco to Persia, gave a great boost to the development of a native intelligentsia, the bearers of a modern national consciousness, in Central Asia. This group grew out of the movement for educational reform among the Muslims of the empire begun by the Crimean Tatar Ismail Bey Gaspirali, a movement that had reached Turkistan in the late 1890s[19] and is well known as the Jadid movement. (This movement and its impact on the contemporary scene is discussed in chapter 4.)

In the last years before the 1917 revolution, Central Asia's Russian rulers were presented with the bill for decades of neglect of the region's needs. Bands of dispossessed Muslim peasants-turned-brigands infested some rural areas and with considerable popular support attacked Russian administrators and settlers. More serious troubles occurred in the protected native khanates, where peasants were taxed much more heavily than peasants in the government-general and the native administrations were even more rapacious and offered even fewer benefits than did the Russian colonial authorities. Several days of rioting between Sunnis and Shi'ites in Bukhara's capital in 1910, suppressed only by the arrival of Russian troops, led Tashkent to again raise the question of the khanate's annexation. The foreign ministry remained wedded to the policy of nonintervention in the protectorates, and Stolypin ruled that while annexation was inevitable in the long run, the present moment was inopportune.

It soon proved impossible, however, to maintain a hands-off attitude toward Khiva, where the khan's regime was mortally threatened by a series of Turkoman revolts between 1912 and 1916. Tashkent's ill-conceived attempts to act as mediator only aggravated the situation, which ended in the establishment of a permanent Russian military presence in Khiva to protect the khan and a plan, forestalled by the 1917 revolution, for a Russian military commissar to supervise the native government and see that needed reforms were implemented.

In Turkistan and the steppe *oblasti*, meanwhile, demands from the liberal Muslim intelligentsia for equal rights for the natives, an end to Russian colonization, and the restitution of lands taken unjustly from the nomads all went unheeded, and popular resentment against Russian settlers and Russian rule kept growing, largely unnoticed by the colonial authorities. World War I added to popular discontent by bringing a fourfold increase in the prices of grain and manufactured goods shipped to Central Asia from the metropole at the same time that short supplies resulting from the cessation of foreign imports led St. Petersburg to impose a ceiling on the price of Central Asian cotton at a level only 50 percent above that of 1913.[20] In addition, special war taxes were levied, draft animals and carts were requisitioned, and natives were conscripted for fieldwork on Russian farms to replace Russians called up for military service.

The spark that ignited this highly combustible situation was the June 25, 1916 decree ordering the mobilization of almost half a million Muslim men in Central Asia for military service behind the front lines.[21] The authorities' failure to explain the rationale for the draft and how it would work helped touch off a chain reaction of rebellion in four major areas: the three core *oblasti* of Turkistan in July, Semirech'e in August, Transcaspia from late August until December, and the four steppe *oblasti* from October to the end of the year. In Turkistan, in spontaneous and uncoordinated local uprisings, urban workers and peasants vented their anger primarily against the native officials responsible for selecting the draftees—officials who were themselves exempt and long detested for their corruption and collaboration with the Russian authorities. In Semirech'e, Kirgiz and Kazakhs attacked Russian officials and peasants, and the latter responded by taking the law into their own hands and repaying the atrocities committed by the natives in kind and with interest. In Transcaspia armed clashes between Turkomans and Russian troops raged for months. In the steppe *oblasti*, by contrast, only in Turgai was the revolt accompanied by much bloodshed; the size and density of the Russian population may have discouraged Muslim attacks.

The uncoordinated nature of the uprisings, which occurred sequentially rather than simultaneously in the four centers of revolt, made them easier to suppress. At no point did they seriously threaten the continuation of Russian rule, but the cost in life and property administered a rude shock to Russia's long-established complacent attitude toward Central Asia. In Turkistan, Russian losses included 2,300 civilians killed and 1,400 missing (over 85 percent of these victims were in Semirech'e); 259 soldiers dead, wounded, or missing (the majority in Transcaspia); 24 Russian and 55 native officials killed; and 9,000 Russian farmsteads destroyed (mostly in Semirech'e). In the steppe Russian losses were only a small fraction of those in Turkistan. Native losses in lives and property far exceeded those of the Russians, and the suppression of the revolt was followed by a mass flight of Kirgiz into Chinese Xinjiang and of Turkomans into Persia. Fewer than 180,000 natives were finally conscripted for noncombat duty.

General A. N. Kuropatkin, who arrived in Turkistan as the new governor-general in August, proposed a number of responses to the problems revealed by the 1916 revolt: more Russian officials at the *uezd* level and more effective administration generally, with Russians assuming greater responsibility for the welfare of the natives; better communication between the colonial administration and the natives; greater protection for the land rights of both nomads and peasants who had fallen deeply into debt; and subsidized grain imports from the metropole and Siberia. Like Kuropatkin's plan for Khiva, these proposals had no chance to be implemented before the tsarist regime collapsed in March 1917.

Kuropatkin's proposed reforms were an implicit indictment of half a century of Russian rule in Central Asia. Drawn into the region in a quest for a secure and stable frontier and by a concern to forestall British influence, Russia from the beginning strove to keep its new responsibilities to a minimum. After the building of the Transcaspian Railroad, Turkistan took

on additional importance as a major source of raw cotton and a market for
Russian products, and subsequently the Steppe became a convenient outlet for some of the surplus rural population of the metropole. When it was
considered at all, the native population was viewed with distrust and contempt, as members of a barbarous and despised religion and culture.

The absence of a concerted Russification campaign like that which was
launched in the Baltic, Polish, and western *gubernii* of European Russia
was testimony to the strength of Russians' confidence in their role as
bringers of civilization to Asia. German and Polish culture were perceived
as dangerous rivals that threatened Russia's own sense of self. The challenge posed by nomads, Turks, and Muslims was much simpler and could
be dealt with through the exercise of superior force. Eventually the
natives of Central Asia would recognize the superiority of Russian culture
and embrace assimilation. Unfortunately for the expectations of both the
tsarist and the Soviet regimes, a century and a quarter has proved not
nearly long enough for this result to be achieved.

Among the positive achievements of tsarist rule in Central Asia must be
counted the establishment of a greater degree of peace and order than had
been known for generations, the abolition of slavery and inhuman punishments, a modest measure of economic development, and a skeletal infrastructure of modern transportation, communications, and irrigation networks.

The failures of tsarist rule can be attributed to two factors that shaped
the fate of the metropole as well as that of Central Asia: the regime's tradition of focusing on the needs of the state and the ruling elite to the virtual
exclusion of any concern for those of society alone, and the limited material means at the disposal of the rulers of a land as economically underdeveloped as Russia was in the second half of the nineteenth century. The
Russians' superior attitude toward the native population only strengthened the operation of these factors in Central Asia. Government was neither honest nor efficient, natives were excluded from administrative and
managerial roles, illiteracy remained the norm, the introduction of
Russian rule and Russian customs inevitably undermined the integrity of
the traditional culture while offering no satisfactory substitute, and the
material condition of the great majority of the native population did not
benefit from the economy's integration with that of the metropole.

The tsarist regime's Communist successors inherited not only the legacy
of half a century of Russian accomplishments and failures in Central Asia,
but the traditions and attitudes that had been responsible for those failures. Seven decades of Communist rule have produced both more substantial achievements and more monumental failures.[22]

N·O·T·E·S

1. For St. Petersburg's policy from 1853 to 1864, see Seymour Becker, *Russia's Protectorates in Central Asia: Bukhara and Khiva, 1865-1924* (Cambridge, MA: Harvard University Press, 1968), pp. 14-17.

2. Quoted in A. L. Popov, "Iz istorii zavoevaniia Srednei Azii," *Istoricheskie zapiski* 9 (1940): 211.

3. "Central Asia, No. 2 (1873)," pp. 70-75, Great Britain, *Parliamentary Papers (1873)*, p. 75.

4. Loftus to Earl Granville [Foreign Secretary], April 16, 1872, "Central Asia, No. 2 (1873)," p. 58.

5. Gorchakov to General N. A. Kryzhanovskii [Governor-General of Orenburg], February 23, 1865, in *Turkestanskii krai. Sbornik materialov dlia istorii ego zavoevaniia*, ed. A. G. Serebrennikov, (Tashkent, 1912-16), 19: 81-84.

6. Quoted in M. A. Terent'ev, *Istoriia zavoevaniia Srednei Azii* (St. Petersburg, 1906), 1: 336-337.

7. P. N. Stremoukhov [director of foreign ministry's Asiatic Department] to Kaufman, 14 October 1869, quoted in Popov, pp. 224-225.

8. Quoted in Terent'ev, *Istoriia zavoevaniia Srednei Azii*, 2: 112.

9. For Russian intervention in Bukhara, see Becker, *Russia's Protectorates in Central Asia*, pp. 46-47 and 218-221; in Khiva, ibid., pp. 81-85 and 231-236.

10. For the Russian administration of Turkistan and the steppe *oblasti*, see Richard A. Pierce, *Russian Central Asia 1867-1917* (Berkeley, CA: University of California Press, 1960), ch. 3-4; and Russia, *Svod zakonov Rossiiskoi imperii*, vol. 2, 1892 edition (St. Petersburg, 1912).

11. Elizabeth E. Bacon, *Central Asians under Russian Rule: A Study in Culture Change* (Ithaca, NY: Cornell University Press, 1966), p. 101; Pierce, *Russian Central Asia*, p. 217.

12. Pierce, *Russian Central Asia*, pp. 165-166.

13. Ibid., pp. 196-198.

14. Ibid., p. 137.

15. For peasant colonization of the steppe, see ibid., ch. 7, and George J. Demko, *The Russian Colonization of Kazakhstan, 1896-1916* (Bloomington, IN: Indiana University Press, 1969).

16. Demko, *Russian Colonization of Kazakhstan*, pp. 98-99.

17. Ibid., pp. 158-161.

18. Ibid., p. 189; see also Bacon, *Central Asians under Russian Rule*, ch. 4.

19. Bacon, *Central Asians under Russian Rule*, p. 115.

20. Pierce, *Russian Central Asia*, p. 267.

21. The following account of the 1916 uprisings is based on ibid., ch. 18, and on Edward Dennis Sokol, *The Revolt of 1916 in Russian Central Asia* (Baltimore, MD: Johns Hopkins University Press, 1953).

22. Two books used for this chapter but not hitherto cited in these notes are P. G. Galuzo, *Turkestan—koloniia (Ocherk istorii Turkistana ot zavoevaniia russkimi do revoliutsii 1917 goda)* (Moscow, 1929), and Edward Allworth, ed., *Central Asia: 120 Years of Russian Rule* (Durham, NC: Duke University Press, 1989).

3

Soviet Reconquest of Central Asia

◆

Stephen Blank

umming up Central Asia's experience of Soviet rule is a daunting task. However, the end of Soviet power allows us to visualize that experience as pure history, not an ongoing process. When one looks for an organizing principle to understand that experience, one finds a fundamental continuity amid the storm of change from 1917 to 1991. That continuity is an abiding Soviet rejection of Central Asia as it was and an attempt to force it to be something other than that reality. Despite the profound changes from Lenin to Gorbachev, neither they nor those between them could accept Central Asia's objective reality. That reality offended their ideas and ideals and had to be swept away by grandiose if ill-conceived transformations or revolutions, socialism, five year-plans, collectivization, industrialization, *perestroika,* antireligious campaigns, national delimitations and cultural revolution, and so on. The Soviet project was always verbally and often in fact a revolutionary and violent one whose fundamental aims remained the transformation of Central Asia by a supposedly superior Russian model, a process entailing ideological, political, and physical coercion and socioeconomic revolution from above. Bolshevism required "holistic social engineering." To accept reality was to confess bankruptcy. Socialism's world-historical project had to replace the intractable reality as the truly real. At the same time this project took root in a Russian culture that not only welcomed grandiose heroic transformations, but also that had and still has a profound ambivalence about its role

in or towards Asia and a deeply rooted Islamophobia.[1] For example, early
Bolsheviks reserved the term *Aziatshchina* for the worst features of
Russian life. Another example is that virtually every commentator on
Stalin and his successors' rule invariably depicts it as Asiatic or Oriental
despotism, terms that carry a conscious choice of opprobrium, even though
few writers have so labeled Nazism.[2]

Thus "Orientalism," as Said used the term, Islamophobia, and ambivalence to Asia are constant but dynamic factors of the Soviet period.[3] And
they were ubiquitous in early political and cultural policies in Central Asia
and toward Russian Islam that laid the durable foundations of Soviet rule.
Bolshevik leaders displayed open colonialism toward minority cultures,
particularly Islam. They regarded Muslims as half-savage, primitive,
patriarchal, religiously fanatical, semibarbarous, stagnant, and barren in
their sociocultural dynamics. European and Marxist theories and Russian
Islamophobia profoundly shaped this outlook that viewed the Orient Fas
both violent yet "ahistorical"; a passive, stagnating, uncivilized receptacle
for the external imposition of a superior dynamic culture totally in contrast to that stagnation.[4] In comparing themselves to Asians, Bolsheviks
instinctively thought in terms of a superior culture, something that was
unthinkable regarding Europe. This orientalism and impatience with
Central Asian reality found political expression in the creation of Muslim
republics and the consolidation of their republican, not ethnic, identity.
Culturally it appeared in policies aiming to create a new Soviet man, by
suppression of Islam and Russification.

Marxism's conception of the Orient updated Europe's cultural hege-
mony over it. It was a discourse of power affirming European and later
Soviet Russian superiority over Asia in general and the Soviet Orient and
Islam in particular.[5] Those views lay at the core of Bolshevik policies.
Russian intellectuals who decried conditions in Muslim societies knew
about them almost exclusively at secondhand, and thereby perpetuated the
"orientalist" discourse. The Communist Party tended to see the Muslim
East as the site where Marxism's world historical perspective would
inevitably be validated as part of a foreordained and vast redemptive project regardless of the wishes of the people involved.[6] But until then the
East's insularity and "inscrutability" was a given. For Bolsheviks, the
Orient inhabited a mysterious, self-contained, uncivilized world largely
immune to western civilization on account of its hermetic social structure,
a structure that always remained a mystery to Bolsheviks even as they
sought to undermine it. Islam and a fanatic religiosity bounded this insular
society and culture, creating a world ruled by clerical elites and tribal or

patriarchal elders. This world lived as an entirely enclosed society within a dense network of mutually reinforcing boundaries of society and culture. Orientalism imparted a closed epistemological boundary to Bolshevik perceptions. Because of this clerical-clannic domination no autonomous self-generated renascence of culture and society could exist within Russian Islam. Since the Orient could not represent itself, the Bolsheviks had to represent it by transforming it from outside in the name of a superior culture. That foreign culture could then dominate, assimilate, and socialize Russian Islam.[7]

Because this hegemonic anti-Muslim viewpoint dominated Soviet thought and practice, Muslim societies were seen as hostile—they were strange, and strange due to their backwardness. Bolsheviks defined them negatively, perceiving them as ontologically inferior yet threatening. Orientalism reinforced Leninism's inherent premodern, mystificating, and magical qualities. According to Said, the Orientalist attitude in general shares "with magic and mythology the self-containing, self-reinforcing character of a closed system, in which objects are what they are because they are what they are, for once, for all time, for ontological reasons that no empirical material can either dislodge or alter."[8]

The ensuing "hegemony of possessing minorities" prevailed after 1917. In June 1921 Lenin warned Miasnikov, Armenia's party secretary, to be scrupulous and cautious toward eastern peoples "who are already awakened, who are in need of education, and who, when enlightened, will complete an even more grandiose overturn than in Russia."[9] Here lie all the canonical elements of Soviet orientalism: the image of the sleeping giant, awakened by an external impulse, but who needs our education; the underlying xenophobia and participation in an ultimately grandiose, vast, and globally redemptive project.

Earlier in 1921 at the X Party Congress, Safarov and Mikoyan attacked the party for treating the Eastern bloc and for forcing communism upon it by "cavalry raids" against religion.[10] After 1921, when the party singled out inequality as the root of national tensions, it instinctively assumed that the Muslim nations were the most backward and unequal. Policies of granting each nation its own language, native cadres, and so on meant raising the nation up to the higher European, if not Russian, culture.[11] In 1920 Zinoviev stated that "We cannot do without the petroleum of Azerbaijan or the cotton of Turkistan. We take those products not as former exploiters, but as older brothers bearing the torch of civilization."[12] He neatly united the frank imperialism and patronizing elder brother rhetoric that came to typify Stalinist and post-Stalinist nationality policy.

THE ATTACK ON ISLAM

The roots of anti-Islamic policy are to be found in the political struggles of
the 1920s. Muslim national Communists such as Mirsaid Sultangaliev and
his followers viewed Islam as an inseparable part of Muslim life and
devoted enormous attention to religious policy. They yielded nothing in
secularism to Soviet officials, but preferred and understood the nuanced
approach as being more likely to succeed and to defend Tatar interests.
They aimed to update or laicizize Islam. Sultangaliev started from
Communists' common accord that both foreign and domestic anti-Islamic
propaganda were needed.[13] He saw Islam as a religious and social force
and spoke of the consequences of that fact to which the party must orient
itself. Since Islam's force and state of development differed across Russia,
propaganda had to be tailored to each region's needs. This was also necessary since Islam, the youngest of major religions, was the most vigorous
and resistant to attack.

This vigor found expression in Islam's ubiquity in civil, social, and political life that strongly implanted it among believers and gave the clergy
high esteem. On the other hand, Muslim cultures were undergoing a modernizing renaissance. Islam now experienced a powerful sense of imperialist
exploitation, seeing anti-Islamic propaganda as an instrument of that
exploitation born of its prior weakness. While Islam was an object of fear
and enmity abroad, believers saw it as an oppressed religion and naturally
took up an embattled solidarity to defend it. In Russia this solidarity was
due to the rash attacks on mosques and Islamic foundations and the use of
hated tsarist missionaries to lead anti-Islamic policy.

To succeed, Soviet leaders had to avoid identifying with past methods
and employ a skillful, careful, and nuanced approach that eschewed
"shouting." Struggle had to appear as antireligious propaganda, not antireligious struggle per se. This propaganda should be conducted in the
course of life itself, by word and deed, not by brochure and letters. Village
atheists' daily lives would produce a demonstration effect that outstripped
literary or verbal efforts because they would refute traditional notions of
unbelievers. The regime must also stop using tsarist missionaries familiar
with Islam lest it run the risk of continuity with the past. Only Muslims
could effectively conduct antireligious propaganda, because Russian intervention would aggravate tensions. Ultimate success depended directly on
Islam's general development.[14] Sultangaliev outlined different conditions of
Islam among different Muslim groups and recommended texts and methods
for each people.[15] To some extent, he succeeded in mitigating the past fury

of anti-Muslim crusades because in 1922-23 republican constitutions tolerated Islam much more than Judaism or Christianity.[16]

His advocacy and his supporters' activity also apparently had a clear impact on administrative rulings and policies.[17] The year 1922 was the high point of Soviet understanding of embattled Islam's immense strength, partly due to his arguments as well as practical difficulties encountered in Muslim regions. Accordingly state agencies received a certain leeway in church and state issues to tacitly overlook the literal enforcement of the law.

But his temporary successes should not blind us to the fact of the countertendency's rising tide. After 1921 a sustained anti-Christianity and anti-Judaism campaign was high on the party's agenda, and not only for religious and political motives.[18] An antireligious apparat was emerging backed by the coercive means at the state's disposal. Before then no real policy had emerged due to the chaos of war. But there were many locally initiated attacks against all creeds. The X Party Congress of 1921 authored a new plan of attack that entailed the suppression of independent "cavalry raids" by a new Central Committee commission. Stalin's client, Emelian Iaroslavskii, devised those new tactics. In 1922-23 the commission drafted a program for central control and for generalizing Russian experience—a chauvinist phrase. It extrapolated from antireligious activity in 29 central Russian *Gubernias* that the Central Committee should place that agitation and propaganda high upon its agenda.[19] Here Moscow arrogated to itself the right to intervene directly in the republics' religious affairs.[20]

Moscow's presumption to decide religious policy by itself repudiated Sultangaliev's reliance on native cadres and initiative. The growing central commitment to a campaign of propaganda in depth, relying on a "scientific approach" under party supervision, was led by Iaroslavskii, whom Stalin installed to lead the policy.[21] His appointment gave control of religious policy to Stalinists who opposed Sultangaliev.[22] Iaroslavskii's goal was to concentrate antireligious propaganda in his own hands, where it would receive the proper "seriousness" of treatment and be used to diffuse party influence on a mass basis.[23] In short, he aimed to centralize his and the party's power, not just set a party line. That did not happen until 1926. For Iaroslavskii success meant deploying a party-led apparat, linked to the masses, to nullify deviant ideas. His appointment and policies soon epitomized the anti-Islamic campaign and its functional value for Stalinist totalitarianism.

Religion, a key indicator or definer of national consciousness, was immediately affected. For Muslims Islam provided the basis of their national identity. The antireligious struggle openly aimed to destroy the basis of their national identification—an intermediate objective to the larger one of undermining Pan-Islamic or Pan-Turkic movements in Russia. Bolshevik writings clearly intend to destroy both religion and its social scaffolding.[24]

Though always a secondary campaign for Soviet authorities, and one that attracted mediocre cadres to the regime, antireligious propaganda and repression was crucial for believers, shaping their hostility to the regime. Though official instructions for antireligion campaigns cautioned against offending believers' sentiments; for the most part such caution was beyond those involved. After 1921 Moscow encouraged boldness, not caution. Lenin admonished the authorities in Shuia during the famine in 1921 to confiscate church property with utmost violence: "Famine is the only time when we can beat the enemy [the Russian Orthodox Church] over the head.—Now when there is cannibalism in famine-stricken areas, we can carry out the expropriation of church valuables with the most furious and ruthless energy.—We must crush their resistance with such cruelty that they will not forget it for decades."[25]

This provocative, violent, and crude behavior showed a radical ignorance of and contempt for believers and minorities. Lenin was clearly ignorant about religion. Before 1917 his sole concern was to use Pan-Islamism against tsarism or imperialism.[26] The party ignored Islam's real social dynamics in different communities and the complexities of how it shapes believers' ethno-communal identity.[27] Thus it kept faith with orientalism's sense of Islam: an exotic, backward, threatening mass fanaticism. Lunacharskii, the commissar of education until 1929, grasped that an anti-Islam campaign that did not "enlighten the masses" would fail, especially since ex-missionaries were often its purveyors. But he regarded scientific propaganda, which was rarely used, as the most reliable instrument. He sought to foster secularization by removing clerics from schools, but not by direct assaults.[28] Yet he also wrote that not only would he not tolerate any religious education at state expense in any form anywhere, but also that the party must combat religious prejudice broadly using the entire educational *apparat*. As an afterthought he stated that this must not be coercive, but then qualified that by ruling out gradualism by unspecified "insignificant" measures.[29] Sixty years later this hostility to religion continued. Gorbachev's 1986 Tashkent speech on Islam was so violent that it could not be published. And he gave it in the context of his political battle directed against Muslim political autonomy and structures.[30]

But lower-level cadres were unimpressed by sophisticated ideas and viewed the issue in terms of the crudest expediency. A Muslim GRU defector recalled Turkistan's Komsomol's party leader commenting on Lenin's letter of 1920 to Ordzhonikidze admonishing him to deal tolerantly with Islam.

> Comrades, of course all of you realize that religion is an opiate and as such is incompatible with Marxism. No one formulated the matter more precisely than Lenin. You must not be confused with the Party's demands to win the confidence of the peasantry and lower clergy in Turkistan by whatever artifice necessary, and the incompatibility of Islam, the most reactionary of all religions, with Communism. You must understand that our effort to win confidence is a temporary tactical move to gain allies. If the devil himself is of some interest to us, we must win his confidence. The incompatibility of our movement with religion is a matter of strategy.[31]

Having little grasp of the effect of ceremony or of ritual upon believers, the government did not fight minority religions on these grounds. Instead it preferred repression, administrative legalisms, and "scientific propaganda."[32] And it remained faithful to this tedious and ineffectual mode of operation right through the 1980s. Therefore, the "peaceful" campaign largely failed before 1929 and again in the 1980s.[33]

Cooperation with Islam and its clergy would have gained more for the regime because Muslim clerics were by no means uniformly anti-Bolshevik. The creation of independent republics and toleration of Adat and Shariat courts after 1920 inclined many clergy to support the regime. Their motives were, of course, mixed. But even hostile clerics had to show a wary neutrality toward Moscow due to these concessions.[34] Though the regime mistrusted them and their neutrality, it eagerly pocketed the benefits of an outlook that foreclosed the possibility of a united, oppositional religious front against it.[35] But that did not suffice since the state was planning a comprehensive attack on Islam as it made those concessions.

Muslim ethnocentrism and its religious-based identification was a threat to Soviet officials from the moment they began ruling over Muslims. One radical Muslim was quoted then as saying "we do not need any cultural assistance. Muslim culture [note, not Tatar or some other branch] is higher than all others. We do not wish to know any advanced Russian culture." In the North Caucasus, for example, strong antireligious attacks helped trigger a massive anti-Soviet uprising in 1920-21.[36]

This uprising and its analogue, the Basmachi rebellion in Central Asia, obstructed the regime's overall Ostpolitik and forced it to make concessions. In November 1920 Stalin allowed the Shariat to govern Muslim customary law in Dagestan and implicitly elsewhere.[37] In 1921 Kirov followed suit. But both men described the concession as one of strict expediency to tame the opposition until the regime could move forward later.[38] Yet the local parties were unreconciled to those concessions.[39]

Ensuing policy was therefore deeply ambivalent. On the one hand, there were significant concessions to believers.[40] On the other hand, there were always insincere tactical retreats until the next round. This pattern later came to typify the overall antireligious policy. Periods of stormy attacks and campaigns were followed by a decline of interest, with the overall trend toward a general Soviet-wide religious revival clearly appearing in the 1980s as communism's exhaustion became all too visible.[41] Despite periods of caution, ambivalence, and hesitancy, the main issue, here as elsewhere, was its arrogation of power to itself to organize its subjects' mental lives. A 1922 circular letter of the CC stated that the central question of all agitation and propaganda was the Communist upbringing of the masses, which could succeed only if Marxism uprooted the religious worldview.[42]

Policy during the 1920s embodied this larger pattern of ambivalence and preparations for an attack. A Central Committee circular to Muslim regional organizations in 1921 reaffirmed the need to approach Islam cautiously, stressed the expediency of concessions to fight the Basmachi, and delivered the usual imprecations against Muslim fanaticism.[43] But other resolutions prove that agitation remained crude and unscientific in execution.[44]

The 1922-23 constitutions of Central Asia and the Caucasus were more tolerant of Islam than of Judaism and Christianity.[45] Many Muslims won the right to religious schools. Indeed, those were years of religious revival in Muslim areas. In some areas of Kirgizia more mosques were built than ever before. In Tatarstan 2,000 Mosques served 4,000 religious leaders. In 1924-25 800 religious schools opened there with 30,000 students under the age of 14 who had finished elementary school.[46] On the other hand, the external "classification" of nationalities from above on the basis of dogma was well advanced by then.[47] And by 1924 pressure to reverse them had begun.[48]

Iaroslavksii also displayed interest in framing religious policy aimed at Islamic exclusivity. In 1923 he traveled to Azerbaijan and found the need for careful tactics in the antireligious struggle because once again Muslim fanaticism was fed by all of the Muslim East. Any aggravation of Soviet Islam's condition would be duly reflected throughout this world too.[49] He made those remarks in 1925, but they certainly colored his thinking during the trip. His views reflected sensitivity to foreign opinion and an ingrained orientalist belief in the universality and intrinsic unity of Muslim fanaticism everywhere as well as Russian Islam's susceptibility to those influences. Therefore Russian Islam had to be insulated from foreign connections and influence. Territorial and cultural policies throughout the North Caucasus and Transcaucasia at this time and after assiduously followed the same goal of severing all ties to Kemal Ata-Turk's Turkey.[50]

The resolutions of the XII and XIII Party Congresses of 1923-24 embodied the view of Islam as inherently *mullah*-ridden, medieval, fanatic, and superstitious; a religion sunk in backwardness because of clerical domination.[51] Hence increasingly restrictive legal action was needed to circumscribe the *mullahs'* influence and then restrict religious activities and rights of Muslim institutions. Later the storming of Islam—a direct outcome of the failure of previous tactics to uproot it—would finish the job.[52]

LANGUAGE POLICY AND EDUCATION

In the creation of new languages and alphabets after 1921, the outcome conformed too closely with Soviet political considerations to be anything other than an engineered result. Here too policy emerged from the interaction of ideological axioms about language policy with practical considerations. Soviet policy continued tsarist efforts to Russify the minorities and stifle their cultural potential. And Brezhnev renewed this effort by pushing Russification in the late 1970s and 1980s throughout the Soviet Union.[53]

Lenin and Stalin exhibited the same ambivalence regarding language and education as they did in education and religion. Several of their premises remained at the heart of Soviet doctrine to the end. One is that language is the social product of culture. Therefore the language problem in multinational polities is an ideological-political, social, and methodological one. Its resolution depends not only on the language's structural aspects, but on ideology, politics, and the social system.[54] Here too we find total politicization and exclusion of linguistic autonomy in the name of those political criteria. Lenin resolutely fought coercion on behalf of Russia.[55] But he would not build real defenses for autonomous minority culture against forcible Russification because he and Stalin held that language was the sole or main cultural factor that identified or denoted national consciousness.[56] Granting linguistic equality would itself reduce tensions that retarded people's inevitable assimilation. Second, by changing social processes and relations, the state could induce a linguistic assimilation that undermined existing national consciousness and promoted a single socialist consciousness and culture.[57] After Lenin died policy continued to emphasize linguistic manipulation as a basis for national identification but embraced open Russification.[58]

The view that language is the common denominator of nationhood remained embedded in Soviet writings.[59] Stalin's 1925 formula promoting languages and cultures that were national in form and socialist in content fit perfectly with the stress on national languages and granted only a purely formal equality and freedom of use. Because Lenin and Stalin believed it is linguistic identification, not religion, that imparts national consciousness to peoples, they remained blind to the realities of Islam. Supposedly minorities cared only about linguistic equality and native language education. By giving them this in a restricted context, the regime would depoliticize and denationalize native languages by social engineering, prepare them for Sovietization, and defang nationalism.[60] Language policy, like overall nationality policy, was to be dialectical. But even considerable pressure for both Russification and linguistic reform of Muslim languages from below allowed the regime first to split Muslims and then to try to Russify them.

This course inevitably placed the regime on a collision course with national intelligentsias. Language reform was the centerpiece of their program and life's work, the basis from which they had moved into politics. While they often envisioned substantial, if not radical, linguistic and cultural changes, they rejected changes whose significance and content would be dictated from without. National regeneration took precedence for them over anything else, even socialism. For them language policy and planning had to facilitate a broader unity, true nationalism, and nativized languages.[61]

But the internal pressures to reform Muslim languages pointed in contradictory directions. Eventually Azeri preference for Latinization clashed with the Tatar resistance to it. Tatars favored a milder orthographic simplification of Arabic to make it a lingua franca accessible to all. Azerbaijan opted to Latinize as part of its resistance to Tatar hegemony in the Pan-Turkic or Pan-Islamic program led by Sultangaliev. When the regime gave serious attention to cultural issues in 1920-21, this rift came to its attention. It offered Moscow a chance to divide the Muslims by supporting Azerbaijan and justifying it later on ideological grounds. But other considerations also operated here.

Moscow now realized that the Muslim masses were strongly resisting communism. Much greater efforts were needed to reach those "illiterate, backward, and fanatical" masses. Scarce resources meant that this could only be done if native languages were equal to Russian and gave equal opportunities for advancement. Lenin's idea that language was the intelligentsia's primary concern clearly influenced Soviet thinking. It suggested that eliminating linguistic discrimination would substantially ease ethnic tensions, reconcile the key class—the local intelligentsia—and promote nativization of the apparat, particularly at its lower levels. These were among the more overt goals of the developing campaign whose real purpose was still more sophisticated and concealed.

The encounter with Muslims and Pan-Islamic or Pan-Turkic trends among them raised the danger of a culturally homogeneous, nationalist, or religious bloc collaborating in the anti-Soviet uprisings that began in 1920. Fear of this specter led Lenin and Stalin to devise a policy aiming, with all deliberate speed, at the fastest possible fragmentation of Muslim unity by all available means but averting violent uprisings. Concessions, such as granting use of the *Shariat* (Islamic laws), bought time while allowing this policy to take effect. And that policy meant exploiting every fissure within the Muslim community as well as using timely tactical retreats, as they did with religion.

This fear of Muslim unity and the fragmentation of it that resulted are the unifying threads of the seemingly contradictory Soviet policies of 1921 to 1924 in religion, nativization, state demarcation, and language policy. In each case the government sought to co-opt the intelligentsia and clergy, Islam's potential leadership strata, to its side. Language policies promoted individual people's separate cultures at the expense of common processes and resources while cloaking itself in the name of self-determination, national cultural development, and the like. That policy already foreshadowed Stalin's formula for national cultures because the fragmentation policy was to promote conditions for most if not all Muslims to fulfill the conditions Stalin had laid down in 1913 for nationhood or identification as such.[62]

The state could then deal with Muslim peoples directly and bilaterally rather than as part of the larger Muslim community. The new nations were tactically conceived attempts to impose Stalin's ideological criteria of nationhood upon formerly relatively undifferentiated clannic and tribal blocs.[63] In time they would become more susceptible to integrative processes associated with Soviet culture and turn away from Islam. This was an ideological and dialectically inspired policy of realpolitik. By individuating elements of the Islamic community along Stalin's lines, the regime would create a basis for their future integration into Soviet Russia.[64]

This policy and the change in views about native language equality with Russian date from about 1920-21. In October 1920 Stalin had placed linguistic equality and nativization at the center of his program for cultural revolution and assimilation. But his 1921 comments on Pan-Islamism demonstrate his real outlook.[65] Throughout his January 1921 speech to Muslim Bolsheviks he identified with Russia and noted that since

Russians had been the ruling nation, Great Russians and Bolsheviks generally had escaped national oppression. Except for certain great power chauvinist tendencies, they had nothing to do with nationalism and had no need to master it. Turkic Communists, on the other hand, still had to reckon with nationalist sentiments and survivals, such as the national deviation in the party. And this comprised their immediate task. Nationalism retarded Communist construction in the East, and Communists had to take responsibility for aborting it and other survivals, Pan-Turkism and Pan-Islamism, just as Lenin had, in 1917, insisted that Polish Bolsheviks and not Russian Communists attack Polish nationalism. Using Russians' prior experience, Muslim Bolsheviks could avoid past mistakes. These facts determined the Central Committee's "relatively soft policy" toward Turkic Communists whom Stalin admittedly already suspected of sedition.[66]

At Sultangaliev's 1923 trial Stalin reiterated his call for nativization, adding that it would strengthen the masses' Communist indoctrination and counter the intelligentsia's drift to republican nationalism.[67] Earlier, at the XII Party Congress, he stressed that language concessions were expedient moves to keep the peace but the dialectical policy of assimilation had to continue. Linguistic equality was a holding operation to encourage the masses' openness to native language Leninism until they were assimilated. Thus,

> Insofar as survivals of nationalism are a useful form of defense against Great Russian chauvinism we grant them as a loyal means of overcoming nationalist survivals. Insofar as these survivals are converted into local chauvinism directed against weak national groups in individual republics, direct struggle with them is the obligation of members of the party.[68]

The party decided whether a survival was useful or not, retaining control over the manipulation of national consciousness through linguistic policies. Meanwhile the inertia of state policy fostered Russification. No defense was made to charges that the army's policy of using Russian as a lingua franca was a deliberate Russifying force.[69] That was the policy's point. Economic, political, and cultural centralization inevitably meant a cumulative momentum from Moscow in favor of Russian.[70]

The policy culminating in Stalin's 1925 formula for cultures was also part of the larger plan to foster a "monolithic" pattern of Soviet culture. He noted that the national question was a global one of revolution and dictatorship, and nationalism's army was the peasantry.[71] By implication the intelligentsia was that army's general staff, and language policy aimed to weaken both groups' nationalist commitment. Stalin repeatedly insisted that the policy aimed to implant a broad range of native language schools and develop national cultures' socialist content. Development of individual cultures was a prerequisite for the later development of a single common culture, which would grow out of each separate culture's democratic component toward assimilation.

In practice, Stalin understood this to mean, as he wrote to Kaganovich in 1926, that Leninism was the highest development of Russian culture, hence indispensable to any proletarian culture.[72] He saw no contradiction between these two ideas despite the overt Russifying tendency of 1926, because socialism, in promoting national entities he defined in 1913, could then "reckon with real nations," which would then adhere to that definition and could foster assimilation. Nations were real only if they followed his criteria.

Undoubtedly formal policy pushed nativization from 1923 to 1929, but the results were limited. Ethnic stratification in politics, media, science, and the like continued and the top layer of government remained basically Russified. Worse, it caused both Russian and minority nationalism to grow steadily.[73] Nativization, which meant Latinization and new alphabets and languages for many peoples, failed to check centralization or nationalism on both sides.[74] Stalin's thinking also became more openly Russian nationalist, moving toward socialism in one country. But the language policy's major accomplishment was the Latinization of Muslim scripts and orthographies—a long-standing aim of many Muslim reformers.

Reformers promoting Latinization were mainly Azeris and North Caucasian; the Tatars favored modernizing the existing language to promote Muslim unity under Kazan's aegis. The Azeris, refusing to submit to Kazan, opted for individual Latinized languages. Until 1921 the dispute had been known but no policy decision had been made. Then many factors caused the situation to change.

Language policy became important in connection with the campaign to overcome illiteracy and the effort to seize control over all cultural policies.[75] The total reshaping of consciousness—creation of a new Soviet man—was diametrically opposed to any Islamic-based identifications. The concurrent compromises in religious policy also led officials to push Latinization to compensate for that forced retreat which offended their sense of propriety. Latinization would help undermine Islam by tightening central control over school curricula. More recently Soviet writers asserted that in the mid-1920s minority languages began to develop strongly in the schools.[76] In the Russian Soviet Federated Socialist Republic (RSFSR) the growth of minority schools teaching in native languages outpaced the increase in Russian schools.[77] The regime had to control that trend lest internationalism lose to nationalism and/or Pan-Islamism.

Latinization served as a way to shatter Muslim unity and lay the groundwork for an eventual turn to Russification. Party fears of Turkic uprisings from 1921 to 1924 only reinforced Stalin's determination to use it to divide Muslims and blunt the threat.[78] Latinization also would estrange Soviet Islam from Ataturk's reforms and isolate Soviet Muslims from that potential alternative "revolutionary" example. As a way to exploit Shi'ite-Sunni and Tatar-Azerbaijani rivalries and co-opt some of the intelligentsia, Latinization had considerable political utility.[79] At the same time it had to be promoted in a way that avoided any hint of Russification, which would have triggered united Muslim opposition.[80] As it took shape, Latinization accompanied the removal of Arabic and Iranian words and constructions from Muslim languages in preparation for future Cyrillicization and Russification.[81] Finally, it was implemented together with the introduction of Russian into schools as a future lingua franca.

Latinization also coincided with attacks against Kazan's cultural position in Soviet Islam, another sign of its divisive impact.[82] In February 1922 Narimanov formed an Azerbaijan committee to implement it there, opening a nationwide debate on Latinization.[83] Soon afterward Lenin called Latinization "a great revolution in the East."[84] And Stalin too carefully supervised Latinization developments. The program involved changing the alphabet, script, and orthography of Muslim languages to Latin letters along with linguistic alteration to a Latin script. But it also meant large-scale cultural engineering. In North Caucasia it meant that there would be no common language for Islam as a whole. Users of the existing religious Arabic script would face a wholly new written and literary language that would divide Muslims in a process directed by Soviet scholars and officials who created the new languages. Given Moscow's strong belief that language was the key to national consciousness, it could boast that it was creating new nations where none had existed, as Stalin had prescribed in 1913. After Narimanov's article the Latinization campaign accelerated rapidly.

Forty-six of 50 Caucasian peoples lacked their own script and used Arabic scripts, schools, and teachers. This explains Lenin's motives for embracing Latinization. The initial phase of creating Cherkess, Kabardinian, and Balkar scripts was organized in Baku with the crucial assistance of Narimanov and the Orgburo.[85] Stalin's Commissariat of Nationalities, Narkomnats, and the CC contributed substantial sums and administrative muscle to the project. They fully grasped Latinization's potential for dividing Muslims. In September 1922 Narkomnats's large collegium resolved to form a commission to reform the Arabic script and Latinize the alphabet in December 1922. This decree called Arabic an intolerant alphabet— a classic case of orientalism—and attributed a state significance to its reform. This reform would convert the basis of Muslim social organization from the clannic and religious and foster the creation of individual Muslim republics and regions within the state.[86]

Arabic's decline meant Russian's rise as the lingua franca since Muslims could no longer communicate meaningfully across national barriers in any Muslim or Arabic language or script. Not by coincidence the first All-Russian Congress for the Liquidation of Illiteracy resolved that it was necessary to study Russian, the language that united workers of different nationalities.[87] Latinization was cited as desirable for all Muslims. The commission also said that the evolution of the Arabic script from a religious one to a national one uniting non-Arab Muslims had been mistaken, thereby broadly implying Latinization's real aim.[88]

An intense public debate began in 1922. In Turkistan the notion that the alphabet needed reform because it was a great obstacle to mass literacy won much support, as it had elsewhere.[89] But many argued that Latinization was not the answer. Latinizers described Arabic as the priests' language, the language of those who sought to keep the population enslaved to the old ways. Therefore no one thought of publishing new works in Arabic. In any case, despite its venerability, few were literate in it. They and the regime disparaged Arabic as the language of religion and Islamic unity and sought instead to promote individual entities based on linguistic criteria of consciousness.[90] Moscow here adroitly exploited nationalists in smaller Muslim communities who wanted their people and each group to have its own dialect, press, or language. Such groups existed in Central Asia and the North Caucasus.[91] Latinizers firmly believed that language was the key to Islam's influence.[92] In 1932 Akmal Ikramov, first secretary of the Uzbek Party, openly admitted that it discarded Arabic, not so much because it was difficult, but because otherwise Uzbeks could never have freed themselves from the "noxious Muslim philosophy and Arabic scholasticism."[93]

Paradoxically the regime, at the same time, was creating local native languages or passing local and central statutes equalizing them with Russian. In the early 1920s Soviet scholars modified Arabic scripts for the Volga Tatars, Kazakhs, Kirgiz, and Uzbeks. Only in 1925 did linguistic policies harmonize and the regime begin to restrict these Arabic tongues.[94] The paradox lies in the emergency confronting the regime in the national

question from 1920 to 1925. Muslims' entrenched opposition to forced
cultural revolution and the scarcity of required materials for that transformation made it clear that Latinization would take years. Second, the
switch to Latinization led some to support it as a way to facilitate a uniform Latinized Turkic alphabet and Muslim cultural unity—directly
against Soviet policy aims. Instead the regime magnified phonetic and linguistic differences among Muslims to divide them over time in advance of
Latinization.[95] Since Latinization could only be a long-term program, the
regime could not idly wait for its acceptance. The linguistic alienation of
largely Russian officials from their subjects was a major cause of discontent that restricted possible avenues of mass support for the regime and
ensured continuing high levels of tension if not violence.[96] It also was a
formidable obstruction to the nativization program. Therefore both the X
and XII Party Congresses and the resolution at Sultangaliev's trial cited
the links among nativization, linguistic equality, dissemination of political
materials, native language education, and calmer local political conditions.[97] This toleration was, however, short-lived. As Paul Henze has recognized, by 1925 official weight had lined up behind Latinization and
elevation of "equal native languages" became watchwords that provided
an ample framework for dividing Soviet Islam. All this showed that while
languages had equal rights, they did not have equal value.[98]

The Volga Muslims sought to lessen Tatar influence over them. But linguistic gerrymandering reached its apogee in the North Caucasus and
Central Asia, where Moscow deliberately created tribal nationalities.[99]
Linguistic and political fragmentation of these regions went hand in hand
precisely to abort such aims and reduce Muslims' access to traditional
sources of culture. These policies fragmented Islam and created "microna-
tionalities," ethnic entities with an artificially contrived territory, economy,
and common culture expressed via languages, often created from above.
These "paper nations" represented efforts to validate Stalin's criteria of
nationhood since he claimed socialism could only reckon with existing
nations, not Pan-Islamic moods. Thus nations had to be created by fiat
from above.[100]

EMERGENCE OF NATIONALITIES

In Central Asia these language policies accompanied the political delimita-
tion of 1924-25 (Razmezhevanie) that created separate republics there.
Many peoples received their own tongue—for example, the Uigurs and
Dungans, who were preserved against the future chance of irredentism

against China. Immigrant peoples, living outside their native lands, except for Russians, were slated for absorption into their host republic by simply denying them schools, press, and a literary language where they lived. Artificial nations, such as the Karakkalpak, whose sole distinctive possession was their native dialect, emerged. Even upgrading of that dialect did not win local popularity. The new republics and nations were artificially created, either squeezed into Stalin's procrustean bed of ideology like the Kazakhs or else created to divide Muslims.[101] Though Stalin claimed that the delimitation made real nations and states feasible for the first time and welded together the toiling masses—significantly not the nationalities but rather a denationalized community including the Russians—with the state, Sir Olaf Caroe's and A. Z. Validov's findings decisively demolished these claims.[102]

Caroe and Validov found that the map contradicted Stalin since the borders are confused and twisted round like a "catherine wheel." The borders did not conform with linguistic boundaries—the 1926 census showed considerable Uzbek minorities in Tajikistan, for example. These were politically imposed borders made to retain central control and that belied true autonomy.[103] The façade of national self-consciousness and autonomy hid the fragmentation of real unity and the Russifying trends that would reduce the people to "disject membra."[104] More recently William Fierman found that the Razmezhevanie failed to divide peoples along linguistic cleavages in its effort to "democratize" the literary languages. The dialects included in Uzbek were so different from each other that there arose the very problem that Moscow claimed to avoid by not creating a single Turkic literary language.[105] It is inconceivable that Moscow did not know these facts, especially since they had parallels in the North Caucasus.[106] Uzbekistan, for example, had to Latinize to gain any common tongue. It had no choice but to opt out of the Turkic family, risk Russification, and consign its minorities abroad either to that fate or assimilation.

Certain consistent axioms governed these overall policies. The inherent disposition of the orientalist mentality to view the West as superior and the Orient as backward, inherently and constantly hostile, and fanatic unashamedly parades itself across scores of Soviet official texts and scholarship. Both the arrogation to Russians of the leadership of the world revolution and the logic of totalitarianism underlay efforts to denationalize Islam and prevent it from becoming a pivot around which Muslims could consciously rally.[107] Equally important is the fact that Soviet policy tried to force reality to conform to ideological dictates of a closed polarized mental universe. Leninism and orientalism postulated landscapes of immutable Muslim hostility and backwardness that were such because they were so proclaimed.

Lenin's refusal to allow minority culture room to breathe must be held accountable for these policies, notwithstanding his consistent opposition to forced Russification. Though he scolded the latter's adherents, he did nothing to stop them, and actively fostered processes and policies that stifled minority autonomy. He too could not resist the Russians' continuing refusal to learn native languages, and legitimate their use, a true sign of their deeply inbred sense of cultural chauvinism and imperial mission. Second, his and Stalin's belief that language denoted or was the foundation of national consciousness led them to try to denationalize minorities by stifling national cultures. Ensuing language policies amplified that line of thought, assuming that introducing linguistic changes with forced socioeconomic transformation would lead minorities to Russian, away from their past national moorings.

Already in the 1920 the sophistication, subtlety, and farsighted quality of this policy and the outlook it stemmed from could be seen. The comprehensiveness of design involved here was a consistent element of Soviet nationality policy. But that grand design and policy paradoxically created republics that developed an intelligentsia—the carrier of nationalist ideas—as the system proved unable to meet their socioeconomic pressure for development and advancement. This crisis and the larger Soviet crisis ultimately led to the creation of truly independent sovereign Central Asian states for the first time.[108] Due to this development several potentially fascinating trends are emerging: republican nationalism, a visible and universally acknowledged Muslim revival whose implications are as yet unrevealed both culturally and politically,[109] massive socioeconomic crisis and some revival of older, perhaps Pan-Turanian drives.[110] As Bernard Lewis recently wrote, the likely alternatives for these states are some form of post-Soviet association, Kemalism, or Khomeinism.[111]

CURRENT DYNAMICS

Certainly all the republics are looking to free themselves from the Russian embrace insofar as it is practicable. The Tajiks' revolt over stationing Russian Commonwealth of Independent States (CIS) troops there, the Kazakh strategy plan authorized by Nazarbayev with its frank criticism of continuing Russian efforts to retard Kazakhstan's economic independence, and the moves toward military autonomy as shown in the treaties of Kazakhstan and Turkmenistan with Russia all point to the Kemalist trend.[112] The negative side of that trend is found in the recent interethnic or communal violence as in Osh and Fergana.[113] Russian economic policy, the attempt to perpetuate a ruble zone and manipulate the terms of trade, plus the collective security and bilateral treaties signed by Russia evince its intention not to renounce its interests in Central Asia and perpetuate some post-Soviet connection, though not yet formally defined.[114] Here too there is a negative potential, as the rioting in Tajikistan indicates.

The attempts by some to project a pan-Turanian union of some sort — either the old idea of Tatarstan, Bashkiria, and Kazakhstan, or that of a revived Turkistan — also bear mentioning here because they counter the divisive impact of nationalism and serve as a secular albeit distorted image of Khomeinist pan-Islamic proclivities.[115] Finally there is Khomeinism. Though everyone acknowledges a rise in Islamic observance and identification, the blunt fact is that Islam differs across each republic and has never been a factor for unity in the Umma as a whole let alone Central Asia. The profound cleavages in each republic, plus the monumental economic problems in all republics, strongly suggest that triumphant militant Islam in one or more republics will awaken an extreme domestic nationalism as in Iran and an equally extreme counterreaction among those menaced by that threat. Charges that the Iranian option is predestined unless the West and the United States intervene are based on fear and ignorance and represent a U.S. variant of the orientalism discussed earlier and a Stalinist or colonialist belief that these states can exist only in the orbit of some other power, not on their own.[116]

What is clear is both the profound internal threats to the orderly progress of the new state and the magnitude of unpredictability that their future development is taking and will take. It is a rash expert who today can claim authoritatively to know or direct that course. And it is a still more rash politician who will emulate Lenin and Stalin and try to lay down that course from both above and outside of Central Asia. If we can say anything for sure as a lesson of Central Asia's Soviet experience, it is that for the forseeable future, no one will likely dare to or succeed in emulating the Bolshevik *folie de grandeur* and make it over in the image of a foreign reality. While that conclusion may not satisfy all the needs of those looking for a way out of the region's terrifying problems, it is not an inconsequential beginning of wisdom for them.

N·O·T·E·S

1. For recent examples see: Susan Layton, "Eros and Empire in Russian Literature About Georgia," *Slavic Review* 51, no. 2 (Summer 1992): 195-213; Milica Bakic-Hayden and Robert M. Hayden, "Orientalist Variations on the Theme 'Balkans': Symbolic Geography in Recent Yugoslav Cultural Politics," *Slavic Review* 51, no. 1 (Spring 1992): 1-15; Mark Bassin, "Russian Between Europe and Asia: The Ideological Construction of Geography," *Slavic Review* 50, no. 1 (Spring 1991): 1-17; Ronald Wixman, "Ethnic Attitudes and Relations in Modern Uzbek Cities," in *Soviet Central Asia: The Failed Transformation*, ed. William Fierman (Boulder, CO: Westview Press, 1991), pp. 159-185; Isabelle Kreindler, "Forging a Soviet People: Ethnolinguistics in Central Asia," in Fierman, ed., *Soviet Central Asia*, pp. 218-231.

2. For example, see the almost gratuitous statement of this in Ambassador Marshall Brement, *Reaching Out to Moscow: From Confrontation to Cooperation* (Westport, CT: Praeger Publishers, 1991), p. 173.

3. Edward W. Said, *Orientalism* (New York: Vintage Books, 1979), passim.

4. Gregory Massell, *The Surrogate Proletariat: Moslem Woman and Revolutionary Strategies in Soviet Central Asia, 1919-1929* (Princeton, NJ: Princeton University Press, 1974), p. 41.

5. Said, *Orientalism*, p. 7.

6. Ibid., pp. 40, 154.

7. Ibid.

8. Ibid., pp. 70, 172.

9. A. N. Mnatsakanian, *Aleksandr' Miasnikov* (Erevan: Alpetrat, 1957), pp. 179-180.

10. Massell, *Surrogate Proletariat*, pp. 44-45.

11. Mary Kilbourne Matossian, *The Impact of Soviet Policies in Armenia* (London: E. J. Brill, 1962), p. 36.

12. Cited in Michael Rywkin, "Searching for Soviet Nationality Policy," in *Soviet Nationality Policy: Ruling Ethnic Groups in the USSR*, ed. Henry R. Huttenbach (New York: Mansell, 1990), p. 70.

13. *Zhizn' Natsional'nostei* (henceforth *Zh.N*) 127, no. 29, December 14, 1921, p. 2.

14. Ibid., 128, no. 30, December 23, 1921, p. 3.

15. Ibid., 127, no. 29, December 14, 1921, p. 2.

16. Alexandre Bennigsen and Chantal Lemercier-Quelquejay, *Islam in the Soviet Union* (London: Pall Mall Press, 1967), p. 144.

17. A. G. Titov, A. M. Smirnov, and K. D. Shalagin, *Bor'be Kommunisticheskoi Partii s Anti-Leninskoi Gruppami i Techeniiami v Posleoktiabr'skoi Period (1917-1934gg.)* (Moscow: Vysshala Shkola, 1974), p. 325.

18. David Remnick, "Coming Out of the Lenin Closet," *Washington Post Weekly*, April 29-May 5, 1991, pp. 18-19; Trotsky later admitted that seizure of church valuables was one motive of the campaign against the Orthodox church.

19. B. N. Konovalov, "Soiuz Voinstvuiushchikh Bezbozhnikov," *Voprosy Nauchnogo Ateizma* 4 (1967): 64-65.

20. F. F. Ganinullin, "Rukovodstvo Partiinoi Organizatsii Bashkiri Anti-Religioznoi Propagandy 1917-1927gg.," *Uchenye Zapiski Oblastnogo Pedagogicheskogo Instituta Imeni N. K. Krupskoi* 277, no. 17 (1971): 254-255.

21. Joan Delaney, "The Origins of Soviet Antireligious Organizations," in *Aspects of Religion in the Soviet Union 1917-1967*, ed. Richard P. Marshall, Jr., Thomas E. Bird, and Andrew Q. Blane (Chicago, IL: University of Chicago Press, 1971), pp 110-112.

22. Ibid., pp. 127-128.

23. Ibid., p. 122.

24. Robert Conquest, *Religion in the USSR* (New York: Praeger Publishers, 1968), pp. 7-9.

25. Ibid.

26. Bohdan R. Bociurkiw, "Changing Soviet Images of Islam: The Domestic Scene," *Journal of the Institute of Muslim Minority Affairs* 2, no. 2, 3, no. 1 (Winter-Summer 1981): 10-11.

27. Maxime Rodinson, *Marxism and the Muslim World*, trans. Jean Matthews (New York: Monthly Review Press, 1981), pp. 12-13; Kemal H. Karpat, "The Turkic Nationalities: Turkish-Soviet and Turkish-Chinese Relations," in *Soviet Asian Ethnic Frontiers*, ed. William O. McCagg and Brian D. Silver (New York: Pergamon Press, 1979), pp. 119-120.

28. A. V. Lunacharskii, *Pochemu Nel'zia Verit' v Boga? Izbrannye Ateisticheskie Proizvedeniia* (Moscow: Nauka, 1965), pp. 236, 238, 288, 304, 310.

29. Ibid., pp. 230-231.

30. James Critchlow, *Nationalism in Uzbekistan: A Soviet Republic's Road to Sovereignty* (Boulder, CO: Westview Press, 1991), pp. 168, 175.

31. Ismail Akhmedov, *In and Out of Stalin's GRU: A Tatar's Escape From Red Army Intelligence* (Frederick, MD: University Publications of America, 1984), pp. 23-24.

32. Aryeh L. Unger, *The Totalitarian Party: Party and People in Nazi Germany and Soviet Russia* (Cambridge: Cambridge University Press, 1974), p. 189.

33. Muriel Atkin, *The Subtlest Battle: Islam in Soviet Tajikistan* (Philadelphia, PA: Foreign Policy Research Institute, 1991); Azade-Ayse Rorlich, "Islam and Atheism: Dynamic

Tension in Soviet Central Asia," in Fierman, ed., *Soviet Central Asia*, pp. 186-218; Critchlow, *Nationalism in Uzbekistan*, pp. 167-190.

34. Massell, *Surrogate Proletariat*, pp. 28-30; Alexandre Bennigsen, "The Soviet Union and Muslim Guerilla War 1920-1981: Lessons for Afghanistan," Rand Corporation Paper no. 1707/1, Santa Monica, California, 1981, pp. 12-13; Alexandre A. Bennigsen and S. Enders Wimbush, *Muslim National Communism in the Soviet Union: A Revolutionary Strategy for the Colonial World* (Chicago, IL: University of Chicago Press, 1979), p. 29; Joseph Berger, *Nothing But the Truth* (New York: John Day Company, 1971), p. 146; Nugman Ashirov, *Evoliutsiia Islama v SSR* (Moscow: Izdatel'stvo Politicheskoi Literatury, 1972), p. 15.

35. Massell, *Surrogate Proletariat*, pp. 28-30; Bennigsen, "Soviet Union and Muslim Guerilla Wars," pp. 12-13.

36. O. P. Osipov, "Protiv Falsifikatsii Roli Religii v Razvitii Natsional'nykh Otnoshenii," *Voprosy Nauchnogo Ateizma* 18 (1975): 65-66; Azade-Ayse Rorlich, "Islam Under Communist Rule: Volga-Ural Muslims," *Central Asian Survey* 1, no. 1 (July 1982): 20-23; N. A. Krylov, "Iz Istorii Propagandy Ateizma v SSSR (1923-1925gg)," *Voprosy Istorii Religii i Ateizma* 8 (1960): 169; M. M. Sattarev and F. G. Kocharli, "Razvitie Ateizma v Sovetskom Azerbaidzhane," *Voprosy Nauchnogo Ateizma* 5 (1968): 47.

37. I. V. Stalin, *Sochineniia* (Moscow: Gosudarstvennoe Izdatel'stvo Politicheskoi Literatury, 1946-51), vol. 4, p. 396.

38. Conquest, *Religion in the USSR*, p. 69.

39. M. M. Magomedov, "Iz Istorii Internatsional'nogo i Ateisticheskogo Vospitaniia Trudiashchikhsiia Dagestana," *Voprosy Nauchnogo Ateizma* 21 (1977): 270; Sattarev and Kocharli, "Razvitie Ateizma v Sovetskom Azerbaidzhane," p. 48.

40. Massell, *Surrogate Proletariat*, pp. 28-30; A. I. Osmanov, *Osushchestvlenie Novoi Ekonomicheskoi Politiki v Dagestane 1921-1925gg.* (Moscow: Nauka, 1978), pp. 68-69.

41. David M. Powell, *Anti-Religious Propaganda in the Soviet Union* (Boston, MA: MIT Press, 1982).

42. *Izvestiia Tsentral'nogo Komiteta RKP* 38, no. 2 (1922): 3.

43. Bociurkiw, "Changing Soviet Images of Islam," p. 13.

44. Bennigsen and Lemercier-Quelquejay, *Islam in the Soviet Union*, p. 144.

45. Ibid.

46. L. I. Klimovich, "Bor'ba Ortodoksov i Modernistov v Islame," *Voprosy Nauchnogo Ateizma* 2 (1966): 78.

47. Ibid; D. Hadjibelyi, "Anti-Islamic Propaganda in Azerbaidzhan," *Caucasian Review*, no. 7 (1957): 26-27; Edward Allworth, "A Theory of Soviet Nationality Policies," in Huttenbach, ed., *Soviet Nationality Policy*, p. 38.

48. Bennigsen and Lemercier-Quelquejay, *Islam in the Soviet Union*, pp. 144-148.

49. D. Hadjibelyi, "The Campaign Against the Clergy," *Caucasian Review*, no. 4 (1956): 80.

50. Paul A. Goble, "Coping with the Nagorno-Karabakh Crisis," *the Fletcher Forum of World Affairs* 16, no. 2 (Summer 1992): 20-21; Stephen Blank, "The Formation of the Soviet North Caucasus," in *Inheriting the Empire: The Soviet Empire From Lenin to Gorbachev*, ed. Michael Rywkin (New York: Massell Publishing Co., forthcoming).

51. *Kommunisticheskaia partiia Sovetskogo Soiuza v Rezoliutsiiakh i Resheniakh S'ezdov, Konferentsii i Plenumov TsK* (Moscow: Izdatel'stvo Politicheskoi Literatury, 1970), vol. 2, pp. 433-472, vol. 3, pp. 86-109.

52. Massell, *Surrogate Proletariat*, pp. 38-45; Abdurakhman Avtorkhanov, *Memuary* (Frankfurt Am Main: Possev, 1982), pp. 99-100.

53. Lubomir Hajda and Mark Beissinger, eds., *The Nationalities Factor in Soviet Politics and Society* (Boulder, CO: Westview Press, 1990); Bohdan Nahaylo and Victor Swoboda, *Soviet Disunion: A History of the Nationalities Problem in the USSR* (New York: The Free Press, 1991).

54. *Zakonomernosti Razvitiia i Literaturnykh Iazykov Narodov v SSSR v Sovetskuiu Epokhu* (Moscow: Nauka, 1969), vol. 1, p. 34.

55. Isabelle Teitz Kreindler, "A Neglected Source of Lenin's Nationality Policy," *Slavic Review* 36, no. 1 (Spring 1977): 86-100.

56. Ibid., p. 98.

57. Ibid., p. 95; Michael Bruchis, "The Effect of the USSR's Language Policy on the National Languages of Its Turkic Population," in *The USSR and the Muslim World*, ed. Yaacov Ro'i (London: George Allen & Unwin, 1984), pp. 129-130.

58. See also Bruchis's books *The USSR: Language and Realities: Nations, Languages, and Scholars* (Boulder, CO: East European Monographs, 1988), and *Nations — Nationalities — People: A Study of the Nationalities Policy of the Communist Party in Soviet Moldavia* (Boulder, CO: East European Monographs, 1984).

59. Kreindler, "Neglected Source of Lenin's Nationality Policy," pp. 86, 95.

60. Erich Hula, *Nationalism and Internationalism: European and American Perspectives* (Lanham, MD: University Press of America, 1982), pp. 25-26.

61. Joshua A. Fishman, *Liberalism and Nationalism: Two Integrative Essays* (Rowley, MA: Newbury House Publishers, 1973), pp. 17, 66.

62. Joseph Stalin, "Marxism and the National Question," in *Marxism and the National Question: Selected Writings and Speeches* (New York: International Publishers, 1942), pp. 7-68.

63. Allworth, "Theory of Soviet Nationality Policies," pp. 24-47.

64. Bruchis, "Effect of the USSR's Nationality Policy," p. 134; Kreindler, "Neglected Source of Lenin's Nationality Policy," pp. 9, 28n. Kreindler emphasizes popular

support from below for these policies instead of a desire to fragment Islamic consciousness. See also Helene Carrere D'Encausse, "La Politique Musulmane des Soviets Dans Une Republique Plurinationale: Le Dagestan," *L'Afrique et L'Asie* 34 (1956): 36; William K. Medlin, Willima M. Cave, and Finley Carpenter, *Education and Development in Central Asia: A Case Study on Social Change in Uzbekistan* (Leiden, The Netherlands: E. J. Brill, 1971), pp. 53-54.

65. Stalin, *Marxism and the National Question*, vol. 5, pp. 1-3, 173.

66. Ibid.

67. Ibid., pp. 358-360; V. I. Lenin, *Polnoe Sobranie Sochineniia* (Moscow: Gosudarstvennoe Izdatel'stvo Politicheskoi Literatury, 1958-65), vol. 53, pp. 28,40, 193-194, 257-258, 294-312.

68. Ibid., pp. 189-190.

69. John S. Reshetar, *The Problem of National Deviation in the Soviet Union with Special Reference to the Ukranian Republic*. Report to the Human Resources Research Institute, Maxwell AFB, Alabama, 1952, p. 6.

70. E. Glyn Lewis, *Bilingualism and Bilingual Education: A Comparative Study* (Albuquerque: University of New Mexico Press, 1980), pp. 54-55.

71. Stalin, *Marxism and the National Question*, vol. 8, p. 71.

72. Ibid., pp. 134-140.

73. K. N. Maksimov, "Korenizatsiia Sovetskogo Gosudarstvennogo Apparata Kalmykskoi Avtonomnoi Oblast (1920-1929gg.)," *Uchenye Zapiski Kalmykskogo Nauchno-Issledovatel'skogo Instituta Iazyka Literatury i Istorii* (Vypusk 10: Elista, 1974), pp. 113-114.

74. George Liber, "Language, Literacy, and Book Publishing in the Ukrainian SSR, 1923-1928," *Slavic Review* 41, no. 4 (Winter 1982): 673-685.

75. I. M. Moiseeva, "Pervye Shagi Sovetskoi Vlasti po Kommunisticheskam Vospitaniiu Trudiashchikhsiia Azerbaidzhan (1920-1922gg.)," *Materialy po Istorii Azerbaidzhana k 50 Letiuum Muzeiia* (Baku: Elm, 1973), vol. 8, p. 52.

76. *Present Day Ethnic Processes in the USSR*, trans. Campbell Creighton, Josef Shapiro, and Sheena Wakefield (Moscow: Progress Publishers, 1982), p. 136.

77. Bruchis, "Effect of the USSR's Language Policy," p. 134; Francis B. Randall, *Stalin's Russia: A Historical Reconsideration* (New York: The Free Press, 1965), pp. 229-230.

78. Ibid.

79. Ibid.; Robert Conquest, *Soviet Nationalities Policy in Practice* (New York: Frederick A. Praeger, 1967), pp. 72-75.

80. Bruchis, "Effect of the USSR's Language Policy," p. 134.

81. *Zh.N.* 148, no. 13, June 26, 1922, pp. 8-9; no. 3-4, 1923, p. 230.

82. M. I. Isaev, *Iazykovoe Stroitel'stvo v SSSR* (Moscow: Nauka, 1979), p. 51.

83. A. T. Baziev and M. I. Isaev, *Iazyk i Natsiia* (Moscow: Nauka, 1973), p. 111-112; D. Korkmasov, "Ot Alfavita k Literaturnomu Iazyku," *Revoliutsiia i Natsional'nostei* 67, no. 9 (September 1935): 35.

84. Kh. G. Beriketov, *Lenin i Kavkaz* (Nal'chik: El'brus, 1970), p. 212.

85. Dzh. B. Guliev, *Pod Znamenem Leninskoi Natsional'noi Politiki* (Baku: Azerbaidzhanskoe Gosudarstvennoe Izdatel'stvo, 1972), p. 373.

86. *Zh.N.* 153, no. 18, September 21, 1922, p. 5.

87. E. Sheudzhen, "Ob Osobennostakh Kul'turnogo Stroitel'stva v Natsional'nykh Oblastiakh Severnogo Kavkaza (1921-1925gg.), *Doklady Mezhvuzovskoi Nauchno-Teoreticheskoi Konferentsii Aspirantov 1969 God* (Rostv na Donu, 1969), p. 22.

88. William Fierman, "Nationalism, Language Planning, and Development in Soviet Uzbekistan (1917-1941)," Ph.D. diss., Harvard University, Cambridge, MA, 1978, p. 45.

89. Ibid., p. 24.

90. Stephen P. Dunn and Ethel Dunn, "The Soviet Regime and Native Culture in Central Asia and Kazakhstan: The Major Peoples," *Current Anthropology* 8, no. 2 (June 1967): 158.

91. Fierman, "Nationalism, Language Planning, and Development," p. 74.

92. Ibid., pp. 47-48.

93. Ibid.

94. Paul B. Henze, "Politics and Alphabets in Inner Asia," *Royal Central Asian Journal* 43, no. 1 (January 1956): 32-33, 49n.

95. Ibid., p. 33.

96. William Fierman, "The Shifting Russian and Uzbek Language Balance in Pre-World War II Uzbekistan," *International Journal of the Sociology of Language* 33 (1982): 129-130; Fierman, "Nationalism, Language Planning, and Development," pp. 191-194.

97. *Kommunisticheskaia partiia Sovetskogo Soiuza v Rezoliutsiiakh*, vol. 2, pp. 246-256, 433-443, 486-494.

98. Henze, "Politics and Alphabets in Inner Asia," pp. 33-49.

99. Alexandre Bennigsen and Marie Broxup, *The Islamic Threat to the Soviet Union* (New York: St. Martin's Press, 1983), pp. 39-39; Bennigsen and Lemercier-Quelquejay, *Islam in the Soviet Union*, pp. 126-128; Alexandre Bennigsen and Chantal Lemercier-Quelquejay, *The Evolution of the Muslim Nationalities of the USSR and Their Linguistic*

Problems, trans. Geoffrey Wheeler (Oxford: St. Antony's College, Oxford University, 1961), pp. 17-18; Ronald Wixman, "Language Aspects of Ethnic Patterns and Processes in the North Caucasus," University of Chicago Geography Department, Research paper no. 191, 1980, pp. 115-117; Edward Allworth, *The Modern Uzbeks: From the Fourteenth Century to the Present* (Stanford, CA: Hoover Institution Press, 1992), pp. 181-209.

100. Wixman, *Language Aspects of Ethnic Patterns,* pp. 115-117.

101. Bennigsen and Broxup, *Islamic Threat to the Soviet Union,* p. 42; Bennigsen and Lemercier-Quelquejay, *Islam in the Soviet Union,* pp. 130-133; Bennigsen and Lemercier-Quelquejay, "Evolution of the Muslim Nationalities of the USSR," pp. 28-33.

102. Bruchis, *Nations—Nationalities—People,* pp. 42-74.

103. Allworth, *Modern Uzbeks,* pp. 181-209; Sir Olaf Caroe, *Soviet Empire: The Turks of Central Asia and Stalinism,* 2nd ed. (New York: St. Martin's Press, 1967), pp. 146-147.

104. Ibid., pp. 148-149.

105. Fierman, "Nationalism, Language Planning, and Development," pp. 36-37.

106. Wixman, *Language Aspects of Ethnic Patterns,* passim.

107. The literature on totalitarianism and culture is too vast to cite here, but its insights are applicable and pertinent to this point.

108. "Central Asia: Valley of Trouble," *The Economist,* August 29, 1992, pp. 30-31.

109. Boris Rumer, *Central Asia: A Tragic Experiment* (New York: St. Martin's Press, 1987); Robert Lewis, ed., *Geographic Perspectives on Central Asia* (New York: Routledge, 1992), and the essays in Fierman, ed., *Soviet Central Asia,* highlight the profound socioeconomic and demographic crises of the region.

110. "Tatarstan President on Summit," *Foreign Broadcast Information Service (FBIS) Central Eurasia,* August 24, 1992, p. 6; "Turkestan Military District Proposed as Basis for Unified Central Asian Country," *FBIS,* August 28, 1992, pp. 82-83.

111. Bernard Lewis, "Rethinking the Middle East," *Foreign Affairs* 71, no. 4 (Fall 1992): 105.

112. Stephen Blank, "Russia and Iran in a New Middle East," *Mediterranean Quarterly* (Fall 1992); "Nazarbayev Statement on Republic Strategy," *FBIS, Central Eurasia,* June 4, 1992, pp. 72-86.

113. Abidin Bozdag, "Crisis and Democracy in Kirgizia," *Aussenpolitik,* English ed., no. 3., 1992, pp. 277-286.

114. Blank, "Russia and Iran"; Martha Brill Olcott, "Central Asia's Catapult to Independence," *Foreign Affairs* 70, no. 3 (Summer 1992): 115-120.

115. Tatarstan president on Summit, p. 6, Turkestan Military District, *FBIS,* August 24, 1992, pp. 82-83.

116. A. D. Horne, "U.S. Loses Specialist Fluent in the Nationalities," *Washington Post,* January 14, 1992, p. A7; David Hoffman, "Iran's Drive to Rebuild Seen Posing New Challenges to West," *Washington Post,* February 2, 1992, p. A1.

4

The Jadid Movement and Its Impact
on Contemporary Central Asia

Abdujabbar A. Abduvakhitov

he Central Asian region with its changing geopolitics demands special
attention from scholars who study interaction between Islam and politics. The resurgence or revival of Islam and the activism of different
groups within the Muslim community give us an opportunity to identify the future trends of this region.

ISLAMIC RESURGENCE

Strategically important regions of Central Asia such as Tajikistan and
Uzbekistan are returning to Islam and are gradually becoming an active
part of the Muslim world, demonstrating that the rehabilitation of Islamic
processes is under way. For the people of Central Asia, the current domination of religious slogans based on traditional Islam is understandable
and is very natural. This development should help us to understand the
nature of rising Islamic activism in Central Asia and to draw conclusions
regarding these trends, which cannot be separated from the Islamic world
and Islamic thought. However, life in the Central Asian societies is influenced by different factors, such as activity of political parties, elite groups
including the armed forces, and the development of economy.

In the Central Asian states two tendencies are visible: first, the emergence of new groups of national elite, and second, the rehabilitation of

those groups that dominated politics before the advent of the policy of *perestroika*. The latter were able to preserve their previous preeminent positions in the social structures. Despite these modest changes in the social structure, Central Asian societies have not yet been altered practically. However, small groups have developed, including the newly organized bourgeoisie, which should be studied. Central Asian tribalism is another important factor. Its role is not merely negative; in some cases it positively balances the social and political life. New contradictions in the tribal system have also appeared that cause conflicts between different groups in the republics, such as in Tajikistan. Except in Turkmenistan and Kazakhstan, no one dominating clan can exercise decision-making power in any one of these republics. New clans are "born", forging connections sometimes spontaneously, and then they confront each other in regional politics. Consequently, regionalism nourishes their local psychology.

In this situation, when Islam is almost completely rehabilitated, the factors of tribalism and regionalism in addition to nationalism are in action in Central Asian republics. Consequently, we should recognize that these republics will follow the way of contemporary developing countries. While the democratic institutions are weak, the role of small ruling elite is rising. Nevertheless, the role of the local army elite at present is insignificant. A national army elite was not created during the Soviet period, and it has not been formed since the advent of independence in December 1991. But it would not take a long time to appear in the Central Asian republics. These states have taken very important steps in forming national army elites by establishing national military units.

The former Soviet Union and Russian empire created a very complicated system of interlocking political, economic, and interethnic relations. The newly independent Central Asian states were parts of this highly unbalanced web of state relations, which still exists. This area still artificially unites many peoples. Social and political relations that should take a natural shape would need a long time to emerge.

When we study the Islamic political movements in the Central Asian republics, we should not analyze them in isolation from the similar processes in the Russian Federation where the Muslim community is also active and the Islamic factor is able to play a considerable role. At the same time we should not separate them from the national liberation movement and Jadidism, which created a liberation psychology, profoundly shaping the future life of the region.

During the course of Central Asia's recent history, the Jadid movement occupied a significant place. It has been an important factor in transforming the society from colony to independent states.

By the end of the nineteenth century the whole territory of contemporary Central Asia (Turkistan) was occupied by Russia, which used these new lands as a source of raw materials to meet the needs of its own economy. At the time, the local society, which was undergoing a crisis, was not able to resist the colonial policy. Because of the high level of feudal fragmentation and absence of a centralized strong state power on the territory, Turkistan easily fell into the hands of Russian empire as a colony. Furthermore, during this colonization process the ideological and political tendencies were unstable in the society of Central Asia. Due to the disunited and uncoordinated level of political thinking of people in different khanates, Central Asia could not resist Russia's colonial policy. Feudal psychology, which was further crippled by the old values and blind dogmas, prevailed.

This social, psychological, and political paralysis was observed not only in Central Asia but also in the whole Muslim world, which had become colonial parts of different empires. To alleviate the conditions of dependency, the national elites began to search for the new ideas and programs that eventually encouraged them to unite the main groups in the society and called upon them to be more active.

The national elites of Turkistan were familiar with religious ideas, and their representatives were often the graduates of the traditional religious schools. Consequently, they attempted to update the religious values to fit in with contemporary life. With this approach, the national elite helped to form new progressive attitudes that denied dogmas and their role in modern life.

THE JADID MOVEMENT: ADVENT OF MODERNISM

It was not accidental that the religious people who formed ideological doctrines in the society were divided into two groups by the end of the nineteenth century. The traditionalists, the biggest group, were against any change in the theory and practice of Islam and the form of education. The modernists, on the other hand, demanded some changes in the theory and practice of the Islamic community, revising old attitudes and adapting religion to the conditions of contemporary life.

The modernists urged their supporters to reform the system of education in the Muslim world. They demanded to include secular curricula in school programs. These demands were justified by the existence of deep contradictions and gaps between the levels of European and Central Asian education and the development of European economy and social thinking.

Jamaluddin Afghani (1838-1897) and his Egyptian disciples, Mahammad Abduh, Rashid Rida, and poet-philosopher Dr. Mohammad Iqbal, led the movement to modernize the system of religious education and defended the idea that the "gate of ijtihad [exercise of independent judgment] is open for renovation which helps the Muslim people to solve the problems of community." Building upon these renovations, the Muslims would transform their society to accept the contemporary technologies of the West and finally achieve cultural, economic, and political independence. While attempting to bring about changes in the system of education and enlightening national activity, while accepting the basic Islamic values and giving them new freshness, the modernists declared national independence to be their main goal. Also, these ideas inspired new ideological orientations for the contemporary movements such as the Ikhwan al-Muslimiyn (Movement of Muslim Brothers) in Egypt and Jama't-i Islamiy in Pakistan.

Among the movements that appeared under the influence of Jamaluddin Afghani and other Islamic reformers was the movement of Jadids in the Muslim part of the Russian empire. In my opinion, the history of this movement, which acted in the educational field, is tragic because its leadership was physically destroyed.

The Jadid movement was born in Crimea in the Russian Empire, where a part of the Tatar Muslim community was concentrated. This segment of the Muslim community in Russia was more educated and informed than other sections; they had made some achievements in learning sciences and arts of European countries, while they also shared the social thought of eastern countries. Under the influence of Jamaluddin Afghani's ideas, the urge to educate the Muslim people within the Russian empire began to grow. The Crimea Tatar Muslims were persuaded to adopt the progressive ideas and to accept the western sciences and technologies in order to eschew the scholastic dogmas both in religion and secular life.

Ismail Bey Gaspirali (1851-1914) was the founder of this movement in Crimea, which came to be known as Jadidism (renewal or renovation). He stands as a model to later leaders and intellectuals. While Gaspirali's slogan — *Dilde, Fikirde, Ishte Birlik* (unity of thought and action) — is widely known, the term *usul-i Jadid* reflects his unique contribution. Originally known as a new method of teaching Turkic languages, including simplified grammar and vocabulary, it came to apply to the style of instruction all subjects, especially in the *maktabs* (elementary schools). The *maktab*-level education, he emphasized, should teach not only the Qur'an, calligraphy, the Prophet Muhammad's traditions, and Arabic, but also geography, arithmetic, and science to create a new Muslim. By 1916 in Kazan (Tatarstan) there were more than a dozen Jadid *maktabs*. Gaspirali visited Central Asia, and under his influence *maktabs* were established in 1898, and in Tashkent in 1901. By the time of the Russian revolution in March 1917, more than 5,000 Jadid schools had been established in "Muslim Russia."[1]

Gaspirali's modernism was based on his education, travel, and social contacts. Educated in Russian schools, he lived for a few years in Moscow and in Paris. He traveled within the Russian Empire and visited Egypt, Muslim India, and the Ottoman Empire. While the comparative backwardness of Muslims everywhere saddened him, he nevertheless believed "that modern life and capabilities were not secrets reserved for Europe and its offshoots, but were available to all societies willing to face the challenge of change, and willing to sacrifice worthless tradition for progress."[2]

His ideas were presented in the newspaper *Terjuman* (Interpreter), which was founded in 1833, and remained in publication until his death in 1914. The language of *Terjuman* was understandable to all Muslim ethnic groups in the Russian Empire and especially to those who lived in Central Asia in the last decades of the nineteenth century. *Terjuman*'s central message focused on the imperative of Islamic updating and renewal in order for the Muslim communities to find an honorable place in the Russian Empire.

Through the Tatar missionaries, who disseminated Gaspirali's ideas, the Jadid movement spread all over Kazan (Tataristan), Orenburg, and Bashkiria. His ideas spread to Turkistan and Bukhara. (The latter was then separated from Turkistan because a "sovereign" empirate of Bukhara was still in existence.) Consequently, the Jadid movement was divided into Bukharan and Turkistani groups.

Tatar missionaries became a bridge between the Central Asian people and the new ideas and achievements of other people in the fields of culture, theater, music, and art. The Tatar language was understood and was linguistically close to the local languages. Tatars' activities in Bukhara and Turkistan, which were then closed societies, helped to change their social and cultural life. However, some scholars have maintained that the Jadid movement had less success in Bukhara, where the political system was less open to its mission, and the *mullahs* were adamant in their opposition to the establishment of Jadid schools.[3] The Jadids, nevertheless, were especially able to politicize the intelligentsia in Central Asia. This local intelligentsia began to be nostalgic about the former glory of their forefathers. During the 1890s the local intelligentsia actively joined the movement searching for the ways to jettison their dependent status.

The religious people in general and Islamic scholars in particular were not receptive to the new trends; they were especially against the reforms in the field of education and religious traditions.[4] Afghani's ideas had spread in the eastern countries with great difficulty and were not universally accepted. Yet some religious scholars who had graduated from the Islamic seminaries joined the Jadid's ranks; some even led the movement. Munavvar-Qari, Abdurashidov, Behbudi, and other activists had obtained religious degrees. It must be recognized that at this time there was not a single secular school in Central Asia. By having religious degrees, these men were able to call for educational reforms.

Also, Jadids established many journals and newspapers, such as *Saдoi Turkiston, Aina, Samarqand, Bukhoroi Sharif, Taraqqiy, Shuhrat, Khurshid,* and *Tujjor.*[6] Through these journals and newspapers they appealed to the intelligentsia.

Supporters of the Jadid movement emphasized the necessity of gaining the experience of European people and of sending Turkistanis to the developed countries to learn in depth of their economy, commerce and culture; at the same time they were determined to preserve their national and religious values. Jadids believed that all this activity finally would awaken the people and make it possible for them to gain national independence. The Jadids were inspired by the ideals of national liberation through modern educational achievement and self-determination. Tawallo (Toliygan Khojjamiarov), one of the Jadid activists, in his book *Rauwnaq ul-Islam* summed up: "Stand up and free your shoulders from those who sit on you; taste the power of education and freedom."

Jadidism from the very beginning united writers, poets, teachers, and other representatives of the Central Asian intelligentsia. There were even some merchants in this movement; rich Uzbeks financially supported Jadid books and journals. Despite these endeavors, Jadidism remained only a national elite movement.

One of the leading Jadids, Munawwar-Qari, stated in his memoirs that the activists of Jadidism did not support Bolsheviks and their actions (though some Jadids joined the Bolshevik Party), but mostly they supported the actions of kadets and the Constitutional Democratic Party and Socialist Revolutionary Party of Russia. Munawwar-Qary himself joined the Bolshevik Party. Subsequently he asserted that the Bolsheviks had continued the Russian colonial policy in Central Asia. Tawallo and some other Jadids joined the Constitutional Democratic Party and were appointed to different positions in the few governments. Some Jadids, realizing the real plans of Bolsheviks, joined the national liberation movement, which was called for many years in the former Soviet Union "*basmachi*" (*korbashis*).

During the first decade of Soviet rule nearly all Jadid movement activists were executed, including Munawwar-Qari, Abdulla Qadiriy, Chulpon, Abdur Rauf Fitrat, Usmon Nosir, Tawallo, and many others. Their deaths do not mean that the movement was defeated. In my opinion, Jadidism succeeded for the following reasons: The movement gave birth to the awakening of national self-determination of Central Asian people, gave them modern education, and brought positive changes in their political thinking. It was due to the Jadids' efforts that there was a cultural renaissance in Central Asia. They wrote outstanding novels, poems, and dramas, which are now famous not only in Central Asia but also in many other countries. Jadidism was a real step forward to the national liberation of the Central Asian people. Even in the field of religion there were many positive achievements, including modernization of attitudes, renovation of past practices, and the adaptation of Islam to modern conditions. Jadidism made Islam a vital force.

During the Soviet period, the Jadid leaders, knowing the aspirations of the Central Asian people, expressed their anxiety about their future and tried to defend them. The participation of Jadid leaders in many national parties during the first years of the Soviet regime was evidence of their developed political mind. In prison Tawallo, when asked why he had not written after 1919, answered that the Soviets showed their true face very early as they were ready to kill an unlimited number of people. He concluded that after 30 to 40 years of such vast killing the Uzbeks and other Central Asian people would disappear or be transformed into slaves. Under these conditions, he did not want to present the negative picture as positive. He also urged Chulpan not to write. Tawallo was condemned for writing *Rawnaq ul- Islam* (1916), a book of poems, and as a poet who composed anti-Soviet and anti-Communist poetry. He was executed in Tashkent on November 10, 1937.

IMPACT OF JADIDISM ON POST-SOVIET CENTRAL ASIA

As part of the history of Central Asia, Jadidism was and still is the most stimulating factor of contemporary political activism in the newly independent republics there. Seventy years of Soviet repression were not able to stop the influence of Jadidism. In independent Central Asian states, Jadid ideas about education, the need to assimilate the progressive experience of developed countries, and the modernization of religion cry out for renewal. In recent years, especially since the dawn of independence in December 1991, the ideas of Jadids have acquired a new direction. Their books and pamphlets have been reprinted. There are many new newspapers and journals aimed at educating people and raising people's consciousness. Some movements and institutions support the Jadids' slogans; in fact, a new organization, the Jadid Party of Uzbekistan, has come into existence. It is supposed to follow the principles of the Jadids beginning in the year 2000. Meanwhile, it will use the slogans and the name to achieve popularity among the people in the republic.

Religion certainly was one of the main areas of concern for the Jadid movement. Under the present circumstances, the revival of Islam in the area is under way. There is a link between Jadidism and the contemporary revivalism in Central Asia. When I asked Abduvali Qari (one of the leaders of Central Asian Islamic revivalism) about the main tasks of the Muslim community, he highlighted the necessity of being flexible concerning renovation of the society and revising some traditions, and educational activity in a mixed system, where both religious and secular education are blended.

This view demonstrates that the orientations of the Jadids and contemporary revivalists are close; in fact, the latter's position is the continuation of the former. But it is important not to think of them as clones of one another. Rather Jadidism and revivalism are two stages of one process of gaining real independence and establishing of a sovereign state. In the process of the national liberation movement, it is appropriate to emphasize that Jadidism and the contemporary Islamic revivalist movement have their own peculiar places: Without the first stage of Jadidism, and without the so-called *basmachi* movement, it is difficult to understand the roots of current movements and parties that have specific features, especially those reflecting extremism among Islamic groups.

During the periods of the Russian and Soviet empires, the policies about religion, in this case the Islamic religion, held a very important place. In the life of the Central Asian republics where Islam occupied a dominant position and Sufi *tariqas* (orders) spread all over the territory, their existence and influence can be observed even today. They are likely to change considerably the future developments in these states. The cultural policy of the former Soviet state and the local authorities was aimed at the suppression of Islamic activities and the destruction of Islamic community. The main objective of the Communist Party was, as it was announced by the local Uzbek atheists, to build a new society "absolutely free of religion." This policy had no effect on the life of Uzbekistan and could not eliminate the development of revivalist trends during the period before Gorbachev's policy of *perestroika*.

NEW PARADIGM OF THE ISLAMIC WORLD

In Uzbekistan a group of young Muslim intellectuals led by Rakhmatulla Alloma, Abduvali, and others began to be active at the end of the 1970s. Their educational activities were effective and made part of this community ready for today's revivalist movement. This movement created many illegal Islamic schools designed to teach young people about Islam. Moreover, it published and distributed many religious books, including some works of Abul Ala Maududi of Pakistan and other ideologists of Islamic revivalism. The movement's adherents endeavored to knit those young people into a group dedicated to building Musulman-abad, the land of Islam. This movement is a natural process based on local conditions and influenced from abroad. The paradigm of Musulman-abad, according to Abduvali, was prepared by Rahmatulla Alloma and contains the following constructs: (1) Central Asia and the Muslim world are a single unified Muslim territory where Islam dominates all over; (2) the *shariat* (Islamic code of laws) rules the relations between the peoples; (3) all the people believe in Allah and the society is ruled by the educated *ulama*. This space where Islam is dominant now should be revived. Historically, one single Muslim state on the territories of the contemporary Muslim world did not exist. Abduvali explained that Musulman-abad means unification of different independent states as one Muslim area in which there would be many states united by Islam.

In order to create Musulman-abad, it was decided to educate people in the ethos of Islamdom. This educational activity was effective right up to the beginning of Gorbachev's era. While the revivalist movement lost its leader, Rahmatulla Alloma, in an accident in 1981, the second tier of leaders emerged in the mid-1980s.

By the end of 1989, they were legally allowed to open a number of schools and mosques and to establish printing houses. By this time the local authorities were unable to stop the process of rehabilitating religion, a process that actually emanated from Russia and, first of all, concerned Christianity. The young Muslims who graduated from the revivalistic schools took a few bold steps and were ready to go on hunger strikes and undertake other political actions in order to revive Islam. These people were then called "Wahabies," the orthodox Muslims.

In Namangan, an important city in the Fargana Valley that is one of the very active centers of the Central Asian revival movement, the revivalists were able to regain the possession of Gumbas Mosque after thousands of revivalists encircled it. In Andijan, which is a revivalist city of no less importance, Jami Mosque has been led by Abduvali Qari, who became a vocal heir to the ideas of Rahmatulla.

Even within the artificial system of official Religious Administration, which had been established by the Soviet Union, things began to change. New radical leaders came to power and changed the system's policy toward radicals, ushering in revivalistic Islamic trends in Central Asia. This new clan of radical leaders came from the Fargana Valley and forced out the Tashkent clan. Despite this change, the new authorities of Spiritual Administration were against the Wahabies.

By the end of 1990, local young people had established several groups of Islamic militia almost spontaneously in the suburbs of Namangan (Uzbekistan). Actually, they were not revivalists. The people who acquired the possession of Gumbas Mosque soon were able to infiltrate the leadership of the militia. Consequently, the Islamic militia became known from the very beginning of its existence as a part of the revivalist movement. Branches were opened in other parts of the valley, and they started to become active revivalist groups.

In December of 1991 they captured the building of the local Namangan branch of the People's Democratic Party and then announced their 15 demands of the government of the republic. Among these demands, they wanted the government to (1) proclaim the establishment of an Islamic state on the territory of Uzbekistan; (2) use only the *shariat* law in ruling the state; (3) stop the policy of drawing close to Turkey; (4) separate the male and female schools; and (5) provide the Muslims with an administrative building in Namangan. Negotiations brought few results but did provide the revivalists with a building in the city. Some promises were made that have yet to be fulfilled.

In April 1992 new examples of revivalist activity in Namangan were visible. The revivalists and the government officials were not able to agree on how to use this administrative building. The local authorities then repossessed the building and closed the city's Islamic center. Some days later outraged revivalists took a few people from the local authorities hostage. Another group of revivalists, who were committed to wage active political struggle against the secular government, emerged as a separate unit called "Tauwba" (repentance), and yet another group united under the name "Baraka" (blessings). In a few days, under the pressure of local Muslim leaders, the hostages were released. These activities of Islamic revivalists opened a new era of relations between the government and true believers of Islam.

Some of the militant activists are currently under arrest and others are functioning illegally. The Muslim community in Uzbekistan is now divided into many factions. In the near future, the community may be drawn into further religio-political conflicts. Yet another area of conflict is the existence of the Russian-speaking community in Uzbekistan. Naturally, their condition would attract the attention of Russia. If Russia decided to intervene by military means, a major conflict would erupt.

The revivalism in Uzbekistan is not only an important factor of the political life of the Central Asian region, it also is a force capable of generating political dynamics in other regions of the former Soviet Union. Its influence must be seen in the new Russian Federation, which has its own large Muslim community. Within this Muslim community the same processes may be observed. The comparative study of the two communities may provide us an opportunity to make prognoses for the future.

N·O·T·E·S

1. Alan W. Fisher, "Ismail Gaspirali, Model Leader for Asia," in *Tatars of the Crimea: Their Struggle for Survival*, ed. Edward Allworth (Durham, NC: Duke University Press, 1988).

2. Edward J. Lazzerimi, "Ismail Bey Gasprinskii (Gaspirali)," in Edward Allworth, ed., *Tatars of the Crimea*, p. 161.

3. Fisher, "Ismail Gaspirali," p. 25.

4. See also Helene Carrere d'Encausse, *Islam and the Russian Empire*, trans. Quintin Hoase (Berkeley, CA: University of California Press, 1988), p. 78.

5. Alexandre Bennigsen and Marie Broxup, *The Islamic Threat to the Soviet State* (New York: St. Martin's Press, 1983), pp. 78-79.

6. See also d'Encausee, *Islam and the Russian Empire*, p. 79.

▲ ▽ ▲

5

Perestroika: Its Impact on the Central Asian Republics and Their Future Relations with Moscow

◆

Melvin Goodman

The Soviet Union collapsed in an unusual and virtually unprecedented manner. It was not the result of war or major acts of violence; it was sudden and totally unexpected. Many of Gorbachev's policies contributed to this collapse, particularly his flawed economic policies and the economic chaos they produced, his depoliticization of the Communist Party, and his policy of *glasnost,* which directly contributed to transforming suppressed nationalism throughout the empire into a revolutionary struggle for self-determination. Gorbachev's waffling on economic policy worsened the domestic chaos, his moves against the party and Politburo ended the legitimacy of the government, and his discussion of autonomy encouraged the republics to assert sovereignty over their resources.

This transformation of nationalism to revolutionary ferment began in the Baltic states but quickly spread to Moldavia, the Caucasus, Ukraine, and even Central Asia. The Central Asian states appeared most willing to maintain ties to Russia and the Commonwealth of Independent States, but they fought long-resented Soviet efforts to integrate the region politically, economically, and culturally with the Russian heartland.[1] Gorbachev never understood the Islamic heritage and cultural vitality of the region, let alone the ethnic differences that contributed to the rivalries among Uzbeks and Tajiks, Kazakhs and Kirghiz. These peoples did not mourn the passing of tsarist rule in 1917, and they shed no tears for the Soviets 75 years later.

Gorbachev and his foreign minister, Eduard Shevardnadze (who was baptized as Georgi in 1992 in a Georgian Orthodox cathedral), were able to build a consensus on foreign policy from 1985 until the latter's sudden and emotional resignation in December 1990, but they had no success on nationality policy. They blazed new trails on arms control and disarmament, East-West and Sino-Soviet relations, pushed for political and economic reform, but were restrained and cautious when dealing with nationality issues. Gorbachev, in hindsight, seemed virtually ignorant on these issues, but Shevardnadze should have helped. He was born and raised in Georgia and is now chairman of the Georgian parliament. He experimented with *glasnost* in Tbilisi long before Gorbachev introduced the policy to Moscow.

There is no doubt that the policy of *glasnost* had the unintended purpose of persuading Central Asians and Balts alike that the Politburo had sanctioned their mass political actions. The policy encouraged acts of nationalism throughout the Soviet Union, including Russia, where an unofficial group (*Pamyat*) held public meetings and demonstrations. The publicity given to these actions contributed to greater ethnic identity. For political reasons, Gorbachev could not apply the policy of *glasnost* selectively, extending it only to those issues he endorsed. He wanted more original thought and personal initiative throughout the empire to stimulate political and economic change. The Soviet Union's last and most radical leader certainly got more change than he bargained for.

GORBACHEV AND ETHNIC POLITICS

Gorbachev's policies brought about the fundamental changes of 1991, but he never endorsed the aspirations for greater political autonomy and cultural differentiation that spread throughout the 14 non-Russian republics. He was determined to repulse the most extreme demands for autonomy and rejected plans for "borders to be redrawn" and "national minorities to be expelled."[2] He condemned "calls for economic autarky," declaring that "their implementation would throw us all a long way back." At the same time, however, he clearly acknowledged nationality grievances and pledged support for expanded republic rights, denouncing the "lawlessness" of the Stalin era. Until January 1991, he was reluctant to risk direct confrontation.

Gorbachev was unprepared for the nationalities' problem. Until his appointment to the Politburo in the late 1970s, his entire career was spent in the North Caucasus, in Stavropol. He rarely spoke on nationalities issues and, when doing so, never veered from the official line. As general secretary in the mid-1980s, his speeches reflected a naive optimism about the problem and, moreover, a tendency to address his remarks to the "great Russian people" and "Russia," instead of the Soviets and Soviet Union. His personnel changes in the Central Asian states were designed to end corruption in the region, but they were insensitive to ethnic politics there.

Gorbachev was confronted by violence on the nationalities' issue from the outset. There were riots in Kazakhstan in the winter of 1986-87, the first nationalist-inspired upheaval in the Soviet Union during Gorbachev's rule, when he unwisely replaced the Kazakh head of the local party organization with a Russian national. The protests were far more extensive and better organized than official accounts described, with thousands of students coming into the city.[3] Scores were killed and hundreds injured, the worst violence of its kind until an attack in Tbilisi in April 1989, when approximately 20 young students lost their lives. The riots made Gorbachev more sensitive to the problem but no more able to develop a solution.

The personnel shift in Kazakhstan was the last of a series of changes throughout Central Asia that replaced indigenous party leaders in Tajikistan, Turkmenia, and Kirghizia for alleged charges of corruption.[4] Months after the riots in Alma-Ata, Crimean Tatars held several widely publicized protests in Red Square and near the headquarters of the Central Committee, including an unprecedented four-day sitdown demonstration near Red Square. As a result, Moscow banned such gatherings in Red Square, around the Kremlin, and in other major downtown squares. Nevertheless, the protests led to more open discussion of the injustices of Stalin's nationality policies, which of course encouraged other nationalities to make their grievances public.

ETHNIC POLITICS AND ETHNIC VIOLENCE

Protests immediately sprang up in the Baltics. Thousands demonstrated in Riga in the summer of 1987 against the annexation of the three Baltic republics in 1940. On the anniversary of the Molotov-Ribbentrop Pact, protests took place in all the Baltic capitals. Moscow forced the introduction of local laws requiring permits ten days before a planned demonstration. With the memories of the riots in Alma-Ata still strong, the Politburo was unnerved.

Confronted by increased violence in Central Asia and the Caucasus as well as in the Baltics, a divided leadership tried to call a plenum of the Central Committee in the summer of 1989 in order to deal with ethnic unrest and make some policy decisions. Differences over policy caused a great deal of heel-dragging and a series of postponements of the plenum scheduled for that year. No draft laws on nationalities appeared in 1989, and the Communist Party's Institute of Marxism-Leninism and the Academy of Sciences failed to recommend policies to the Politburo. Eventually the Politburo approved a "draft platform" on nationality policy and forwarded it to republic party organizations, but the document ignored Gorbachev's warnings about the "growing danger of an exacerbation of interethnic relations" and his assertion that the "fate of restructuring and the integrity of our state" depend on the resolution of nationality disputes.[5]

MOSCOW AND THE POLITICS OF ETHNICITY

Moscow's handling of the problem pointed to the political sensitivity of the ethnic issue. Gorbachev, on the one hand, argued that a policy solution was "not a matter for the distant future," but he offered only vaguely defined commitments to equal rights for all citizens and the "free development of language and culture."[6] The Central Committee held a conference in May to prepare materials for the plenum on nationalities but the meeting went unreported in the media. The fact that party secretary and KGB chairman Viktor Chebrikov addressed the conference was never mentioned. When the Institute on Marxism-Leninism finally met in July, there was no mention of specific proposals regarding the ethnic issues on the agenda.[7]

The reticence of the Soviet media probably reflected the divided responsibility for nationality issues within the leadership. In addition to Gorbachev's role as president and general secretary of the party, Premier Nikolai Ryzhkov headed the Politburo Commission on Questions of Interethnic Relations and Secretary Vadim Medvedev led the Central Committee Commission on Ideology, which also dealt with nationality issues. Chebrikov chaired the party conference in May but rarely spoke publicly on nationalities issues. When doing so, however, he took a harder line than did his colleagues, presumably as part of an overall political effort to maintain pressure on the liberal policies of Gorbachev. Chebrikov and "First Secretary" Fedor Ligachev were Gorbachev's leading critics, believing that the policy of *glasnost* was directly responsible for the unleashing of nationalism in the Baltics, the Caucasus, and Central Asia.

Medvedev led a faction that was willing to allow greater economic autonomy in the various republics; Chebrikov had consistently taken a harder line toward economic reform and economic independence in the

Baltics. During a visit to Estonia in July 1989, Medvedev was friendly to the notion of economic reform in Tallinn.[8] A month later Chebrikov told an interviewer that economic independence could come only through integration; he explicitly rejected any notion of economic autarky.[9]

The leadership differences over the nationalities' issues probably explains the tepid "draft platform," entitled "Draft Nationalities Policy of the Party Under Present Conditions," which was Gorbachev's effort to reach consensus on this divisive and ultimately explosive issue.[10] Approved by the leadership in July but withheld from the press for more than a month, the document offered no detailed solutions for specific problems and adhered to previous defined limits on republic rights. No new ground was broken on ethnic grievances over redrawing republic borders and the superiority of national laws over republic laws that had led to confrontations with Moscow since the riots in Alma-Ata in December 1986.

The plenum platform implicitly acknowledged that the leadership continued to be divided over the nationalities' issue and that no Soviet leader was willing to sponsor more than limited compromises. The platform declared that the "fragmentation of the USSR by nationality is fundamentally unacceptable" and that "political documents" could be adopted only "within the limits of the Communist Party program." The document refused to expand any of the provisions for economic independence, emphasizing that the Soviet Union had the right to define nationally the principles for the use of land and mineral resources. There was no endorsement of Lithuanian and Estonian draft laws to give the republics unrestricted authority to control natural resources. The platform, moreover, contradicted the efforts of the Baltic states to gain legitimacy for the application of national legislation within their territories.

In a move that was a harbinger of the Yeltsin government's protection of ethnic Russians in the non-Russian former republics of the Soviet Union, the draft platform asserted that Russians too have suffered under past policies and endorsed new Russian institutions in the Russian republic to bolster its autonomy. The most significant of these institutions was a party leadership body for the Russian republic, which had no republic-level party organization since the abolition of the Russian Bureau of the Communist Party Central Committee in 1966.

Gorbachev, in a televised address, made it clear that he was unwilling to go beyond the limited concessions expressed in the platform.[11] He rejected Armenia's demand for the transfer of Nagorno-Karabagh and refused to endorse the Balts' autonomy plan. His policies may have contributed to eth-

nic violence by demonstrating that he would use force against those groups—
such as the Balts—that were trying to avoid violence, but not against those
groups—such as the Ukrainians—that were prepared to resist. Given the
intractability of the nationality conflicts, the rebellious mood within the non-
Russian elements in the party, and the hesitancy of Gorbachev on ethnic
issues, it was inevitable that push would come to shove.

THE LEADERSHIP AND THE NATIONALITIES' PLENUM

When the nationalities' plenum was finally held in September 1989, it
turned out to be a great political success for Gorbachev but broke no new
ground in dealing with the country's increased economic and ethnic problems. In a remarkable show of political strength, probably his last at this
level of party politics, Gorbachev ousted several of the Politburo members
most objectionable to the Balts and Central Asians and least supportive of
reform, including KGB Chairman Chebrikov and Ukrainian party leader
Vladimir Shcherbitsky. Chebrikov was Gorbachev's major nemesis on
nationality issues, and Shcherbitsky was becoming increasingly unpopular in the Ukraine.

Chebrikov's removal was the most surprising since he had been prominent over the summer, installing the new first secretary in Kazakhstan in
June, acting as a spokesman on nationality issues in August, and attacking the Balts in September. He was a member of the Politburo commission
in charge of preparations for the plenum on nationalities and the main
spokesman for hard-line views on nationality affairs. As secretary in
charge of internal security, however, he was responsible for handling the
tragedy in Tbilisi while Gorbachev was out of the country. Chebrikov
admitted that he was the Politburo member in contact with Georgian
leaders when the order to the military and police was given to crush the
demonstration.[12]

Shcherbitsky's opposition in the Ukraine included nationalist and
reformist groups that had been calling for his retirement. At the same
time, one of his protégés, Andrey Girenko, was named to the Secretariat,
indicating the limits of Gorbachev's power and the residual strength of
Shcherbitsky. Like Shcherbitsky, Girenko was opposed to making
Ukrainian the state language of the republic. Shcherbitsky's departure
from the Politburo, however, left only two non-Russians in the top leadership body, a Belorussian and a Georgian.

THE LANGUAGE ISSUE: THE THIN EDGE OF THE NATIONALITY WEDGE

Since the leadership failed to come up with an effective program to deal with nationality issues, the republics themselves began to address these sensitive problems. The republics were alert to the problem of provoking a Russian nationalist backlash or a showdown with Soviet officials but, nevertheless, began to enhance the status of their local languages. As with other issues affecting republic autonomy, Estonia took the lead on the language issue and, in January 1989, adopted a law making Estonian the language of government and business and establishing deadlines for public institutions to switch all communications to Estonian. In order to mollify Moscow, military personnel in Estonia were exempted from the law entirely and Russian-language primary schools were permitted to conduct administrative business in Russian.

The other Baltic states also adopted language laws, and Moldova, Belorussia, Ukraine, and Tajikistan followed suit.[13] Lithuania made Lithuanian the state language but ensured that all public institutions provided services in any language acceptable to their employees. Like Talinn, Vilnius exempted military personnel from any language requirements and allowed non-Lithuanian schools to keep records in their own languages. Latvia's law was similar but went further in appeasing Moscow: Russian was specified as "one of the means of international communication" along with Latvian.[14] Moreover, the law was not declared to be operative until 1995 in regions heavily populated by Russians.

The first sign of a protest movement in Uzbekistan took place in Tashkent in November 1988, when a student group demonstrated to promote the Uzbek language and reduce the use of Russian on television, in classrooms, on street signs, and in courts. A mass rally took place a year later, in which the agenda had been broadened to include ecological and economic issues as well as linguistic resistance. With the appearance of popular front movements in Uzbekistan and an increase in ethnic militancy, nearly 100,000 Russian speakers fled the country, leaving such vital installations as the republic's largest thermal electric power station without skilled maintenance personnel.[15]

Russia as well as the non-Russian republics wanted to avoid confrontation over the language issue, and Moscow appeared to accept the conciliatory language of the various decrees. The Soviet leadership conceded that local nationalities had faced discrimination in the past and expressed a willingness to allow republics to adopt laws protecting their languages. Gorbachev even acknowledged that "linguistic Russification" was a problem and defended the right of every ethnic group to understand its own roots and develop its own culture. He told cultural and scientific leaders that Moscow "cannot permit even the smallest people to disappear, the language of even the smallest people to be lost."[16]

Gorbachev's willingness to compromise on the language issue encountered criticism from the leadership, particularly KGB chairman Viktor Chebrikov. Gorbachev's opponents presumably believed that his conciliation on this issue was merely another effort to appeal to moderate reformers in the non-Russian republics, which it almost certainly was. Gorbachev, in addition to shoring up the moderate elements within the republics, was trying to undermine the influence of nationalist extremists and strengthen popular support for *perestroika*. Chebrikov, on the other hand, shared neither Gorbachev's objectives nor, of course, Tallinn's anxieties about preserving its language. During his visit to Estonia in November 1988 at the height of the constitutional crisis, he mocked the notion that "someone is encroaching on your language."[17]

Differences within the Soviet media reflected the leadership division, although most publications supported a greater role for non-Russian languages. *Izvestia* acknowledged the problem of "linguistic Russification" on Moldavia, and *Pravda* regretted the decrease in the "number of national schools."[18] A senior researcher with the Institute of Marxism-Leninism, however, denounced the granting of state-language status to any language, arguing that minorities eventually would be "unable to study their native languages."[19] Additional articles denounced language laws as efforts to "establish . . . the inequality of the population speaking languages other than the indigenous language."[20]

The anticipated nationalist backlash was not long in coming, particularly from Russian intellectuals and ethnic Russian organizations in non-Russian republics. In November 1989, at the plenum of the Russian Writers Union, a separate "Russian" writers organization was created in Leningrad to counter the allegedly Jewish-dominated Leningrad union amid a chorus of extremist attacks on Jews and reformers. The Russian nationalist writers, the most open opponents of *perestroika*, had taken control of many of the prominent intellectual journals in the country, including *Nash Sovremennik, Literaturnaya Rossiya,* and *Oktyabr;* and were finding a more receptive audience among workers and peasants in local elections. In the winter of 1989-90, moreover, the Yedinstvo movement, which represents Russians living in other republics, joined the Russian Writers Union and the United Front of Russian Workers to form Rossiya, an organization to "help maintain permanent links" among legislative deputies, voters, workers, and public organizations.[21]

GEORGIAN VIOLENCE AND RECRIMINATIONS OVER REFORM

The clumsy and brutal attack in Tbilisi in April 1989, which left 20 people dead, led to a nationalist upsurge in Georgia and elsewhere as well as to a sharper debate in the country over the impact of democratizations and *perestroika* on nationality problems. The attack, now known throughout Georgia as "bloody Sunday," was conducted by Soviet forces and Internal Affairs Ministry troops against a group of young people in the central square of the capital, where the troops had sealed off the exits before bludgeoning the demonstrators with trenching shovels. The tragic incident should have convinced Gorbachev that the use of the military in "police actions" was counterproductive, but he resorted to the same tactics in January 1991 against the Lithuanians, with similarly devastating consequences.

The first accounts of violence in Georgia suggested that *glasnost* had never been introduced, condemning nationalists for provoking the troops, exonerating the political leadership, and attributing the fatalities to a panic that led to the trampling of demonstrators on the streets of Tbilisi.[22] Nearly two weeks later Yegor Yakovlev, then chief editor of *Moscow News* and a reformer who lost his position as chief of Moscow's radio and television center in the winter of 1992-93, traveled to Tbilisi and filed the first Soviet accounts of a "peaceful" demonstration that had made no "call for violence or any other unlawful action."[23] Yakovlev's trip to Georgia was part of a parliamentary delegation that made the first Soviet references to deaths from "chemical agents" and described the attack as a "deliberate provocation . . . to sap the growing prestige of . . . Gorbachev."[24] As late as mid-May, the Soviets were officially denying any use of chemicals and refused to cooperate with the efforts of Andrei Sakharov to identify the agents in order to develop an antidote for the hospitalized victims in Tbilisi.[25]

The leadership in Moscow was aware that any debate over the causes and consequences of the violence in Georgia would lead to recriminations over the reform process and attempted to downplay the attack from the outset. Gorbachev and Shevardnadze were the only Politburo members to address the issue, and they carefully avoided the rhetorical extremes of the reformist and conservative accounts. Gorbachev confined his remarks to a defense of his nationality policies and emphasized that *perestroika* did not mean a "redrawing of borders or breaking up the country's ethnic state structure."[26]

Shevardnadze made himself particularly unpopular in Tbilisi by coupling criticism of the Georgian nationalists with denunciations of the republic party leaders' handling of the demonstrations. He spent a week in Georgia in April, never mentioning the use of poisonous gas, and argued that both sides were "unable to display tact, restraint, or calm, and to build dialogue with the other."[27] His unusual exoneration of General Igor Rodionov, the commander of the Transcaucasus Military District who was eventually censured for his actions, served to place responsibility on the local Georgian leadership.[28] Shevardnadze's exoneration of Rodinov may have been designed to legitimize the professional military's opposition to the use of regular army forces to quell disturbances, but it did not play well in Tbilisi. His continued unpopularity in certain circles in Georgia, where he is head of state and chairman of the parliament, stems in part from his lackluster investigation of the incident.

The battle between nationalists and reformers over the Tbilisi incident revealed a far greater split within the leadership over nationality policy and suggested that Gorbachev would never be able to resolve the differences. Concern was growing within the leadership that the policies of *glasnost* and *perestroika* were energizing nationalist movements in the Baltics, Caucasus, and Central Asia. At the same time, nationalists were badgering Gorbachev and his minions for increased regional autonomy. The general secretary was trying to balance the rival factions, but, in his closing speech to a Central Committee plenum in April 1989, he revealed increased displeasure with nationalist independence movements, accusing "anti-Soviet elements" of trying to "exploit long-neglected" nationality policies.

PERESTROIKA AND CENTRAL ASIA

The four pillars of *perestroika* throughout the Soviet Union were democracy, *glasnost*, political renewal, and economic modernization, which in turn led to the formation of civil rights groups, writers' groups, cultural institutes, and environmental groups demanding change. Civil rights groups were formed in Turkmenistan and Kirghizia, and cultural studies throughout the region made comparisons between the Afghan mujahideen and the anti-Soviet guerrilla movements of the 1920s and 1930s. The Central Asians long had a case for affirmative ecological action, particularly for water redistribution, and in the late 1980s began to make their case. Protest movements began to appear, particularly in Uzbekistan, where the leader of a popular front exhorted crowds to "take control of their own land. We must feel that we are the true masters."[29]

The creation of such movements, however, was hampered in Central Asia by the lack of organizational skills and political sophistication. The exception to the rule was Kazakhstan, where there was a tradition of some cooperation between Russians and Kazakhs and the mutual concern with environmental problems led to the formation of several ecology groups. The most prominent of these was "Nevada-Semipalatinsk," the only binational unofficial group in Central Asia, formed to protest nuclear testing but expanded to include other ecological and political issues.[30]

Tajikistan and Uzbekistan were the quickest to hold demonstrations to defend nationality issues, particularly linguistic independence, and to form popular fronts based on the Baltics model. The Uzbek group known as *Birlik* (Unity) became a growing political force, with an agenda that was nationalist and strongly influenced by Islam.[31] The increase in demonstrations in the region, particularly the violence in Uzbekistan's Fergana Valley, added to the popularity of these groups. Similarly, the demographic shortfalls in the region, particularly high infant mortality and lagging immunization, provided additional grist for the mill of protest.

When more than 100 people were killed and 1,000 wounded in the Fergana Valley, *Birlik* tested the power of its grass-roots movement in the capital city and organized an unauthorized rally in Lenin Square, the parade ground of the Uzbek Communist Party.[32] The people who rallied to *Birlik's* cause should have been natural allies of Gorbachev's *perestroika* because they also were demanding economic and political renewal. But Moscow's worries about Afghanistan and the rise of Islamic fundamentalism in Iran in the 1980s increased the political distance between the Kremlin and the Central Asian capitals. The cultural differences between the Russians and the Central Asian Muslims were also a force for separation. Gorbachev was able to make a decision to withdraw Soviet forces from Afghanistan for geopolitical reasons, but the Soviet mindset had not moved sufficiently from Leonid Brezhnev's rationale for the invasion: to prevent the uniting of the diverse peoples of Central Asia against the Russian heartland.

THE CENTRAL ASIAN STATES AND NATIONAL SECURITY

Just as the Crimean War had been the undoing of Tsar Nicholas I and the Russo-Japanese War of 1905 had begun the unraveling of the reign of Tsar Nicholas II, the invasion of Afghanistan was the final nail in the coffin of Brezhnev. The Soviet invasion of Czechoslovakia in 1968 had encouraged cynicism and disappointment among Russian intellectuals, but these thoughts were primarily private ones that were not translated into political action. In the case of Afghanistan, however, the Russians spoke openly of their opposition and lack of understanding of Brezhnev's decision to invade a weak border state at a time of political uncertainty and economic weakness in Moscow.

Despite differences over nationality issues, Russia will continue to play a key role in the security interests of the new Central Asian states because of their political and economic backwardness and their concerns with the geopolitical aspirations of Turkey and Iran. The Central Asians are concerned with a "Balkanization" of the region and see the chaos and uncertainty in Afghanistan as a catalyst for revolutionary change throughout the region. Some cooperation between Moscow and the Central Asian capitals will be needed in order to withstand the pressures and rivalries among Turkey, Iran, and Pakistan in the region.

The Commonwealth of Independent States (CIS) is not a genuine political entity and will not be a factor in the defense and security policies of Central Asia. The CIS, in fact, is a fig leaf for an unwieldy alliance of republics that must determine responsibility for its borders, its treasure, its army, and its military assets. The agreements that formed the commonwealth sidestepped many of these matters as well as the most serious issue confronting the member states—the collapse of their joint economy.

There is a tendency among western analysts to invoke the nineteenth-century model of the "great game" for Central Asia, which tends to exaggerate the role and influence of Turkey, Iran, and China in the diplomacy of the region. Despite the sudden and unexpected collapse of the Soviet Union and the military and economic weakness of Russia, there is a tendency to exaggerate Moscow's influence among the Central Asian states. These states are, of course, weak and unstable, but they are wary of external influence, either from ultra-nationalists in Russia or Islamic fundamentalists in Iran. The Central Asians are introducing themselves to the process of nation-building and national identity, and are not friendly to the notion of replacing Soviet influence of the past 70 years with foreign influence of another stripe.

At the same time, the Central Asians are aware of their military weakness and political vulnerability and, as a result, are willing to cooperate with Russian military forces over the near term. They are wary of Turkish and Iranian influence in the region, and Tajikistan particularly fears Turkish encroachment. Both Kazakhstan and Kyrgyzstan, moreover, have significant Russian populations, and the Muslim republics lack the officer corps to create viable armies and the economic resources to support a military network. As a result, they favor short-term cooperation with Russia in order to build their military forces, train personnel, and procure weaponry.

In the beginning, some of the Central Asian states believed they could get along without an army and were unwilling to contribute to the unified armed forces of the commonwealth. Several months after the formation of the CIS, all the Central Asian states except Tajikistan signed a collective security arrangement with Russia that committed the parties to military cooperation and mutual assistance in case of aggression. One year after the formation of the CIS, only Kyrgyzstan had not created its own army. President Askar Akayev proclaimed a neutral Kyrgizia that would not "enter any military blocks . . . create its own army, or take military units on its territory."[33]

Kazakhstan President Nursultan Nazarbayev reversed his pledge against a national army within several weeks. At the CIS summit in Minsk in February 1992, Alma-Ata supported the notion of a centralized CIS force, with a "single system of support and maintenance, a single military education system, and an extraterritorial manning of the Strategic Forces."[34] After several days of rioting at the Baikonur space center, which was provoked by the arrest of one Kazakh soldier by the military police, Nazarbayev reversed himself and established a Republican Guard. The Guard is made up of volunteers and is not part of the CIS Unified Armed Forces. When Russia created its own armed forces, Kazakhstan followed suit and, in May, reorganized the State Committee for Defense into the Defense Ministry. Nazarbayev then transferred all commonwealth forces on his territory to the Defense Ministry.[35] At the CIS summit in Tashkent, also in May, Kazakhstan joined Russia and several other Central Asian republics in a common defense treaty and declared that the armed forces of one CIS state could not be used against another.[36]

Soon after the formation of the commonwealth, Uzbekistan organized a National Guard and placed Russian troops on its territory under Tashkent's jurisdiction. The parliament withdrew Uzbeki soldiers stationed in the Baltics and the Caucasus, allowing its soldiers to remain their only on contract. When Boris Yeltsin created the Russian armed forces in May, President Islam Karimov did the same in Uzbekistan.[37] At the CIS summit in Tashkent that month, Karimov explained that "events in Afghanistan and Tajikistan required a closer relationship with Russia."[38] Since then, he has called for Russian, Kazakh, and Uzbeki cooperation in peacekeeping operation in the region.

The civil war in Tajikistan—the poorest of the independent states that emerged from the detritus of the Soviet Union—has led, of course, to a greater dialogue between Russia and the Central Asia states on national security. Moscow fears the success of the Islamic-dominated coalition in Dushanbe, and ethnic Russians have fled Tajikistan because of the appearance of Tajik troops from Afghanistan, where they fought for Gulbuddin Hekmatyar, the fundamentalist Muslim leader. The ethnic, religious, and clan unrest that has swept the southern rim of the former Soviet Union has kept Russian troops in the region, nominally under the command of the commonwealth. Increased violence in Afghanistan has added to the refugee situation and unrest in Tajikistan.

Uzbekistan (nearly one-fourth of the population of Tajikistan is Uzbek) and Kyrgyzstan (with only 2 percent of the population in Tajikistan) have sealed their borders against refugees from the fighting and increased controls against their political opponents. Kyrgyzstan still has not formed its own army—the only former Soviet republic not to do so—and has signed a treaty with Russia for defense cooperation. It has formed a National Guard, but a far smaller one than now exists in Uzbekistan and Tajikistan. The Kyrgyz Supreme Soviet has refused to participate in peacekeeping actions in Tajikistan.

Tashkent has been far more aggressive in protecting itself against the instability across the border. President Islam Karimov has stopped flights between Tashkent and Dushanbe, closed party newspapers, and seized assets of opposition banks. He particularly fears the influence of Hekmatyar in the region and has called for a United Nations peacekeeping force in Tajikistan. In the meantime, Uzbekistan's Supreme Soviet dispatched an Uzbek battalion to Tajikistan to participate in the multinational peacekeeping force under CIS command.[39] Karimov's policies have made Tajiks more nervous in Uzbekistan, where they represent only 4 percent of the population but are an important part of such key cities as Bukhara and Samarkand.

Like Kazakhstan, Turkmenistan did not want to form its own army; like Kyrgyzstan, it signed an agreement with Russia for defense cooperation. President Saparmurad Niyazov said defense cooperation was necessary to guarantee "social protection of the military and pensions for the officers."[40] The civil war in Tajikistan was the more likely cause of the closer ties between Russia and Turkmenistan.

PROSPECTS FOR ETHNIC POLITICS

Ethnic politics and ethnic violence will be sources of friction and conflict for the Russian leadership for an indefinite period. Unlike Gorbachev, however, Boris Yeltsin is addressing the problem at the highest level of Russian politics, including the appointment of one of his most capable advisors as deputy premier and chairman of the State Committee for Nationality Policy. In early November 1991, only several weeks before the winter session of the Congress of People's Deputies, Yeltsin appointed

Sergey Shakhray as a member of the Security Council and a viceroy for the North Caucasus in addition to his position as nationalities' supervisor.

Shakhray replaced two officials who lacked Yeltsin's confidence, councillor for interethnic affairs Galina Starovoytova and chairman of the State Committee for Nationality Policy Vlery Tishkov. Shakhray is an outspoken reformer and, in addition to Deputy Premier Aleksandr Shokhin and economics advisor Gennady Burbulis, strengthens what is left of Yeltsin's original economics team. They are lined up against such conservatives as Security Council chairman Yury Skokov and administration leader Yury Petrov on a series of domestic issues. When Shakhray resigned from the government in March, he cited his differences with both Petrov and Skokov, particularly their efforts to exclude him from decision making.[41]

Several days after his return to the highest levels of government, Shakhray was dispatched to the Caucasus to be "head of the temporary administration on the territories of North Ossetia and the Ingush Republic."[42] He supervised the State Committee for Nationality Policy while deputy premier from December 1991 to March 1992, but left the administration at that time due to pressure from the conservatives and to serve as Yeltsin's floor manager at the spring session of the Congress. Shakhray was a logical choice for the delicate assignment in the northern Caucasus, having been raised in a Cossack community, a serious student of interethnic relations, and claiming the Caucasus as his homeland.

Yeltsin, of course, will need all the help he can muster. The fighting has increased in Central Asia and the Caucasus, a renegade Russian general commands forces in Moldova, controversies over ethnic issues continue in the Baltics, and Ukraine is dragging its heels over ratification of the START treaty and other disarmament issues. These non-Russian regions harbor great distrust and suspicion of Moscow, but the worsening state of their economies and the importance of national security problems demand some cooperation with Russia. These regions and states would have more independence and flexibility if they could count on western economic and security guarantees, but, barring a U.S. effort to lead an international arrangement, they ultimately have to negotiate with the Kremlin. The Central Asian states, with greater concerns on their borders with Afghanistan, China, and Iran, will be the most conciliatory of all toward Russia.

N·O·T·E·S

1. See Martha Brill Olcott, "Central Asia: The Reformers Challenge a Traditional Society" in *The Nationalities Factor in Soviet Politics and Society*, ed. Lubomyr Hajda and Mark Beissinger (Boulder, CO: Westview Press, 1990), pp. 253-280.

2. *Izvestia*, July 2, 1989, p. 3.

3. See Martha Brill Olcott, "Central Asia: The Reformers Challenge a Traditional Society," in Hadja and Beissinger, eds., *The Nationalities Factor in Soviet Politics and Society*, pp. 253-280.

4. There was another series of changes among local party leaders in 1988, when Gorbachev named a new first secretary in Uzbekistan, Armenia, and Azerbaijan. The following year, new local leaders were named in all the Baltic states as well as Ukraine and Moldova. Thus, Gorbachev changed every republic leader where there had been ethnic disturbances. Unlike his Kazakh mistake, he made sure to appoint indigenous leaders, not ethnic Russians.

5. *Pravda*, July 16, 1989, p. 3.

6. TASS, July 2, 1989.

7. *Sovetskaya Rossiya*, July 5, 1989, p. 5.

8. *Izvestia*, July 7, 1989, p. 5.

9. *Pradva*, August 19, 1989, p. 3.

10. *Pravda*, August 19, 1989, p. 1.

11. *Izvestia*, July 2, 1989, p. 3.

12. *Moscow News*, no. 37, September 1989, p. 3.

13. The three Transcaucasus republics—Armenia, Azerbaijan, and Georgia—granted state language status to their languages in the 1930s.

14. *Sovetskaya Latviya*, February 1, 1989, p. 2.

15. Murray Feshbach and Alfred Friendly, Jr., *Ecocide in the USSR: Health and Nature Under Siege* (New York: Basic Books, 1992), p. 87.

16. *Pravda*, January 7, 1989, p. 3.

17. *Pravda*, November 15, 1988, p. 3.

18 *Izvestia*, February 1, 1989, p. 3; *Pravda*, December 30, 1988, p. 4.

19. TASS, February 2, 1989.

20. *Izvestia*, January 8, 1989, p. 4.

21. TASS, January 24, 1990.

22. *Pravda*, April 10, 1989, p. 1.

23. *Moscow News*, no. 17, April 23, 1989, p. 5.

24. Ibid.

25. Author's interview with U.S. ambassador to the Soviet Union Jack Matlock in Moscow on May 12, 1989. The author led the first foreign delegation into Tbilisi in May 1989, when Moscow lifted the ban on foreign travel to Georgia.

26. TASS, April 12, 1989.

27. TASS, April 20, 1989.

28. *Izvestia*, April 26, 1989, p. 3. Roald Sagdeyev, Gorbachev's leading space scientist, referred to "bloody Sunday" as "our Irangate," and General Rodionov as "our Colonel Ollie North."

29. Feshbach and Friendly, *Ecocide in the USSR*, p. 86.

30. See Martha Olcott, "Central Asia," p. 275.

31. See Timur Kocaoglu, "Demonstrations by Uzbek Popular Front," Radio Liberty, *Report on the USSR*, vol. 1, no. 17 (April 1989): 13-16.

32. See Hedrick Smith, *The New Russians* (New York: Random House, 1990), pp. 297-298.

33. *Krasnaya Zvezda*, March 6, 1992, p. 5.

34. *Komsomolskaya Pravda*, February 24, 1992, p. 5.

35. *Nezavisimaya Gazette*, May 15, 1992, p. 3.

36. Ibid.

37. *Krasnaya Zvezda*, May 13, 1992, p. 3.

38. *Nezavisimaya Gazette*, May 13, 1992, p. 5.

39. The CIS peacekeeping force is to comprise Russian units, including the 201st Motorized Division already stationed in Tajikistan, and units from Kazakhstan.

40. *Komsomolskaya Pravda*, March 3, 1992, p. 4.

41. TASS, March 29, 1992.

42. *Rossiyskaya Gazeta*, November 14, 1992, p. 5.

6

Impact of Afghanistan's War on the Former Soviet Republics of Central Asia

◆

Victor Spolnikov

To explore the level of influence of Afghanistan's war on the former Soviet republics of Central Asia, a few questions may be asked about the nature of society in these republics, their social life, economics, religion, and culture. If we try to define the main peculiarity of Central Asia society, we can say with confidence that this peculiarity is its traditionalism. Terms such as tradition and traditionalism have many meanings. Traditionalism includes active disallowance, rejection, or negation of new elements into the customary and traditional way of life, as a permanent addition to the society that is rooted in the remote past. It does not matter whether this model is Islamic or Christian or something else. The main principle is that the society must not depart from the "ideal model." You may ask 100 or 1,000 respondents in the Central Asia region: According to what laws do you live? What defines the way of your life? The answer to the first question, as a general rule, will be: According to the precepts of our fathers, in the Muslim way. The answer to the second question will be: Tradition.

The mechanism of traditionalism includes the system of transmission of information from one generation to another. The next generation receives only that information that helps to preserve the traditional way of life; all contrary information is blocked out. Such an objective-oriented selection of information includes family members, close relatives, methods of production, cultural values, and religion. I do not intend to imply any moral or ethnic deprecation of these aspects of life of the Muslim society of Central Asia, which are traditional. The objective of this analysis is to point out some factors that maintain traditional stability in Central Asian society. Here it may be appropriate to point out that in the Oriental studies centers of the former Soviet Union, a paradox had developed. A strange "division of labor" appeared. The Oriental studies centers in Moscow and St. Petersburg studied foreign states of the East, while the Oriental studies departments of the Central Asia republics monopolized the history, culture, and religion of the Central Asia region. (There were exceptions to this rule; for example, in Moscow and St. Petersburg archaeology and demography of Central Asia were studied.) Consequently, important problems of religious trends and activism, aggravation of interethnic relations, and increasing social tensions were ig nored.

For example, the spread of Islamic fundamentalism in the region was avoided completely and was not mentioned even in research articles; the press ignored it as well. The press sometimes covered only those facts that were not possible to hide—such as demonstrations, meetings, and clashes in the streets, but there was no information about the aspirations and demands of the participants. The Central (Moscow) and republic authorities in particular did not want to disclose the real reasons for the mass opposition—the motivating factors of these actions, especially their economic, ethnic, and religious aspects. Attempts to analyze these situations were opposed by local authorities and "national intellectuals."

An interesting example illustrates this situation. Even before mass opposition demonstrations and clashes with tragic consequences began, Professor Igor P. Beliaev wrote an article entitled "Islam and Politics," which was published in two issues of a Moscow newspaper. In this article, the connection between ideas of the Arabic Muslim Brothers and events in Afghanistan on the one hand and facts of Islamic fundamentalism in Central Asia on the other were highlighted.[1]

A reaction followed immediately. In the same newspaper Professor Talib Saidbayev, director of the Institute of Philosophy and Law of the Uzbekistan Academy of Sciences, a specialist in Islam, wrote a sharp rejoinder against Beliaev's analysis, stating that "Islam does not play any role in economy, politics, law and educational system of our region, though it takes some place in social psychology, influences the world outlook and vital values of many people.[2] No comments are necessary.

After the bloody events in Dushanbe in February 1990, the capital of Tajikistan was in the hands of pogrom-makers for three days. Only troops saved the population of the city from more bloodshed. What happened after that? Were the underlying reasons of the incident investigated, identified, and analyzed? The answer is no! Only in April 1990, at a conference in Dushanbe, did the republic's ruling clique attempt to assess the mass demonstrations. The published report of the conference said

> that representatives of various strata of society took part in them. There were first of all the most radical intellectuals demanding immediate changes without taking into consideration the realities of economy of the city and the republic. They were joined by students of institutes, and of technical secondary schools, who were dissatisfied with the conditions of everyday life and study. The second group of the participants consisted of people who were compromised or offended by the political system and the Republic's authorities, and also young people with narrow understanding of national interests. The second group is the most destructive ideological and organized force, who pursued their own political and ambitious interests, skillfully articulating them in national and religious tones.[3]

This analysis sounds very strange if we take into account that from February 12 to February 14, more than 700 crimes were committed in the city and that during the curfew hours about 3,000 automatic weapons were confiscated. In this analysis, not a single word was said about the calls to seize political power and to create an Islamic state.

The language of the analysis needs to be "translated" from the official party jargon into normal language; the following social groups took part in the riots: "The most radical part of intellectuals" who demanded changes "without taking into consideration existing realities" means local national democrats; "the most destructive force" means Islamic fundamentalists plus declassed elements of the population. Here it may not be out of place to mention that in neighboring Afghanistan, contemporary Islamic fundamentalism was born during the 1960s at Kabul University and among the declassed elements. The same strata of society were the fertile soil of Islamic fundamentalism in the Arab world. We shall return to the astonishing alliance between local democrats and fundamentalists later.

TRADITIONALISM OF THE CENTRAL ASIAN SOCIETY: IS IT SURVIVAL OF EARLY FORMS OF SOCIAL CONSCIOUSNESS?

In the Soviet Union traditionalism in the Central Asian republics was looked upon just in a superficial way—as an early form of social consciousness. But Islamic traditionalism is not merely "survival of the past"; economic factors and the ideology of Islam constitute the base of Islamic traditionalism. In the economics of Central Asia, Islamic tradition means the way of life based on the specific character of the household structure. This specific character consists of the combination of irrigated agriculture and extensive stock-breeding and a very important role of mediatory trade. The foundation of the traditional society of Central Asia is first of all the community, which combines existence derived from the irrigation system belonging to the state and the ownership of private or community land. Land cannot be separated from the irrigation system and therefore from any community as a collective user of the irrigation system. Thus, there are two levels of owners in Central Asia, the state and the community. In communities where agriculture is based on artificial irrigation systems, it makes no difference from an economic point of view what kind of state provides the irrigation system. The main point is to preserve the internal structure of the community. External forms of the community may be different, but the essence remains the same.[4]

If the foundation of the community (the combination of the community use of water and the possession of a plot of land) is preserved, despite all possible changes at the state level, the community will regenerate and function again. This principle also applies to the stock-breeding part of the Central Asian society. The only difference is that in this case, instead of the irrigation system, only the community pasture and irrigated lands produce livestock.

Before the Soviet system was introduced in Central Asia, two forms of state structures had existed there. The first was the Khiva and Kokand Khanates and the Bukhara Emirate, where a variety of Islamic states existed. The second form of state structure in Central Asia was the land possessions of tsarist Russia. In Russia's land possessions some former Islamic upper state structure was replaced by tsarist administration, which provided for the irrigation system and the regulation of pasture use. The tsarist regime did not touch the essence of the community. As a result, the cell, which under favorable conditions is capable of regenerating the whole organism, was preserved. Thus, at the everyday level, all traditional socioeconomic structures were preserved.

Strange as it may seem, after Soviet power was established in Central Asia, the same picture was observed. The "state" part of Islam was liquidated—that is, the state system at the highest level was changed—but the structure of the traditional society of Central Asia was not altered. It remained the same for the Muslims: The Soviets took away the khan's power as well as all big irrigation systems and pastures. The state built and repaired large irrigation systems, but small irrigation systems remained in charge of the *kishlak* and *mahallia* (the district community in the city and in the big village), that is, at the disposal of communities. The structure of communities was not demolished, only the land was redistributed.

The way of production remained the same. The lands that were "socialized" and included into *kolkhoz* were regarded as "state land" (in the past they were "khan's land"); the worker of the *kolhoznik* plot of land near his home was looked upon and is still being looked upon as *mulk*, or private property. At the *kishlak* (village) level, the earlier types of property have been preserved as well. The uniting of *dehkans* (peasants) into *brigades* and *zvenijas* (small labor teams) in *kolkhoz* took place in conformity with the family or neighborhood (*mahalla*) principle. We can see this principle in *kishlak* *Avchi* (Ganchin district, Leninabad Region in Tajikistan). At first, 13 collective farms were organized there in accordance with the number of *avlod* (large family units). Later on these collective farms were united into one, and 13 *avlods* became big *brigades*.

When private land plots (irrigated before the introduction of the Soviet system) were distributed, the borders of the former tribes and *avlods* domains were strictly observed. The land that was some other people's "property" could be taken only after the ritual of sale and purchase was completed, or treated as a registered gift. All actions of sale and purchase of land took place with the participation of a "non-official" *mullah* according to the rules of *Shariat* (Islamic laws) and *adat* (custom). The same order of things is also observed in the city when the procedure of sale and purchase of land plots for the building of private houses takes place. Here the details are under the control of the *mahalla* authorities.

Obviously, before the introduction of the Soviet system and during its existence, the Central Asian community preserved its stability by adapting to one or the other form of state. This adaptation probably will continue in the future regardless of the forms of rule that might exist in the Central Asian republics, secular or Islamic. Thus, when the so-called democratic forces in Russia accuse the leaders of the Central Asian republics of conservatism, of unwillingness to carry out deep social and economic reforms particularly in the use of land, they ("democrats") make a gross mistake. The reason for the opposition to deep changes in the system of land usage (and in other areas too) is not that the heads of some republics of the former Soviet Union are dull "partocrats." The fact is that they realize (some more, some less) the danger in the breaking up of the community, which is the foundation of the social and economic structure of Muslim republics.

Let us remember that the Afghan resistance began not at the moment when Islamic opposition called upon the peasants to struggle, but when the new leadership of the country rudely attempted to carry out the land reform and then the land-and-water reform. The peasantry considered these reforms to be a threat to the existence of the traditional community. These events were the manifestation of the connection of Islamic traditionalism with politics.

Table 6.1
FORMS OF LAND PROPERTY AND POWER STRUCTURE AT THE VILLAGE LEVEL

Islamic State (before creation of the Soviet Union)	Under the Soviet Government
Forms of Property and Taxes	
Land belongs to the state, to khan, to community. Income taxes are a part of harvest.	Land belongs to the state (to *kolkhoz*). Fixed taxes in the form of state plan of production.
Rent of land from the state, private owner. Taxes are a part of harvest.	Rent of land from *kolkhoz*. Taxes are a fixed part of harvest.
Private land (*mulk*). Taxes from the income.	Plot of land near the house (private land). Taxes are fixed. Payment for the land plot.
Pastures—community land, without taxes. Taxes on livestock. Payment to the herdsman.	Pastures—community land, without taxes. Taxes for livestock in the form of insurance. Payment to the herdsman.
Waqf (endowment)—property of cult (religious) structures. No taxes.	*Waqf* (endowment)—property of cult (religious) structures. No taxes.
Rule Structure	
Rais—representative of an administration, custodian of Islamic law, collector of taxes.	*District committee*—Representative of administration. Leader of community life, custodian of the Islamic law, creator of social opinion. *Rais*—head of district committee.
Mullah—state employee, *imam* of mosque, leader of religious life, collection of taxes, observer of rituals. Teaching in *maktab*. In charge of *waqf* (endowments).	*Mullah*—district clergyman, *imam* of mosque, leader of religious life, collection of taxes, teaching in *maktab*, in charge of *waqf*.

CENTRAL ASIAN TRADITIONALISM AND POLITICS

In politics Central Asian traditionalism asserted itself most vigorously when attempts were made to break ruthlessly the main norms and forms of the traditional society (the same is the case in Afghanistan); this was the uprising in Central Asia and Kazakhstan in 1916.[5]

The encroachment of tsarist administration upon the traditional rules—namely, the mobilization of Muslims to work in the rear of the front during World War I—led to the uprising in Russian-controlled Central Asia. Some Soviet historians endeavored to present this uprising as "antifeudal," but this contention does not hold water. The uprising did not spread to the territories of the Central Asian Islamic states of the Bukhara Emirate and Khiva khanate, which according to those historians were "feudal-despotic" states. The uprising was of anti-Russian character. In most places the insurgency's leaders were clergymen. The slogan of the uprising was the rejection of all *kafir* and non-Muslim elements, which were identified as Russian. Their actions against local "feudals" took place only if these "feudals" supported Russia's administration. This uprising became the beginning of the *basmatchi* movement. Thus the *basmatchi* movement originated not in the years of Soviet system but before it, and at the beginning it was directed against the encroachment of tsarist administration upon the basic principles of Central Asian traditional society.

After the fall of the tsarist regime in February 1917, the uprising calmed down. However, in October it erupted with new force because the Soviets took the first steps to redistribute land and livestock. In the 1930s the main forces of *basmatchis* were liquidated, but the movement continued until the end of 1941. The activity of *basmatchis* was noted not only in the remote areas of Pamir, but also in the *Asht* district of the Leninabad region of Tajikistan, where most of the *basmatchis* were liquidated. In October 1941 some of them went to Afghanistan.

During the war years (1941-1945) orders of the Communist Party of the Soviet Union (CPSU) narrowed the frames of Central Asia traditionalism to the borders of *kishlak*, or village. However, traditionalism was revived when the postwar recovery of the Soviet economy started. This revival reached a high level in the 1960s and peaked in 1985, when a general weakening of the state power and of the ruling party began.

Let us take a look at the social and economic situation in the Central Asian republics at the moment of disintegration of the Soviet Union, since many things that happened there clarify what was going on in the 1990s in this region.

Economics

By the mid-1980s, the economies of rural Central Asia were divided into two parts: the state sector and the family economy. The state sector, based on industry, was regulated by the state. Its lower level of structure was the *kolkhoz* (collective farm) and the *sovkhoz* (state farm). The results of production of this sector can be controlled to a certain extent. The second part of the rural economy is what is called the personal or family economy, which included a plot of land near the home of the collective farm member. This family economy, which is not under the control or regulation of the state, plays a very important role in the life of the population.

The agricultural conditions of the region are suitable for cultivating fruits and vegetables, which do not grow in other parts of the country and therefore yield great profits when traded. Narcotics are grown here as well. Consequently, the income of the family part of the rural economy exceeds very much the income of the state sector. As a rule, the personal (family) economy is oriented toward the market.

We must now touch upon the demographic situation and the problem of unemployment, which are the sources of social tension. These problems play and in the future will play a very important role. The monthly wages in the state sector of the economy do not bring in enough income to support the family of seven to eight or more dependents. There are many "irrational" expenses in the Central Asia family that are unavoidable. The growing of grapes, other fruits, and cotton demands manual labor, but even this low productive labor does not provide adequate employment to the population. Typically, the head of the family is mostly busy with trading, while other members of the family work in the gardens and fields.

By the end of the 1970s and the beginning of the 1980s, the term demographic explosion was used in research works regarding the population growth in the Central Asian republics. This term is imprecise. I believe the population growth was not the result of any "explosion," but rather the result of gradual qualitative change that took place in the society. It sounds rather strange, but the fact is that the joining of Central Asia to Russia created favorable conditions for population growth. For example, from 1870 to 1931 the number of people in the Leninabad region (*khogent*) increased 3.5 times; by 1985 the number had increased 10.5 times.[6]

Up to 1931 the main factor causing a population increase was the cessation of internal conflicts and establishment of relative political stability. These factors were also responsible for an increase in longevity for the adult population, an increase in marriages and, correspondingly, an increase in the number of farms. Beginning in 1931 social programs to aid the population began to rise: Child mortality was sharply reduced, thanks to the rising standard of living and the development of health services. Also, constant factors stimulating the increase of the Muslim population were early marriages and the prohibition of abortions. Another supplemental factor was economic—the desire to have more hands in the family to assist in the family economy. Unlike what occurred in other Muslim countries in the Central Asian republics, the migration of the rural population to the cities has been limited.

As a result of the population increase, the problem of absolute and relative overpopulation has appeared: A substantial number of people in the rural population (that is most Central Asians) do not do any productive work. This sharp increase in population was not accompanied by a corresponding development of the rural and city economies. As an example, the population of the Leninabad region increased 10.5 times, while the land for agriculture increased only 2.5 times. This increase took place in the flat lands of the region. In the mountain areas the irrigated land was reduced sharply. This change created serious ecological problems: The water regime broke down, the stock-breeding population started to live a settled life in oases and in the valleys, and as a result, vast areas of pasture were reduced and a shortage of land ensued. Working in the state sector has become unprofitable; the main source of income has become private plots of land, trade, and profiteering beyond the state boundaries.

National and Local Intellectuals

National intellectuals have played a special role during the recent events in Central Asia. (In Russia, the national intellectuals are called the intelligentsia.) This fact deserves to be discussed in some detail. First, a few words about the Central Asian schools are in order. Recently, as a rule, schoolchildren went to work for two months every year in the fields to help harvesting (especially cotton). Thus, the complete course of studies (ten years) was shortened by twelve months. Consequently, the children in rural areas are more poorly educated than schoolchildren in other regions of the country. In addition, many families in need of hands for their private plots take their children out of school after five or six years, believing that beyond the ability to write, read, and count, school was not necessary. Also, the current level of education in rural schools does not correspond to today's advanced standards. The same is true about the training of specialists at the rural institutes.

An overwhelming majority of Central Asian students receive education in humanities, while there is a permanent shortage of students at the technology faculties. Only the youth of non-Central Asian nationalities want to enroll there. Students of Central Asian nationalities prefer to study history, especially history of their own people or that of the bordering Muslim countries. They concentrate mostly on studying ancient and medieval history, ethnography, and archaeology.

The Central Asian intellectuals believe that all that is theirs is "good." The source of this perception lies in the denial of everything that contradicts tradition. Their own national values are given preference. The idea of the "golden age" (the pre-Russian period) is in circulation, while a "silver age" view (the period of the tsarist empire) also exists. Alternative researches in the history of Central Asia receive damnable criticism. The period of Arab conquests is pushed forward in historic researches; the conquests are considered to have coincided with the introduction of the advanced state system and culture. Pre-Islamic culture is ignored as a rule. Sometimes strange interpretations are offered. At the second congress of Turkicologists in 1976 in Alma-Ata (Kazakhstan), a member of the Kazakhstan Academy of Sciences insisted that Chinggis Khan (1206-1227) was a Muslim and spoke the Kazakh language in his *kibitka* (nomad tent). Despite the fact that there is no proof that the original Kazakh language existed in the thirteenth century or that Chinggis Khan was a Muslim, the audience roared with approval.

Here is a fresh example of Uzbekistan's connection with Timur (1336-1405) from a local newspaper:

> construction and architecture in Uzbekistan never reached the scale of the [Timurid] period, when the republic was headed by Sharaf Rashidov. Let us ask sincerely: Were there ever many such buildings in Uzbekistan since the time of Amir Timur? How many traitors and slanderers who tried to bury the great Timur's memory in oblivion sank in the lake and those who remained active were unmasked, but the name of Amir Timur goes on living in centuries.[7]

This newspaper compared Rashidov, a former candidate member of the Political Bureau of the CPSU and first secretary of the Central Committee of the Communist Party of Uzbekistan, who was condemned for corruption, with Timur, creator of a state with its capital in Samarkand. Timur crushed the Golden Horde and conducted expansionist marches to Iran, the Trans-Caucasian region, India, and Asia Minor.

In all Central Asian republics the technical intelligentsia is very small in number, because technical professions do not enjoy much respect. There are many reasons for this: Technical professions take specialists away from the rural community and from its way of life; and technical professions demand a good knowledge of the Russian language. Russian was taught at a low level in most of the rural communities; only a few people knew Russian, mainly those who engaged in trade beyond the region. In Tajikistan the exceptional nature of the Tajik people and their history has been propagated. Consequently, nationalism and fundamentalism among the national intelligentsia have been thoroughly espoused.

Corruption

To speak about corruption in Central Asia in 1992 at a time when corruption in Russia has reached the highest level is a bit tactless. Yet this phenomenon is so typical of Central Asia and so different from "savage capitalism" in Russia that it seems necessary to pay attention to it.

The conservation of strong family, clan, and tribal relations brings about family protection as well as mutual protection. Misappropriation at the state sector factories is considered wrong. In Islamic theory and practice there is no juridical concept of bribery. In social consciousness a bribe is looked upon as payment for "service," for a "fulfilled job" done by another person. For example, the head of the district committee (*mahalla*) takes payment for his signature on a document or for the official stamp of the committee. From reports in the world mass media, it is well known that bribery exists at the government level in the Central Asian republics—in Uzbekistan, for example.

Mahalla (residential district). The *mahalla* is in fact a form of Asian traditional community of neighbors. The predecessor of the *mahalla* was *avlod*, the community of the big family. When the big family began to divide, the *avlod* transformed into the *mahalla*, while both institutions coexisted for a long time. At present, the *avlod* has given way to the *mahalla*; the latter is significant only at the level of family relations. In economic and social life the *mahalla* has very great significance, especially in cities and *kishlaks* (big villages). At the head of the *mahalla* is a committee led by the elders. The *mahalla* is officially recognized as a structured unit of the city and big village. The *mahalla* is not only a territorial but a religious organization as well; it controls social and private life of the inhabitants of its territory, supports religious schools (*maktabs*), forms public opinion, observes adherence to the norms of the *Shariat*, and punishes those who violate these norms. No one can sell his own house without permission of the committee; if members of the committee do not like the buyer for some reason, the deal does not take place. If the buyer of the house ignores the opinion of the committee, he will find himself in such an uncomfortable position that eventually he will have to leave the district. In rural areas the *mahalla* has a real economic basis; the local irrigation system also increases the influence of the *mahalla*.

Respect for the Elders

The Muslim way of life emphasizes respect for the elders in the family and in society. The explanation for this can be found in Islamic religion and in economic features of the Muslim family and community.

But some other special features cannot be ignored. Respect for the elders is cultivated within the framework of Muslim tradition; all that is beyond it is not recognized and not respected. The tradition of respect for the elders has a selective character: The nearer a young or not so young Muslim is to the place of his residence, the more respect for the elders this Muslim displays. However, when Muslims come from Central Asia or the Caucasus to Russian cities to trade or for another purpose, they do not always demonstrate "inborn" feeling of respect for elders. Also, when recruited by Islamic fundamentalist parties, young Muslims killed even old men and women in Central Asia.

Moreover, religious upbringing encourages a dogmatic attitude discouraging the need for explanations: why one must not do this or that act. To these Muslims it is quite enough to know such concepts as *halal* (permitted) and *haram* (prohibited). Ask any Muslim why he is not allowed to eat pork and in most cases he will answer: it is *haram*.

Attitude Toward State Laws

In everyday life only those laws are observed that do not obviously contradict *Shariat* (Islamic law). There are not many such laws. On the contrary, violation of the laws of land usage, possession of weapons, bribes, and misappropriation of state funds have become normal behavior. Rich people, even if known to be criminals, are considered "respectable." The stealing of private property or funds in the neighborhood only is considered wrong. Misappropriation in the state sector is not considered to be a shameful act.

"Official" and "Nonofficial" Islam

This is very important and a very difficult subject. Ideally, Muslim society regardless of its geographical location claims to be based on canons of Islam. However, there are plenty of "local Islams" with their own specific features. In Central Asia Islam is divided horizontally and vertically. The horizontal division breaks Islam into Sunnism and Shiism, with further subdivisions into orders and sects. The vertical division means "official" and "nonofficial" Islam. The overwhelming majority of Central Asian Muslims are Sunnis. Among them, some special features are visible. For instance, Turkmen, since the seventeenth century, were considered to be Sunnis, but in their everyday life Shiism also spread, especially under the influence of radio broadcasts from the Iranian city of Gorgan. This radio propaganda emphasized the conception of the Shiite Islamic state persistently. Shiism in Turkmenistan is so marked that in neighboring Uzbekistan there is a saying: "When a Turkman is praying, an Uzbek is spitting."

Ismailism, a denomination of Shiism, has spread in the mountainous areas of Pamir. In the mushrooming of orders, sects, and worship of *mazars* (graves of local "saints"), Central Asia has beaten all records in the Islamic world. This is one of the very special features of "local" Islam. However, the so-called Wahabism in Tajikistan is another name for Gulbeddin Hekmatyar's fundamentalism and nothing more.

The vertical division of Islam is complicated. "Official" Islam is a Soviet-instituted system that includes Islam in the structure of society. "Official" *ulema* and *mullahs* as a rule received education in *medrese* (traditional Islamic college); they maintained more or less close relations with the state religious boards and were registered in the councils of religious affairs, the official part of the republican state administration. This category of clergy functioned openly, organizing Friday prayers in mosques, weddings, and funerals. Community elders provided contacts between mosque and members of the community.

The activity of the "nonofficial" clergy is not controlled by the state authorities. Nonofficial *mullahs* usually were educated in illegal *maktabs.* These *mullahs,* in addition to conducting religious activity, function in the state or cooperative sectors, while the *imam* of the registered mosque in districts or villages meet them daily. Nonofficial *mullahs* are not always thoroughly educated, but they exercise great influence in the community daily. They contributed to the politicization of the community in opposition to the state authorities. Most of them are Islamic fundamentalists, like Hekmatyar of Afghanistan.

Relations between official and nonofficial clergy were always complicated and even hostile. Before the disintegration of the Soviet Union, official and nonofficial clergy struggled for influence in Muslim society. Official clergy who were connected with state authorities used their position to compromise nonofficial clergy, labeling them as extremists who did not understand Islam and erroneously explained the Quran. Despite this visible conflict, many official *mullahs* maintained secret contacts with nonofficial ones, while nonofficial *mullahs* blamed official ones for deviating from Islam, for selling themselves to the authorities and making Islam serve the regime. Eventually, nonofficial Islam became the foundation for the birth of Islamic fundamentalist parties in Central Asian republics. They are now struggling for political power.

This was the social and economic landscape in Central Asia even before the Soviet intervention in Afghanistan. The Central Asian situation remained unchanged during the intervention in the early 1980s. Clearly, this situation could not continue for long without further development.

CENTRAL ASIA AND THE WAR IN AFGHANISTAN

What kind of influence did the war in Afghanistan have on the Central Asian republics of the former Soviet Union? Americans were the first to theoretically touch this problem. On May 9, 1979, the U.S. Embassy in Kabul informed Washington by coded telegram no. 3626, which was signed by B. Amstutz, chargé d'affaires:

> Why did the USSR decide to intervene? Afghanistan, unlike Angola, Ethiopia, or Yemen, borders on the Soviet Union. Indeed, this turbulent country abuts several sensitive Muslim, Central Asian republics of the USSR. Moscow is understandably concerned about the possibility of an unbroken band of conservative Islamic states stretching along its southern frontier, from Iran to Pakistan. This situation could happen should an Ikhwan-dominated alliance ever topple the khalqi regime.[8]

The U.S. Embassy in Moscow received a copy of this telegram for comments. The embassy staff there did not agree with their Kabul colleagues' assessment. In telegram no. 3088 on May 24, 1979, to Washington, the embassy reported:

> We do not consider that concern about the Muslim population of the Soviet Central Asian republics by itself would be an important incentive for the Soviet leadership to adopt an interventionist course in Afghanistan. All the information we have been able to gather about this region indicates that Moscow has the situation well under control. Frequent visits by Embassy officers to Soviet Central Asia in recent months have uncovered few signs of discontent. The Central Asian republics have made significant social and economic progress under Soviet rule and enjoy a significantly higher standard of living than in neighboring areas of Afghanistan and Iran. And, should discontent nevertheless surface in the coming months, the Soviets can be counted on to move quickly and effectively to crush in.[9]

The telegram was signed by Ambassador Malcolm Toon. When Amstutz in Kabul foresaw the Soviet military intervention, he was right, though his perception was based on political conclusions only, without confirmation by any hard facts. (This does not, however, belittle the value of his forecast.) The U.S. Embassy in Moscow proceeded from traditional (for that time) views about the stability of "friendship of the nations" in the Soviet Union and from the visual observations of American diplomats who had visited local rich markets and derived "knowledge" from the press. Did Moscow possess reliable information about the political processes in the Central Asian republics? I assume it did. But Moscow was already helpless to do anything to correct the situation, or perhaps it hoped that everything would somehow be settled positively.

Long before the events in Afghanistan, I had the opportunity to read the KGB analysis of the Central Asian republics for the CPSU's Central Committee and for the Soviet government. The reports indicate that in some republics of Central Asia, for example, in Turkmenistan, there was a diarchy of structures. In other words, official structures (district committees of the party, *kolkhozs*, courts) were functioning on the surface, but in reality all of them were no more than outward forms of the traditional Islamic structures. The intelligence information from Turkmenistan indicated that in the south of the republic, *kolkhozes*, villages, and courts remained on paper, while real power and economics were in the hands of traditional leaders. In 1980 Yuri Andropov, then the chief of the KGB, told me that Soviet power in many mountainous regions of the Caucasus did not exist at all.

The question was not whether Moscow knew about the developments in Central Asia. An explosive situation had developed and some remedial action was necessary. The only remaining question was the timing of the action. Even if the well-known events in Afghanistan did not take place, the Islamic revival in the Soviet Union was bound to turn into an important political factor. This dynamic was only accelerated by the war in Afghanistan and the disintegration of the Soviet Union.

The sources of fundamentalist and nationalist movements in Central Asia should be looked for elsewhere. The inspiration for these movements came from the activating of Islam, which began in the Muslim world with the fall of the colonial system, the rejection of western culture, and the aggravation of economic conditions of the Muslim masses in Muslim countries. The Islamic movements were not spawned by capitalism or socialism. Islamic fundamentalism in Central Asia came to life with the disintegration of the unitary state system of the Soviet Union. The developments forced Muslims in the world and in Central Asia in particular to find their own way to economic and political development, a way that would be in harmony with their own religious and cultural values and be an alternative to capitalism and socialism.

In Central Asia resurgent Islam was slowed down by the Soviet power and World War II. Afterward, this process gained momentum. While the unitarian state did not encourage the religious feelings of its citizens, the base structure of the traditional Muslim society and its main economic cell—the traditional community—remained. All the reforms and *perestroika* did not touch the essence of the Muslim community. The middle and upper administrative structures, including the former or surviving Soviets, and their external construction coincided with the classical Islamic form of management, the principle of *shura* (consultative body).

The banning of communist parties in Central Asian republics created a political vacuum in the middle and upper echelons of power. Consequently, the competing forces of "national democrats" and particularly the Islamic fundamentalists are now attempting to fill the vacuum. The former legitimize their claim with the slogans of democracy, revival of national culture, and revival of the historical conception of state; the latter attempt to build an Islamic state in some form.

I have maintained elsewhere that the alliance of "democrats" and Islamists is by definition unnatural. If an alliance comes about and takes power, it would soon collapse because the more aggressive fundamentalists leaning on lumpen strata will save themselves from the "democrats," who are supported by the Moscow "democrats."[10]

This is precisely what happened in Tajikistan. "Democrats" of Russia who supported the Islamists in their struggle against the former "partocrats" proved to be politically blind; they stimulated the growth of the Islamic fundamentalists. At the last stage of the struggle for power in Tajikistan, local "democrats" headed by Shodmon Yusupov, chairman of the Democratic Party of Tajikistan, realized that they were doomed, but it was too late. The political stage was under the control of the fundamentalists, who did not hesitate to shed blood, commit political murders, and incite hatred against the Russians. Yusupov's appeal to Russians "not to leave land of Tajikistan"[11] did not sound convincing. After this appeal he himself left the political arena.

Independence came to the Central Asian republics not as a result of a victory of the national-liberation forces; it came as a "present" after the liquidation of the Soviet Union by the three leaders of the Slavic republics: Russia, the Ukraine, and Byelorussia. The Central Asian republics, especially Kazakhstan and Kirgistan, decided to preserve close relations with Russia. Others by choice or default became the objects of expansion of Iran, Turkey, Saudi Arabia, and Pakistan. But the main theater of instability in Central Asia is Tajikistan. It is not an accident; in this republic all negative peculiarities typical of Central Asian republics reached their apex: deformed and weak economy, overpopulation, unemployment, low level of mass culture, religious fanaticism, and arrogance of local intellectuals. Last, but not least, Afghanistan, where the dominating forces were not "moderate" Islamic organizations but Hekmatyar's furious fundamentalists, is contiguous to Tajikistan.

Let us remember that it was not the overthrow of the king of Afghanistan in 1973, or the overthrow of Prince Muhammad Daud in April 1978, or the Soviet intervention in Afghanistan and the beginning of Islamic jihad that caused the political stir in Tajikistan. Tajiks fought in Afghanistan in the ranks of the Soviet military. Most of the translators in the 40th Army and military and civil advisors of all ranks were Soviet Tajiks. The main Soviet legal advisor to Babrak Karmal was the former minister of Tajikistan, Radjabov. In Afghanistan he was arrested by the Soviet counterintelligence for smuggling gold from Europe to Kabul and was sentenced to prison. (Currently, he is free and is politically active in Tajikistan.) Nevertheless, the breakthrough of Islamic fundamentalism into Central Asia has taken place via Tajikistan with the help of Afghan fundamentalists. This impact was the first, but not the last one.

Some Moscow Islamic specialists assured us that Islamic fundamentalism in Central Asian republics were defeated as a united movement; that Turkmenistan is "a quiet and safe" republic; that "attempts to organize political Islam" turned out to be bankrupt; that the fundamentalist movement is discredited.[12] Do they really think that any political movement, including the fundamentalist one, can be "organized"? Every political movement can arise or "disperse" (the term belongs to the quoted specialist), but nobody knows how and when this will happen.

The fact remains that fundamentalist Islam has openly broken into the former Soviet Union through Tajikistan and now it threatens Uzbekistan. Islam Karimov, president of Uzbekistan, at a press conference in September 1992, said that Russia did not fulfill its duty to secure the southern borders of the former Soviet Union and that there was fighting at the borders of Tajikistan and Afghanistan and at the borders of Turkmenistan and Iran as well.[13]

Karimov's anxiety is well founded. Unlike the optimistic Moscow Islamic specialist, the presidents of Kazakhstan, Kirgizstan, Uzbekistan, and Russia are worried. In their statement to the Tajik people they expressed anxiety about the disturbance in Tajikistan and the unsettled situation on the southern borders of the republic.[14] Turkmenistan did not sign this statement, a fact worthy of speculation. It is noteworthy that

Karimov at his press conference said openly that if Russia does not realize its own strategic interests in Central Asia, Russian southern borders will approach quite near the Islamic countries.

At this stage, let me quote from one more document of the U.S. Embassy in Kabul that discusses events in Afghanistan before the Soviet intervention. The embassy telegram no. 6251 of August 16, 1979, informed the State Department that the victory of the opposition could have many favorable consequences for the economic and political interests of the United States in this region. The manifesto of the Islamic party of Afghanistan calls for restoration of the veil for women. The inevitable mass extermination of the *khalqis* could be a violation of human rights. The regime of opposition apparently does not include social and economic reforms in the list of its urgent tasks. But, nevertheless, "our larger interests would, probably, be served by the demise of the Taraki and Amin regime, despite whatever setbacks this might mean for future social and economic reforms within Afghanistan."[15]

Washington apparently realized the danger of making such a statement known to others; consequently, the U.S. mission in the North Atlantic Treaty Organization (NATO) was warned: "You may draw from Kabul 6251, which is an analysis of the opposition to the Taraki regime as well as a discussion of a possible development in Afghanistan. You should not, *rpt., NOT* pass on Kabul's conclusions about the effects on US interests or the desirability of the demise of the Taraki/Amin regime."[16]

As for Tajikistan, the developments in this republic remind me of the Afghan scenario. In fact, civil war is raging there. President Nabiev resigned under the threat. The function of parliament is paralyzed. The stream of refugees from the areas of fighting increases daily, and ethnic conflict between Tajiks and Uzbeks is likely to break out.

Just like the futile attempts of the former Kabul regime to close the Afghan border with Pakistan, Russia's ineffectual attempts to close the border with Afghanistan will not yield results. Clearly, the border troops cannot protect the border with all-round defense. Weapons and ammunition continue to cross the border from Afghanistan. According to the deputy chief of the Russian border troops stationed in Tajikistan, groups of fighters from Tajikistan, including not only Tajikis but Uzbeks as well, receive military training in the Afghan province of Kunduz. Hekmatyar's commanders head the forays into Tajikistan.[17] The power-grab process by the Afghan fundamentalists that was predicted is apparently under way.

In 1972, during the reign of King Zahir Shah, Habib ur-Rahman, one of the founders of the Islamic party of Afghanistan, said:

Existence of an independent Islamic state in Afghanistan will influence the feelings of millions of Muslims in Russia, where their mosques are turned into theaters, dancing clubs and museums. . . . The day will come at last when they will rise in the arms against despotism of Communists and overthrow the bloody government of Russia. . . . We do not recognize borders. The day will come when Muslims of all the world will live under a common flag with the same coat of arms. If we attain power we shall struggle for Islam in Afghanistan and in the whole world, where our brothers live under the yoke of communism. Are the inhabitants of Bukhara, Samarkand and Tajikistan not Muslims? What about the Tatars? Are they not our brothers?[18]

These statements are reflective of true intentions.

Certain conclusions can be drawn. Afghan (and other) fundamentalists consider their struggle for power as a component of worldwide Islamic revolution. Their power in Kabul is not the ultimate aim, but only a stage in the development of this Islamic revolution. What might be the next stage is not difficult to imagine, judging by the events in Tajikistan.

What about the current leadership of Russia? What are Russia's intentions and practical steps in this situation?

One of the biggest mistakes of Russian diplomacy was the unpromising policy of "two Afghanistans," when two parallel negotiations were conducted with Najibullah and the Mujahideen. Najibullah was given assurances and plans were worked out to create "democratic" Afghanistan with the help of the United Nations (UN). Consequently Najibullah resigned in order to fulfill these plans. However, under the pretext of freeing Soviet prisoners, negotiations were conducted at different levels with the Mujahideen's leaders. Naturally, this contradictory policy of sitting on "two chairs" collapsed: Najibullah was overthrown; the UN plans were ruined; Kabul was captured by the Mujahideen's mutually hostile groups; terror against the population began; and the evacuation of the Russian Embassy personnel was clumsily done at the eleventh hour.

War came to the borders of the former Soviet Union and crossed over them. Here we have a comparative study of the principle of morality in policy. Gorbachev and Shevardnadze espoused it with passion, and so does the current Russian minister of foreign affairs, A. Kozyrev. Yet this concept is alien to the political philosophy of the extremist wing of Islamic fundamentalists, whether in Iran, Afghanistan, Egypt, Tajikistan, or Uzbekistan. The achievement of agreements with them with or without compromises is often presented as success. As a rule, however, these agreements are fundamentalists' successes, not the other side's. Islamic fundamentalists make agreements when they are profitable for political, military, and economic reasons. The party that is ready to deal with Islamic fundamentalists loses the game from moral and political points of view.

Normal negotiations with fundamentalists need not be avoided. However, these negotiations must not end in a deal, but be concerned with principles only. Let us listen to the words of the representative of Islam, the religious leader of Muslims of the Kulyab region of Tajikistan, Haidar Sharifzoda:

> I pray to Allah so that everybody should understand: Supporters of fundamentalism are not true interpreters of Quran. They bring only evil, we have seen it in our republic. Now they have decided that their time has come. For their own dirty aims they have chosen the most terrible course—to shed blood. Now I see how right I was when I opposed in the parliament the registration of the Party of Islamic Revival.[19]

Only recently the Russian foreign policy decision makers were ready to make another fatal mistake: On September 2, 1992, when civil war in Tajikistan was raging, the Russian government was planning to sign a treaty between Russia and Tajikistan, according to which Russia's troops were to take various economic projects in Tajikistan under their protection and to seal the border with Afghanistan. Apparently, the experience in Afghanistan taught Russia almost nothing. There is very little possibility of a quick settlement of the conflict in Tajikistan. But there is a real danger that this conflict will spill over into other Central Asian republics. It is difficult to predict the consequences and to be optimistic for future developments.

N·O·T·E·S

1. *Literaturnaya gazeta,* May 13, 20, 1987.

2. Ibid., July 10, 1987.

3. *Vechernii Dushanbe,* April 30, 1990.

4. C. Poliakov, *Istoricheskaya etnographiay Srednei Azii i Kazahstana* (Moscow, 1980), p. 107.

5. Vosstanie 1916 goda v Srednei Azii i Kazahstane. Sbornik statei. M, 1960.

6. Issledovaniay po istorii i culture Leninabada. Dushanbe, 1986, s. 175.

7. *Pravda Vostoka,* June 25, 1992.

8. Asnad-e lane-e josusy, no. 29, Afghanistan (1) (Tehran), p. 94.

9. Asnad-e la ne-e jo susy, no. 29, Afghanistan (1) (Tehran), p. 121.

10. *Azija i Africa segodnia,* no. 9, 1992, p. 29-30.

11. *Komsomolskaya pravda,* September 12, 1992.

12. A. Malashenko, "Islam v SNG," *Nezavisimaya gazeta,* September 18, 1992.

13. *Nezavisimaya gazeta,* September 4, 1992.

14. Ibid., September 5, 1992.

15. *Asnad-e lane-e jo susy,* no. 30. Afghanistan (2) (Tehran), p. 31.

16. *Asnad-e lane-e jo susy,* no. 30. Afghanistan (2) (Tehran), p. 40.

17. *Nezavisimaya gazeta,* September 23, 1992.

18. Habib-ur-Rahman, *Afghanistan* (Tehran, no date).

19. *Pravda,* September 29, 1992.

7

Russia's Relations with the Central Asian States Since the Dissolution of the Soviet Union

◆

Yuri V. Gankovsky

n analyzing the foreign policy of any state, it is necessary to carefully consider all factors that exert influence on the formation of the foreign policy, its aims, as well as the hierarchy of these aims and the methods employed to achieve them. In the final analysis, the foreign policy of a state is determined by the interests of the social forces (or strata) that exercise power in that state. Also, the foreign policy decisions are taken under the influence not only of internal factors (including the historical, socioeconomic, and political development), but also within the framework of the international balance of power.

The foreign policy of the Soviet Union was a fragmentary yet a pragmatic policy of "one day." In practice, the Soviet Union undertook uncoordinated political, military, or economic actions in order to achieve political breakthroughs or change in the balance of forces at the global level. (I am sorry to say that Russia's foreign policy has inherited the worst features of the Soviet foreign policy, especially of the later years of its existence.)

IS ISLAMIC FUNDAMENTALISM DANGEROUS TO RUSSIA?

Russia's emerging relations with the Central Asia republics, including Kazakhstan, must be analyzed without often-repeated myths. The biggest myth would have us believe that Muslim fundamentalism is dangerous for

Russia or for Russia's state interests. Muslim fundamentalism has existed for about 1,000 years. In the Middle East and South Asia it appeared at the end of the thirteenth and the beginning of the fourteenth century. Scholars of Islamic history usually connect the emergence of Muslim fundamentalism in this region with the activity of Fakhruddin Zarradi (d. 1326). In the eighteenth century, the prominent scholar of Islamic fundamentalism was Shah Waliullah (1703-1762). The disciple of his son, Abdul Aziz, was the famous Sayyid Ahmad Barelwi (1786-1831). Muslim fundamentalism itself is not dangerous. Among its leaders there were and are figures deserving respect.[1] The determining factors are the leaders' orientation; their social, economic, and political aims; and finally the methods they employ in order to achieve Islamic fundamentalism. Academician V. V. Barthold (1869-1930) stated very aptly in 1914: "Islamic slogans are always used as a doctrine and not a religious one, but as a political doctrine and mostly as a means of attaining quite definite political aims."[2]

The second myth is about the Soviet Union being a socialist state. Two rhetorical questions may be asked: What kind of society was built in the Soviet Union? And who ruled the Soviet Union? Lenin's characterization of Soviet society has been published many times and need not be repeated.

The Soviet society as it emerged by the middle 1930s and remains at present is a society of state capitalism rather than "developed socialist society" or "administrative-commanding and barrack socialism." The system of state capitalism gave the upper crust of Soviet bureaucracy the proprietary control over the means of production and a unique capability to appropriate the greater part of the newly created wealth and products in the state economy. The upper strata of the Soviet bureaucracy is no more than a quarter of 1 percent of the country's population; its members are practically uncontrolled. Not a monolith, the bureaucracy consists of a large number of territorial, ethnic, and professional clans and groups. They compete for power and their combats often take extreme forms.

Against the landscape of political infighting in the Commonwealth of Independent States (CIS) republics lurks the struggle for power between various clans and groups of the upper crust of the bureaucracy. To attain their aims, they purposely create economic hardships and tensions, including ethnic conflicts.[3]

As a result, in some of the Central Asian republics and Kazakhstan "national-patriotic" regimes have come into being. These regimes are the product of an alliance between former local bosses of the Communist Party and some segments of the nationalists. The authoritarian character of these regimes is obvious. The leaders of these regimes aim to establish "order" and "strong-hand rule." Does all this mean that democracy has no chance to flourish in the republics of the CIS? If liberal democracy means the rule of law, respect for human rights, and individual freedom, then its chances are slim indeed in the short run. These republics do not have even the elementary conditions necessary for liberal democracy. Moreover, they are going through political, economic, and social crisis, which invite strong-arm tactics and centralized executive authority.

CURRENT DYNAMICS IN RUSSIA

Very largely, the fate of the CIS will be determined by what is now happening in the political life of Russia.

Peoples of the Russian Federation did not have any democratic experience before the October Revolution, nor after it; nor are they ready for democracy. Objectively, the Russian Federation has now two options of development: either return to the Stalinist model of totalitarian order, or establish an authoritarian form of rule with some element of democracy. No other model of political development is possible. There is no need to discuss the Stalinist model's consequences for the people of the CIS and the political situation in the world.

Some foreign leaders by their encouraging words lend support to the forces of the extreme right in Russia, especially when they announce the necessity of limiting Russia to its 1552 borders.[4] They encourage territorial claims on Russia, assert that Russia lost the Cold War, and attach political demands to their assistance to Russia. These thoughtless words and actions assist the rise of fascism in Russia with all of its negative consequences.

As far as the privatization of state enterprises and the transition to a market economy are concerned, they will not lead to democracy under the existing conditions in the CIS republics. The corrupted upper strata of bureaucracy and "kings" of the "black market" are striving to turn billions in paper money, which they have accumulated, into real property by transferring this paper money to joint ventures, retaining control over state property, and buying state plants, land, and houses. If they succeed, their power will become formidable.

The territory of Central Asia is 4 million square kilometers, and the population is little more than 50 million. The political situation within the republics of this region influences their foreign policy to a great degree. It also influences strongly Russia's policy toward the countries of this region. Their volatile political situation impacts on the relations between the Russian Federation and countries of the Middle East and South Asia.

During the last four years political organizations have appeared that may be called traditionalist or populist and nationalist. All of them were formed by local intelligentsia, and they actively use Islam and nationalist slogans. They are not very large, but the economic instability continuously nurtures them.

Proclaiming the slogan of "Turkistan for Turks" and encouraging followers to create the Islamic Republic of Turkistan, the traditionalist Alash became most active in Kazakhstan in 1990 to 1992. The same year two organizations, Birlik and Erk, sprang into action. They urged the need to establish a federation or confederation of Muslim republics in the region. In Tajikistan, Rostakhoz became well known. Its leaders made territorial claims on Uzbekistan. In Kirghizia, the Ashar Party and another one called Osh Aimagi were officially registered. The latter party's activity, encouraged by the local bureaucracy, led to bloody conflicts in Osh. From the perspectives of orthodox Islam, these organizations pretended to be defenders of people, called upon justice, and criticized corrupt rulers.

The official leaders of the ruling bodies of Islam are against the participation of *ulama* in any political party or organization since, in their eyes, their participation would contradict the Holy Quran and *Shariat*. However, in the 1990s at least ten Islamic parties existed in the region. These parties are not very large and their structure is in the formative stage. Muslim *ulama* take an active part in their leadership. In the past, the *ulama* played an important part in the region. Since the religious parties continue to increase rapidly, one can also expect a substantial role and influence for the *ulama*.

On the political spectrum center and the left parties are characterized by a variety of orientations, including the progressive adherents of socialist orientation, democracy, and pluralism of opinions and of economic and political liberties. These parties hope to achieve their aims through a genuine reform of the state administrative structures in the region. They are not at all strong numerically. The left groups have not been successful in wooing the working classes. The silent majority of the population is not on the side of the left either. All attempts at consolidating the left-wing parties have been frustrated by the personal ambitions of their leaders. The absence of any well-considered program of actions also hindered the consolidation of these parties.[5] The conservative bureaucratic elite occupies a right-wing position in the political arena and is devoted to strengthening its position and preserving its privileges. The struggle of various groups in the ruling bureaucratic upper circles of the local society is a complicating factor in Central Asia.

RUSSIAN FOREIGN POLICY ORIENTATION

At present, Russian foreign policy is at the crossroads. This is, first of all, due to the inner problems of the Russian Federation. Second, Russian foreign policy is greatly influenced by the political processes in the world. These processes are marked by complications and contradictions. Currently in Russia there is public emphasis on the "common European home." However, this policy orientation moves Russia away from Asia. On April 24, 1992, President Boris Yeltsin issued a decree to promote coordination in the relations of member states of the CIS.[6] In response to this decree, the Ministry of Foreign Affairs presented him in September 1992 with an extensive report on the priorities of the foreign policy of Russia in the CIS. These priorities are: (1) ensuring human rights (including the rights of ethnic-national minorities); (2) achievement of stability and safety; (3) equal rights of all states; (4) obligatory fulfillment of agreements by all states; and (5) strengthening the security of Russia's borders.

In October this report was discussed and its shortcomings were pointed out: The report gave no clear definition of the state interests and aims of Russia; it has no strategy of foreign policy; it does not indicated how the foreign policy of Russia must be coordinated. The report does not define the precise place and role of Central Asia in the CIS. The absence of definite aims and concrete definitions has led to contradictions in Russia's decisions, dissipating national resources.

Russian experts believe that reliance on foreign aid is an illusion and whatever aid the Central Asian republics can get would not solve their economic problems; nor would the creation of free zones help. The foreign capital might be invested, but decentralization of the economies and great domestic political instability will make it impossible to mobilize the essential means for the revival of this vast region.

Russian expert opinion urges the Russian government to hold regular meetings of the ministers of foreign affairs of Russia and the Central Asia republics, leading to summit meetings of the CIS countries in order to promote not only multilateral but also cooperative bilateral relations. This flexible approach is recommended to find mutually acceptable solutions to smothering ethnic conflicts and fixing ecological disasters.

Economics factors exert tremendous influence on the political situation within Russia and on its policy toward the Central Asian region and vice versa. In the Soviet Union a common economic system was created, and it functioned.

In the 1920s and 1930s, a sizable portion of the budgets of the Central Asian republics was covered by subsidies from the budget of the Russian

Federation. In Tajikistan, for example, between 1924 and 1929, from 46.5 to 79.9 percent of the republic's expenditures were provided through Russian subsidies. Rapid industrialization of the outlying districts was accompanied by development of labor forces, and illiteracy was eliminated. The *Pakistan Army Journal* acknowledged in June 1992: "All republics have almost one hundred percent literacy rate."[7] The real incomes of the local population rose sharply. The *Financial Times* in April 1987 pointed out: "Material living standards have risen in the Muslim countries, but also faster than those in Russia itself."[8]

From 1929 to 1932 the Turkistan-Siberian railway (TURKSIB) connecting Kazakhstan and Central Asia with Siberia was built. Subsequently, common power and electricity systems were built and gas lines were laid, supplying gas from Central Asia to the center of Russia. The Russian Federation provided Central Asia and Kazakhstan with oil, cars, excavators, timber, paper, cement, and radio and electric equipment. The Central Asian republics, including Kazakhstan, supplied animal produce, vegetables, and fruits to the Russian Federation. Russia received 97 percent of cotton produced there, and more than 80 percent of the Central Asian commodity trade was with Russia.

The disintegration of the Soviet Union has created enormous economic difficulties, not only in Russia, but in all the other republics of the former Soviet Union. In June-July 1992 the gross national product declined by 18 to 20 percent as compared to 1991; average output of industrial products and food became sharply reduced.[9] Costs of consumer goods have increased dozens of times. For broad masses of the population, living conditions have worsened. According to official data, during just the seven months from November 1991 to June 1992, workers' income decreased by 43.7 percent and that of pensioners by 55.4 percent.[10] These destructive processes caused the growth of social tensions and sharpened political instability.

Economic difficulties and social tension that followed the disintegration of the Soviet Union encouraged the centripetal tendencies in the political development of the Central Asian republics.

On April 23, 1992, in Bishkek, the capital of Kirghizia, the presidents of Kirghizia, Kazakhstan, Uzbekistan, Turkmenia, and the first deputy of the prime minister of Tajikistan proclaimed their desire to consolidate the CIS. There is nothing extraordinary about this proclamation, as a Pakistani expert appropriately wrote in June 1992: "Other republics need Russia more than Russia needs them. The leaders of the Muslim states have been worried about their economic viability, therefore, they were inclined toward the idea of CIS, with the center having the responsibility for foreign affairs, economy, defense, communications, etc."[11] On May 25, 1992, in the Moscow Kremlin, presidents of the Russian Federation and Kazakhstan signed an agreement of friendship, cooperation, and mutual assistance.

Five days later, on May 30, the Treaty for Inter-States Relations, Friendship, and Cooperation between the Russian Federation and Uzbekistan was signed in Moscow. Operative for ten years, the treaty envisages cooperation in the spheres of economics, education, science, and technology. The treaty also provides that the territories of Russia and Uzbekistan will be included into a common military strategic region. After signing the treaty, the president of Uzbekistan said that "Uzbekistan doesn't envisage its future without Russia. Russia is guarantor of stability and peace in our region, and guarantor of the stability of our boundaries."[12]

In August 1992 the president of Kazakhstan suggested the creation of an Economic Council of the CIS in which all participants will have obligations to create a CIS Banking Council to make the ruble common currency; organize an Economic Court and Coordinating Economic Council; create an Inter-Parliament Assembly; and establish a Defense Union for CIS. These suggestions were supported by the presidents of all the republics of Central Asia, as well as the presidents of Armenia, Moldavia, Byelorussia, and Russia.[13]

In Bishkek at a meeting in October 1992, the CIS heads decided to create a united ruble zone, a Consultative Economic Group under the Council of States and government heads, in addition to an Inter-State Bank and an Economic Court, whose members will be appointed by the CIS parliaments. They also agreed to work out interstate (CIS) regulations. Finally, an Inter-State Radio-TV Company will be organized, and some newspapers—for instance, *Izvestia,* will get the legal status of Inter-State publication.

In order to promote amity and reduce arguments and contradictions between the CIS leaders, the president of Kirghizia proposed a pragmatic idea: namely, the integration at various levels, where each CIS member would determine its own status, selecting the status of a full and equal member or associate member or even an observer. Each country will thus assume its own well-defined obligations.

The centripetal tendencies have also become obvious in the military sphere. However, the CIS Council of Defense Ministers and Chief Command of the United Military Forces have also been set up. Their functions are controlled by Russia's president and the commander-in-chief of the CIS United Military Forces. Mobile forces capable of rapid reaction have been organized.[15] This military cooperation is developing not only collectively, but on a bilateral basis as well. Thus, in June 1992, an Agreement of Mutual Defense between Russia and Turkmenia was signed, establishing a joint military force in Russia and Turkmenia, which at present numbers more than 110,000 men.[16]

Many foreign and Russian scholars focus on the issue of the Russian constructive role in solving various territorial and boundary disputes that are likely to emerge in the Central Asian region.

In this connection, it is useful to repeat that on April 23, 1993, at the meeting in Bishkek, leaders of the Central Asian republics announced their recognition of "the territorial integrity of each other and of the permanence of existing boundaries between them."[17] They have assured that they will conduct coordinated policy as far as regional security is concerned and that they will not allow the use of force in their relations. In June 1992, on the eve of his visit to the United States, the Russian minister of Foreign Affairs articulated the Russian Federation's policy on this issue: "Russia does not exclude the possibility of revising the boundaries inside the CIS, but only on the basis of mutual agreements."[18]

Excluding the problem of the South Kuril Islands and a few very small islands on the Amur, all disputable boundary problems are likely to arise only during the demarcation of western Russia's boundaries.

However, one must not ignore the fact that not only in Russia, but in the Central Asian republics as well, there are ultra-nationalist organizations that insist upon the revision of the existing boundaries. Against this background, it might be useful to survey the ethnic composition of the population of Kazakhstan and Central Asia.

With a population of 17 million, Kazakhstan's territory contains 2.7 million square kilometers. The Kazakhstan Autonomous Republic was created on August 26, 1920, in the Russian Federation. The autonomous republic included some regions of southwestern Siberia, mostly populated by Russians. On December 5, 1936, the autonomous republic was reorganized into the Kazakhstan Union Republic, where Kazakhs comprised 36 percent of the population; Russians, 41 percent; Ukrainians, 6 percent; Germans, 6 percent; Uzbeks, 2 percent; and Byelorussians, 1.2 percent. Uighurs, Azerbaijanis, Dungans, and Koreans live in Kazakhstan as well. However, Germans and Koreans were evicted from their former places of habitation in Kazakhstan in the years of Stalin's rule. About 1 million Kazakh people live in Xinjiang (China); about 100,000 Kazakh people live in Mongolia.

In Uzbekistan's territory of 447,000 square kilometers, the population is 20 million. The Uzbekistan Union Republic was formed on October 24, 1924. At present, Uzbeks are 69 percent of the population; Russians,

11 percent; Tatars, 4.2 percent; Kazakhs, 4 percent; Tajiks, 4 percent; Kara-Kalpaks, 2 percent. Koreans, Kirghizes, Ukrainians, Jews, Turkmen, and Azerbaijanis live in Uzbekistan as well. About 1.5 million Uzbeks also live in Afghanistan.

Tajikistan's territory is 143,000 square kilometers, and the population is 5.1 million. The Tajikistan Republic was created in 1924. Tajiks comprise 59 percent of the population; Uzbeks, 23 percent; Russians, 10.4 percent. Tatars, Ukrainians, Jews, and Turkmen live in Tajikistan as well. About 3 million Tajik people also live in Afghanistan.

Kirghizia's territory is 199,000 square kilometers, and the population is 4.3 million. The Kirghiz Republic was created in 1924. Kirghizes comprise 48 percent of the population; Russians, 26 percent; Uzbeks, 12 percent; Ukrainians, 3 percent; Germans, 3 percent. Tatars, Uighurs, Kazakhs, and also Tajiks live in Kirghizistan. Eighty-nine percent of all Kirghizs live in the territory of the Kirghiz Republic.

Turkmenistan's territory is 448,000 square kilometers, and the population is 9 million. The Turkmenistan Republic was formed in 1924. Turkmen comprise 64 percent of the population; Russians, 12.6 percent; Uzbeks, 8.5 percent; Kazakhs, 3 percent. Tatars, Ukrainians, Armenians, Azerbaijanis, and Baluchis live in Turkmenistan as well. About 1 million Turkmen also live in Iran and Afghanistan.

In Kazakhstan and Central Asia, Russians comprise 23 percent of the total population. In Kazakhstan, they are the most numerous ethnic group.[19]

In their struggle for power, rival groups of the ruling upper strata frequently use the ethno-national factor. It is known that Uzbekistan's leadership had information regarding the tragic events that developed in the Ferghana Valley but did not take effective measures to prevent their occurrence. Officers of the Ministry of Home Affairs of Uzbekistan took part in pogroms in Ferghana in 1989. Another example is the events of Kirghizia in the summer of 1990. As a consequence of ethnic conflicts, 42,000 Meshetian Turks left Uzbekistan. All of them are Sunni Muslims and have found refuge in Russia.[20] These provocative ethnic conflicts create deeper anarchy and fatal confrontations.

RUSSIA: A GREAT POWER?

The disintegration of the Soviet Union has led to tremendous changes, not only in Eurasia, but in the whole world. The causes of the Soviet Union's disintegration have not been studied in detail. One can hardly be satisfied with the conclusions made by a group of American experts: "The Soviet

Union collapsed because its leaders and institutions were too insular, too rigid, too bureaucratized and, most of all, too closed to adapt to a world of microchips, modems and mobile money."[21] This assessment gives no explanation of the consequences of the Soviet Union's disintegration to our small planet.

The negative results, not only to the CIS, but to the whole world, that will be spawned by the increasing external interference in the internal affairs of the CIS, including Russia, Kazakhstan, and Central Asia, have not been assessed. No one paid any attention to the statement made by the commander-in-chief of the CIS United Military Forces that such an interference may become the cause of World War III.[22]

One can cite well-known cases of interference into the inner affairs of Tajikistan from Afghanistan; its negative consequences are harmful not only to Tajikistan, but to Afghanistan as well. Why are some western countries attempting to destabilize the situation in Uzbekistan? Is it just the thoughtlessness of some Western leaders? To answer these questions, it would be useful to combine the efforts of scholars of our two countries.

Last, but not least, it is necessary to consider that Russian public opinion polls demonstrate that 69 percent of Russia's inhabitants are adamant that Russia must remain a great power even if this position worsens its relations with the world.[23] Therefore, those in the West who are glad that the bells toll for the Soviet Union are to be told: "Ask not for whom the bell tolls, it tolls for thee."

N·O·T·E·S

1. For more details, see: Aziz Ahmad, *Islam in India* (Edinburgh, 1969); Hafeez Malik, *Moslem Nationalism in India and Pakistan* (Washington, DC, 1963); I. H. Qureshi, *Ulema in Politics* (Karachi, 1972); G. Allana, *Our Freedom Fighters* (Karachi, 1969); I. P. Petrushevsky, *Islam in Iran* (Leningrad, 1966) (in Russian).

2. V. V. Barthold, *Panislamism — Complete Works*, vol. 4 (Moscow, 1966), p. 402 (in Russian).

3. For more details, see: Yu. V. Gankovsky, "Marxist Theory and Historical Practice — Who Rules the Soviet Union?" *Journal of South Asian and Middle Eastern Studies* 14, no. 3 (Spring 1991): 77-85.

4. "A Round Table Conference," *Soviet Muslims Brief* 4, no. 1 (May-June 1988).

5. For more details, see: M. Makhkamov, "Islam and the Political Development of Tajikistan after 1985" in this volume (chapter 11).

6. *Moscow News*, N19 (614), May 10, 1992, p. 7 (in Russian).

7. Major Shaukat Zaidi, "Central Asia," *Pakistan Army Journal*, 33, no. 2 (June 1992): 50.

8. Edward Mortimer, "Soviet Central Asia: Where Glasnost and Islam Meet," *Financial Times*, April 14, 1987, p. 25.

9. For more details, see: *Izvestiya* (Moscow), April 10, May 5, July 27, 1992 (in Russian).

10. Academician N. Petrakov, "Reform: Riding a Camel," *Moscow News*, N28 (623), July 12, 1992, p. 16. For more details, see: *Arguments and Facts* (Moscow), N20 (605), May 1992, p. 4 (in Russian); *Izvestiya*, April 24; May; June 3, 5, 8, 16; July 7. 24, 1992.

11. Zaidi, "Central Asia," p. 50.

12. *Pravda* (Moscow), June 2, 1992.

13. *Literaturnaya Gazeta* (Moscow), August 19, 1992.

14. *Izvestiya*, October 12, 1992.

15. *Izvestiya*, May 25; October 8, 14, 1992.

16. *Izvestiya*, June 6, 1992; "Moscow News," N29 (623), July 12, 1992, p. 4.

17. *Izvestiya*, April 23, 1992.

18. *Izvestiya*, June 9, 1992.

19. For more details, see: S. I. Burk, *Population of the World* (Moscow, 1986), pp. 123-176 (in Russian).

20. *Izvestiya,* October 15, 1992.

21. Report of the Conference on Global Changes and Domestic Transformations: New Possibilities for American Foreign Policy, University of Iowa, April 30-May 2, 1992, p. 6.

22. *Izvestiya,* May 21, 1992.

23. *Moscow News,* N30 (625), July 26, 1992, p. 2.

Central Asia and American National Interests

◆

Graham E. Fuller

T
he emergence of Central Asia onto the world scene is one of the more
extraordinary phenomena of the end of the Cold War. A region that
was almost unknown in the West, fabled and obscure even in the nineteenth century, has now joined the ranks of international politics as
states that never existed as such in the past.

In this chapter an attempt is made to define the character of American
strategic interests in this distant region. The task is a challenging one,
because the definition of strategic interests anywhere in this post-Cold
War era requires a lot of new thinking. It is striking to note that the entire
area of the former Soviet Union is itself in the throes of attempting to
define its own strategic national interests anew. After 70 years in which
virtually every part of the globe had come to play its role on the Cold War
chessboard, the end of the Cold War has taken away the ready ability of
most large states to determine their national interests.

The states of Central Asia themselves are confronting the same urgent
necessity. But before these strategic interests can be assessed, the states
must first determine who they are and what their own identity is. This
might seem to be elementary, but it is not, for the new states have never
before faced the world as independent entities. What is their national
character? Are they "westerners" — as a result of inclusion for over a century and a half in a western (Russian) state? Or are they Asians, looking
more toward the East? Or are they Muslims, looking mostly south to the

rest of the Muslim world? Or are they Turks, associated first and foremost with other Turkish states and especially Ankara? These very questions themselves were forbidden in the past, but now are essential to the formulation of new nation-states, especially when those states are often heavily multinational in character. Only when they are answered can the Central Asian republics decide who their friends are and from where threats to their security will emanate. The answers will have direct bearing on Washington's decisions about its own national interests in this area.

But we need not wait indefinitely before offering some of our own answers to these questions. As Americans looking at the new post-Cold War order (or disorder), we can already say a few things about what is and is not desirable to see in this region. Strategic and tactical policies will then flow from those interests.

In briefest terms, American national interests in Central Asia are quite limited and are primarily "negative" in character; that is, they seek to prevent or avoid undesirable developments in the region. These interests can be reduced to six basic areas, four of which are negative and two of which are positive:

1. Arranging our policies all over the former Soviet Union so as to avoid the reemergence of any kind of Russian radical or ideological expansionism that could return the world to global nuclear confrontation.
2. Avoiding or maintaining damage control over further civil war or breakup of nations that will spill over into neighboring states, keeping the world in a state of disorder and mayhem.
3. Avoiding nuclear proliferation.
4. Avoiding the development of radical antiwestern forms of political Islam in the region.

Two other positive U.S. national interests are:

5. Supporting the growth of human rights, democracy, free market economics and a cleaner global environment.
6. Enabling the United States to play a role in the economic development of the region, especially its raw materials.

THE PRIORITY OF MANAGING OUR RELATIONS WITH RUSSIA

The highest American priority in Central Asia is Russia. The key American, indeed global, interest is to see Russia evolve as a democratic and moderate member of the international community. There can be no return to the

Cold War era. American policies in the former Soviet Union must devote priority attention to that goal.

What does this mean in practical terms? To defer to Russian interests above all else in the region? Not at all. But it does mean that we need to keep a very clear eye on the nature of relations between Russia and the Central Asian republics, especially when it involves the welfare and lives of Russians who still live in these republics. Washington has no business protecting the rights and welfare of Russians in these states. But the fact remains that abuse of Russians in these republics is perhaps the single most volatile issue for Moscow politics, the one seized upon by Russian extreme nationalists and expansionists as potential justification for sending in Russian forces or reimposing some kind of imperial relationship upon the region. If future Russian politics should adopt that kind of extreme right-wing chauvinistic or neobolshevik ideology and action plan, then some kind of ideological confrontation with the West will not be far behind.

The fact is there are over 25 million Russians who live outside of Russia in the new republics, a high proportion of them in Central Asia. They are the butt of nationalist movements that seek their departure. It is hardly the role of the West to protect Russians there, but the West can at least do something to address the problems of this decolonization process—for that is what it is. We need to undertake frank discussions with Moscow of our vision of the problem of expatriate Russians and also undertake discussions with the individual republics as to what they think is the best way to alleviate potential ethnic confrontation. For we should be in no doubt: There will be confrontation with the Russians, most explosively in Kazakhstan above all else.

The Russians will need to face the reality that their days as the elites of Central Asia are numbered. It is a terrible shock to Russians, many of whom were born there and contributed to the building of the Central Asian economies, to realize that it is no longer "their" country. Local nationalities now seek the Russians' previous authority, power, jobs, housing, and other privileges. Their early departure will in many cases negatively affect the local economies, where the Russians possess unique skills and experience in technology, administration, industry, and agriculture. But nationalist impulses are not inclined to consider cold economic factors, and they generally want the Russians out, the sooner the better.

Kazakhstan is the most potentially volatile region, for there are more Russians there than in any other republic, both proportionally—some 40 percent of the population—and in absolute numbers. The Kazakhs, however, are literally beside themselves with anguish over the fact that they constitute a minority in their own republic, and they will devote every waking moment to eventually rectifying that situation so as to take control. The fact that Kazakhstan today in the person of President Nursultan Nazarbaev possesses the most able leader in any of the post-Soviet republics only serves to veil the problem for the moment. Kazakhstan's present stability and moderation cannot last. When nationalist confrontation takes place, the primarily Russian-populated northern industrial areas could well secede and join Russia, creating a massive confrontation with Kazakh nationalism and affecting the other republics to the south as well. This problem should be high on the list of American interests; in effect, the United States should determine how to encourage an early long-range look at this problem by all parties out of recognition that, for better or for worse, nationalism will be the reigning impulse of the region in the years to come. Pleasant talk about a binational state simply will not wash.

US world goals would thus suggest that we have an interest in facilitating the peaceful evolution and continuing decolonization of the region in such a way that does not offer ammunition to Russian extremist or expansionist forces. It is hoped that the Western presence in Central Asia can be viewed by Moscow and the republics as benign and positive as the region evolves new relationships and forms of governance.

If avoidance of dangerous confrontation between Russians and the republics is important to American interests and global stability in the future, realistic American ability to substantively prevent this eventuality is nonetheless extremely limited. America cannot be policeman of the world, and our presence and advice could well be resented and shunned on occasion. Nor can resolution of these problems be primarily an American problem. But the fact remains that this issue is of single critical importance in this region, even if American action is limited primarily to the diplomatic realm. Washington will require creativity to think constructively about the kinds of approaches and mechanisms that will serve to alleviate confrontation.

DAMAGE CONTROL OVER NATIONALIST SEPARATISM

Avoiding civil war and maintaining damage control is a close corollary of managing our relations with Russia, but it is slightly less directly critical to U.S. interests since, when Russian citizens are not involved, there is less likelihood of sparking resuscitation of nationalist extremism in Russia and resuscitation of global ideological polarization. The primary destabilizing element in Central Asia is the "artificial" nature of the republican boundaries drawn by Stalin, which leave many nationals outside the boundaries of their own republics. Kazakhstan in particular suffers most from this problem due to its role as "prison of nationalities" during Stalin's time when all nationalist dissidents, and sometimes whole nationalities, were deported to Central Asia during World War II, such as the Crimean Tatars and the Chechen. Kazakhstan today has well over 100 nationalities represented within its borders.

Will the present boundaries of Central Asian states serve to meet the human rights and citizenship rights of all their citizens of so many different nationalities? Will the evolution of the nation-state in each of the republics, designed first and foremost to protect and promote the interests of the titular nationality, prove to be a stable and progressive vehicle for all citizens of the state? Given the pent-up character of these long-frustrated nationalisms, it is difficult to be optimistic about solutions for this mosaic of complex nationalist conflicts. The multiethnic state and society is a worthwhile goal, but how feasible is it in this age of aggressive nationalist expression?

Key regional ethnic conflicts include large Tajik minorities in Uzbekistan; even larger Uzbek minorities in Tajikistan, Kazakhstan, and Kyrgyzstan; Uighur minorities in Kazakhstan; Kazakhs in Uzbekistan; and so on. In addition, large numbers of Caucasian nationalities such as Azeris, Armenians, and Chechens play prominent roles in the private economy, as do Dungans, Koreans, Germans, and others. To date the pattern is for the smaller nationalities all to identify with each other and with the local Russians against the titular nationality that is now seeking to create the new nation-state for its own people and culture. These conflicts are the potential bases for bloody nationalist conflict and for efforts by smaller groups to break away, declare local autonomy, or adjust borders. This kind of turmoil will create political and economic instability and discourage outside investment or trade, worsening economic conditions and creating the groundwork for extremism.

Breakaway nationalist movements are unfortunately not limited to states within Central Asia. Emergent nationalism has already had major impact on neighboring states that could have grave international consequences. At the top of the list is the impact on Turkey, a state that in modern times has always linked its vital interests and orientation toward the West; today Turkey is tempted by the new opportunities that a more pan-Turkist policy can offer among the five new Turkish states of the former Soviet Union (including Azerbaijan). Turkey has moved swiftly to occupy the most prominent position of any external state in the affairs of the new Central Asian states, so far without abandoning its interests in the West.

This Turkish posture is in direct rivalry with Iran, which considers Central Asia historically part of the great Iranian cultural continuum and a natural extension of its interests. More important, the new pan-Turkist orientation of independent Azerbaijan now challenges Iran's very territorial integrity by calling for union with Iranian Azerbaijan. Iran, as a multinational Persian empire in its own right, is vulnerable to the emergence of new nationalist and breakaway trends in the region. Turkey and Iran may be rapidly moving into a confrontational course with the most serious consequences as these two great nationalist traditions compete.

Afghanistan, a small multinational Pashtun empire, is also threatened by the new politics of Central Asia. If the dominant Pashtuns of Afghanistan are not willing to accept a far greater degree of power sharing than in the past with the large Tajik and Uzbek minorities, the Tajiks and Uzbeks of northern Afghanistan may well break off and even possibly seek union with their respective republics to the north. Tajikistan in particular would have the greatest interest in this in order to increase its demographic power vis-à-vis that of the Uzbeks.

The breakup of Afghanistan leads to major complications in Pakistan, also highly multinational in character, where Pashtuns might once again seek to unite in a new state of greater Pashtunistan. India too, with its own growing Hindu-Muslim tensions, is already unhappy that the former friendly Soviet Union has disappeared, giving way to a slew of new Muslim states in the same area, which in geopolitical terms strengthen Pakistan's own "Islamic strategic depth."

China too will be inexorably affected as its empire faces likely collapse with the fall of Communist rule there. The Tibetans have long since enjoyed world sympathy for their aspirations for independence; the 8 million Turkish Uighurs of Xinjiang province have equal claim to independent status, despite Chinese efforts to assimilate the region by forced massive population resettlement of Han Chinese to the Uighur homeland.

As this process of ethnic conflict, separation, and reunification evolves, the Central Asia states will not, unfortunately, be masters of their own fate. They are caught in the center of Asia between such other giants as Russia, China, and India. As geopolitical conflict evolves or diminishes between these states, Central Asian priorities will be directly affected. Will these republics lean toward Russia as a counterweight against China? Or with China against Russia? How will they react if Sino-Indian rivalry begins anew? These are major questions for the geopolitics of the Asian continent in the decades to come.

The region thus faces the prospect of potentially massive change. Once again, it cannot, and should not, be the role of the United States to preserve the status quo and existing boundaries and authorities of the governments of the region against separatist nationalist aspirations. Indeed, it is beyond the power of the United States to do so even if it wished. But the phenomenon of breakup will be important to U.S. interests elsewhere, and the United States cannot absent itself from world efforts to manage the process.

It is furthermore highly debatable whether the breakup of multiethnic states along narrow ethnic lines is truly desirable. The issue is not so much whether it is desirable, but whether it is possible to arrest these trends. If the cost of breakup is high, how much higher might be the cost in blood, treasure, and stability of forcibly repressing all such aspirations? The fact is that we are living in a period when nationalism is once again able to assert itself broadly after the chilling affect of the Cold War. These processes cannot be stopped, only channeled, and the damage limited. One of the paramount tasks of the world and the United Nations in this decade will be to try to evolve a series of alternative approaches and methods to handle breakaway nationalist aspirations by small—or sometimes not so small—nations and peoples who seek fulfillment of ethnic aspirations. What kind of creative new arrangements and methods can be brought to bear: guarantees and arrangements including combinations of autonomies, commonwealths, federations, or confederations? The next century may well be the era of ministates created to fulfill nationalist aspirations, but in which the concept of sovereignty is sharply and voluntarily delimited by the realities of living in a community of nations in which isolation is economic and social death.

American interests then will need to focus on the early identification of ethnic conflict, its potential dimensions, and possible methods of solution. While the United States cannot take on this obligation on its own, it has experience, insights, and a tradition of leadership that should assist in new regional efforts to reach solutions. That process will include looking for means that can protect and satisfy the aspirations of small ethnic peoples short of tearing apart the states in which they live. Russia itself could also be well positioned to assist in these efforts, as long as the nationalities involved do not feel that Moscow is somehow seeking to reassert its former imperial authority. The process of nation breaking and nation formation will be the hallmark of the next decades; Central Asia is but one area where broad international—and American—interests are affected.

PREVENTION OF NUCLEAR PROLIFERATION

The collapse of the Soviet Union dictated that Kazakhstan would be the one Central Asian state where strategic nuclear missiles are located. President Nazarbaev has played a very canny game in relation to the disposition of these weapons. Although the weapons are under the operational control of Russian forces, Nazarbaev has clearly sought to use Kazakhstan's "nuclear" status as a springboard for international prestige and attention. While denying any desire to develop an independent nuclear capability, Nazarbaev has insisted that Kazakhstan must be included in any discussions of the disposition of its weapons and that it must receive guarantees about its eventual security if it should relinquish these weapons—given Kazakhstan's location among nuclear neighbors in China, Russia, India, and Pakistan. Nazarbaev's calculated ambiguity about his intentions have undoubtedly served to put Kazakhstan on the geostrategic map—to the benefit of Kazakhstan. But U.S. interests—and Russian—dictate that Kazakhstan not attain any true independent nuclear capability.

The United States—indeed the world—has a keen interest in preventing the spread of nuclear weapons anywhere in this region, given its potential for conflict and its strategic location between other nuclear powers. It is unlikely that Nazarbaev intends to retain an independent nuclear capability controlled by Kazakh nationals: Russia itself will surely take the lead in preventing it. The United States and other security council members will be carefully following the prospects for proliferation—or sale—of nuclear weapons in Central Asia, as in the rest of the world.

Proliferation concerns affect not only actually deployable weapons, but nuclear materials and technology as well. It would seem probable that the ranks of nuclear physicists and engineers of the former Soviet Union include some citizens of the Central Asian republics, especially in Kazakhstan and Uzbekistan. International policy will attempt to prevent this knowledge from emigrating to create any new nuclear capabilities among or beyond the Central Asian republics. The sale, or even theft, of nuclear weapons or components from any of the republics, especially in periods of chaos, is another concern. Highly enriched uranium, produced in Tajikistan and Kazakhstan, should also not be openly available on the international market.

Last, the United States in principle is also concerned about the massive spread of conventional weaponry to volatile areas of the world, such as the Middle East. Washington has recently criticized Russian arms sales to Syria and Iran, for example. On the other hand, the United States itself has not set a particularly good example of restraint in selling major weapons systems; commercial concerns, as with all other countries, figure powerfully in all national calculations; debate then ensues only about which recipient states are more "responsible" than others. The prospects for a meaningful conventional arms regime in the region seem slight; commercial stimuli to sales are at least as powerful as the strategic and ideological incentives of the Cold War period.

PREVENTION OF ANTI-WESTERN POLITICAL ISLAM FROM DOMINATION

This interest is hardly unique to the United States, but is shared by all western states, Russia, and a high proportion of states of the Muslim world itself. Few states in the world welcome the emergence of any kind of radical global movement that can only destabilize the international political order. The United States, however, is poorly equipped to do much to prevent the emergence of radical Islamic movements. Indeed, any serious effort to do so can often lead only to exacerbation of the problem. But the national—and international—interest is still there.

It is important to be clear about this. American interests are not opposed to Islam or to Muslim states and societies. Western concern is focused on the phenomenon of transnational, politically radical, ideological movements that seek global polarization or struggle between Islam and non-Islamic societies, especially when violent means are employed. Since the demise of communism, Islamic radicalism is the most "global" radical ideological movement in the world. The problem is with radicalism and not with Islam.

Radical political Islam, like many other radical ideological movements, tends to flourish when political, economic, and social conditions are desperate, provoking the public to turn to more radical remedies. Islamic radicalism often feeds off the grievances of Muslim societies that have suffered in the past in one way or another from western imperialism, colonialism, or interventionism. Islam—as has Christianity in the past—can then serve as the vehicle for these resentments, political struggles, or even political ambitions of one state versus another. As noted earlier, there is little that the United States can do directly to stop the emergence of radical Islamic forces. The primary American contribution can be to help identify such problems as might play into Islamic radicalism and to seek international cooperation for their alleviation. The goal of taming radical political Islam is indeed not focused exclusively upon Central Asia, but characterizes American interests elsewhere in the Muslim world as well.

My personal belief is that domestic political Islam can be dealt with only by managing its eventual controlled integration into the political process; there it will be forced to develop concrete political agendas that must meet public testing at the ballot box, and it will be required to find compromises in working with other political parties that do not share all Islamist values. Only in this manner can radical Islam eventually become politically tamed. When radical Islam becomes state policy expressed in the foreign policy of any state, then that state may eventually evoke international sanctions until its behavior conforms more closely to international norms.

Yet many Central Asian regimes feel threatened by the inevitable Islamic resurgence that is under way in the region. After 70 years of repression, it is not surprising that Islam is enjoying a powerful renaissance, and that—as elsewhere—Islam should serve as a vehicle of nationalist expression or opposition to unpopular regimes. The problem is exacerbated because the institutions of "establishment Islam" in Central Asia—long dominated and puppetized by the Communist state—do not enjoy prestige and respect of the people as a result of their too cozy relationships with the state. Unofficial Islam or Islamist movements then inevitably fill in the vacuum, gain adherence and legitimacy among the people, and can often be able to impose powerful demands upon the state itself and threaten its legitimacy.

The states in Central Asia, especially in Uzbekistan, seem unwilling to allow establishment Islam the necessary independent authority and legitimacy that is crucial to its ability to compete with the highly vibrant and growing "Islamic fundamentalists." While Islam is almost certain to gain a far more powerful position in Central Asian society than ever before, I do not believe that it necessarily presents a powerful threat to western interests. There are no direct grounds for Central Asian grievance against the United States, although there are indirect perceptions that America has in the past been insensitive to Islamic societies and has often supported its enemies. The adoption of a more Islamic agenda domestically need not take Iranian form, and may not differ much from the Pakistani or Saudi forms, both of which are highly Islamic in their own way. Islam may threaten the legitimacy of Central Asian regimes, but it is partly the regimes' own obligation to maintain their own legitimacy among their citizenry. Only if the region sinks into economic crisis, social chaos, or popular despair, or becomes involved in direct and ugly confrontations with Russia and Russians will political Islam have an opportunity to come to power overall.

The American interest then is to help create the international and regional environment, through means described in the next section, to help avoid the emergence of radical Islamic movements. We basically have little influence or control over the process, but the goal is no less of interest to the West as one of several "negative interests" that require close watch.

The remaining two national interests are not designed merely to prevent negative developments from occurring, but are positive goals in themselves. They tend to be mirror images of the anxieties just expressed above.

THE EMERGENCE OF DEMOCRATIC GOVERNMENTS

Part of American interests in the rest of the world at large includes the assisting of democratic governments that respect human rights, allow open political dialogue, have free market economies, and exhibit concern for the global environment. They are desirable not because they are nice ideals, but because they are increasingly perceived as instruments and mechanisms critical to the establishment of healthy, stable, and developing societies over time. If fundamental human rights are not observed at the start, few areas are as vulnerable to violent ethnic struggle as is Central Asia.

U.S. policy will likely watch the emerging governments of the region with an eye to encouraging increasing democratization, human rights, and privatization of large portions of the state-run economy. Washington undoubtedly recognizes, however, that these goals cannot be pursued simplistically. Issues as "simple" as democracy become highly complex when a variety of nationality interests are in competition and when, as in Kazakhstan, the Kazakhs feel that they are not fully in charge of their own state. The same problems apply to the issue of privatization, always complex, but especially volatile when the winners and losers in the process may be one nationality—especially the Russians, or the titular nationality—over all other nationalities.

Last, the United States has an interest in helping all the republics of the former Soviet Union clean up the terrible ecological catastrophe that was the product of 70 years of communism. The full dimensions of this catastrophe are only slowly emerging. Central Asia has suffered its full share of them: the disappearance of the Aral Sea and the emergence of destructive salt flats that are replacing it; the inundation of Central Asian fields with pesticides and fertilizers in quantities that have poisoned the fields, the water table, and large portions of the population; and dirty industries that foul the air. It will take a long time to clean up these problems. Others, such as unsafe nuclear reactors, figure less prominently in Central Asia, but are nonetheless of global concern. U.S. policy will undoubtedly keep an eye on the region's ability to cope with its own ecological problems.

U.S. policy will thus base much of its willingness to assist and cooperate with republican governments on the extent to which the new governments of Central Asia move toward further reform in all areas of life. But Washington must also beware of an unrealistic search for stability for its own sake. When stability is imposed at the cost of reform and political and social evolution, it is not true stability but only the suppression and repression of problems that will explode even more violently when the lid is eventually lifted.

U.S. INTEREST IN DEVELOPING CENTRAL ASIAN ECONOMIES

The Central Asian states are mercifully blessed with a number of resources that enable them to enter upon the world stage with viable economic prospects. While much of the region's industrial potential is of dubious quality, its resources and raw materials are of much promise. Nearly all the republics have oil, gas, gold, other valuable metals, agricultural products, or potent hydroelectrical resources. U.S. investors are undoubtedly interested in looking at these resources as sources of investment. None of these resources is "critical" in the sense that the economy of the United States or the world depends on them.

While the United States will have an interest in the oil of Kazakhstan and Turkmenistan, those resources of course will enter the international oil market as a fungible commodity at international prices and will not serve U.S. interests at the expense of other national economies. The United States will also have an interest in the stability of the region, shared with other regional states, to ensure the smooth development of natural resources and their export, especially when construction of pipelines over politically volatile territory is involved. For the first time, too, the peoples of the region itself have the dominant voice in the disposition of these resources.

The United States will continue to encourage the emergence of broad, free markets. Positive signs are already developing with the number of cooperative trade zones proposed by regional states such as the Commonwealth of Independent States' (CIS's) own ruble zone; the Black Sea Consortium proposed by Turkey; the Caspian zone proposed by Iran, the extension of the Economic Cooperation Organization of Turkey, Iran, Afghanistan, and Pakistan to include the new Central Asian states; potential Central Asian economic cooperation unions; and so on. It is as yet unclear which of these trade zones will prove viable, and a great deal of politics and rivalry is involved in the process. But the emergence of inclusionary, rather than exclusionary, market regions is of the greatest interest to the United States.

CONCLUSION

At a time when the United States itself is struggling to reformulate a new vision of its own national goals, Central Asia is also doing the same. With the end of the Cold War, Central Asia can now be taken largely on its own terms, rather than as an extension of some greater global strategy. Russia, in one way or another, will of course remain America's greatest interest in Central Asia, but that fact need not imply that the interest is either to the disadvantage of Russia or of Central Asia.

Central Asia will be sharing the problems of much of the rest of the world as it seeks to develop economically, politically, and socially and to establish new links on the international scene. The pitfalls of this process are heightened by the contemporary world environment in which virulent nationalism and the redrawing of borders create a chaotic environment for the development of all nations. In one sense, the United States has almost no "special interests" in Central Asia. But it has many broad interests, often shared with other states. It is hoped that the United States will be able to play a meaningful and constructive role in helping the new states of Central Asia to negotiate the dangerous shoals of the new post-Cold War international order.

9

The Problem of Nagorno-Karabagh: Geography versus Demography under Colonialism and in Decolonization

Tadeusz Swietochowski

arly in the nineteenth century, the region of Transcaucasia, the isthmus between the Caspian and the Black seas, passed under the rule of Russia as the result of wars against Iran ending in the treaties of Gulistan in 1813 and Turkmanchai in 1828. The new state frontiers were drawn hastily, and primarily on the ground of strategic interests of Russia, with the view of future penetration of Iran or outflanking Turkey.[1] The territorial changes were carried out on the lines that one day would be emulated by France in Lebanon: a strategic foothold in the rimland of the Middle East with the large proportion of Christian population as the mainstay of the colonial rule. As the chief Christian group at the time, the Georgians, were not numerous enough or fully reliable, in Russia's eyes, so immigration of the Armenians from Iran and Turkey was encouraged.

In 1834, an imperial decree established the Armenian *oblast'* (district) comprising the territories of the just-abolished Azerbaijani khanates (principalities) of Erivan and Nakhichevan, an act that some wished to see as restoring to the Armenians their ancient lands of Eastern Armenia. As the recent research on the region's demographic change by George Bournutian confirms,

> prior to the Russian conquests the Armenians accounted for some 20 percent of the total population of Eastern Armenia and the Muslims for 80 percent; following the

Russian annexation, 57,000 Armenian immigrants arrived from Persia and the
Ottoman Empire. By 1832, therefore, the Armenians formed 50 percent or half of
the population.[2]

The influx of Armenians, who often displaced the Muslims by buying out
their lands with the government's assistance, portended a potential for
ethnic tensions, but remarkably, for a long time the relations between the
two groups appeared to be free of major instances of violence. These
Christian immigrants were not regarded as European settlers comparable
to Russian or German peasants also brought in by the tsardom, but as
newcomers from the familiar environment of the Middle East.

The Armenian immigration produced a spotty pattern of population
distribution, and one of the Armenian enclaves in the Muslim territory
was Nagorno-Karabagh, a mountainous part of the former Azerbaijani
khanate of Karabagh. With its slopes, rivers, and valleys, Nagorno-
Karabagh was open toward the rest of Karabagh, and under the Russian
rule it was included into the *guberniia* (province) of Elizavetpol (Ganja),
which together with that of Baku was called Eastern Transcaucasia, or
future Azerbaijan.

There were major upsurges in the influx of Armenians to Transcaucasia
after each of Russia's wars with the Ottoman State during the nineteenth
century—the Crimean War of 1853 to 1856, the 1876 to 1878 War—as
well as after the mid-1890s massacres of Armenians by Kurdish tribesmen
under Sultan Abdulhamid II's regime in Turkey. By this time the number
of the Armenians in Transcaucasia had reached 900,000.[3] These last waves
of immigration arrived during a period of rapid industrialization and
urbanization, conditions that were apt to generate increasingly higher
degrees of ethnic tensions.

The antagonism between Armenians and the Azerbaijanis had with
time transcended cultural-religious differences. In the eyes of some west-
ern observers, the position of Armenians in Azerbaijan resembled that of
Jews in the parts of Europe where they were both threatened and feared.
Observers with a Middle Eastern perspective noticed similarities with the
Maronites and Copts.

As had other Christian minorities in the Middle East, the Armenians had
developed a special relationship with a European power having expansionist designs, in this case with Russia. The Armenians association with
Russia turned out to be one of the most fateful alliances in history, even
though Russia in general lacked in goodwill and generosity toward the
Armenians, who clearly enjoyed preferential treatment among the peoples

of Transcaucasia. The alliance was based as much on the religious affinity as on the long-range political calculations—restoration of an Armenian state at the expense of Turkey—but its flaw was too great an imbalance between the power of Russia and that of the Armenian nationalism. Russia's far-flung interests and commitments all too often did not coincide with aspirations of the Armenians, and in times of trials Russia was unwilling or unable to come to the rescue of its small ally. At the same time, the friendship with Russia helped poison the atmosphere for the Armenians coexistence with Turkey, whose territory most of them inhabited.[4]

Meanwhile, in Transcaucasia, Muslim-Armenian relations had gradually developed into a complex, multifaceted antagonism. Apart from the perception of the Armenians as a comparatively privileged group, it involved economic and social factors, such as grievances of the fledgling Muslim bourgeoisie beset by ruinous competition, the conflict of interests between the unskilled "Tatar" laborers and Armenian entrepreneurs and merchants, and the animosity of the predominantly rural Muslims toward the largely urbanized Armenians. The differences in socioeconomic structure of the two communities had their parallel in the degree to which each of them was politically organized. Unlike the Muslims, the Armenians had produced political parties, and their nationalist movement was dominated by the Armenian Revolutionary Federation, *Dashnaktsutiun*.

The massive eruptions of violence in the form of mutual intercommunal massacres began with the 1905 Russian Revolution, and would reemerge each time the Russia state was in a condition of crisis or overhaul—during the Civil War in 1918 and during the *perestroika* from 1988 on. At such periods, not only was the Russian government not able to perform its peacekeeping functions, but in fact, it was directly or indirectly inciting the two communities to the violence.[5] One of the centers of the intercommunal fighting in the 1905 revolution was Nagorno-Karabagh, and particularly the town of Shusha.

The final downfall of the tsardom in 1917 led to the renewal of the ethnic conflict, with Nagorno-Karabagh passing on several occasions from one authority to another. The Armenian forces that had come to control this part of the emerging independent Azerbaijan relinquished it in the summer of 1918, when the Ottoman army entered Transcaucasia. By the fall, Turkey had lost the war and withdrawn its troops, and Armenian forces under General Andranik seized Nagorno-Karabagh. This time their aim was not only to possess an Armenian-populated territory, but also to create a base for further expansion eastward and form a strategic corridor extending into Nakhichevan. Armenia was on the winning side in the war, and it seemed that no moment could be more auspicious for the fulfillment of its aspirations aimed at the creation of a large state of a Greater Armenia.

By contrast, Azerbaijan, tainted by its association with Turkey, had negligible political influence in western capitals. Furthermore, Transcaucasia passed into British control; yet as it turned out, it was the British commander, General L. Thomson, who ordered the Andranik forces to withdraw at once from Nagorno-Karabagh and to transfer it to the Azerbaijani administration. Thomson's concern was not the political, diplomatic, or historical considerations, which would be debated by statesmen in the Versailles Conference just about to convene; rather he was guided by practical reasons as a military governor. By its geography, economy, and transportation network, Nagorno-Karabagh was linked to Azerbaijan, and from Armenia it was separated by mountains.

Thomson said, "The fact is that in Azerbaijan some Armenians are much disappointed that the British occupation is [not an] opportunity for revenge. They are reluctant to accept that the peace conference is going to decide, not the military force."[6] On Thomson's insistence, Nagorno-Karabagh had to accept the authority of the Azerbaijani governor, Khosrow Sultanov. For all protests that greeted him, Sultanov over the next several months succeeded in getting the Armenian Assembly in Nagorno-Karabagh to accept formally Azerbaijani rule, an act that recognized the realities of the geographical situation of this ethnic enclave. Nagorno-Karabagh was to retain its administrative and cultural autonomy, and conditions were specified to restrict the size and placement of Azerbaijani garrisons in peacetime.[7] This first attempt to reconcile Nagorno-Karabagh's geography with demography would set an example for future arrangements.

The 1919 Nagorno-Karabagh-Azerbaijani agreement could not be isolated from the general state of Azerbaijani-Armenian relations, as not a single stretch of the border between the two republics was undisputed. While in Nagorno-Karabagh infractions of the agreement were a common occurrence, in the Nakhichevan region there was intermittent fighting. Volunteers included men from the Turkish Nationalist forces of Mustafa Kemal Pasha, who was anxious to establish land communications with Soviet Russia.[8]

In Nagorno-Karabagh the growing tensions broke out in a major Armenian uprising in March 1920, on the eve of the invasion of Azerbaijan by the Red Army. The Azerbaijani high command stripped its border with Russia of troops to deal with the insurgency. The outcome was a virtually bloodless invasion and the end of the independent Azerbaijani Republic on

April 28, 1920. Communist propaganda at the time had it that the purpose of the Red Army's entry was to march across Karabagh and Nakhichevan to Anatolia to help the Turkish war of liberation.[9]

One of the first acts of the newly established Soviet government in Baku, the *Azrevkom* (Azerbaijani Revolutionary Committee), in May 1920 was to send an ultimatum demanding the withdrawal of the Armenian forces from Nagorno-Karabagh and Zangezur, with which the Erivan government promptly complied. Several months later, by December 2, the local Communists took over power in Armenia, although their hold on it was still very weak. Intending to prop up the position of the Armenian comrades, the head of the Communist party of Azerbaijan (CPAz), Nariman Narimanov, came out with his famous statement of December 1, 1920:

> Soviet Azerbaijan . . . declares that from now on no territorial questions could become the cause for spilling of blood between the two peoples who for centuries lived as neighbors: the Muslims and Armenians. The laboring peasantry of Nagorno-Karabagh is given herewith the full right for self-determination; all military operations in the Zangezur region are to end forthwith and the forces of the Soviets to withdraw.[10]

Narimanov's declaration only opened a new chapter in the politics of intractability that the Nagorno-Karabagh problem proved to be. When it came to definite arrangements, the contradiction of geography versus demography reappeared. The arguments raised for retaining the status quo stressed economic integration of Nagorno-Karabagh with Azerbaijan, while those for the unification with Armenia emphasized the fact of the indisputably Armenian composition of its population. The compromise solution included the creation of an autonomous administrative unit within the Azerbaijani Soviet Republic, and the establishment of supreme Communist authority over Transcaucasia, the *Kavbiuro*, with the participation of Stalin (who was still far from the height of his power), decided in principle on this course of action in July 1921. It took another two years of complex maneuvering and controversial debates before the *Kavbiuro* arrived at concrete recommendations. On July 7, 1923, the decree of the Azerbaijani Executive Committee of the Soviets created the Nagorno-Karabagh Autonomous *Oblast'*. The new unit covered 2,600 square miles, or 5.1 percent of the republic's territory, and had its capital in the town of Khankend, later to be renamed Stepanakert.[11]

The case of the other disputed region, Nakhichevan, larger in population and area, involved international negotiations. The March 1921 Friendship Treaty of Moscow that normalized relations between the

Soviet Union and the Ankara regime acceded to the Turkish insistence on having a link with an Armenian territory. One of the treaty's provisions was that Nakhichevan would not be included in Soviet Armenia, but rather would be formed into an administrative unit under the jurisdiction of Azerbaijan even though it was separated from that republic by a belt of Armenian territory. In the words of a historian of Armenia, "Soviet Russia sacrificed the Armenian question to cement the Turkish alliance."[12]

The October 1921 Treaty of Kars, which the Ankara government signed with the Soviet republics of Georgia, Azerbaijan, and Armenia, confirmed the stipulations reached earlier in Moscow. After the formation of the Soviet Union in 1922, Nakhichevan received the status of the Autonomous Soviet Republic as a part of the Azerbaijani Soviet Socialist Republic (SSR). While the local administration in Nagorno-Karabagh was in the hands of the Armenians, in Nakhichevan the Azeris were in control. In an additional act of balancing, Zangezur, which formed a barrier between Nagorno-Karabagh and Nakhichevan, was given outright to Armenia. The overall result of these territorial arrangements was a chessboard pattern, a condition boding ill for the prospects of a stable intercommunal harmony, but the firm grip of Soviet power seemed to assure that at least violence could be avoided.

Indeed, the manifestations of the ethnic antagonism had to remain in hibernation throughout most of the Soviet period. Only in the post-Khrushchevian years did the Armenians begin occasionally to challenge in public the status quo. On April 24, 1965, the fiftieth anniversary of the Armenian deportations by the Ottomans, a crowd of 100,000 came out to the streets of Erivan calling for the restoration of the "territories," the term referring to the eastern provinces of Turkey as well as to Nagorno-Karabagh and Nakhichevan. Before the day was over, the crowd had clashed violently with the militia.[13]

Irredentist claims, and particularly those to Nagorno-Karabagh, served as a means of mobilizing the community for the cause of Armenian nationalism. Another form of action was petitioning for the transfer of the Autonomous *Oblast'* to the Armenian SSR. In 1966, an appeal under 45,000 signatures was submitted to Moscow, and likewise a letter signed by tens of thousands was sent to the Twenty-seventh Congress of the Communist Party of the Soviet Union. The replies were negative, and the standard explanation was that the accommodation of the Armenian demands would create a precedent for other territorial disputes in the Soviet Union.[14] Nonetheless, the irredentist agitation created the antecedents for the rise of the Armenian dissident movement, one of the first of its kind in the Soviet Union.

Even though the manifestations of intercommunal tensions were isolated and restrained, a deep current of demographic change under way in both Azerbaijan and Armenia, a process of national homogenization, cast its shadow on the relations between the two Soviet republics. The first instance was large in scale and brutal in character, in keeping with the spirit of the Stalinist epoch. In 1948, approximately 100,000 of the Azerbaijan inhabitants of Armenia were forcibly deported to Azerbaijan and resettled in the Mugan Steppe, which was ill suited for habitation.[15] The justification was the need to provide the space for the expected influx of Armenians from abroad, a repatriation that failed to materialize on any large scale. Beginning in the next decade, a slow but steady reverse trend was noticeable, the outmigration of the Armenian minority from Azerbaijan.

As the twilight of the great age of Baku oil set in after World War II, the incentives that had been attracting immigrants to Azerbaijan were no longer in force. An additional cause for the outmigration of Armenians was, in the words of a demographer, the fact that the "historical antipathy between the members of the two groups has crystallized in recent years to encourage mutual avoidance and resettlement."[16]

As Gorbachev's *perestroika* got under way, soon the signs of structural crisis of an overextended empire with typical prospects for decolonization were obvious. All these were clearly in evidence: diminished returns from the conquered lands as natural resources were depleted; economic stagnation combined with pressures of a growing population; consolidation of native elites with their rising expectations for a greater share of government responsibilities, a problem compounded by the specifically Soviet condition of bureaucratic overcentralization.

The nationality question, not among the initial concerns of *perestroika*, turned out to be the weakest link in the chain that held the Soviet Union together. The ethnic tensions appeared in outbreaks of widely scattered intercommunal clashes, first against the Russians in the Baltic republics and Kazakhstan, then on the larger scale among the native communities in Transcaucasia, in a manner reminiscent of the winding up of colonial rule in India, Palestine, Cyprus, or Angola. "An interethnic conflict or decolonization crisis?" an Armenian scholar aptly asked.[17]

The old Azerbaijani-Armenian conflict, kept in check for almost 70 years by the Soviet regime, erupted again and with pent-up fury in February 1988 when the Armenian SSR formally announced its claims to Nagorno-Karabagh, apparently on the assumption that the structure of the Union had weakened enough that an attempt to change the status quo would be successful. Upon Moscow's rejection of the petition by the *oblast'*

Soviet for unification with Armenia, a series of mass protests began in Erivan involving street demonstrations, industrial strikes, and school boycotts. Similar events unfolded in other towns of Armenia and in Nagorno-Karabagh. These demonstrations were followed by outbreaks of ethnic violence in both republics, the most notorious of which were the riots in the Azerbaijani city of Sumgait in which scores of Armenian residents were killed or wounded.[18]

In an effort to reduce the tensions and to restore order, Moscow resorted to various extraordinary measures. A package of economic aid was put together for Nagorno-Karabagh and some high-ranking officials were dismissed, including the first secretaries of the republican party organizations, Kamran Baghirov in Azerbaijan and Karen Demirchiyan in Armenia. Troops were brought into the area, and the *oblast'* was put under the direct rule of Moscow through the appointment of a special committee headed by a Russian official, Arkadii Vol'skii.

Among the Azerbaijanis, the revival of ethnic conflict produced the political awakening comparable to the effects of the Tatar-Armenian War of 1905 to 1907. The Armenian action was understood as an opening gambit in the quest for a greater Armenia: the natural hinterland of Nagorno-Karabagh and other parts of Azerbaijan into which Armenian expansion would have to take place. Likewise it became painfully clear to the Azerbaijanis that their adversaries had the advantages of better organization and the powerful support from the diaspora worldwide. Moreover, the sympathies of the Russian and western public were overwhelmingly on the Armenian side, a circumstance that infused an element of the West-versus-East confrontation with the inevitable undertones of a clash of the Christian world against the Muslim.[19]

Meanwhile, it was becoming increasingly obvious that the Communist Party of Azerbaijan, in essence a bureaucratic structure, was incapable of providing leadership in a national emergency. The field was left open for grass-roots initiatives of diverse forms, beginning from ad hoc relief committees, collection of funds, distributing leaflets and *samizdat* publications. A familiar sight in Baku became huge crowds filling the square in front of the Stalinist-style House of the Soviets, once the site of official parades. From the stony podium built for the Communist dignitaries, the crowds were now addressed by new men who came from their ranks.

As the ethnic violence kept spreading, Baku was soon inundated with waves of refugees: Azerbaijanis from Armenia, Nagorno-Karabagh, or the border areas of the two republics where a state of war existed. The officially registered number of refugees, most of them expelled from Armenia in retaliation for similar Azerbaijani actions, reached 165,000 by the end of 1988, and the actual figures were estimated at some 50,000 more.[20] The effect was the sudden upsurge in the ongoing process of the population exchange between the two republics, on the scale that elsewhere, notably in Yugoslavia, would be called "ethnic cleansing." This was a new element in an almost century-long Azerbaijani-Armenian conflict. The plight of these homeless, hungry, and desperate people with bleak prospects for the future in a country where the rate of chronic unemployment hovered around 25 percent stimulated some voluntary action groups to assume political character and to merge into larger associations. A survey of the Azerbaijani "informal" organizations—those without legally recognized status—gave the figure of "close to 40" by the end of 1988.[21] Of this number very few had been in existence prior to the outbreak of the ethnic strife.

Among the new political groups, the one that was most viable and enjoyed the broadest measure of mass support became the Popular Front of Azerbaijan (PFA), an "open door" association accepting the followers of all political trends, including Communists. The PFA rejected the principles of centralism, strict discipline, and accountability; it accepted the struggle of ideas within its ranks, and consequently encouraged factionalism.

Although the front sponsored various actions related to the Nagorno-Karabagh dispute—not only mass protest rallies and strikes, but also a quite effective boycott of rail transit to Armenia—in its program and policy declarations it was not preoccupied with the ethnic conflict, and the emphasis was given to such goals as the reassertion of national identity, economic revival, closer relations with Turkey and Iran, especially south Azerbaijan, and respect for Islam as a part of national heritage.[22]

The front grew rapidly to the position of the main center of political activity in the country, rivaling and soon overshadowing the Communist Party. In fact, the party chief, Abdurrahman Vazirov, felt compelled to conclude in the fall of 1989 a series of agreements with the front's leaders. In return for abandoning the wave of protest strikes that idled tens of thousands of workers, including the general strike of September 4, and calling off the boycott of the rail transit to Armenia, the regime agreed to grant a series of concessions. Together with such steps as lifting the curfew, drafting legislation on the economic independence of the Azerbaijani SSR, free elections, and legalizing the People's Front, the republic's Supreme Soviet adopted the Sovereignty Law. The law reaffirmed the Azerbaijani sovereignty over Nagorno-Karabagh and Nakhichevan and stipulated that the frontiers of the Azerbaijani Republic could not be changed without the approval of the Azerbaijani nation. There was provision for the right of secession from the Soviet Union after a referendum put forth before the entire population of the republic. Even though the Azerbaijani Sovereignty Law was short of a declaration of independence, the Presidium of the Supreme Soviet in Moscow pronounced it invalid on the grounds that it contradicted the Soviet constitution, "which charges the Supreme Soviet with guaranteeing the uniformity of legislative norms throughout the USSR." To those embroiled in the Nagorno-Karabagh dispute, this rejection was seen as another token of support for the Armenian position.[23]

The shadow of the Nagorno-Karabagh conflict kept hanging over the liberalized political life of Azerbaijan. The news that the Autonomous *Oblast'* was incorporated into Armenia's budget and was given the right to vote in that republic's elections sparked bloody anti-Armenian riots in Baku in January 1990. These events in turn served as the pretext for the Soviet military intervention that took place after the riots had run their course, resulting in far higher Azerbaijani than Armenian casualties.[24]

The tragic events of January 1990 seemed to offer a ray of hope for the issue that had given the prime impetus for the convulsions shaking Azerbaijan since early 1988. The Nagorno-Karabagh conflict at last became the subject of direct negotiations between the Azerbaijanis and Armenians at the level of their respective national movements. In February the delegates of the PFA and the Armenian National Movement began direct talks in the faraway capital of Latvia, Riga. Yet the situation in Transcaucasia—a not-quite-unusual switch from killings to embraces—failed to materialize. The talks proved to be more exploratory than productive, and behind their failure was the perception of the PFA's weakness. An Armenian delegate in Riga described this perception later on:

> We learned that the Azerbaijani People's Front as a political organization does not exist. The PFA includes all political forces, from the intellectuals fighting against totalitarianism . . . to the mobs involved in ransacking of Armenian homes. . . . By their own account, their organization, unlike the Armenian National Movement, is unable to assume responsibility for the whole of Azerbaijan."[25]

While the People's Front and the opposition in general experienced a dramatic if temporary decline after the January intervention that was followed by wholesale arrests of political activists, the Communist Party revived like a "phoenix from ashes of the burnt membership cards," in the words of a currently circulating parable. Under circumstances that raised widespread suspicions of rigging, the Communists won overwhelmingly the parliamentary elections in September 1990. Nearly a year later, party leader Ayaz Mutalibov confidently gave his support to the perpetrators of the August 1991 Moscow coup. Several days later, on August 30, he found himself presiding over Azerbaijan's Declaration of Independence, as the Soviet Union had entered the final stage of its disintegration.[26]

Following the declaration, Mutalibov made conciliatory gestures to the opposition, including a power-sharing arrangement that would give each party 25 seats on the National Security Council. By now the People's Front seemed to be a poorly equipped army of irregulars that kept losing most of the battles, yet the war was turning its way. The Azerbaijani president also showed his readiness to wind down the dispute over Nagorno-Karabagh, where the *oblast'* legislature had proclaimed the establishment of the republic and secession from Azerbaijan. He accepted the mediation of Boris Yeltsin and the prime minister of Kazakhstan, Nursultan Nazarbayov, in signing an agreement that basically restored the status quo ante. The agreement was destined, however, to remain a dead letter, and the fighting in Nagorno-Karabagh soon resumed, a veritable time bomb for Mutalibov, with no prospects of being defused.

Reacting to the secession vote, the Azerbaijani parliament abrogated the autonomous status of Nagorno-Karabagh on November 27. In a countermove, Nagorno-Karabagh held a referendum on December 10 in which the overwhelming majority voted for independence. The newly elected regional parliament proclaimed independence on January 6, 1992, an act that was not recognized by any government, including that of Ter-Petrosyan in Armenia. This refusal contributed nonetheless to deepening of the political division between the moderate and radical Armenian approach to the dispute with Azerbaijan.[27]

The Azerbaijanis were waking up to the realization that the most invidious effects of the Soviet rule was their lack of military experience. While under the tsardom, they had been exempt from the compulsory service altogether, under the Soviets they often discharged their military duties in construction battalions. An indication of Moscow's distrust, this practice had not been applied to the Armenians, who with their better training, equipment, and field commanders usually had the upper hand in fighting at equal strength. As the situation in Nagorno-Karabagh kept worsening, Mutalibov showed himself unbelievably sluggish in putting together the national army. Four defense ministers in six months coped with all manner of shortages, from trained reserves, to arms, uniforms, native officers, and last but not least, the sense of discipline.[28] The ministry was accused of sabotaging the formation of the army for fear that the new government would not be able to keep it from being influenced by the opposition. Meanwhile, the reverses that the Azeri side suffered in Nagorno-Karabagh grew increasingly painful.

In February 1992 the Armenian forces seized Shusha and Lachin, a success that opened the road link with Armenia around the mountain barrier. They met with negligible resistance. By this time, the People's front began to call for the resignation of Mutalibov. It took the tragedy of the town of Khojali to bring the simmering political crisis to the boil. The grisly images of hundreds of massacred Azerbaijanis—women and children whom the army had left to the tender mercies of the attackers—produced in the public a shock that the Mutalibov regime could no longer survive.

On March 5, the Azerbaijani parliament gathered for an extraordinary session, while outside of the building the People's Front held a mass meeting. After two days of intense maneuvering and bitter recriminations, Mutalibov resigned. Provisionally, the presidency passed into the hands of a PFA figure, Isa Gambarov, pending the new presidential elections. The voting took place, as scheduled, on June 6. The fragmented and discredited *nomenklatura* failed to put up a candidate. The front-runner in the polls was the leader of the People's Front, a 53-year-old Arabic scholar, Abulfaz Elchibayli, an ascetic-looking man who, like Ter Petrosyan in Armenia, was considered a political moderate. He scored a solid electoral victory, and with this act the book was closed on the last of the Communist practices (the practice of making cosmetic changes in the government under new conditions).

Azerbaijan, one of the slowest ex-Soviet republics to begin its political reawakening, was also the last one to make a deep break with the Soviet past, and symbolically the new regime refused to join the Commonwealth of Independent States (CIS). The Nagorno-Karabagh conflict, it appeared, has fulfilled its function of political mobilization in both Azerbaijan and Armenia. The respective national movements coalesced around passions arising from the ethnic strife, grew in strength, and passed to larger issues of independence. Yet the lives lost, the suffering of the deported and uprooted who have little hope for rebuilding their lives, will loom behind attempts to reach a solution to a dispute about a small stretch of mountainous territory, which epitomizes the contradiction between geography and demography.

Nagorno-Karabagh lends itself to being a bridge between the two countries, even though it has been a bone of contention. In the end, Azerbaijan and Armenia will have to settle the dispute themselves. The worst course of action that the outside world could take would be an involvement without even-handedness. Meanwhile, the historic process of decolonization will go on. For this part of the former Soviet Union, it will most likely result in the reintegration of Transcaucasia into the Middle East, from which it was pulled out almost two centuries ago.

N·O·T·E·S

1. On the Russian expansion south of the Caucasus range, see: M. Atkin, *Russia and Iran 1780-1828* (Minneapolis: Minnesota University Press, 1980); F. Kazemzadeh, "Russian Penetration of the Caucasus," in *Russian Imperialism from Ivan the Great to the Revolution*, ed. T. Hunczak (New Brunswick, NJ: Rutgers University Press, 1974), pp. 239-283.

2. G. A. Bournoutian, "The Ethnic Composition and the Socio-Economic Condition of Eastern Armenia in the First Half of the Nineteenth Century," in *Transcaucasia: Nationalism and Social Change*, ed. R. G. Suny (Ann Arbor: University of Michigan Press, 1983), p. 79; see also Bournoutian's *Eastern Armenia in the Last Decades of Persian Rule, 1807-1828: A Political and Socio-Economic Study of the Khanate of Erivan on the Eve of the Russian Conquest* (Malibu, CA, 1982).

3. For the approximate figures on the Armenian immigration in the second half of the nineteenth century, see: N. I. Isharov, *Novaia ugroza russkomu delu v Zakavkaz'e* (St. Petersburg, 1911), pp. 59-61.

4. For a review and general discussion of the Armenian-Russian relations under the tsardom, see: R. G. Hovannisian, *Armenia on the Road to Independence, 1918* (Berkeley: University of California Press, 1969); C. J. Walker, *Armenia: The Survival of a Nation* (New York: St. Martin's Press, 1980).

5. For the accounts of fighting, see: L. Villari, *The Fire and Sword in the Caucasus* (London, 1906); J. D. Henry, *Baku: An Eventful History* (London, 1905); Walker, *Armenia*, pp. 73-81. For an Azerbaijani view, see: M. S. Ordubadi, *Ganli illar* (Baku: Karabagh Yardim Komitasi, 1991).

6. T. Swietochowski, *Russian Azerbaijan 1905-1920: The Shaping of National Identity in a Muslim Community* (Cambridge: Cambridge University Press, 1985), p. 143; on Azerbaijani-Armenian relations in the period of independence, 1918 to 1920, consult also: A. Altstadt, *The Azerbaijani Turks: Power and Identity under Russian Rule* (Stanford, CA: Hoover Institution Press, 1992), pp. 100-106; R. G. Hovannisian, *The Republic of Armenia* (Berkeley: University of California Press, 1982), vol. 2, pp. 168-206.

7. On the Azerbaijani-Armenian agreement on Nagorno-Karabagh, see; Hovannisian, *Republic of Armenia*, vol. 2, pp. 195, 211.

8. On the fighting in Nakhichevan and the involvement of Kemalist Turks, see: K. Krabekir, *Istiklal harbimiz* (Istanbul: Turkiye Yayinevi, 1960), pp. 328-330. On the Soviet-Kemalist rapprochement, see: G. Jaschke, "La role du communisme dans les relations russo-turques," *Orient* 2, no. 26 (1963): 31-46.

9. On the downfall of the independent Azerbaijani republic, see: Swietochowski, *Russian Azerbaijan*, pp. 173-184.

10. Kommunisticheskai Partiia Azerbaidzhana, Institut Istorii Partii, *K istorii obrzovaniia Nagono-Karakhskoi Avtonomnoi Oblasti AzSSR, 1918-1925. Dokumenty i materialy* (Baku, 1989), p. 41.

11. Ibid., p. 64.

12. R. Hovannisian, "Caucasian Armenia Between Imperial and Soviet Rule: The Interlude of National Independence," in Suny, ed., *Transcaucasia*, p. 291. On the Nakhichevan dispute, see also Altstadt, *Azerbaijani Turks*, pp. 127-128.

13. On the 1965 Erivan demonstrations, see: B. Nahaylo and V. Svoboda, *Soviet Disunion: A History of the Nationality Problem in the USSR* (New York: The Free Press, 1990), pp. 147-148.

14. On the petitioning campaign, see Radio Free Europe, RADS Background Report/39, March 11, 1989; C. Mouradian, "The Mountainous Karabagh Question: An Inter-Ethnic Conflict or Decolonization Crisis?" *Armenian Review* 40, no. 2-3 (1990): 9-12.

15. USSR, People's Deputies from Azerbaijan, *On Forcible Deportation of Azerbaijanis from Armenia*, n.d., p. 2.

16. B. D. Silver, "Population Redistribution and Ethnic Balance in Transcaucasia," in Suny, *Transcaucasia*, p. 377.

17. See: Mouradian, "Mountainous Karabagh Question"; see also: M. Saroyan, "The Karabagh Syndrome and Azerbaijani Politics," *Problems of Communism* (September-October 1990): 14-27.

18. On the Sumgait riots, see: Z. Bunitov, "Pochemu Sumgait. Situatsionnyi analiz," *Elm* (Baku), no. 19 (1989); for an Armenian view, see: *The Sumgait Tragedy: Pogroms Against Armenians in Soviet Azerbaijan* (Cambridge, MA: Zoryan Institute, 1990).

19. See: L. Iunusova, "End of the Ice Age: Azerbaiajna: August-September 1989," *Chronicle of Central Asia and the Caucasus* 8, no. 6 (1989): 12; M. Ibragimov, "Zavtra budet pozdno," *Vyshka*, September 2, 1989.

20. On the refugee problem in Azerbaijan, see: I. Mardanov and V. Rasulov, "Gachynlar va igtisadiyyatimiz," *Vatan sesi*, no. 11 (1990): 5.

21. L. Iunusova, "Pestraia palistra neformal'ykh dvizhenii v Azerbaidzhane," *Russkaia mysl'*, (September 22, 1989): 7. For a list of unofficial and opposition publications, see Altstadt, *Azerbaijani Turks*, pp. 228-230; see also: R. Motika, "Glasnost in der Sowjetrepublik Aserbaidschan am Beispiel der Zeitschrift 'Azerbaycan,'" *Orient*, no. 4 (1991): 573-590.

22. "Program of the People's Front of Azerbaijan," *Chronicle of Central Asia and the Caucasus* 8, no. 4 (1989): 7-10.

23. E. Fuller, "Moscow Rejects Azerbaijani Law on Sovereignty. A Moral Victory for Armenia?" RFE/RL Research Institute, *Report on the USSR*, December 1, 1989, pp. 16-18. On the PFA, see: A. Balaev, *Apercue historique du Front Populaire d'Azerbaïdjan*, n.d.

24. For an official account of the Baku January Days, see: Azerbaidzhanskaia SSR, Verkhovnyi Sovet, *Zaiavlenie Kommissii po rassledovaniiu sobytii imevshikh mesto v gorode Baku 19-20 ianvaria 1990 goda* (Baku, 1990); see also: *Chernyi ianvar'. Dokumenty i materialy* (Baku, 1990).

25. *Armenian Update*, no. 3 (March 1990).

26. On the Declaration of Independence, see *FBIS*, NES-90-31; also *New York Times*, September 4, 1991.

27. On the creation of the independent republic of Nagorno-Karabagh, see: *Transcaucasus: A Chronology. A Publication of the Armenian National Committee of America*, vol. 1, no. 88, August 1, 1992.

28. On the formation of the Azerbaijani national army, see: *Bakinskii Rabochii*, December 20, 1991; *Financial Times*, March 10, 1992; *The Guardian*, June 9, 1992.

▲ ▽ ▲

10

Tragedy in the Aral Sea Basin: Looking Back to Plan Ahead?

◆

Michael H. Glantz, Alvin Z. Rubinstein, and Igor Zonn

For the first time in modern history, Central Asia has acquired global importance. The unanticipated, precipitous dissolution of the former Soviet Union brought the Muslim states of Central Asia and Kazakhstan independence and membership in the United Nations. Kazakhstan, Uzbekistan, Turkmenistan, Tajikistan, and Kyrgyzstan, however, had never really been groomed for independence. Rather, they were tactically set up after 1924 as conveniences to help Moscow rule the region in a colonial way in accordance with Stalin's pronouncement of "socialist in content, national in form." Constituting the western part of "Turkistan" prior to 1924, Central Asia and Kazakhstan were reconstituted as union-republics: Uzbekistan and Turkmenistan in 1925, Tajikistan in 1931, and Kazakhstan and Kyrgyzstan in 1936. The present political boundaries in the region are, therefore, of relatively recent vintage. Thus, nation-building within the newly independent Central Asian republics will, at best, be a difficult and problematic process. With the collapse of the Soviet system and Russia's apparent acceptance of the end of its imperial age, the independent Central Asian republics and Kazakhstan arrived on the scene with constraints from the past that will likely impede their efforts to establish themselves as viable, truly independent nation-states.

The five republics have little experience in self-government or international cooperation, lacking trained indigenous administrative and technical elites. They are beset, to varying degrees, by ethnolinguistic as well as territorial tensions within and across their borders. Their economies are distorted, as a consequence of past forced dependency on Moscow for central economic planning and financial resource allocation. Their economic dependency on the Russian federation for personnel, skills, resources, markets for new materials, and structure, for example, rivaled what had been the case in the African colonies in the 1950s and 1960s when they gained independence from the British and French. In addition, the Soviet Union's legacy of environmental problems to the Central Asian republics and Kazakhstan is in need of redress.

While the term *perestroika* was given great importance by Mikhail Gorbachev in his attempt to restructure the Soviet political system, successive Soviet governments since the "Great October Revolution" had been attempting to restructure nature in order to exploit it. *Ecoperestroika* is a term recently used to describe the Soviet Union's historical approach to human interactions with the natural environment. Government decisions, one after another, sought to assure the dominance of human activities over nature by restructuring the relationship between society and the natural world. Soviet leaders believed that, armed with Soviet engineering and know-how, rivers could be diverted, precipitation increased at will, deserts made green, and so forth.

The socialist transformation of nature was supported by members of the scientific community as well as party and government officials. For example, in 1953 Viktor Kovda captured the spirit of socialist transformation when he wrote "the Party . . . and the Soviet government are doing everything possible to transform nature, to do away with deserts, to attain a further big rise in agricultural productivity. . . . The grand projects outlined by Stalin's genius . . . will make it possible to master the forces of nature in the USSR."[1] Khrushchev later asserted that his society could not wait for nature to produce benefits and that society must extract those benefits from nature. Russian environmentalist Ruben Mnatsakanian recently linked the roots of the ecological crisis in the former Soviet Union and the attack in the 1930s on objective scientific research. The crisis, he noted, ". . . was clearly foreseen as early as the 1930s by distinguished Russian philosophers and scientists . . . ; other scientists and dissidents also mentioned the threat. However, these domestic critics went unheeded by the Communist Party chiefs."[2] This situation has apparently recently changed. R. G. Darst has noted that "after decades of neglect, environmental protection is becoming an increasingly vital component of Soviet economic policy. Soviet economic planners have come to realize that the unintended ecological consequences of industrial and agricultural initiatives have a direct and pernicious impact upon growth and efficiency."[3] Thus, Soviet Communist rule has bequeathed a legacy of unparalleled widespread environmental degradation, impoverishment, and mismanagement.[4] This may prove to be one of history's bitterest condemnations of Soviet socialism — its wanton treatment of nature.

This baleful condition is dramatically, tragically, and chronically evident in the Aral Sea basin, where the sea level has sharply declined since the early 1960s. As of the late 1950s, the Aral Sea was the fourth largest inland body of water in the world (by surface area), and the location of successful fishing, hunting, navigational, and recreational activities. It was also considered a favorable environment for livestock rearing and for waterfowl.[5] During the past three decades, the Aral Sea basin has become an ecological nightmare and a socioeconomic tragedy.

POLITICAL ROOTS OF THE CRISIS

Economic development activities often exact a heavy price from the environment. In theory, with prudent resource management and a positive perspective about the future, including concern about intergenerational equity, the development process can be sustainably managed. Practice, however, is more often than not another matter: The pressures of population growth rates and increasing affluence, demand for maximum profits, and ever-expanding production targets enable decision-making elites to focus only on immediate and short-term needs, to the neglect of longer-term plans. In economic terms, they heavily discount the future. In a similar fashion, major river basins are also in trouble — the Nile, the Jordan, the Tigris-Euphrates[6] — but none is so close to irreversible ecological damage as the Aral Sea basin.

The environmental problems of Central Asia and Kazakhstan began in the late 1950s when Nikita Khrushchev pushed his "Virgin Lands" scheme, the aim of which was to grow wheat on the arid and semiarid steppes of Kazakhstan.[7] At the same time, the cultivation of cotton took on a new salience. As of the mid-1960s, "about half the sown area in Uzbekistan was in cotton (the rest was divided among grains, vegetables, and fodder). By 1990, cotton was sown on about two-thirds of the agricultural lands in Uzbekistan."[8] Its production was expanded as a cash crop, with the raw cotton shipped to the textile plants around Moscow and to other large Russian cities. In the process of imposing a cotton monoculture on Uzbekistan and Turkmenistan, to the neglect of other food crops and of established objective principles of agricultural management that, for example, allow the soil fertility to be retained, the economic development decisions of successive Soviet leaders aggravated the degradation of the land and the sea and misused scarce regional water resources.

A sizable portion of Central Asia's agricultural production is dependent on irrigation. Irrigated agriculture in the region predates by millennia the era of tsarist conquests of the eighteenth and nineteenth centuries. What is new about irrigation in the region, however, is the huge amount of water diverted from the major rivers and, in turn, the large proportion of arable land devoted to cotton production. The stream flows of the two perennial river systems, the Amudarya and Syrdarya, have in the relatively recent past sustained a relatively stable Aral Sea level. Over the centuries, about half the flow of the two rivers reached the Aral; a major expansion of irrigated cotton production altered this ecological balance. Beginning in the late 1970s, no water from the Syrdarya reached the Aral Sea, and the Amudarya supplied only a minimal and ever-decreasing volume.

Large diversions, poor irrigation construction and maintenance, and mismanagement of water resources have been identified as major causes of the decreased flow to the Aral Sea. For example, about 15 percent of the flow of the Amudarya has been diverted since the construction of the Karakum Canal in the mid-1950s in Turkmenistan. This canal's diversion from the Amudarya is "more than the entire stream flow in the upper portion of the Syrdarya."[9] One view contends that there is little doubt that the rapid desiccation of the Aral Sea has been integrally linked to the canal. Turkmenistan officials, among others, have challenged this view.[10]

By the early 1980s, Soviet officials were beginning to reevaluate the causes, consequences, and costs of the economic and ecological problems that decades of dogmatic attempts at development had fostered. Under Gorbachev's policies of *glasnost* and *perestroika*, the full range of issues came to be discussed in public forums with a new openness and in an informative, somewhat objective fashion.

The nuclear meltdown at Chernobyl on April 26, 1986, was a catalyst for *glasnost*. Its transboundary nuclear fallout served to break through decades of secrecy and bureaucratic inertia and paved the way for more serious scrutiny by the public of Soviet environmental problems. Only two months earlier at the Twenty-seventh Congress of the Communist Party of the Soviet Union (CPSU), there had been no specific proposals for examining, let alone resolving, the Soviet Union's environmental problems. Changes, however, came slowly, and there were no significant increases in environmental expenditures until 1988; indeed, "from 1985 through 1987, governmental outlays on behalf of the environment were not significantly ahead of where they were during the Brezhnev era."[11]

Soviet press coverage anticipated, if not prompted, governmental action. The Aral Sea situation was publicly acknowledged to be a catastrophe. *Pravda*, for example, ran an occasional question-and-answer column in which a government official or environmental expert responded to readers' questions. A growing number of articles drew the attention of the public to the gravity of the situation in the Aral Sea basin. Slowly stories emerged about drastic ecological changes that were altering nature on a large scale, as well as adversely affecting the lives of hundreds of thousands of people near the Aral Sea, especially in Karakalpakistan. The themes of ensuing news reports were invariably similar: As a result of poor land use planning and inefficient water resource management practices, the Aral Sea was drying up and, at the existing rate of desiccation, would likely disappear by the year 2010.[12] Throughout these articles there has been much finger-pointing at the Soviet bureaucracy and ministries that, by focusing only on the need to fulfill cotton production planning quotas, ignored consideration of the possible consequences of their policies that were generating environmental disasters. The Aral Sea situation was regarded as "completely intolerable," but, apart from detailing "scandalous instances of a barbaric attitude toward water use," the experts could not agree on a preferred course of action.[13]

Probing articles appeared in *Novyi Mir* and *Nauka i Zhizn*. One of the bitterest critiques of the Soviet establishment's blindness, ineptness, and blundering was presented by Andrei Monin, corresponding member of the USSR Academy of Sciences. He castigated academician Yevgeny Federov of the Department of Oceanology, Atmospheric Physics and Geography (OOFAG), of the USSR's Academy of Sciences, for legitimating a dubious procedure for predicting the level of terminal lakes. Monin charged that "in the period of stagnation [e.g., the Brezhnev era], bureaucratic centralism, and the flourishing of subjective principles of administration, a branch of science was often assigned the role of servant to certain powers that be."[14] It was responsible for planning and setting in motion a "very real large-scale ecological disaster" in the Caspian Sea region, as in the Aral Sea basin. With regard to the Aral Sea situation, Monin referred to a piece written by V. Sokolov in *Literaturnaya Gazeta* (November 18, 1987) in which Sokolov cited optimistic projections from the 1960s of expected increments in irrigated land and yields of cotton, rice, and various fruits and vegetables, but the facts, he noted, proved to be otherwise:

The total area of irrigated land in the Aral Basin has not doubled—it has only increased by a half; nor have the hypothetical yields of cotton and rice doubled. As far as foodstuffs are concerned, per-capita production in most prosperous Central Asia is 26 percent of the medical norm for meat, 42 percent for milk, 53 percent for fruits and vegetables. . . . What had increased? The use of chemicals. Cotton fields are inundated with ten (!) times more pesticides than on average elsewhere in the Soviet Union or in the USA. What else has increased? Consumption of irrigation water.[15]

Monin also criticized Turkmen officials for hiding the fact that ever-increasing percentages of irrigated land were becoming permanently salinized and taken out of production. Behind their "scientific phraseology" was a harsh reality that "If one were to travel by car from Khiva to Tashauz to Nukus, then one would see a white, as a snow-covered steppe, lifeless plain from horizon to horizon."[16]

For Monin, the key question was: Where were the scientists during this period? After exposing the shortcomings of academic and governmental bureaucratic in-fighting, he identified OOFAG (of which he was an estranged member) as the prime culprit, arguing that it must bear the responsibility for the failures of the scientific community to properly advise those who were attempting to develop Central Asia's natural and economic potential. Others, however, have blamed the academy's Institute of Water Problems and its director, G. Voropaev.[17]

In September 1988, *Novyi Mir* collaborated with *Pamir* and several environmental groups to organize an expedition across the Aral basin. The group, which included scientists, writers, and journalists, traveled more than 8,000 miles through Central Asia, talking to local officials, observing, and learning about regional conditions. The resulting seminar attended by scholars from the Central Asian republics, Kazakhstan, and Moscow examined the origin and nature of the existing degradation of the region and possible options. They called the Aral "a symbol of the calamity" that was already evident in the rivers, seas, and lakes throughout the country.

For most of the Gorbachev period, the Soviet government was slow to respond to its environmental crises, of which the Aral Sea problem was but one. It was aware of widespread concern: the frequent discussions in the press, the lobbying of newly established "green" groups, the growing weight of incontrovertible evidence that told of the rising incidence of innumerable human health problems that were attributable to environmental pollution, and the post-Chernobyl critiques that came as *glasnost* took hold. Some measures were taken, but they often proved to be inadequate to the magnitude of the problems. Government commissions set up to investigate environmental problems had no mandate to act; many of those appointed to develop solutions were the same officials responsible for the neglect of the problems in the first place. For example, the Ministry of Water Resources Construction (formerly the Ministry of Land Reclamation and Water Resources) was charged with wasting large sums of money in trying to restore the Aral by proposing the same method that had caused the problem, namely, canal construction.

Moreover, emerging attention to the environmental problems coincided with turmoil in government and party leadership. Gorbachev's attempt to reform the party paralyzed the administrative system and depressed the economy. The struggle for power at the highest levels precluded any systematic action on the everyday problems at the local level. The passiveness of Central Asian and Kazakh government leaders in this process contributed to Moscow's inertia. As Rusi Nasar has noted, the Aral Sea problem had been out of reach for Central Asian writers. "Only in the wake of the 27th CPSU Congress has a serious effort been made to educate and mobilize public opinion to save the Aral Sea."[18] The Gorbachev period was in a way no different from previous ones: problems were solemnly discussed, resolutions passed, new governmental bodies created, action programs planned, but few decision makers came close to grappling with the core problems themselves, especially if it required deviation from the economic five-year plan targets set by Gosplan.

In April 1987, the central government created a Commission on the Aral Sea, under the chairmanship of Yu. A. Izrael, head of the Soviet State Committee on Hydrometeorology. The commission included academicians and the presidents of the Academies of Sciences of the Central Asian republics and Kazakhstan. It agreed on a far-reaching program of actions for adoption, and its recommendations were discussed at meetings of the Soviet Council of Ministers and of the Politburo of the CPSU's Central Committee. All of this led to the adoption in January 1988 by the Central Committee and the Council of Ministers of a resolution "On the Radical Restructuring of Environmental Protection Work in the Country."

Andrei A. Gromyko, then a member of the Politburo and president of the Soviet Union (as the chairman of the Presidium of the Supreme Soviet was referred to in the West), wrote a key article in the party's authoritative journal, *Kommunist*, calling attention to the ecological problems facing the country.[19] Acknowledging that "until recently, important environmental protection tasks were being carried out in an unsatisfactory manner," he ranged widely across the country's major ecological problems, blaming, among other things, "the 'cost-is-no-object' principle of economic management," "a certain deformation of public awareness," and the failure of "some departments" to adhere to or properly enforce existing legislation on protection of the environment. Aside from calling for improved legislation and administrative oversight, he announced the decision to set up an All-Union State Committee for Environmental Protection. As a follow-up, on September 30, 1988, the Central Committee and the Council of Ministers adopted a resolution "On Measures for a Fundamental Improvement of the Ecological and Sanitary Conditions in the Aral Sea region, and for increased effectiveness in the utilization, strengthening, and safeguarding of water and land resources in this basin."[20] The need to improve the quality of drinking water and water conservation measures received special attention. Nevertheless, a rapidly deteriorating economy became the controlling factor throughout the last days of the Soviet Union, and, as a result, the Kremlin was unable to direct adequate financial resources to "new" problems.

Constrained by a lack of funds and increasingly engaged in a life-or-death struggle to control the political forces he had unleashed, Gorbachev could do little. Research continued, albeit at relatively low levels compared to the magnitude of the Aral basin problems, but no new environmental programs were undertaken. The increasingly persistent calls for emergency measures from Central Asian and Kazakh leaders went unheeded. On June 23, 1990, the presidents of Kazakhstan, Uzbekistan, Turkmenistan, Tajikistan, and Kyrgyzstan signed a joint declaration, stating that the growing deficit and pollution of water resources put the Aral Sea basin on the edge of ecological ruin and that the problems were so acute that they "could not be solved by regional efforts alone." What was needed was for the central government to "declare the Aral region one of national calamity and to provide real help."[21]

Their sense of urgency and their willingness to publicly put pressure on decision makers in Moscow came, however, too late. In December 1991, the Soviet Union was dissolved, and constituent independent republics (states) now assumed full responsibility for their respective territorial problems. At the least, the *glasnost* era under Gorbachev had revealed that "the state of the Soviet environment is in far poorer shape" than had previously been admitted — or realized in the West — and that the Aral Sea basin problem was one of the worst.[22]

ARAL SEA DESICCATION:
SOCIAL AND ECOLOGICAL CAUSES AND CONSEQUENCES

At the beginning of the 1960s, the Aral Sea was the earth's fourth largest inland body of water in surface area, behind the Caspian Sea, Lake

Superior, and Lake Victoria. This terminal (no outlets) saline lake is bordered by the Karakum and Kyzylkum (deserts) and the Ustyurt Plateau, and, as noted earlier, its water supply has been replenished primarily by the annual flows of two major perennial rivers, the Syrdarya and the Amudarya (*darya* is Turkic for river). The 1,578-mile-long Amudarya rises in Afghanistan's Pamir Mountains and flows through Turkmenistan and Uzbekistan (sometimes forming their border) before emptying into the Aral Sea; the 1,370-mile-long Syrdarya begins in Kyrgyzstan and flows through Tajikistan and Kazakhstan, and then into the Aral Sea.

About 90 percent of the water in the sea is drawn from these two rivers, with the Amudarya transporting about 73 cubic kilometers (cu km) per year on average, and the Syrdarya about 37 cu km per year prior to 1960. Given the high rates of water use, evaporation, and transpiration, about half the water in these rivers was "lost" before reaching the sea.

In 1960 the mean level of the Aral Sea was measured at 53.4 meters, its surface area at 66,000 km^2, its volume at about 1090 km^3, and its salinity at about 10 grams/liter (g/l). A flourishing sea fishery industry existed, based on the exploitation of a variety of commercially valued species. The forests and wetlands surrounding the sea and in the Syrdarya and Amudarya deltas were quite productive, as flora and fauna had adapted to the natural saline characteristics of the sea. The levels of the Aral Sea had fluctuated less than a meter in the first half of the twentieth century and by up to four meters during the preceding 200-year period.

Since the beginning of the 1960s, the Aral Sea level has dropped continually and dramatically. This was a direct result of the reduction in stream flow of the Amudarya and Syrdarya that was able to reach the sea; from between 50 and 60 km^3 to between 20 and 30 km^3 in the 1970s and 1980s and, finally, to 5 km^3 in 1989-90.[23] In the late 1970s and in the 1980s, there were years when virtually no water reached the Aral Sea from either of these rivers. At first, the drawdown of the sea did not spark much concern within Soviet government organizations. By the mid-1970s, however, concern increased because of ". . . a more rapid drop of the water level than expected."[24] In fact, the annual average rates of sea level decline has accelerated; 0.21 meters/year (m/yr) (1961-70), 0.6 m/yr (1971-80), and 0.8 m/yr (1981-86).[25]

The primary cause of declining sea levels centers on the continual, increasing, and excessive diversions of water from the Amudarya and the Syrdarya for the purpose of expanding the agricultural hectarage devoted in large part to cotton production and, to a lesser extent, rice. In 1950, only 2.9 million hectares of land in Central Asia had been irrigated. By the

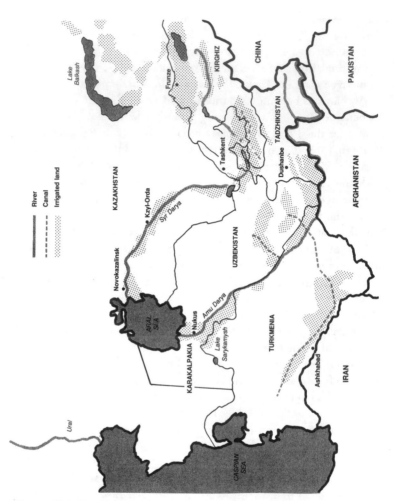

Figure 10.1. The Aral Sea Region. (Source: *Environment* 33, no. 1
[January/February 1991]: 7. Reprinted with permission of the Helen
Dwight Reid Educational Foundation. Published by Heldref
Publications, 1319 18th Street, N.W., Washington, D.C. 20036-1802.
Copyright 1991.)

late 1980s, the irrigated area had been expanded to about 7.2 million
hectares.[26] Figure 10.2 depicts the proportional use of the Amudarya and
Syrdarya water for various agricultural purposes.

Decisions to pursue a "cotton independence policy," made in Moscow
in the early postwar decades by the central government, called for the all-
out exploitation of the most important natural resource in the Aral

basin—water. The goal was to make the country self-sufficient in cotton production at the national level and to expand textile production in factories outside Central Asia and Kazakhstan.[27]

By the beginning of the 1990s, the Aral Sea level had dropped considerably, its surface area had been reduced by half, and its volume reduced by two-thirds, as a result of increasing volumes of water diverted from these rivers. Today the Aral Sea has dropped to sixth place in terms of surface area. P. Raskin, E. Hansen, and Z. Zhu noted that "without any action to reduce the demands or to increase the supplies in the future, the sea would continue to shrink at roughly the same rate as it did in the 1980s."[28] The quality of the seawater has also deteriorated. Figure 10.3 graphically displays the evolution of the sea's characteristics.[29]

In the late 1980s, the sea divided into the "Little Aral" in the north and the "Big Aral" to the south.[30] The sea is shallow at its eastern edge and deepens toward its western shore, and if the sea level were to decline to below 33 m or so, the Big Sea would likely divide into an "East" Sea and a "West" Sea.

The year 1960 serves as a benchmark for the predicament in which Central Asians and Kazakhs find themselves with regard to the Aral Sea. At that time about 5 million hectares were irrigated in the region. Between 1960 and 1990, the level of the Aral Sea dropped from 53.4 meters to about 38 meters, a 15-m (46-foot) drop. A declining sea level caused by the withdrawals of water from the two major rivers in the region has led to many changes in the ecological and societal conditions in the Aral basin. For example, the salinity of the lake water increased markedly from the pre-1960 level of 10 g/l to today's high of above 30 g/l, approaching that of seawater in the open ocean! In addition, large expanses of the lake's previously submerged sediments became exposed to wind action, leading to the formation of live sand dune fields and to other long-term destructive desertification processes. As a result of desertification, the frequency and intensity of springtime salt-laden dust storms have increased, with major dust storms having been identified by Soviet cosmonauts on spaceflight missions as early as the mid-1970s.[31]

There has been considerable discussion in the scientific literature and popular media about the impacts on the environment, agriculture, and human health of dust and salt storms. Dust particles have been carried by prevailing winds from the desertified areas along the eastern shores of the sea to distant agricultural fields. In the mid-1970s Soviet scientist V. M. Borovsky, commenting on the adverse impacts of such storms, observed that "In view of the hazardous nature of the salt composition in the young solonchak soils being formed on the exposed Aral seabed, the

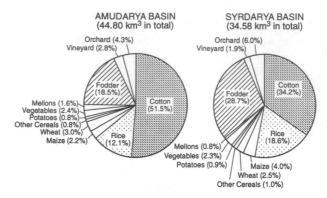

Fig. 10.2. Agricultural water use in the Amudarya and Sydarya basins. (Source: H. Tsutsui, "Some Remarks on the Aral Sea Basin Irrigation Management," Nara, Japan, 1991, mimeo.)

windborne transfer of these salts to the east of the Aral Sea poses a serious danger for plants and soils in the farm land of that region."[32] Salts and other chemicals deposited on these fields have apparently contributed to lowered soil fertility and reduced crop yields as far away as several hundred kilometers from the sea coast.

With irrigation development and an increasing amount of desert land devoted to cotton production in Central Asia and Kazakhstan, it was necessary to increase fertilizer applications as well as the use of pesticides and

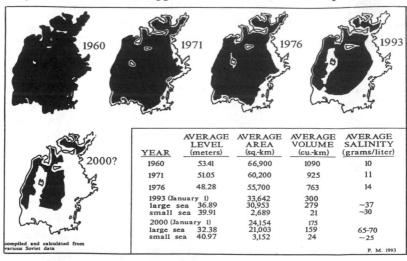

Figure 10.3. Chronology of Aral Sea Changes. (Source: Philip Micklin, *The Water Management Crisis in Central Asia* [Pittsburgh: University of Pittsburgh Center for Russian Studies, 1992], p. 67.)

herbicides (defoliants used to facilitate cotton harvesting). In past years, when the major rivers still reached the sea, a significant portion of these chemicals polluted (some say poisoned) the waters of the lower reaches of both the rivers and of the sea.

To reduce the amount of toxic chemicals and salts flowing into the rivers and sea, drainage water collector systems have been and are still being constructed throughout the irrigated agricultural areas in the Aral basin. A significant portion of the polluted drainage water is returned to the rivers; some has been diverted to desert depressions, resulting in the creation of large, highly polluted, terminal drainage lakes—Lake Sarykamysh (in Turkmenistan) and Lake Arnasay (in Uzbekistan).

As another example of the ecological consequences of reduced stream flow into the sea, the degradation of the highly productive Amudarya and Syrdarya deltaic regions has become increasing pronounced during the past 30 years. One of the consequences of a drying out of the delta region has been the diminution of vegetative cover, a loss that destroyed habitats for wildlife and migratory birds. K. D. Frederick highlighted the economic importance of the deltas, noting that they provided a "feeding base for livestock, a source of reeds for industry, spawning grounds for fish, and sites of commercial hunting and trapping."[33] Each of these ecological and societal processes has either been sharply curtailed or ended.

With regard to changes in biological productivity in the Aral Sea, several Soviet newspapers reported in the late 1960s that "a reduction in spawning areas in the shallow reaches of the lake [*sic*] resulted in a decline of the annual fish catch from about 40,000 tons in 1962 to about 20,000 in 1967." By 1970 only about 8,000 tons of landings were expected.[34] In its heyday, the fishing industry had supported thousands of workers. However, the commercial fish population and, therefore, the industry had been destroyed within a few decades (between the early 1960s and the early 1980s), as a direct result of adverse changes in water chemistry. Both were victims of the consequences of the steadily increasing river diversions, resultant declining sea levels, and sharply reduced river and seawater quality. The Soviet government, until recently, had shipped fish caught in the Atlantic Ocean and the Far East into the now-defunct fishing port of Muynak for processing in order to provide a stopgap employment measure for factory workers. In fact, representatives of these fish processing factories visited other factories throughout the country to obtain fish for their Karakalpak factories to process.

The Aral Sea, as a transportation route, was also affected by the mid-1970s. The several-meter drop in sea level prompted the need for "extra dredging, relocating port facilities and reducing ships' draughts by light loading or new designs."[35] Thus, as the sea receded, it became increasingly difficult to keep the ports of Muynak and Aral'sk accessible to ships. As a result, Muynak on the southern shore of the Aral Sea became a land-locked city situated more than 40 kilometers from the coast. Aral'sk, on the northern edge of the sea, suffered a similar fate. In the early years of the genesis of the Aral Sea problem, Shul'ts had considered the possible navigational losses of the Aral Sea unimportant because of the low level of economic activity along its shores and the shallowness of the waters.

Health Effects of Monoculture

The consequences of the dependence of several Central Asia republics on cotton monoculture have not only wreaked havoc on the physical environment by upsetting ecological balances in many parts of the Aral basin but have also had a devastating impact on human health. Such documented regional effects have only recently been exposed to the public: high infant mortality and morbidity rates, a sharp increase in esophageal cancers directly attributable to "poisoned" water resources, gastrointestinal problems, typhoid, high rates of congenital deformation, outbreaks of viral hepatitis, the contamination of mothers' milk, and a life expectancy in some areas about 20 years less than that for the Commonwealth of Independent States (CIS) in general, and so forth.[36] Adverse impacts of all-out cotton production on human health have been compounded by the absolute dearth of medical and health facilities in the Aral basin. In addition, water treatment facilities in the region are wholly inadequate (and in many areas nonexistent), necessitating the use for domestic purposes of untreated surface waters from the rivers, irrigation canals, and drainage ditches. Groundwater supplies, too, have been contaminated as a result of the widespread and wanton use of chemicals on the cotton fields. By all statistical measures, the region's human health profile fares poorly in comparison to the rest of the CIS.[37]

By way of illustration, one typical, tragic situation may be mentioned, namely, the condition of the Karakalpak, the Turkic-speaking people of autonomous Karakalpakistan in northwest Uzbekistan. More than 1 million people have been affected:

> There is a shortage of clean water, and there is not enough even for drinking. In several parts of the region the consumption of water per person per day is about 5 liters, compared to an average of 200 to 300 liters. The mineralization (salt content) of this water stands at 2 to 4 grams per liter, and the bacteria content exceeds

the maximum permissible concentration by 5 to 10 times. Through the dispensary system the Ministry of Health discovered a truly tragic picture: 60 percent of those examined—children and adults—have serious health problems; 80 percent of pregnant women suffer from anemia; intestinal infections are widespread; the infant mortality rate is much higher than national average figures and in several regions reaches 82 in 1000 newborns. Diseases never before seen here are appearing, for example gallstones and kidney stones.[38]

In the absence of any major improvement in regional health care or in detoxifying water and land resources in the Aral basin, the only way out for regional inhabitants, other than perpetuating the status quo, has been emigration. However, despite previous Soviet plans to encourage those most directly and most negatively affected (the people from Karakalpakistan) to migrate to those areas outside Central Asia in need of laborers, few have opted to leave the homelands of their forefathers. Thus, in the absence of meaningful actions to improve the health of the people or the environment in the Aral basin, it must be recognized that the total sum of misery can only increase, as the region boasts an extremely high population growth rate of about 2.6 to 3.2 percent. With a present-day regional population estimated at more than 30 million, a doubling to 60 million is expected in the early decades of the twenty-first century.

OBSERVATIONS ABOUT THE DECLINE OF THE ARAL SEA

In the following section, we present evidence that many if not most of the devastating ecological and socioeconomic impacts of excessive water diversions from Central Asian rivers for the purpose of cotton monoculture had been known at least as early as the 1960s, when major increases in diversions began. The evidence underscores the view that problems, as well as solutions, were known early in the process of degradation but were not dealt with, as a result of political tactics to achieve an economic development strategy that would eventually prove to have been unsustainable in the long term.

Declining Sea Levels: Crisis or Not?

A crisis can be defined as the existence of a high threat, a high cost associated with inaction, and a short time to respond. While the degradation of the Aral Sea can be considered an ecological tragedy, it is not necessarily a crisis. The contemporary Aral Sea situation has evolved over three decades. Not only have political and socioeconomic causes of the declining sea level been identified by various Soviet researchers beyond a reasonable doubt in the earliest stages of that process of degradation, but several of the adverse environmental and societal impacts had also been identified. The rapid change that did occur in the mid-1980s was in the fact that "the ecological catastrophe in the Aral Sea basin . . . burst suddenly in the consciousness of many people."[39] Some observers suggest that *glasnost* and the Chernobyl disaster in the mid-1980s prompted Central Asians and Kazakhs to become more vocal about their republics' environmental problems, only the most glaring of which happened to be the declining levels of the Aral Sea.[40]

There is a high threat to those in the Aral region. The Aral Sea could be converted to an Aral Desert (or Aralkum) within the next few decades in the absence of effective intergovernmental intervention in the near future.[41] There has been a high cost of inaction associated with the changes in the Aral Sea, and the push toward cotton monoculture. Many of those costs have already been paid by local and regional populations faced with the deterioration of ecological conditions and human health in the Aral basin.

Today, the sea has become the main focus of attention of Central Asian states and Kazakhstan as well as of some members of the international community (e.g., Japan). Although interest in the fate of the sea and its possible restoration appears to remain high among Russian scientists, the extent to which leaders of the Russian Federation are truly concerned about the desiccation of the sea remains unclear. V. Rich reported that "although the Supreme Soviet acknowledged that the Aral Basin is an 'all-union' problem, it hands over much of the responsibility for restoring the region to the local republics."[42] It is also not yet clear how contemporary anti-Russian activities and policies in the Central Asian states will affect the future involvement of the Russian Federation in the resolution of the Aral Sea catastrophe, a catastrophe viewed by some writers as second only to Chernobyl.

Aral Water: Of What Value?

Not everyone who has witnessed the decline in Aral Sea level has considered it in an adverse light. In fact, not everyone views the preservation or restoration of the sea as an important objective. A lack of concern over the fate of the Aral Sea was apparently expressed at least as early as the turn of the century, when Russian scientist Voyeykov argued that the sea was an unimportant body of water.[43] He suggested that in order to put the Aral water to beneficial use, the sea should be allowed to dry up and the rivers' waters used to irrigate agricultural fields. Ellis captured this lingering sentiment when he wrote that "the Soviet Union has more than achieved its goal of self-sufficiency in cotton: a fact that still justifies, for some, the sacrifice of the Aral Sea."[44]

Images of the sea's future have included the planned desiccation of the sea as well as allowing the sea level to decline to any one of a number of predetermined levels at or below its current level of about 38 meters. Still others have foreseen the partitioning of the sea into a number of small saline lakes with perhaps a few of them being replenished by minimal flows of the Syrdarya and Amudarya or of drainage water. Yet some scientists continue to call for all-out attempts to increase the flow of the rivers into the sea in order to restore it to its pre-1960s level. Still others believe it would be impossible (politically if not hydrologically) to restore the sea to its original level.[45] Such a restoration could be accomplished in several decades if republics were to forgo diversions from the Amudarya and Syrdarya, on which their economies have become dependent. In the midst of wide-ranging proposals to restore the Aral Sea, N. T. Kuznetsov appropriately asks those concerned with the Aral Sea's future state to consider "What properties can or must the Aral Sea possess at different stages in the decline in its level and then its subsequent restoration and what functions must the sea perform?"[46] These questions have yet to be answered.

Cost/Benefit Considerations and Aral Sea Water

A review of the scientific writings of the 1960s and 1970s supports the assertion that cost/benefit considerations (however informal, anecdotal, or erroneous) had in fact been made with regard to reduced stream flow, increased diversions, increased cotton production, declining sea level and their consequences. The perceived value of water in the Aral Sea was compared at least in a qualitative way to the expected value of water for other uses. For example, scientists have suggested that the value of water used to irrigate cotton fields would be several times higher than letting that same amount of water flow into the sea. The diagnostic study of the United Nations Environment Programme (UNEP) for the rehabilitation of the Aral Sea basin succinctly states the reasons behind the push for increased cotton production: "It was thought this increase would provide clothing material for the entire country, and drastically increase the export of cotton products. Cotton production in the republics of Central Asia and Kazakhstan in the period between 1960 and 1975-80 almost doubled. After those years, however, production declined."[47]

With regard to the decision to construct the Turkmenian Karakum Canal, Feshbach and Friendly noted that "At the time, a number of water management and desert development experts believed this a worthwhile tradeoff: a cubic meter of river water used for irrigation, they calculated, would be more economically beneficial than the same volume delivered to the Aral Sea."[48]

The loss of vegetation around the sea coast (rushes, reeds, trees, etc.) was also considered by some to be a positive change because such a reduction in vegetation would reduce moisture losses to the atmosphere as a result of evaporation and transpiration. V. L. Shul'ts wrote that "it is necessary to drain the Aral Sea in the future. . . . The time has come for the rational use of the water resources of the Aral basin for the benefit of the Soviet people building communism."[49] Reasoning similar to that used to justify the expansion of irrigated cotton production was used to justify the projected demise of the Aral Sea fishing sector. Borovsky, quoting Geller (1969), wrote in 1978 that "It has been estimated that the use of the water for irrigation will be 100 times more cost-effective than the Aral Sea fish catch."[50]

Value (or cost/benefit) assessments such as these were strictly based on inappropriate economic considerations (e.g., water was seen as a free good), with environmental aspects being given little, if any, attention.[51] Had broader perspectives (which did exist a few decades ago in the USSR and elsewhere) of economic development been considered or an objective, realistic cost/benefit analysis been undertaken and the possible long-term ecological and societal factors been considered, the consequences of the destruction of natural vegetation and biological productivity, such as the loss of reeds and other vegetation in the deltas and of wildlife, fish, and bird populations, would likely have been considered negative.[52]

Scientific Opposition to Drawdown Existed

Contrary to popular belief, opposing views about the fate of the Aral Sea were expressed in the scientific literature and at meetings and conferences in the early years of the sea's drawdown. Some scientific writings in the 1960s and 1970s cautioned readers about the likely environmental costs associated with declining sea levels. Such views were not just presented in these articles as generalities, but they identified specific problems that would most likely ensue as the sea level dropped.[53]

Concern about the sea's fate was raised as a result of the consumptive nature of water withdrawals from the Amudarya and Syrdarya. The fate of those inhabiting the lower reaches of these rivers was also discussed. Water taken from these rivers would be permanently lost to the deltas as well as the sea. These opposing scientific views and assessments, however, were ignored by decision makers in favor of pursuing the policy of rapid growth in cotton production in the Aral basin.

Drawdown "Spin Doctors"

In the early postwar decades there appeared what we now might refer to as "spin doctors": those who sought to put a positive image on the environmental changes that were expected to occur, as the river diversions increased and the sea level declined. In their public writings some scientists couched several of the forecasted adverse impacts of a declining sea level in their public writings in positive terms. I. M. Chernenko, for example, suggested that "the draining of flooded shore areas and the drying up of reed growths will make water available through savings in evaporation and transpiration." He also believed that "nine-tenths of the present stream flow into the Aral Sea can be diverted for other purposes without causing the sea to dry up."[54] Another author argued that returning drainage water from the irrigated fields to the Aral Sea would be beneficial because "they are particularly valuable in that they are rich in biogens."[55] Geller argued that "the only chemical sediment that would be subject to blowing would be the sediment precipitating out in the first stage and consisting of gypsum and lime, which not only present no hazard to soils, but actually play a positive role in soil reclamation."[56]

With regard to regional and local climate changes that might accompany a drying out of the Aral Sea, some researchers suggested that desiccation would have little impact on regional climate because the expanded irrigation system would compensate for losses of seawater and would provide an increase in evaporation and transpiration processes that would return moisture to the region's atmosphere.

These positive "spins," among many others, put on expected environmental degradation have proven wrong. With regard to the last example, regional climate change, winters in the Aral Sea region have in fact become colder, summers warmer, and the growing season shortened. This last change has prompted a shift from cotton to rice production in some locales. Since 1961, "the character of seasonal fluctuations [in sea level] changed. The lake no longer rose in the spring. At best the level remained constant during the first half of the year, while in the second half it fell sharply."[57]

Adverse Consequences Were Known

Throughout the first 20 years of the Aral Sea problem (1960-1980), signs of change were appearing everywhere: wind erosion, salt-laden dust

storms, destroyed spawning grounds, the collapse of the fisheries, secondary salinization, increased salinity of seawater, waterlogging, disruption of navigation, the likely division of the sea into separate parts, the
need for extra-basin water resources to stabilize the sea level, the loss of
wildlife in the littoral areas, the large reduction of stream flow from the
two main tributaries, a change in the regional climate, the disappearance
of pasture lands, and so forth. Each one of these adverse changes was
mentioned in the Soviet scientific literature in the 1960s and 1970s.

In the 1960s sea level dropped 3 meters; in the 1970s large dust storms
were spotted from space, and their occurrence seemed to have become
more frequent. Wildlife disappeared from around the delta and forests
became decimated as the soils dried out or became salinized or water-
logged, depending on local soil conditions. Kuznetsov supported this view
of the early detection of adverse impacts when he wrote that "the degradation of wetland soils in the deltas was noted quite clearly as early as the
second half of the 1960s. For the preservation of the most fertile soils of
the Amudarya delta it was proposed that they be artificially irrigated, for
which it was recommended that 3.0-3.5 km³/year of river water be used.
However, professional water managers and land reclamation specialists
paid no heed to this recommendation, nor to many others."[58]

At a 1977 Conference on the Environmental Impact of a Drop in the
Level of the Aral Sea," a paper prepared by two Uzbek republic scientists
reported a sharp reduction in fish landings.[59] They suggested that a
demise of the fishery was likely because of the destruction of fish spawning grounds. Borovsky also had suggested that the depletion of the Aral
Sea fisheries would be one of the first consequences of declining sea levels.[60] Reteyum recently wrote that "in 1965, the Council of Ministers of
the USSR passed a special resolution, On Measures to Preserve the
Fishery Importance of the Aral Sea."[61] This was one example he cited to
support of his belief that signs of deterioration in the Aral basin were seen
as early as the mid-1960s.

As for concern about the adverse human health effects of a demise of
the Aral ecosystem, Kuznetsov recently noted that "Unfortunately,
secrecy over an entire series of research results in the 1970s, especially
medical-epidemiological data, precluded their publication at that time and
the predictions associated with them did not become available to the public in time."[62]

Solutions to the various environmental changes associated with the Aral
Sea situation were known almost at the outset of the drop in sea level. Its
potential consequences for economy and ecosystems were presented in the

Soviet literature and at Soviet conferences throughout the 1960s and 1970s. Adverse signs appeared but no one in authority seemed to care.

Ecosystem Replacement

A natural ecosystem, the Aral Sea, is being replaced by man-made ones. For example, the construction of the 1200-km Karakum Canal in Turkmenistan, beginning in the mid-1950s, has been responsible for a sizable diversion of Amudarya waters at Kerki (about 15 percent of its average annual flow). This is in essence a man-made river. In fact, all the main canals that divert water from the rivers can be viewed as man-made distributaries, created at the expense of the perennial rivers and the Aral Sea ecosystem. In addition, as a final example of this anthropogenic transformation of nature, the large drainage lakes such as Sarykamysh are also ecosystems fabricated by humans at the expense of the Aral Sea. Diverting Amudarya and Syrdarya water to irrigate desert sands can be viewed as an attempt to transform one natural ecosystem, the desert, into a man-made one, a "garden," "a grandiose project that was to transform the region from an arid wasteland into a fertile oasis."[63]

Coping Options

There has been no paucity of ideas over the years on what or how to deal with these cotton production-related environmental changes in the Aral Sea basin. What has been lacking is a unified position about the fate of the Aral Sea. To "save" the Aral Sea itself will require major coordinated decisions at the highest levels of governments of the newly independent states that made up the former Soviet Union, in addition to financial and technical support from the international donor community. Yet some government representatives from Kazakhstan and the Central Asian states still challenge the desire to save the Aral Sea at the expense of the region's dominant agricultural activity—cotton production.

In 1990 an open competition was sponsored by the Soviet government to identify possible solutions to the Aral Sea dilemma. The competition yielded over 200 proposals, of which seven were selected for further consideration. In addition, international support has been sought by the Soviet Union, as well as its successor, the CIS, the Central Asian republics, and Kazakhstan. For example, at the request of the Soviet Union (and later, the CIS), the UNEP created an International Experts Working Group to provide "Assistance in the Development of an Action Plan for the Conservation of the Aral Sea," to prepare, for example, a diagnostic study of the ecological, epidemiological, and socioeconomic situation in the Aral Sea basin, with the ultimate goal of developing an Action Plan for the basin's rehabilitation.[64] Japanese industrial leaders, through their Global Infrastructure Foundation (GIF), have also become interested in Central Asia's Aral Sea problems and have recently been involved in developing plans to rehabilitate the basin.[65] In the early 1990s, the U.S. National Academy of Science launched a short-lived Central Asian program. Most recently, the World Bank in its role as part of the Global Environment Facility (GEF) along with UNEP and UNDP has chosen to pursue a Central Asian interest with a focus on the Aral Sea basin.[66]

Many of the standard approaches to solving the Aral Sea problem have been proposed by various groups, individuals, or agencies. These include but are not limited to the following: the diverting of north-flowing Siberian rivers to Central Asia, letting the Aral Sea break up into numerous small saline lakes, preservation of only a portion of the sea surrounding the deltas, reducing diversions to irrigated areas, transferring water from the Caspian Sea, increasing irrigation efficiency, shifting to crops that consume less water (e.g., reduce cotton and rice production), artificially inducing the melting of glaciers in the Pamir Mountains, and returning highly polluted drainage water directly into the sea.

The most controversial and contentious proposals to rehabilitate the Aral Sea have centered on the demand by Central Asians for transbasin diversions. Central Asian and Kazakh leaders see water diversions from north-flowing Siberian rivers as the only key source of new water for maintaining the level of the sea and human activities in the basin. Those outside the Central Asian republics and Kazakhstan call for the reduction of irrigated acreage devoted to cotton and rice specifically, and the reduction of the regional agricultural dependence on growing cotton in general. Yet another more extreme suggestion had been to reduce or terminate diversions to Turkmenistan's Karakum Canal. Regardless of the options one might pursue to restore the sea to its pre-1960 level, it appears to be an almost impossible task, if not because of the lack of available water resources or of engineering know-how, then because of the lack of interrepublic collective political will.

Transbasin Diversions

The literature prepared during the early years of the Amudarya and Syrdarya diversions shows that concern about the fate of the Aral Sea was not high among Soviet decision makers, agricultural planners, and water resource specialists. How was this possible, when signs of degradation were visible and their numbers growing? One key reason was that in the back of everyone's mind was the likely possibility that water would be transferred to the Aral basin as a result of the Siberian river diversions. When the Communist Party Congress called for "research and development preparing the way for the transfer of part of the flow of northern and Siberian streams to Central Asia and Kazakhstan and into the Volga basin,"[67] many scientists believed that it was no longer a question of whether such transfers would take place but when. Several scientists, however, did seek to persuade policymakers to link future Amudarya and Syrdarya diversions for irrigation directly to the transfer of Siberian river water into the Aral Sea. However, in the early 1980s Soviet scientist Michael Borovsky asserted that in his view "not one drop of transferred Siberian water would go to save the Aral Sea" (personal communication).

There exist a considerable number of publications on the plans to transfer Siberian river water to Central Asia.[68] Water was to have been transferred in part to allow for expanding regional cotton production. This would have entailed building a 1,600-mile-long diversion canal (Sibaral—the Siberia–Aral Sea Canal) drawing water from the Ob' and Irtysh rivers of western Siberia to the Aral Sea. However, soon after his coming to power in March 1985, public pressure resulting from *glasnost* pushed Gorbachev to decide that the costs of such a project would have been prohibitive and, in August 1986, a joint resolution of the party's Central Committee and government's Council of Ministers shelved the proposal. Central Asians had seen the "Sibaral" diversion as the solution for the economic development of their region, as well as the only way to save the Aral Sea. Despite the apparent ban on the implementation of such diversions, scientific investigations focusing on a smaller-scale diversion continued and supporters of the idea continued to discuss its advantages.[69] In the beginning of the 1990s, Kazakh and Uzbek specialists became increasingly active in arguing the project's merits.[70] The collapse of the Soviet Union, however, inevitably changed Moscow's environmental agenda to a focus on problems most urgent to the Russian Federation.

However strong the argument for saving the Aral Sea might be, it is not apt to command much in the way of resources from a Russia that is no longer politically responsible for either the well-being or the long-term developmental prospects of the newly independent Central Asian states. Given the tumultuous times facing the fledgling Russian democratic system (including strong, nationalistic opposition to interrepublic diversions), Moscow simply does not have the wherewithal to seriously consider such an enormous undertaking. Moreover, the environmental objections that were raised before the breakup of the Soviet Union remain as compelling as ever: exorbitant costs, impacts of inundation of historical sites, ecological impacts on land to be flooded, effect on fisheries of the Ob' and Irtysh, "degradation of water quality downstream from points of diversion, deterioration of flood plain meadows with agricultural value downstream from points of withdrawal owing to reduced spring flooding, and the worsened low-flow navigation conditions below points of diversion."[71]

Philip P. Micklin and A. R. Bond have suggested that the best argument that Central Asians might muster in favor of a scaled-down version of the original grandiose interbasin water transfer scheme would be an environmental one.[72] With so many adverse environmental consequences of declining river flow and sea level, only a large infusion of transbasin water resources might reverse or at least mitigate some of the adverse impacts on regional environment, ecosystems, and health. International politics, not necessarily environmental or human health considerations in the region, will likely determine the fate of such interbasin, interrepublic water transfers. Interrepublic water diversions as a solution to the Aral catastrophe raise serious doubt about the utility (if not impracticability) of applying the concept of sustainable development to the Aral basin.

To most observers, the status quo in terms of present conditions—cotton monoculture, expanding populations, declining availability of regional water resources—cannot be maintained for long. Internal adjustments will clearly be required, such as a shift from dependence on cotton production to more environmentally friendly crops, a greater efficiency in the use of local and regional water resources, and, perhaps, policies related to population issues. As a result of an in-depth assessment of the Siberian rivers diversion project, Darst concluded that "Even the most draconian measures to conserve water in Central Asia will not obviate the necessity of outside water if the population continues to grow . . . and its economy continues to be based overwhelmingly upon agriculture [e.g., cotton monoculture]."[73]

But external adjustments will also have to be made, not only to stabilize the current conditions but to improve them as well. That means that water resources will likely have to be transferred into the basin from water-rich areas, if current levels and conditions of water use are maintained. Is it possible, therefore, to pursue policies of sustainable development in Central Asia and Kazakhstan when the region must rely on water resources from elsewhere to improve the quality of life of its citizens and the quality of its environment?

Natural Variability and Human Trends

According to A. Ye. Asarin, "an increase in water withdrawals for irrigation in the 1950s did not appreciably affect the Aral Sea level because of generally large water resources during those years."[74] The 1960s, however, proved to be relatively dry years (with the exception of 1969) when compared to the preceding 35-year period (1926 to 1960). According to Aladin, the reduction of river flow into the Aral Sea between 1962 and 1980 was about 47 percent when compared to the period from 1911 to 1960 and was to some extent attributable to a natural decrease in precipitation in the Pamir Mountains in this period.[75] The dry 1960s coincided with the beginning of declining water levels in the Aral Sea. The fact that the Caspian Sea level was also falling in the 1960s and drastically in the 1970s prompted concern about a possible regional-scale desiccation. This reinforced the view that at least some part of that decline was related to natural variability as opposed to human activities. Expectations about reduced stream flow under such dry conditions perhaps served to mask the anthropogenic impacts of water diversions from the Amudarya and the Syrdarya in that decade. By the early 1970s, however, it had become clear that "the intensive decline of the water level since 1961 [was] attributed mainly to a growth in consumptive withdrawals from . . . the two main tributaries [*sic*] of the Aral Sea."[76] Human activities had eventually overwhelmed natural fluctuations in stream flow.

Intergenerational Inequity

With respect to human populations, one generally refers to a generation as a 20-year period: for example, grandparents, parents, children. For potential decision makers, however, a generation must be viewed in a different way—that is, in terms of their tenure in office. With respect to the desiccation of the Aral Sea, a generation of decision makers (in the 1950s and 1960s) relied primarily, if not solely, on ideologically biased economic criteria when considering the transformation of nature in Central Asia. The situation in the Aral Sea basin draws attention to the concept of intergenerational equity. Today's decision makers in Russia appear to be under some pressure (internationally if not nationally) to take environmental factors into their value assessments. Russian geographer V. M. Kotlyakov recently referred to this new focus on the interactions between human activities and the environment as the "ecologization" of the natural sciences, a shift in focus that he claims actually began in the 1960s.[77] In retrospect, one generation of decision makers has doomed a later generation of decision makers in the newly independent states of the former Soviet Union to cope with the environmental mess it had set in motion a few decades earlier. The Aral Sea situation provides a possible analogy for those researchers concerned with environmental justice and intra- (as well as inter-) generational equity issues.

Regional Political Realities

With the breakup of the Soviet Union, political relations in the Aral basin have obviously changed markedly. Problems related to the environment that recently occurred within one country (the Soviet Union) have now become international problems. The Aral Sea, for example, is in the territories of Kazakhstan and Uzbekistan, and within Uzbekistan is the quasi-autonomous republic of Karakalpakistan, which borders directly on the sea. The Amudarya, whose origin is in the Pamir Mountains of Afghanistan, now flows through the independent republics of Tajikistan, Uzbekistan, Turkmenistan, and the autonomous region of Karakalpakistan. The Syrdarya begins in the Tien Shan Mountains in Kyrgyzstan and flows through Kyrgyzstan, Uzbekistan, and Kazakhstan. The north-flowing Siberian rivers from which, it is hoped, water will come to the arid republics of Central Asia and Kazakhstan are within the Russian Federation. The Caspian Sea, from which some researchers have proposed to transfer water, is an international sea whose shores fall within Azerbaijan, the Russian Federation, Kazakhstan, Turkmenistan, and Iran. Clearly, the international diplomatic obstacles to replenishing the Aral Sea are quite formidable, especially because the governments of the newly independent republics have had little, if any, experience in dealing with international resource management.

Even when the Soviet Union was intact, regional conflicts related to environmental issues existed. Darst observed that "The demand for environmental protection in the Soviet Union is further complicated by the fact that efforts to ameliorate environmental degradation frequently pit the inhabitants of one region against others perceived as holding the keys to the solution of the problem, frictions which are all too often exacerbated by national differences."[78] As one scholar noted, "[W]hen Central Asian leaders meet among themselves, as they did in April 1992 in Bishkek [Kyrgyzstan], they find little of substance on which to agree. Under Soviet rule the leaders competed for Moscow's favor. Now they are competing for investment from a far greater pool, and each is striving to define the uniqueness of his republic."[79]

Although the Central Asian republics and Kazakhstan are no longer directly controlled by political leaders of the Russian Federation, their dependency in several ways remains significant and will be extremely difficult to diminish greatly for some time to come. Although they can act on their own, their residual bureaucratic inertia and regional and domestic cleavages are yet to be overcome. They look to Moscow for assistance, as much out of habit as need, but their futures may hinge on how well they can pioneer openings to the outside world. This, however, will not be easy. The outside world is remote, separated from them by an Iran that is torn between fueling resurgent "Islamicization" and normalizing relations with the West (though not necessarily the United States); by a ravaged Afghanistan that is free of Soviet and Communist rule but hopelessly mired in divisive tribal, ethnic, religious, and personal rivalries; and by a China that is mainly interested in stronger ties to the industrialized world and not to an underdeveloped Central Asia. In addition, all three of these neighbors are constrained by their own economic problems from offering very much assistance to Central Asia and Kazakhstan.

Outside assistance may be needed to bring the interested parties together to work out an action program to save the Aral Sea basin. The World Bank, GEF, the United States, and possibly the United Nations are potential sources of assistance. Their enticements might take the form of sizable investment funds combined with proposals for setting up turnkey food processing, textile, and other types of industrial plants that might provide jobs and access to foreign markets. Leadership in Central Asia and Kazakhstan has yet to be convinced that only through regional cooperation can they attract foreign investment on the order of magnitude that will enable them to reduce high levels of unemployment, pave the way to foreign markets, and reduce dependency on the Russian Federation, while at the same time contributing to the long-term amelioration of the Aral Sea problem. Thus, with the individual Central Asian states and Kazakhstan groping for ways to promote domestic stability and reluctant to take domestically unpopular political steps, incentives from outside the region may prove to be the key to the development of a comprehensive integrated regional plan for addressing the Aral Sea problem.

Central Asia's problems are heavily economic, the doleful legacy of flawed human engineering that ultimately precipitated the sudden collapse of the Soviet empire.[80] It would be a mistake, however, to think that the looming economic tragedy, for example, in the Aral Sea basin, could be avoided without taking into account attendant cultural, political, and technocratic impediments that have been integral to the region's problems and prospects.

CONCLUDING COMMENTS

The Aral Sea is limnologically a closed system. As such it lends itself to close scrutiny of the interactions among the various physical, socioeconomic, and political processes at play in the basin. Close scrutiny of the numerous processes that contribute to the degraded environment in the Aral basin clearly underscores the complexity of the interactions between society and ecosystems within the basin. If one cannot successfully investigate the causes and consequences of the recent Aral Sea desiccation, one most likely would be unable to do so with a more complex system. Another important feature of an investigation of the Aral Sea situation was suggested by Australian limnologist W. D. Williams. He noted that "since most of the world is semiarid and arid, and worldwide waters have been and are being diverted from salt lakes, management of the Aral Sea basin provides a most important case study."[81]

We have witnessed the incremental degradation of the sea and its littoral over a period of three decades. It is important to identify the past levels of awareness of the potential consequences of Amudarya and Syrdarya diversions in order to support a major expansion of irrigated cotton production. A review of past literature underscores the fact that decisions were made to exploit the Central Asian environment (perfect climatic conditions for growing cotton) with the existing knowledge that the long-term effects of large water diversions and of a dependence on cotton monoculture could well be deleterious.

The current highest explicitly stated political priority centers on the improvement of regional water quality for human consumption. Epidemiological studies support the belief that much of the region's long list of health problems is directly related to contaminated water resources above- as well as belowground. Many suggestions have been made on how to improve water quality, but who will pay for such a wide-ranging improvement of potable water supply systems? Despite mounting evidence about the deleterious effects of high levels of water diversions from the Amudarya and Syrdarya beginning in the early 1960s, today one continues to hear pleas for the further expansion of irrigated cotton production in Central Asia and explicit calls for the demise of the Aral Sea.

It is now popular to come up with estimates of how much water might be saved for use in the basin if: (1) less cotton were grown, (2) water-demanding rice production was ended, (3) water efficiency could be enforced, (4) nonproductive lands could be removed from production, (5) drainage water were to be returned to the sea, (6) a realistic system for pricing water were established, and so forth. Each of these tactical measures to allow more water to flow into the sea carries with it water resource savings measured in cubic kilometers per year.

Enforcing such required changes in current water use in the basin would be a major task. Yet there is still considerable dissension in the basin as to what the problem really is and how best to resolve it. Inter-republic rivalries are only just beginning to surface. Even with regard to water-saving plans related to the Aral Sea, the Russians, Uzbeks, and Kazakhs each have put forth an approach, and the remaining republics are allegedly busy developing their own.

At a recent meeting on the Aral Sea in which representatives of the Central Asian republics, Karakalpakistan, the Russian Federation, and Kazakhstan were present, representatives of ministries associated with water resources joked about the importance of their respective republics. The Turkmen representative boasted about the Karakum Canal and its contribution to the prosperity of his republic. The Uzbek representative told of the "white gold" (e.g., cotton) for which his republic has become well known. After listening to their boasts, the Tajik representative made a simple gesture with his hands by pretending he was shutting off a water faucet. The truth of the matter is that the states in the upper reaches of the Amudarya and Syrdarya have the water but little arable land, whereas those in the lower reaches are totally dependent on stream flow for their survival. A considerable amount of bargaining remains ahead among these newly independent countries which have little if any long-term experience in international negotiations.

Perhaps the international lending institutions (World Bank, GEF, GIF, UNEP) will serve to catalyze regional cooperation for improving the quality of life in the Aral basin, especially the quality of life for those closest to the Aral Sea in Karakalpakistan. The ability of these countries to cooperate remains dim in light of the numerous ethnically based regional conflicts that have emerged as a result of the demise of the former Soviet Union.

Decision makers in the Central Asian states and Kazakhstan have yet to agree that the sea itself should be saved and, if so, at what level. While they negotiate these crucial points, the sea level will have declined further, barring any sharp long-term natural increase in river flow. Even then, it cannot be taken for granted that decisions would not follow to expand agriculture in the basin, if the flow is perceived to have increased as a result of secular changes in climate. (N.B.: Russian scientist Mikhail Budyko has suggested that rainfall in Central Asia would likely increase in the event of a global warming of the atmosphere.[82] Budyko's view is not widely supported in the Russian scientific community.)

Most observers of the catastrophe in the Aral basin acknowledge the urgent need for a restructuring of the economies in Central Asia. A reduction in dependence on cotton and rice, two high-water-consuming crops, and a shift away from its primary sector role (raw materials, mining) to enhance its manufacturing sector (textiles, irrigation equipment) is recommended by most reviewers of the Aral situation. The trick will be accomplishing this with only minimal additional pressures on the population and environment of these republics.

The role of the Russian Federation in the rehabilitation of the Aral Sea basin remains unclear. In 1990, while the Soviet Union was still intact, Central Asian writer Nasar commented on the underlying animosity that existed (and one might argue still exists) with regard to the relationships between the Central Asian republics, Kazakhstan, and the former Soviet Union. "No writer has publicly acknowledged that Central Asia's problem, symbolized by the water shortage and the Aral problem, is fundamentally a colonial one. . . . Unless systematic changes are undertaken to break the traditional colonial relationship between Moscow and Central Asia, I cannot see how the core problems, including the Aral's disposition, can be solved."[83] Thus, the Russian Federation's apparent former colonial relationship with these republics may stand in the way of their future meaningful involvement.

Like other spurned metropoles, it is not too far-fetched to expect that only minimal attention will be given to the problems of former "colonial subjects." As for accepting responsibility for the widespread regional environmental and human health degradation, the leaders of the Russian Federation are not likely to feel any moral pressures to clean up the situation that their political predecessors had created. We would expect that only for political advantages would Moscow decision makers ever agree to implementing a modified Siberian rivers diversion project. From the Russian standpoint, economic and environmental reasons to do so are not very persuasive, despite the pleas from Central Asian and Kazakh leaders.

The Aral Sea will most likely be allowed to continue to decline as a result of inaction (which is also a form of action in favor of "business as usual") by governments. The quality of water from the Amudarya and the Syrdarya, however, cannot be allowed to decline without consequence. As W. D. Williams has recently suggested, "when they are only slightly above their present salinities, they will become less and less useful for irrigation and I suspect they will no longer be diverted. Thus, if inaction prevails with regard to river water quality, an ecological solution will be imposed, whether or not we like it."[84]

Decisions are being made on how to use water more efficiently (e.g., pricing water, reducing allocations); others are being discussed (e.g., privatization of land and water). People fear change and are reluctant to do so. Perhaps when the Aral Sea level drops to below 34 meters and the Big Aral is on the verge of further dividing into two more serious assessment of the true value of maintaining a healthy Aral Sea, healthy rivers such as the Amudarya and Syrdarya, and a healthy human population will override the tendency of policymakers to pursue short-term economic benefits at the expense of long-term economic and ecological stability.

N·O·T·E·S

1. Quoted in G. E. Hollis, "The Falling Levels of the Caspian and Aral Seas," *Geographical Journal* 144 (1978): 77.

2. Ruben A. Mnatsakanian, *Environmental Legacy of the Former Soviet Republics* (Edinburgh: University of Edinburgh, Center for Human Ecology, 1992), p. viii.

3. R. G. Darst, Jr. , "Environmentalism in the USSR: The Opposition to the River Diversion Projects," *Soviet Economy* 4, no. 3 (1988): 223.

4. For example, see Mnatsakanian, *Environmental Legacy*; Murray Feshback and Alfred Friendly, Jr., *Ecocide in the USSR: Health and Nature Under Siege* (New York: Basic Books, 1992); and Barbara Jancar, "Democracy and the Environment in Eastern Europe and the Soviet Union," *Harvard International Review* 12, no. 4 (Summer 1990): 13-18, 58-60.

5. Michael H. Glantz and Igor Zonn, "A Quiet Chernobyl," *The World and I* (September 1991): 325.

6. Peter Rogers, "International River Basins: Pervasive Unidirectional Externalities," paper presented at the conference entitled "The Economics of Transnational Commons," April 25-27, 1991, at the Universita di Siena, Italy, mimeo.; see also *Water International* 15, no. 4 (December 1990), special issue, "Water, Peace, and Conflict Management. "

7. Leonid Brezhnev, *Virgin Lands* (Moscow: Progress Publishers, 1978); see also Igor Zonn, "Virgin Lands of the Former Soviet Union," in *Drought Follows the Plow*, ed. M. H. Glanz (Cambridge: Cambridge University Press, forthcoming).

8. David Smith, "Culture and Water," *Cultural Survival Quarterly* 16, no. 1 (Winter 1992): 49-50. See also James Critchlow, *Nationalism in Uzbekistan: A Soviet Republic Road to Sovereignty* (Boulder, CO: Westview Press, 1991), esp. chap. 4, pp 61-75.

9. Critchlow, *Nationalism in Uzbekistan*, p. 51.

10. B. T. Kirsta, "The Problem of the Aral Sea and Karakum Canal," *Problemy Osvoeniya Pustyn*, no. 5 (1989).

11. Philip R. Pryde, *Environmental Management in the Soviet Union* (New York: Cambridge University Press, 1991), p. 3.

12. V. Shcherban, *Izvestia*, June 23, 1987, p. 1.

13. For example, see V. Magay, "Sud'ba Aral'skovo More" (The fate of the Aral Sea), *Pravda Vostoka*, April 30, 1987, p. 4.

14. Andrei Monin, "Zastoinye zony" (Stagnant zones), *Novyi Mir* 7 (July 1988): 163.

15. Ibid., p. 164.

16. Ibid., p. 165.

17. Sergei Zalygin, "Reversal: The Lessons from One Discussion," *Novyi Mir* 1 (1987): 3-18.

18. Rusi Nasar, "Reflections on the Aral Tragedy," presented at University of Indiana conference entitled "The Aral Sea Crisis: Environmental Issues in Central Asia," July 9-13, 1991, Bloomington, Indiana, mimeo.

19. Andrei A. Gromyko, "The Urgent Task of the Soviets," *Kommunist* 3 (February 1988): 12-26, in Foreign Broadcast Information Service, April 15, 1986, Annex, pp. 3-12.

20. "V Tsentral" nom Komitete KPSS i Sovete Ministrov SSSR," *Pravda*, September 30, 1988, pp. 1, 3.

21. Philip P. Micklin, *The Water Management Crisis in Central Asia* (Pittsburgh: University of Pittsburgh Center for Russian and East European Studies: The Carl Beck Papers), 905, August 1991, pp. 66-67.

22. Pryde, *Environmental Management in the Soviet Union*, p. 2.

23. "Concept for Preserving and Restoring the Aral Sea and Normalizing the Ecological, Public Health, and Socioeconomic Situation in the Aral Region," *Post-Soviet Geography* 33, no. 5 (1992): 283-295.

24. N. T. Kuznetsov, "Geographical Aspects of the Future of the Aral Sea," *Soviet Geography* (December 1977): 163.

25. Mnatsakanian, *Environmental Legacy*, p. 104.

26. A. Ye. Anayev, "Aral: Anatomy of a Dying Sea," *Soviet Life* 8, no. 395 (August 1989): 14.

27. See, for example, K. D. Frederick, "The Disappearing Aral Sea," *Resources* (RFF Newsletter) 102 (Winter 1991): 11-14; and V. Rich, "A New Life for the Sea that Died?" *New Scientist*, April 13, 1991, p. 15.

28. P. Raskin, E. Hansen, and Z. Zhu, "Simulation of Water Supply and Demand in the Aral Sea Region," *Water International* 17 (1992): 64.

29. Micklin, *Water Management Crisis*, p. 92.

30. A scientific expedition to the Little Aral Sea in May 1992 discovered that its sea level had increased about 20 centimeters and that its salinity had notably declined. These were the first signs of any improvement in the region in about 30 years. At the present rate of improvement, some scientists estimate that the Little Aral Sea level could be at pre-1960 levels in about two decades (Aladin, personal communication, September 11, 1992).

31. United Nations Environment Programme (UNEP), *Diagnostic Study for the Development of an Action Plan for the Aral Sea* (Nairobi, Kenya: UNEP, 1992), p. 36.

32. V. M. Borovsky, "The Drying Out of the Aral Sea and Its Consequences," *Izvestiya Akademii Nauk SSSR, seriya geograficheskaya* 5 (1978), English translation in Scripta Publishing Co, 1980, p. 74.

33. Frederick, "Disappearing Aral Sea," p. 12.

34. T. Shabad, "News Notes," *Geographical Abstracts* (March 1969): 146.

35. Hollis, "Falling Levels of the Caspian and Aral Seas," p. 70.

36. L. I. Elpiner, "Medical-Ecological Problems in the Eastern Aral Region," paper presented at University of Indiana Conference entitled "The Aral Sea Crisis: Environmental Issues in Central Asia," July 9-13, 1990, Bloomington, Indiana, mimeo.

37. For an account of the devastating health conditions in the Aral basin, see Feshbach and Friendly, *Ecocide in the USSR*; UNEP, *Diagnostic Study*; and W. S. Ellis, "The Aral: A Soviet Sea Lies Dying," *National Geographic* (February 1990): 83.

38. B. Rudenko, "Solenye Peski Aralkum" (The salty sands of the Aral), *Nauka i zhizn* 10 (October 1989): 44. Additional details on the excesses of pesticides and their effects on children are discussed in N. Skripnikov, "Khimizatsiya, zdorovye i zakon" (Chemicalization, health, and the law), *Pravda Vostoka*, March 4, 1989, p. 1.

39. A. U. Reteyum, letter in Overview section, *Environment* 33, no. 1 (1991): 3.

40. Critchlow, *Nationalism in Uzbekistan*, p. 77.

41. See, for example, I. S. Zonn, "The Problem of the Aral Sea in the Light of New Geopolitical Policy," paper presented to the Second International Planning Meeting of the Global Infrastructure Foundation, May 21-24, 1992, in Istanbul, Turkey.

42. V. Rich, "New Life for the Sea that Died?" p. 15.

43. Quoted in Borovsky, "Drying Out of the Aral Sea," p. 64.

44. Ellis, "Aral," p 83.

45. For example, see Kirsta, "Problem of the Aral Sea," p. 8.

46. N. T. Kuznetsov, "Geographical and Ecological Aspects of Aral Sea Hydrological Functions," *Post-Soviet Geography* 33, no. 5 (1992): 324.

47. UNEP, *Diagnostic Study*, p. 77.

48. Feshbach and Friendly, *Ecocide in the USSR*, p. 224.

49. V. L. Shul'ts, "The Aral Sea Problem," *Soviet Hydrology* 5 (1968): 491-492.

50. Quoted Geller (1969) in Borovsky "Drying Out of the Aral Sea," p. 66.

51. See, for example, Sultangazin et al., "Concept for Preserving and Restoring the Aral Sea, and Normalizing the Ecological and Socioeconomic Situation in the Aral Region," *Problemy Osvoeniya Pustyn* 4 (1991): 9.

52. See, for example, N. Precoda, "Requiem for the Aral Sea," *Ambio* 20, no. 3-4 (1991): 114; and UNEP, *Diagnostic Study*, pp. 76-77.

53. M. Ye. Gorodetskaya and A. S. Kes', "Alma-Ata Conference on the Environmental Impact of a Drop in the Level of the Aral Sea," *Soviet Geography* 19, no. 10 (1978): 728-736.

54. I. M. Chernenko, "The Aral Sea Problem and Its Solution," *Soviet Geography* 9, no. 6 (1968): 489.

55. A. V. Volodkin, "Irrigation Construction and the Fish Industry of the Sea of Aral," *Geographical Abstracts* 72C/0097 (1969): 28.

56. Quoted in Borovsky, "Drying Out of the Aral Sea," pp. 8-12.

57. N. V. Aladin, "The Changes in the Aral Sea Ecosystems During the Last Thirty Years," paper presented at University of Indiana Conference entitled "The Aral Sea Crisis: Environmental Issues in Central Asia," July 9-13, 1990, Bloomington, Indiana, mimeo.

58. Kuznetsov, "Geographical and Ecological Aspects," p. 325.

59. Gorodetskaya and Kes', "Alma-Ata Conference."

60. Borovsky, "Drying Out of the Aral Sea," p. 66.

61. Reteyum, Letter, pp 3-4.

62. Kuznetsov, "Geographical and Ecological Aspects," p. 327.

63. Annette Bohr, "Turkmenistan under *Perestroika*: An Overview," *Report on the USSR*, March 23, 1990, p. 24.

64. UNEP, *Diagnostic Study*.

65. H. Tsutsui, "Some Remarks on the Aral Sea Basin Irrigation Management," Nara, Japan, 1991, mimeo.

66. World Bank, "Environmental Issues in the Aral Sea Basin," preliminary draft version, April 3, 1992, ENVAP/03/92, mimeo.

67. M. I. Lvovich, "Geographical Aspects of a Territorial Redistribution of Water Resources in the USSR," *Soviet Geography* (October 1977): 558.

68. See, for example, Darst, "Environmentalism in the USSR"; Philip P. Micklin and A. R. Bond, "Reflections on Environmentalism and the River Diversion Projects," *Soviet Economy* 4, no. 3 (1988): 253-274; Micklin, *Water Management Crisis*.

69. Peter Sinnott, "Water Diversion Politics," RFE/RL, RL 374/88, August 17, 1988, pp. 1-7; and Ann Sheehy, "The Central Asian Siberian River Diversion Lobby Hits Back," RFE/RL, RL 243/87, June 29, 1987, pp. 1-5.

70. *Pravda vostoka*, February 9, 1991, p. 2, as translated in JPRS-UPA, Environmental Affairs, April 12, 1991, pp. 61-62.

71. Philip P. Micklin, "The Fate of 'Sibaral': Soviet Water Politics in the Gorbachev Era," *Central Asian Survey* 2 (1987): 72.

72. Micklin and Bond, "Reflections on Environmentalism."

73. Darst, "Environmentalism in the USSR," p. 230.

74. A. Ye. Asarin, "The Water-balance Components of the Aral Sea and Their Impact on Long-term Level Fluctuations," *Soviet Geography* 15, no. 7 (1974): 408.

75. Aladin, "Changes in the Aral Sea Ecosystems," p. 1.

76. Asarin, "Water-balance Components of the Aral Sea," p. 408.

77. V. M. Kotlyakov, "Geography and Ecological Problems," *Soviet Geography* 29, no. 6 (1989): 569.

78. Darst, "Environmentalism in the USSR," p. 223.

79. Martha Brill Olcott, "Central Asia's Catapult to Independence," *Foreign Affairs* 71, no. 3 (Summer 1992): 126.

80. See Boris Z. Rumer, *Soviet Central Asia: "A Tragic Experiment"* (Boston: Unwin Hyman, 1989); for a relevant Soviet assessment, see Yu. G. Aleksandrov, "Srednyaya Aziya: spetsificheskii slychai ekonomicheskoi slaborazvitosti" (Central Asia: A specific case of economic underdevelopment), *Vostok* 5 (1991): 142-154.

81. W. D. Williams, private correspondence, September 29, 1992.

82. M. Budyko and Yu. S. Sedunov, "Anthropogenic Climatic Changes," in *Climate and Development*, ed. H.-J. Karpe, D. Otten, and S. C. Trindade (Berlin: Springer-Verlag, 1990), pp. 270-284.

83. Nasar, "Reflections on the Aral Tragedy."

84. Williams, private correspondence.

▲ ▽ ▲

11

Islam and the Political Development of Tajikistan After 1985

◆

Mavlon Makhamov

In order to analyze the interaction between Islam and politics in Tajikistan, it is appropriate to highlight (1) its economic condition; (2) regionalism; (3) the rise of Islam-oriented political parties; and (4) external influences, especially those of the neighboring states of Southwest Asia.

Administratively, Tajikistan is divided into four provinces: Leninabad, Hatlon (former Kuliab), Kurgan-Tyube, and the autonomous province of Mountainous Badakhshan. Special administrative units include the capital of the republic, Dushanbe, and four regions subordinated directly to the central authorities of the republic. They are: Garms, Hissar, Leninabad and Ordjonikidzeabad region. According to the 1989 census, the population of Tajikistan totaled 5.1 million persons;[1] 78 percent of all Tajiks reside in Tajikistan. There are some Tajiks in Uzbekistan, Kyrgyzstan, Kazakhstan, and Turkmenistan. Also, there are Tajiks in Afghanistan, Iran, and Pakistan. Tajikistan is a multiethnic state. Besides Tajiks, 3.8 million Uzbeks, 580,000 Russians, and a total of 70 nationalities,[2] including Tatars, Kirgizs, Ukrainians, Jews, Germans, and Turkmen, live in the republic.

To the west and north Tajikistan shares borders with Uzbekistan; to the north and northeast, with Kirgizstan; to the east, with China; and to the south, with Afghanistan. Tajikistan appeared on the map of the Soviet Union on October 14, 1924, as a result of national and state division of Central Asia, when the Tajik autonomous republic was formed as a part of

Uzbekistan. In October 1929 the autonomous republic was reorganized and became the Tajik Soviet Socialist Republic. On September 9, 1990, Tajikistan became an independent state as a member of the Commonwealth of Independent States (CIS).

The distribution of the republic's population in its provinces is not even. The least populated province is Mountainous Badakhshan; the most populated is Hatlon. The majority of the population, especially Tajiks, Uzbeks, Kirghizes, and Tatars, are the Sunni Muslims; most people of the province of Mountainous Badakhshan are Ismaili.

The majority (67 percent) of the republic's population lives in the rural areas; only 33 percent is urbanized.

TABLE 11.1
Population Density in the Provinces
1989 Census

Region	Population	Remarks
1. Badakhshan	161,000	mostly Ismailis
2. Leninabad	1,559,000	
3. Halton	1,703,000	
4. Dushanbe, including four regions of Garms, Hissar, Lenin, Ordjonikidzeabad	1,689,000	

Source: *Social Development in Tajikistan* (Dushanbe, 1984), p. 24.

Tajikistan is potentially rich in natural resources; in 1989 it ranked second after Russia and first among the states of Central Asia in hydroelectric power potentials.

The economic development of Tajikistan is identical to the economic patterns of other Central Asian states. However, it has some specific features caused by geographical and natural peculiarities of the republic and by the lifestyles and traditions of its population. Cotton is the basic agricultural product—nearly 1 million tons of raw cotton are produced annually—and its cultivation takes up most of the cultivated land. Tobacco is cultivated only in some mountainous regions; cattle breeding is developed fairly extensively. Tajikistan is rich in various mineral resources, including oil, lead, antimony, zinc, bismuth, mercury, tungsten, molybdenum, and gold. There are considerable reserves of precious and semiprecious stones. Besides the cotton industry, there are ore mining and processing enterprises, nonferrous metals and rare metals mining, and dressing works.

Despite considerable natural resources and extensive economic development potential, Tajikistan is now encountering serious economic difficulties.

The recession in its economy was caused by the fractured economic ties with the republics of the former Soviet Union. The construction of many industrial enterprises has been stopped. Various projects of economic development of the autonomous province of Mountainous Badakhshan and socioeconomic development of the capital, Dushanbe, have stopped. The agrarian economy has been seriously damaged as a result of natural calamities.

Political instability has badly hurt the economy of the republic. The instability is caused by economic as well as by ethnic exclusivity, aggravated by the influence of traditional mentality and traditional law (aðat) and behavior. Moreover, the political instability in the republic is worsened by the events in neighboring Afghanistan, where there is a substantial Tajik population. Despite the fall of Najibullah's government, civil war still rages in Afghanistan.

Another important destabilizing feature of today's Tajikistan is the rapid politicization of Islam, which followed in the wake of the disintegration of the Soviet Union. Many leaders of political parties and movements acting in Tajikistan made the most of Islam to further their chances for power. Due to the less mature secular culture of the population, the politicization of Islam ran to an extreme and produced unpredictable consequences.

The republic's authorities failed to cope with economic difficulties, which lowered living standards of workers, peasants, intellectuals, and nearly all social classes. Students and teachers, physicians, scientists, scholars, and other professionals were left destitute. Even before 1985 these social groups had lived under trying conditions; the housing conditions were especially poor. Hundreds of scholars and scientists working in academic institutes waited for apartments for 15 to 20 years. No wonder that opposition parties and movements first appeared in research institutes of the Academy of Sciences of Tajikistan. Students and intellectuals became active members of these movements.

Unemployment, especially among young people, grew into one of the most serious problems. In the autonomous province of Mountainous Badakhshan alone more than 76,000 persons out of the total population of 161,000 had no job in 1991. Of those who had jobs, mostly worked only temporarily. Many families subsisted on monthly compensation paid by the state to support children. Many unemployed women found no way to increase the income of their families except by giving birth to one more child in order to receive more state money. Trying conditions caused a high rate of infant mortality, especially in the countryside. Also, the death rate of adults increased considerably.[3]

The discontent with economic difficulties increased further when the republic's government did not appear to take active measures to improve the situation. Clan rivalries and corruption corroded the will of the ruling circles of the state. From spring 1987, high government circles even thwarted all attempts of law enforcement bodies to root out criminal organizations that were gaining strength. Thus, the state authorities lost prestige and could no longer influence the population. Continuing social and property stratification complicated the situation in the republic, causing a widespread sense of relative deprivation. These abominable conditions caused a crisis in Tajik society and further encouraged the formation of opposition political parties and movements in 1989 and 1990, especially in the cities and large towns. The rural society mostly stayed out of the process of politicization of social life.

In February 1990 in Dushanbe, young people and intellectuals came out in the streets and started demonstrations against the government; many were killed and wounded in the process. Rostokhez and the Democratic Party of Tajikistan were the most conspicuous organizations opposed to the government. They were the first to create stable organizations that managed to arrange conferences of protest. On August 10, 1990, in Dushanbe the Constituent Conference of the Democratic Party of Tajikistan (DPT) took place; it was attended by 108 delegates. According to the Tajik opposition press, a considerable number of DPT supporters were pressmen and other mass media office employees, research workers, and members of independent professions.[4]

At the conference the DPT's program and charter were adopted. The party's main aim was capturing political and state power. With this objective in view, the DPT decided first to involve the *ulama* (Islamic religious leaders) of democratic orientation in it; second, to work out syllabi for all educational institutions of the republic that might begin to be used in 1991. The DPT's program especially emphasized that no militia or the personnel of the public prosecution organizations should be members of any political party; and the army should be a professional one, and act only within the boundaries of Tajikistan.[5]

Subsequently, on January 19-20, 1991, the Constituent Conference of Rostokhez took place, with 323 delegates participating. The conference was thoroughly prepared by Rostokhez.[6] Rostokhez proclaimed a comprehensive program to make radical changes in all spheres of the state and social life of Tajikistan; ensure socioeconomic and cultural development of the republic; improve material well-being and spiritual culture of the population; secure social justice; revive the Tajik language, traditions, and best customs of Tajik ancestors; infuse the society with the spirit of values common to all mankind; eradicate oppression and exploitation, social inequality and injustice, corruption, deception, immorality, and total fear. Finally, the Rostokhez program called for a truly democratic state based on law, which would hand over all power to the people and would take care of the natural environment and public health.[7]

While the program paid much attention to economic problems, which were most important to people, political objectives were recognized as paramount. The leaders of Rostokhez explained that the main cause of the crisis in Tajik society was the peculiarities of the existing political system and the way it functioned.[8] They insisted that the state and the Communist party machine had lost the capability to represent the interests of the population. It is burdened with clannish, tribal and regional loyalties. Rostokhez pointed out bluntly that "higher circles of the state apparatus were controlled by natives of Leninabad," and demanded that this injustice be removed. In order to implement this demand, the Central Council of Rostokhez proposed on June 2, 1990, that the Leninabad province should be entitled to elect only 30 deputies to the new parliament. Ironically, one-fourth of the republic's population lived in Leninabad, while Rostokhez's supporters were to elect 50 deputies. In Dushanbe, where Rostokhez was expected to win the elections, 100 deputies were to be elected.[9] In Rostokhez's eyes this reshuffling of electoral seats would have rectified the "wrongs" of the past.

The DPT supported Rostokhez's claims. The leaders of these organizations were conscious of their shaky position; consequently, they sought out the support of Islamic parties and movements, especially of the recognized Islamic scholars. Consequently, the society splintered, and Tajikistan found itself on the edge of a bloody civil war.

In the summer of 1992, several other organizations, parties, and political clubs became active in Tajikistan, including Ehya-i Khojent (Revival of Khojent); the sociocultural association of Samarkand; Oftab-i Sugdian (the Sun of Sogdiana); Vahdat (Unity); a popular front of supporters of reconstruction; Oshkoro (Publicity); society Maihan (Homeland); and Haverim (society of the friends of Jewish culture). The influence of some of these organizations is nearly imperceptible, but they continue to be active. The most influential are still DPT and Rostokhez. The latter calls itself a popular movement rather than a political party in order to consolidate its influence and guide all democratic forces of opposition. The organization Lal-i Badakhshan (Rubis of Badakhshan), which appeared in 1991, is another active force. These organizations are supported by politically active intellectuals—teachers, medical workers, scientists, pressmen, students, and even teenagers. After the disintegration of the Soviet Union in 1991, some elements of state and party bureaucracy went over to the opposition. Their participation did not lend prestige to the opposition because turncoats had a very bad reputation and pursued their own interests. The broadening of political activity in Tajikistan was closely related to the political processes that were taking place in other republics of the former Soviet Union. Thus, the process of party-making or the functioning of democratic opposition took place directly under the influence of similar organizations and movements, which became active in Russia and in the Baltic republics during 1989-90. Representatives of Russian and Baltic republics' opposition parties often visited Tajikistan. They found some local activists holding similar views who were ready and willing to cooperate with them. Moreover, earlier issues of opposition newspapers were printed in the Baltic republics and then brought to Tajikistan for distribution. However, the lack of unity and mass support and rivalry among the leaders of "democratic opposition" prevent them from engaging in a serious competition with state authorities.

Nevertheless, the Islamic opposition functioned much more successfully. *Ulama,* representing the official Islam, at first found itself in an advantageous position because it was supported by the state authorities, who wanted to control with the assistance of the *ulamas* the political and religious situation. The government did not hamper the construction of mosques or the repair of cemeteries and *mazars* (mausoleum of the saints). Moreover, the government encouraged the organizing of *haj* (pilgrimage) to Mecca. From January 1989 to January 1990 the number of officially registered mosques increased from 17 to 47 and continued to grow.[10] In July 1991 the number reached 2,700. Mosques were being constructed spontaneously in nearly every neighborhood. With the help of authorities some *ulama* were elected to the parliament of the republic. Representatives of official Islam regularly called on their followers to remain loyal to the government and to observe state laws. Thus, a temporary compromise was reached between the government and official Islam.

But soon the *ulamas* registered their displeasure with the fact that the government allowed them only the opportunity to engage in purely religious matters. They wanted to determine state policy, insisting on transforming Tajikistan into an independent Muslim state. Akbar Kahharov Turajonzoda, the head of official Islam, appointed to the post by the government in 1988, took more interest in politics than in religion,[11] claiming at the same time to be the only true adherent and protector of Islam and Muslims in the republic. Kahharov and his adherents emphasized the advantage of the Islamic way of life, maintaining that Saudi Arabia and the United Arab Emirates had achieved great success in economic development and secured high living standards for their population only through their devotion to Islam. Leaders of official Islam visited Saudi Arabia, Jordan, and Pakistan, where they met in May 1990 Gulbeddin Hekmatyar, with whom they made an arrangement of cooperation and mutual aid.

The Muslim Department of Tajikistan condemned the government for allowing pig breeding in the Muslim country, which is forbidden in Islam, and the slaughtering of cattle without the observance of Muslim rites. The Muslim Department demanded that the government proclaim Muslim holy days as nonworking days and that it ensure the fulfillment of Muslim customs when cattle are slaughtered; in addition, it demanded that the off days be changed from Saturday and Sunday to Tuesday and Friday. The Supreme Soviet and the government of Tajikistan complied with some of these demands, but ignored others, explaining that it was impossible to fulfill them. Then leaders of official Islam openly opposed the government and were supported by the democratic organizations mentioned earlier.

Despite these developments and changes, Kahharov failed to become an all-Tajikistan Muslim leader. Yet another Islamic organization appeared on the political scene, which claimed to be the supreme political power in the republic. It was the Islamic Renaissance Party (IRP). Unlike other parties and political organizations, the IRP had declared that any Muslim residing in Tajikistan could join the party. Those who refused to support this Islamic party were declared infidels (*kafirs*).

THE ASTRAKHAN CONFERENCE: EMERGENCE OF THE IRP

The IRP of Tajikistan was created according to the resolution of the Constituent Congress of the Islamic Renaissance Party of the Muslims of the Soviet Union, which took place in Astrakhan (Russian Federation) in June 1990. About 140 participants attended the congress, mostly Islamic fundamentalists of Dagestan (60 delegates), Abkhazia (2 delegates), Tajikistan (24 delegates), Azerbaijan (2 delegates), Abkhazia (2 delegates), Tatarstan (1 delegate), and some other regions.[12] They elected party leaders, including Saidibrahim Gadoev, who became deputy chairman of the party. The IRP declared its main objective to be the struggle for consolidation of all Muslims of the Soviet Union under the aegis of a unified coordinating body to counterbalance the existing official Muslim Departments, which collaborated with the Soviet authorities. After returning from Astrakhan, the members of the Tajik delegation started to organize in July and August 1990 the Islamic Renaissance Party. The principal aim of the IRP was the establishment of an Islamic state in Tajikistan. The program and charter of the party were distributed. The program stated that the IRP was a sociopolitical organization guided by the ideals and cultural values of Islam, consolidating all faithful Muslims devoted to the revival of Islamic principles, which were revealed in the Quran and Sunna. The IRP wanted true Islam to become the creed of the people. The economic life of the country also had to be determined by the principles of Islam.[13] A 17-member organizing committee was established, and a campaign for the collection of signatures and applications in the favor of the party started. In August 1990 the organizing committee unsuccessfully sought to have the government's permission to hold the Constituent Conference in Dushanbe.

Nevertheless, the Constituent Conference of the IRP took place on October 6, 1990, in the village of Chortut (Lenin region) in the suburb of Dushanbe. About 300 delegates and guests participated. Among them were representatives of "democratic parties" and organizations. For the council of *ulama*, 27 persons were elected; Abdussamad Himmatov[14] was elected chairman (*amir*); Dawlat Usmonov and Saidibrahim Gadoev became his deputies.

The attempt to establish a political Islamic party was criticized by the Supreme Council of the republic. Leaders of official Islam, in particular the Qazikalon Akbar Kahharov, opposed the establishment of the IRP; they declared it to be against Quranic principles. This declaration was only a political trick since the representatives of official Islam abruptly changed their position when they severely criticized the government and supported the IRP.

The first congress of the IRP took place in October shortly after the aborted coup of August 1991 in Moscow. It was attended by 657 delegates and 310 guests. Thus the IRP's activity was legalized. Its chairman, Himmatov, informed the delegates that the IRP had decided to leave the Islamic Renaissance Party of Muslims of the Soviet Union, which had been created in June 1990 in Astrakhan, but that the IRP-Tajikistan would continue its activity regardless of the latter's fortune and existence in the Soviet Union. At the congress organizational problems, strategy, and tactics of the party in the course of the next presidential elections were discussed. The proposal of the chairman's deputy, Usmanov, was accepted when the IRP decided to support the nomination of D. Khudanazarov, who had become the representative of democratic organizations. With more than 10,000 active members,[15] the IRP was able to involve a considerable number of the indigenous population in the new exhausting political struggle.

SUFI ORDERS AND THE PIRS' ROLE

In analyzing the influence of Islam on the political and social life of contemporary Tajikistan, one cannot disregard the so-called unofficial Islam, consisting of the Sufi orders headed by *pirs* and *ishans*.

It is well known that Sufis, particularly of the Nakhshbandiya and Qadiriya orders, had played an important role in the spiritual life of Muslims in the areas that in 1924 were included in the Tajik republic. This was especially true before the revolution of 1917. Judging by the available evidence of Sufi orders in Tajikistan, as well as in other republics of Central Asia, one can safely say that they were destroyed by the Soviets during the 1920s and 1930s. At present the overwhelming majority of Muslims in Tajikistan is almost unaware of the Sufi orders. But the institution of *pirs* (spiritual and religious mentors), though somewhat transformed, has survived in Tajikistan, particularly in the rural areas. *Pirs* were not officially registered, but they directed all ceremonial rites in the rural area. *Pirs* are regarded with greater reverence than *ulama,* representing official Islam. Some *pirs* have disciples and adherents (*murids*), and this fact is not concealed. They function openly, thought not very actively. This phenomenon may be explained by the fact that the destruction of the Sufi tradition in Tajikistan created a spiritual vacuum, which was filled by the *pirs*. Muslim theologians who understood Sufism perfectly and enjoyed authority had no opportunity to hand down their spiritual heritage. After they ceased to exist, no other religious authority of their eminence could effectively lead Sufi orders. The social and religious condition of the Ismaili community of the autonomous province of Mountainous Badakhshan is not dissimilar. Since Islam is resurgent in Tajikistan, the revival of Sufi orders is quite probable.

The politicization of Islam worried the secular Tajik intellectuals who understood the aims of the IRP leaders. They preferred to support politicians who could maintain stability in the republic and ensure the necessary economic reforms.

PRESIDENTIAL ELECTION OF NOVEMBER 1991

The presidential elections of November 1991 became the first serious trial of strength for the parties. Despite the strenuous efforts made by the "democrats" and their Islamic supporters, they lost the election. Rahman Nabiev[16] was elected president of Tajikistan, demonstrating the fact that the Tajik people preferred a secular form of government. But the supporters of Islamization did not stop fighting; they gathered themselves up to find an opportunity to grab power. The events of 1992 were characterized by the rising tide of Muslim self-consciousness and nationalism, when the opposition leaders united and sometimes even consolidated to struggle for political power. However, nationalism was often concealed under Islamic verbiage and religious views were advanced under the slogans of national interests.

EXTERNAL INFLUENCES ESPECIALLY FOR TURKEY, IRAN, AND PAKISTAN

It is appropriate to emphasize that the current political dynamics in Tajikistan were generated primarily by internal problems of a social, economic, and political nature, but they are also closely related to the changes within the Soviet Union from 1985 to 1991. Simultaneously, the external factors originating in Afghanistan and Iran profoundly influenced Tajikistan's political development. This influence need not be overestimated; but to disregard it would be a mistake.

The disintegration of the Soviet Union gave the ruling circles of Muslim states in Southwest Asia an opportunity to strengthen their position in Central Asia. This opportunity to take advantage of the economic, scientific, and technical difficulties of this vast area was not available when Central Asia and Kazakhstan were part of the Soviet Union. In Tajikistan they started to pay special attention to various Muslim parties and movements. They attempted to popularize their models of socioeconomic development as Muslim states. These neighboring Muslim states openly competed with each other in highlighting their own achievements.

At first, Saudi Arabia, with its financial capabilities and as the locale of sacred Islamic shrines, attempted to strengthen its position in Tajikistan. Pilgrims who returned to Tajikistan after accomplishing their *haj* in 1990—and there were 8,000 *hajɖ* from the Central Asian republics— praised to the sky the life in Saudi Arabia, whose government had paid their total traveling expenses. However, in addition to Islam, the political orientation of the Tajikistanis has always been greatly influenced by the ethnic and linguistic factors that they share with Iran. The Iranian leadership has used these factors skillfully.

At present, Iran's influence is spreading widely in Tajikistan because of nationalistic groups of Tajik intellectuals, who give preference to nationalism over religion (Islam). To them the national revival of Tajikistan is impossible to achieve without Iran's help. Iran's geopolitical location is another factor in their consideration. But the first contacts with Iran demonstrated that cultural and linguistic affinity has its own limitations; the exchange of official delegations to Iran in June 1992 yielded no significant results, especially when no contract of economic cooperation was signed.

Since the fall of Najibullah's regime relations between Tajikistan and Afghanistan have also remained complicated. In Tajikistan the Afghan war was always looked upon as a vexation, because of the long boundary between the two neighbors. Moreover, a large number of Tajiks live in Afghanistan and have relatives in Tajikistan.

The secular section of Tajikistan's population, which is engaged in thwarting attempts to transform the republic into an Islamic theocratic state, is afraid that the Islamic opposition will seize power in Afghanistan. But the IRP and its allies hope to get economic and military assistance from Kabul for their struggle in Dushanbe. Afghanistan's assistance to the IRP cannot be excluded because these contacts were established before the collapse of Najibullah's regime. Arms, narcotics, and religious propaganda literature from Afghanistan continuously cross over into Tajikistan, while Tajikistan's government follows the policy of noninterference in the domestic affairs of Afghanistan and expects reciprocity. The problem of mutual noninterference was one of the most important topics discussed during the visit of Tajikistan's premier, A. Mirzoev, to Kabul. Nevertheless, both governments agreed to maintain friendly and mutually beneficial relations.

Relations between Tajikistan and Pakistan are of great importance. Recently contacts between the leaders of these states have taken place. In July 1992 the Tajik delegation headed by President Nabiev visited Pakistan. Special attention was paid to the start of economic cooperation especially in the field of electric engineering and road construction. It was agreed that Tajikistan would deliver electric power to northern Pakistani provinces in exchange for consumer goods and manufactured products. The construction of a vehicular road connecting Tajikistan and Pakistan is planned. Increased economic cooperation will guarantee friendly relations between Tajikistan and Pakistan.

The establishment of close economic ties between the two Muslim states would cause anxiety in India, which might look upon it as a prologue to close political ties. Already there are indications that India is displeased with the strength of Islamic parties and movements in Tajikistan and in other Central Asian states. India perceives this process to be operating against its interests, weakening its economic and political ties with the Central Asian republics.

THE LURE OF SO-CALLED MODELS

At present, China seems to be developing a general strategy of relations with the states of Central Asia. No doubt friendly and mutually beneficial relations are in the interest of Tajikistan. The economic relations have already been established: In Isfara a factory producing electronic equipment, color television sets, and telephone apparatus is being constructed, and several porcelain works have been constructed. Other economic projects are being discussed. Tajikistan and other Central Asian republics are likely to adopt the Chinese model of economic development since their existing economic system has more in common with China's than with Iran's or Turkey's. This possibility may induce China to accelerate its economic and political programs in these republics.

Recently, Turkey has also initiated a great deal of activity in the Central Asian states, proposing its own economic and political model as most suitable for them. To strengthen its position, particularly in Turkic-speaking states, Turkey relies on ethnic and linguistic affinity. This was confirmed by numerous visits of leaders, particularly by the visit of the Turkish premier, S. Demirel, to the republics of Central Asia. But Turkey's economic capability is rather limited. Therefore, it can hardly take a leading position in these republics in the near future. In Tajikistan, Turkey's influence is conspicuously absent.

Despite the Soviet Union's disintegration, Tajikistan is still strongly influenced by Russia. This is so not only because a fairly large number of Russians live in the republic. An additional important fact is that Tajik intellectuals are aware that the republic's national independence is most closely associated with Russia. The material contribution made by Russia to the development of the Tajik economy and culture is widely appreciated in the republic, especially Russian nonrefundable subsidies provided to Tajikistan during the 1920s and 1930s. Industrial plants of Tajikistan form an integral part of the economic system that functioned within the Soviet Union's boundaries. Even now Tajikistan is within the zone of rubles circulation. Tajikistan is unlikely in the near future to introduce its own currency. In light of these factors, the relations between Tajikistan and Russia cannot be broken off without the greatest possible damage to the economy, science, and culture of the republic. Moreover, Tajikistan signed a military agreement with Russia, accepting Russia to be the guarantor of its security and independence.

CONCLUDING COMMENTS

The fate of Tajikistan depends mainly on the main political forces that govern it and define its home and foreign policy. Recent events demonstrate that if the IRP's leaders and their allies come to power, Tajikistan would be threatened by disintegration. In that case, the more developed northern Tajikistan (Leninabad region) is likely to drop out of the republic in order to create a separate state. But the bloody events in May 1992 undermined the influence of the IRP's leaders. They lost a considerable part of their supporters, retaining some influence only in Dushanbe and the regions subordinated to the republican authorities, including Garms, Hissar, Lenin, and Ordjonikidzeabad. They are not likely to come to power, at least in the near future.

The so-called democratic leaders of Tajikistan allied themselves with the IRP, hoping to derive advantages, but this alliance made them lose some of their influence and prestige. Leaders of the older generation, who are well known in the republic and who are well informed about Tajikistan's economic, social, and ecological problems, have been ignored. Their place is occupied by young functionaries, who rely upon persons of their own generation. Tajikistan's democratic forces suffer (and have always suffered) from such shortcomings as nationalism, clannishness, and regional narrow-mindedness. However, the democratic leaders of the new generation could lift the democratic movement to a much higher level because, unlike the older generation, they are less burdened with nationalism and other prejudices. They are staunch adherents of the secular state. They believe in retaining, broadening, and strengthening mutually beneficial relations with Russia and other states that are the members of the CIS. They also stand for the restoration of broken relations with Afghanistan and for the development of contacts with other Muslim states of the region.

Only the establishment of civil peace will enable Tajikistan to overcome the current political and socioeconomic crisis. The forceful seizure of power by any party or group will only accentuate tension and armed conflicts and lead to civil war. Islamic fundamentalists and the democratic forces representatives' attempt to grab power led to the refusal of two provinces, Leninabad and Kuliyab, to recognize the newly formed government. The current political situation in Tajikistan is complicated and highly unpredictable and will remain so in the near future.

N·O·T·E·S

1. *Social Development of Tajikistan SSR* (Dushanbe, 1989), p. 24.

2. Ibid, p. 25.

3. Adult mortality was caused mainly by defective blood circulation, malignant tumors, accidents, poisoning, injuries, and respiratory diseases.

   Leader of the Democratic Party of Tajikistan (DPT) Shodmon Yusupov, Ph.D, is a staff member of the Department of Philosophy of the Tajikistan Academy of Sciences. Before the events of February 1990, he worked in the department as a senior research fellow. He studied in Saratov and defended his thesis there.

   Rahim Musulmangulov is deputy chairman of the DPT's board. Members of the board are Nyazov Jumabay, Khalifaev Madrizo, Sattorov Abdunabi, and Bobonazarova Oynihol.

4. *Rostokhez*, N:4 (Dushanbe. October 1990), p. 6.

5. Ibid.

6. *Public Movement in Tajikistan* (Moscow, 1990), p. 116 (in Russian).

7. Leader of Rostokhez Tahir Jabborov (Abdujabbarov), Ph.D., is a senior research fellow of the Council of Studying of Productive Forces (Tajikistan Academy of Sciences), Deputy of the Supreme Council of Tajikistan. He took his postgraduate course at the Institute of Oriental Studies, Moscow (the Pakistan Department). In 1974, he defended his thesis, entitled "The Northwest Frontier Province of Pakistan. Economic Outline."

   Deputies of the chairman of the Central Council of Rostokhez are Khalifbaba Hamidov and Sharafuddin Imomov. Members of the Central Council are Mirbaba Mirrahimov, Muhabbat Ghonoatov, Ahmad Janzoda, and others.

8. *Public Movements in Tajikistan*, p. 38.

9. *Rostokhez*, N:2, July 1990.

10. *Public Movements in Tajikistan* (1989-March 1990) (Dushanbe, 1990), p. 41 (in Russian).

11. Akbar Kahharov was born in 1954, in the village of Turkabad (Orjonikidzeabad Division). His father was Ishan Turajon. He went to madrasa in Bukhara, then studied at the Islamic University in Tashkent and in Jordan.

12. *Hidayat* (Publication of the Tajik Branch of the Islamic Renaissance Party [IRP]), N:5 (July 1990), pp. 1-2.

13. "Programme of IRP," *Komsomolets Tajikistana* (Dushanbe), November 21, 1990, p. 2 (in Russian).

14. Leader of IRP Himmatov Abdusamad (Himmatzoda) worked at a pumping station in Orjonikidzeabad (where A. Kahharov was born). He was born in 1951. Until

1990, he was practically unknown in the republic. He is said to be a graduate of the Polytechnical Institute (Dushanbe).

15. *Soglasie* (Dushanbe), November 1, 1991, p. 5.

16. Rahman Nabiev, president of the Republic of Tajikistan. He was born in 1930. Before 1985, he was the first secretary of the Communist Party of the Tajikistan Central Committee. From 1971 to 1973 he was deputy to the Supreme Council of the USSR. From 1976 on he was a member of the Central Auditing Commission of the CPSU.

▲ ▽ ▲

12

The Politics of Polarization in Tajikistan

◆

Muriel Atkin

Tajikistan has been the scene of intense political drama since it declared its independence on September 9, 1991—far too much drama for the thousands of its citizens who were killed, wounded, or made refugees. A widely heard characterization of the power struggle there was that it was being waged by two diametrically opposed camps: one representing secularism and stability and led for much of the period by the president, Rahman Nabiev (deposed in September 1992); the other representing radical Islamic "fundamentalism."

"Fundamentalism" is a poor term to describe the views of Islamicizers in Tajikistan or elsewhere, but it has become a common designation for a bogeyman in the former Soviet states, in imitation of western usage.

According to that view, there was no middle ground—no groups were willing to make compromises, accept pluralism, or work for a peaceful transition to a new political, social, and economic order. The cause of the conflict was allegedly the Islamic radicals' attempt to overthrow the legitimate, secular government. This interpretation presented a distorted picture of conditions in Tajikistan, but there was a danger that the intransigence of its leading proponents might make real precisely that fiction that they manipulated for their own purposes.

Another misperception of the political turmoil was that it was just about the rivalry among cliques, usually defined in regional terms, with the long-dominant position of northerners (Khujandis) under attack by factions

from other parts of the country. The definition of contending camps by
such nonideological factors as region, extended family, patron-client networks, and even criminal ties was indeed part—but only part—of the picture. In Tajikistan, as in other countries, the fact that some political groups
had pronounced regional associations did not preclude their also having
political platforms. The outcome of the power struggle will determine not
only who will govern but also toward what ends they will do so, whether
the political clock will be turned back to the Brezhnev era or whether
some form of post-Communist political system will evolve.

Although the Manichaean view of secularism assailed by religious
extremism could be found in western and Russian reports, its leading pro-
ponent was the Communist old guard in Tajikistan. These were people
who remained unreconciled to the Communist Party's loss of its monopoly
of power and privileges. However, they also realized that changing circumstances made it impolitic for them to justify themselves publicly in
those terms. Therefore, they attempted to play on the fears of all those at
home or abroad who would not want to see a radical Islamicizing regime
take power in Tajikistan. For example, when Nabiev was nearly driven
from office by demonstrators early in May 1992, he went on the radio to
warn that the only way to preserve a secular form of government in
Tajikistan was to keep him in power.[1] Similarly, just before he was ousted
in September 1992, he told anyone who would listen, including the
Associated Press and *Izvestiia*, that the current political crisis was caused
by Islamic radicals who wanted to make Tajikistan an Islamic state like
Iran. This allegation was intended to prompt intervention by other countries to defeat his opponents for him. He signaled that by including the
warning that his ouster by Islamic "fundamentalists" would pose "a threat
to all neighboring states and others."[2]

This was another version of Nabiev's pattern of trying to use any foreign contacts, including the United States, Iran, and the Commonwealth
of Independent States (CIS) to enhance his own position. For example, at
the time of the May 1992 crisis, he had sought military support from Boris
Yeltsin and other CIS leaders.[3]

That line was not unique to Nabiev but was a recurrent theme of the old
guard's propaganda. Communist hard-liners in the southern province of
Kulyab, who took the lead in the 1992 fighting to restore the old order,
used the same kind of rhetoric. For example, Rustam Abdurahimov, head
of the political group Oshkor (*glasnost*) in the province, claimed that
"'Iranization' has begun in Tajikistan. . . . They want to make us a colony
of Iran."[4] The deputy chairman of the province's executive committee,

Mahmadsaid Ubaidulloev, told a Russian reporter, "I think that Islam, which today they try to foist upon us, is frightening not only for us but also for you. . . . Islamicization is dangerous for you Russians, too! You still do not understand that!"[5]

The old guard's leaders were not simply secularists. They were Communist Party careerists who did well in the Brezhnev era and used every means possible to maintain the power and privileges they enjoyed under the old order. Nabiev himself was first secretary of the Communist Party of Tajikistan from 1982 to 1985, when he was removed from office as part of Gorbachev's purge of the party leadership in Central Asia. He kept looking for a way to make a comeback in subsequent years; he found his opportunity in 1991, when his successor was ousted for supporting the junta that attempted to overthrow Gorbachev that August.

The old guard, for all its railing against the alleged Islamic menace, manipulated Islamic themes to advance its own aims. Indeed, in a country where the vast majority of inhabitants are Muslim in some sense (whether in religious or cultural terms, or both), every party that sought a broad following had to declare itself in favor, at a minimum, of full religious freedom for Muslims.

One example of the rather crude way the old guard tried to play on Islamic loyalties comes from April 1992, during a period of sharpening confrontation between the regime and its opponents. The 'Id al-Fitr, the holiday marking the end of the Ramadan fast, fell at that time. Nabiev used the occasion to send his holiday greetings to "all the noble Muslims of Tajikistan" and pointed to the just-completed Ramadan observances as proof that "our people are faithful to national religious traditions."[6] He did not mention that for years Communist propaganda had railed against fasting during Ramadan, including on the grounds that it is bad for the health. Nor did he mention that Tajikistan's leading Islamic figure, the *qadi*, Akbar Turajonzoda, had waged a tough political fight in the fall of 1991 to get the Tajikistan Supreme Soviet to make the main Islamic holidays state holidays as well. Nabiev also used his 'Id al-Fitr remarks to argue that *his* regime embodied Islamic values while his opponents' did not. He identified the relevant values as "unity, friendship, brotherhood, and cooperation," and faulted participants in the growing demonstrations against him for being divisive.[7]

After surviving the spring 1992 challenge to his authority, Nabiev visited Iran and Pakistan at the end of June and beginning of July. On his return, he sought to convey to Tajikistanis his respect for Ayatollah Ruhollah Khomeini as a religious leader.[8]

The opposition to the old guard was not monopolized by radical Islamicizers, despite the old guard's attempt to create that impression. There was a middle ground occupied by non-Communists and those Communists willing to work with them.

Some veteran Communists showed greater willingness than the old guard to reach an accommodation with non-Communists. Representative of this group was Akbarshoh Iskandarov, who, at the age of 42, became acting president of Tajikistan after Nabiev's ouster in September 1992. He had a conventional career in the party and state for a rising apparatchik; during the political crisis of August-October 1991, he seemed to be just an ordinary follower of the party hard line.[9] However, during the spring 1992 crisis, he broke with the hard-liners and openly supported an accommodation with the opposition. During his short term as acting president he was vilified by the hard-liners. He and other members of the coalition government resigned in November 1992 in an effort to placate Communist hard-liners and facilitate an end to the civil war.

Some of the major opposition parties advocated a reformist state in which Muslims have complete religious freedom but that would not attempt to govern according to Islamic law. Prominent among these were the Democratic Party of Tajikistan, the popular front organization, Rastokhez, and a newer reformist group, Loli Badakhshon. (The latter group drew support primarily from members of ethnic and religious minorities from the republic's southeastern mountains. As such, they were influenced not only by the growth of the reform movement in the Soviet Union as a whole in its last years but also by a minority's special perception of the advantages of tolerance of diversity.)

The Democratic Party of Tajikistan grew out of the reform movement that gained importance in the late Soviet period both at the center and in several republics.[10] It maintained contact with democratic reformers from various parts of the former Soviet Union, including the Democratic Party of Russia, the United Democratic Party of Belarus, and parties from the Central Asian republics.[11] Its platform advocated such things as the establishment of a market economy, work within legal political institutions, and cooperation among all who favor reform.[12]

Rastokhez's political platform advocated civil liberties and amicable relations among nationalities as well as a strong emphasis on Tajik nationalism.[13] Far from advocating a retreat into chauvinistic isolationism, the head of Rastokhez, Tohir Abdujabbor, favored the preservation of the union, albeit in revised form, until the union collapsed for reasons that had nothing to do with Tajikistan's politics.[14] The old guard tried to paint Rastokhez as an extremist menace, even when it had good reason to know otherwise.

The Islamicizers were not monolithic either. Many outside observers who warned of an Islamic menace did not distinguish between a desire to have a secular state, in which Muslims would have complete religious freedom, or an Islamic state, in which those in power see themselves as governing according to Islamic law. Moreover, even those who favored a larger public role for Islam disagreed among themselves. The republic's leading religious figure, the *qaði,* Akbar Turajonzoda, who became an open critic of Nabiev in the fall of 1991, repeatedly expressed doubts about the feasibility or desirability of establishing an Islamic state in Tajikistan for a long time to come. The leaders of the Islamic Rebirth Party disagreed over how far to press Islamicization.[15]

A number of Islamic Rebirth Party activists spoke, at least publicly, of an Islamic state as an *ultimate* goal, but one that they expected to achieve only after a long process of public education and consent. Party leaders talked of a period of several decades before the public might accept an Islamic state. The reason Islamic Rebirth Party members gave for this approach in essence acknowledged that the idea of government according to Islamic rule was unpopular in Tajikistan in the early 1990s. They also insisted that whatever kind of Islamic state evolved would be one of local design, not an imitation of any foreign example.[16]

One of the founders of the Islamic Rebirth Party, Davlat Usmon, tried to reassure the United States that his party did not espouse the kind of extremism and anti-Americanism that the United States tended to associate with Islamicizers because of the Iranian example. Thus, he told American visitors during the spring 1992 demonstrations that he advocated good relations between Muslims and Christians and believed in human rights and democracy.[17] He also spoke positively about the United States to Washington's chargé d'affaires in Dushanbe.[18]

Even though one cannot be certain how parties that have had at best sharply limited power would behave if they were in full control, it is worth noting that in the large demonstrations in Dushanbe organized by the opposition coalition between August and October 1991, when the supporters of the old order were particularly vulnerable, the rhetoric did not have a fanatical tone and could best be characterized as a local variant of the political climate that existed among reformers in various parts of the Soviet Union after the failure of the August coup attempt. Respect was shown for national pride and Islam as well as for democracy and for those in Moscow who had defied the coup plotters. The demonstrators called for the ouster of Tajikistan's political leaders for having been all too ready to cooperate with the junta.[19] In early October, the demonstrators gave a friendly reception to Anatolii Sobchak, hardly an advocate of Islamic fundamentalism. His remarks to the crowd stressed the importance of freedom for all; that the Tajiks deserved freedom and so did the Russians—and freedom for either required freedom for the other.[20]

In the fall 1991 presidential campaign, the Democratic Party, Rastokhez, *Qaði* Turajonzoda, and some members of the Islamic opposition joined to support the candidacy of filmmaker Davlat Khudonazarov instead of Nabiev. Khudonazarov, then head of the all-union cinematographers' union, had been a member of the Communist Party and supporter of Gorbachev's reforms but quit the party in reaction to the hard-liners' intransigence. Since that fall he has advocated the nonviolent pursuit of political objectives and an accommodation among contending political groups.[21] During the 1992 conflict, he made several attempts, sometimes at personal risk, to resolve disputes through negotiations among contending factions.[22]

In the power struggle between the Communist hard-liners and their various opponents, it was the hard-liners who bore much of the responsibility for thwarting compromise and using violence. This was not a situation in which both sides were, from the outset, similarly ruthless in their determination to crush the other. Rather, the hard-liners behaved repressively while the opposition showed considerable moderation, given the circumstances.

Anti-Communist feeling in Tajikistan was embittered by the hard-liners' repression at the end of the Soviet era and the first year of independence. A turning point was the clash in Dushanbe in February 1990, when a government attack on peaceful demonstrators voicing economic and political grievances provoked riots. Twenty-five people died and more than 800 were injured.

The government of Tajikistan ordered an investigation of the February events by a commission of the republic's Supreme Soviet. The commission's report showed that some key political figures, including the then-party first secretary, Qahhor Mahkamov, had responded with heavy-handed ineptitude to what began as peaceful demonstrations and therefore were largely to blame for the ensuing violence. The report also showed that the security forces were guilty of acts of unprovoked, excessive, and indiscriminate violence that sparked the riots in the first place and caused innocent casualties during the course of the troubles.[23]

This report disproved the official version of events, which had blamed the turmoil on a number of factors, from unemployment and dissatisfaction with the pre-*pereótroika* style of rule to Rastokhez machinations and a conspiracy of Islamic fundamentalists who used drugs as an aid in whipping up mob violence (as the head of Tajikistan's KGB had claimed) and killing innocent bystanders.[24]

The government impeded the commission's inquiry while it was under-way and then suppressed its report. Some of the central news sources also carried distorted versions of what had happened. However, reformers were able to get a copy of the report and publish it in Moscow.[25]

The regime reacted to the February troubles by imposing a prolonged state of emergency, which was used not only to stop the rioting (which had ended after a few days) but also to repress the opposition. The leadership prohibited state radio and television from carrying stories about a score of people who criticized the harshness of the regime but did not advocate a radical alternative, Islamic or otherwise. For example, one of the pro-scribed was Shodmon Yusuf, a founder of the Democratic Party of Tajikistan.[26] The regime falsely accused Rastokhez of inciting the February riots. The Supreme Soviet's special commission found it innocent of that charge.[27] Nevertheless, one year later, Tajikistan's prosecutor-general's office charged the leaders of Rastokhez with fomenting the riots.[28]

The regime's readiness to kill citizens of Tajikistan and lie about it after-ward deeply scarred republican politics. In early September 1991, as demonstrators in Dushanbe pressured a temporarily uncertain regime to make reforms, the demonstrators raised the issue of the February troubles as a grievance in its own right and symbol of long-standing oppression. They demanded that Lenin Square, where the government forces first opened fire on demonstrators in February 1990, be renamed Martyrs' Square. The Supreme Soviet complied. As resentment against the old order became increasingly open and intense after August 1991, people recalled the 1990 troubles as an example of the regime's hostility toward its own citizens and its readiness to shed their blood. As one critic of the hard-line government noted, it "can speak only the language of cannon and guns."[29]

Tajikistan's old guard often presented the power struggle there as an assault upon the duly elected president and legislature. However, those elections conveyed less legitimacy than the old guard claimed. First of all, elections do not mean much when the party in power tries to prevent all others from operating openly or freely contesting elections. Although else-where in the then-Soviet Union, non-Communist parties acquired legal status, the regime in Tajikistan blocked that from happening within the republic until mid- to late 1991 (depending on which party). In any event, the formal legalization of other parties did not constitute a serious step toward political pluralism because the hard-liners were willing to arrest, even kill, opponents, regardless of which parties enjoyed legal recognition.

It should come as no surprise that 95 percent of the seats in Tajikistan's Supreme Soviet were held by Communists; though that was no proof of public support for the party.[30] The most recent legislative elections were held in late February 1990, while the country was still under the state of emergency imposed because of the Dushanbe riots shortly before; organized political opposition was still illegal when the ballots were cast. The legislative representatives elected at that time have refused to allow their mandate to be put to a real test. For example, the Supreme Soviet rejected opposition calls in October 1991 for a plebiscite vote of confidence in it.[31]

Tajikistan's first direct presidential election, on November 24, 1991, provided scarcely more legitimacy than the legislative election. According to the official returns, Nabiev won with 58 percent of the vote; Khudonazarov came in second in the eight-man field, with 30 percent. Some of the vote for Nabiev can be explained by a backlash against the economic hardships caused by the Gorbachev reforms, the inertia resulting from nearly 70 years of Communist rule in the republic, and the hard-liners' substantial (though not total) control over the mass media. However, the outcome was also the result of election fraud. Khudonazarov charged ballot stuffing and voter intimidation.[32] The Communists used their organizational network, including their control over the workplace, not only to promote Nabiev's candidacy but also to malign the opposition.[33]

Khudonazarov did not claim that he would have won the election but did contend that he actually received 37 percent of the vote, not 30 percent.[34] Under the circumstances, that figure, taken with the perhaps 10 percent of the vote that went for several other candidates, was not an inconsiderable vote against an entrenched political establishment in the country's first direct presidential election.

While hard-liners at the Soviet center failed in their attempt to seize power in August 1991, their counterparts in Tajikistan succeeded a few weeks later in overthrowing those fellow Communists who had been willing to make some accommodation to the pressures for change. The tone of the junta's comments was reminiscent of the heavy-handed Communist propaganda of the past: patronizing and designed to give the impression that there was no legitimate basis for opposition. While demonstrators against the attempted coup in Moscow won international admiration, the makers of the successful coup in Dushanbe derided those who demonstrated against it as irresponsible youths manipulated by others as well as workers, white-collar workers, teachers, girls, scholars, and poets [sic] run amok, to the detriment of their jobs and family relations.[35] These comments also, unintentionally, reveal the social diversity of the opponents of the coup. The Dushanbe junta showed its true colors when it declared, "we are not ready for peaceful multiparty relations."[36] These were the people who returned Nabiev to the apex of power in Tajikistan.

The comparison between the attempted coup in Moscow and the successful one in Dushanbe was not lost on advocates of change. One reformist Tajik journalist described the group that seized power in Tajikistan as the "Tajik Iazov, Kruchkov, and Pugo."[37] A group of 31 Tajik writers, people who were not radical outsiders by the standards of the Gorbachev era but had made their way within the system, protested the Dushanbe coup as an attempt to turn the clock back to Brezhnev-style rule.

> The despotic apparatus of the Communist Party has deceitfully and brazenly made its own servant, the infamous leader Rahmon Nabiev, head of the government. This new government, which is a perfect copy of the . . . [junta] of August 19-21 . . . in Moscow, prevents society from progressing and developing. . . . They have only one objective. To hold on to power by any means, to keep the oppressed people of Tajikistan in ignorance.[38]

Nabiev's first press conference as president showed the aptness of such comparisons. Sitting next to him were the prosecutor-general, the minister of internal affairs, and the head of the republic-level KGB.[39]

Even in symbolic terms, it is notable that the Communist Party of Tajikistan kept its name; in contrast, party organizations in many formerly Soviet republics adopted new names, which did not conjure up images of the old order. The activities of the Communist Party of Tajikistan were suspended but not banned by a presidential decree of October 2, 1991, issued in token recognition of anti-Communist sentiment following that August's attempted coup. This fell far short of the demands of the demonstrators on the streets of Dushanbe, who wanted the party banned outright.[40] The decree had little practical impact since the party retained its property and party officials were still paid their salaries.[41] Shortly before the decree was issued, the party renamed itself Socialist. This illusion of change was abandoned in December 1991, when the party resumed the name Communist.

After their return to power, the hard-liners showed how unwilling they were to tolerate the existence of any opposition, let alone share power with it. The more time passed, the more dissenting voices could be heard in Tajikistan's press. In reaction to that, a new press law was enacted in the spring of 1992; it contained the kind of loose wording that facilitates a crackdown on the press. The new law made it illegal to run a story that interfered with the life of an individual citizen or is libelous or provocative. Government officials, public organizations, and other groups or individuals were to be protected from anything the authorities chose to construe as displaying these objectionable characteristics.

In addition, mass media organizations had to obtain official permission for changing such things as their structure, name, or language.[42] This represented the kind of government involvement in the functioning of the mass media that far exceeded legitimate concerns over any possible press abuses. The law seemed designed to provide a convenient device for harassing those who expressed opinions displeasing to the regime.

The Communist Party meeting of September 23, 1991, considered ordering the arrest of Tajikistan's *qadi,* though ultimately it backed down, perhaps because it saw that a considerable number of citizens were willing to take to the streets to protect him.[43] Rumor has it that when Nabiev's supporters attempted to seize Dushanbe (October 24-26, 1992), one of their prime targets was the *qadi,* although they were unable to capture him.

Less fortunate was the former mayor of Dushanbe, Maqsud Ikromov. Although a veteran Communist himself, he incurred the wrath of the hard-liners by taking a tolerant stance toward demonstrators' demolition of a statue of Lenin in downtown Dushanbe, when, in the aftermath of the August 1991 attempted coup, advocates of change thought they would win. The Supreme Soviet promised Ikromov that he would not be punished for his conduct on that occasion. Despite that, he was arrested early in 1992 on corruption charges. Opposition demonstrators in Dushanbe in the spring of 1992 perceived Ikromov as a victim of a political reprisal and demanded his release.[44]

What happened to members of non-Communist parties was at times much worse. Scores of members of the Democratic Party of Tajikistan, Rastokhez, and the Islamic Rebirth Party were arrested in the first few months of 1992.[45] During the May 1992 crisis, opposition supporters temporarily seized the Supreme Soviet's building. They found spots of blood on the cellar walls where some 50 members of the opposition had recently been held captive.[46]

Not content with using existing law enforcement agencies for the purpose of political repression, Nabiev tried to organize a private army answerable directly to him to crush his opponents. This took the form of both a national guard and local militias. He tried several times to establish a national guard funded from state revenues and controlled by him (rather than by the ministers of defense or interior). The first attempt came in December 1991, followed by attempts in April, May, and June of 1992. Each attempt provoked strong criticism.[47]

He also used his patron-client network to create private militias in various parts of Tajikistan. These were unsavory associations used as tools of crude repression. The head of the pro-Nabiev militia in the southern province of Kulyab was Sangak Safarov, a 64-year-old who had spent more than 20 years in prison for nonpolitical crimes, including vehicular homicide.[48] He publicly acknowledged that he killed the head of Kulyab's provincial executive committee, Jumakhon Rizoev, in October 1992, and added, "It is necessary to kill enemies."[49] Safarov advocated the return of the old guard to a monopoly of power and the restoration of the Soviet Union. In keeping with the old-guard line, he equated opposition to the old order with radical Islamicization and blamed all Tajikistan's troubles on this alleged Islamic menace. The notion of a political compromise was alien to his thinking. He dismissed those Kulyabis who had fled to Dushanbe as people who "sold themselves to the Islamists."[50] Although the restoration of Nabiev apparently became a moot point in November 1992, when the Supreme Soviet accepted his resignation, Safarov's militia fought on, in pursuit of victory for other Communist hard-liners.

Much of the worst political violence in the country during 1992 took place in the southern province of Qurghonteppa, where support for the reformers was strong. The violence was largely the doing of the Kulyab militia. In August and September 1992, the assault on Qurghonteppa was particularly grim. Militia members murdered eight opposition activists at their homes or offices.[51] They took noncombatants hostage, including doctors and patients at a hospital and a group of about 100 interrupted during their prayers at a mosque.[52] The militia's assault on the city of Qurghonteppa is said to have cost hundreds of lives.[53] When the Kulyab militia attacked Qurghonteppa, it freed some 400 hardened criminals, who went on a rampage in the provincial capital. In the words of militia chief Safarov, "sincere, honest people who happened to be behind bars" joined his group.[54]

Tajikistani television, then controlled by reformers, claimed that the fighting in the southern part of the republic caused 18,500 deaths in the half year following the May 1992 crisis.[55] Late in November 1992 came word of many more casualties in Qurghonteppa as a result of the Kulyab militia's attack on refugees who had fled farther south within the province (to the Shahrtuz district). The number of victims was uncertain but may have been about 500.[56]

On October 24, 1992, the Kulyab militia pressed northward and attacked Dushanbe in an attempt to restore Nabiev to power. By the time the attack ended two days later, 600 people had been killed, according to the anti-Nabiev camp.[57] Supporters of the old guard finally seized the city in December of that year.

When faced with the need to make compromises with the opposition — and so reduce tensions — the Communist hard-liners have, like Nicholas II, repeatedly sought to take back as much as possible of what they had yielded so grudgingly.

In April 1992, an apparent compromise between the regime and opposition demonstrators included the promised removal of Safarali Kenjaev, the speaker of the Supreme Soviet, in return for an end to the demonstrations. He was disliked by the opposition as an embodiment of old-guard intransigence and made no secret of his personal animosity toward individuals who favored change. As speaker of the legislature, he did such things as threaten to block the sale of issues of *Izvestiia*, after it came under the control of reformers, and prevent the broadcast of television programs from Moscow if these carried reports that he considered disruptive. Access to outside sources of information was a particularly sensitive issue because of the old guard's efforts (not entirely successful) to control political reporting by the mass media within the republic. The opposition also accused Kenjaev of corruption.[58]

At first, the old guard refused to comply with the agreement to remove him. When that caused increased tensions in Dushanbe, Nabiev simply transferred Kenjaev to a different position, if anything an even more objectionable one from the opposition's point of view — leadership of the republic's successor to the KGB (the National Security Committee). Before long, Kenjaev returned to his position as head of the Supreme Soviet.[59] Not surprisingly, opposition demonstrations resumed in Dushanbe.

After coming so close to being ousted in May 1992, Nabiev appeared to agree to power sharing with the opposition. The plan was hammered out during the night of May 10 in negotiations at the CIS army barracks in Dushanbe between Nabiev, members of opposition parties, and *Qadi* Turajonzoda; the commander of CIS troops in the city, Colonel Viacheslav Zabolotnyi, presided over the meeting. Nabiev was allowed to retain his office, although his powers were supposed to be diminished. The Communist Party was not banned but its property was supposed to be nationalized. Kenjaev was removed as head of the Supreme Soviet; other prominent hard-liners were also ousted. Kenjaev fled the capital but returned in October, in conjunction with the attack by the Kulyab militia, and briefly claimed the presidency.[60]

According to the May agreement, eight government positions were to go to members of the coalition that advocated change. Even though these positions accounted for only one-third of the cabinet, they included many of the key offices, including those that controlled the security forces and broadcasting. Both sides were to disarm. The Supreme Soviet was to be replaced by a new legislature, a National Assembly, in which members of the opposition would have half the seats; this was to exist until new legislative elections could be held at the end of the year.[61]

Among the members of the opposition who now entered the government were Davlat Usmon, of the Islamic Rebirth Party, who became deputy prime minister, and Mirbobo Mirrahim, of Rastokhez, who took charge of the state radio and television committee.

Hard-liners were soon at work to undermine the coalition government. For example, deputies of the Supreme Soviet who supported the old order claimed that the new coalition government was illegitimate.[62] Hard-liners began attacking Tajikistan state television, no longer under their control in the coalition government, in essence because it had ceased to report only their version of events, a situation they portrayed as divisive rabble rousing.[63] In Qurghonteppa, hard-liners demanded that opposition members of the post-May coalition government resign and that all members of opposition parties leave the province by late August.[64]

The proposed National Assembly never got off the ground. The Supreme Soviet refused to give way to it.[65] Nabiev denied having agreed to the assembly's creation, accused the opposition of violating the terms of the May agreement by advocating its creation, and claimed that such a body could not be created unless the Supreme Soviet voted to do so.[66]

Under the circumstances, what is striking is not that the opposition resorted to violence but how much restraint it showed.[67] Many in the opposition avoided the use of force even during political crises. The example from the ruins of Yugoslavia of the terrible consequences of the unwillingness to compromise coupled with the willingness to use violence were not lost on some members of Tajikistan's opposition.[68]

The members of the old guard who reacted to the destruction of the Lenin statue with moral outrage (for example, Tajikistan's Council of Ministers condemned it as an act of "barbaric vandalism")[69] did not seem to have noticed that the sole "victim" was an inanimate object. Given that the supporters of the old order were in temporary disarray at that time, if the demonstrators had wanted to attack members of the Communist Party leadership then assembled in Dushanbe, there would have been little to stop them. However, such assaults were not even attempted. The mass demonstrations remained peaceful even after the government tried to prevent public meetings and, on one occasion, kept demonstrators waiting for an hour and a half in the late summer's heat before providing loudspeakers or electricity.[70]

When Nabiev won the presidential election, the opposition did not let its objections to the way the election had been conducted drive it to violence.

As the political confrontation intensified in the spring of 1992, many of the opposition's moves were reactions to threatening gestures by the Nabiev regime. As demonstrations grew in Dushanbe in late March 1992, the demonstrators called for an end to the persecution of non-Communists and for the replacement of the Supreme Soviet by a newly elected legislature. The coalition of opposition parties voiced frustration that the government was unwilling even to negotiate with them.[71]

The end of April and beginning of May 1992 saw ominous moves by the old guard. The Supreme Soviet authorized Nabiev to rule by decree, and he threatened a crackdown on the still-peaceful opposition demonstrators. This effort at intimidation proved counterproductive. The opposition reacted by marshaling its own armed supporters in Dushanbe and holding its ground.[72]

On May 10, 1992, Nabiev and representatives of the opposition were supposed to meet to sign an agreement to establish a coalition government. He did not arrive at the scheduled meeting and could not be located by the opposition. That caused several hundred demonstrators to go to the (renamed) KGB headquarters in the expectation of finding him there. Exactly what happened at that point was disputed, but in the end government forces fired on demonstrators, according to some accounts, opening fire without warning and without shots having been fired at them. In any event, Tajikistan television claimed eight people were killed.[73]

In reaction to this event, some members of the opposition, especially in the Islamic Rebirth Party, called for Nabiev's ouster. However, others, including Shodmon Yusuf, of the Democratic Party of Tajikistan, wanted Nabiev to remain in office. Although he was highly critical of Nabiev's repressive measures, he opposed ousting the president on the grounds that that posed too great a threat to the country's stability. *Qaḍi* Turajonzoda, whom hard-liners repeatedly accused of wanting to oust Nabiev in order to seize power himself, agreed with Yusuf's position.[74] In the end, the Islamic Rebirth Party also reconciled itself to Nabiev's continuance in office for the same reason.[75]

It was at this point that the fragile agreement to establish a coalition government was hammered out. Demonstrations in the capital subsided.

However, the hard-liners' bad faith was demonstrated over the next few months by their reneging on the May agreement and the bloodshed in

Qurghonteppa. Therefore, on August 31, 1992, opposition demonstrators seized the presidential palace as well as the offices of the Council of Ministers and took hostages, among them prominent officials and Nabiev aides, to press for their demands, including Nabiev's ouster. Some of the hostages were released quickly, but more than a score remained captives. Although roughly 1,000 members of the opposition, some of them well armed, participated in the seizure of the building, none of the hostages was harmed. The demonstrators opened negotiations with government representatives, led by Akbarshoh Iskandarov, then head of the Supreme Soviet.[76] Once again, the opposition chose to end a confrontation peacefully. An agreement was concluded on September 4; the demonstrators left both the buildings they had occupied without a fight.[77]

When Nabiev was finally forced from office on September 7, 1992, he was not arrested or harmed physically even though he had been captured by opposition demonstrators. The terms of his resignation statement, which had the opposition's assent, allowed him to keep various perquisites, including a house in Dushanbe.[78] By the terms of his resignation, he promised he would "not initiate any provocation or intrigue in any part of Tajikistan or outside it."[79]

Granted, the resignation must have been made under duress, despite the opposition's attempt to make it appear otherwise, but Nabiev did not abide by this commitment any more than he had to any other commitments he made to the opposition previously. He returned to his home province of Leninabad (Khujand), in the north of the republic, where his supporters remained powerful. At the same time, his supporters in the south fought on.

In an attempt to end the civil war, Tajikistan's acting president Iskandarov and most of the coalition cabinet resigned in November 1992, so that the Supreme Soviet could name a new government. The legislature met not in Dushnabe but in the northern city of Khujand, a hard-liner stronghold. The legislators formally accepted Nabiev's resignation and then formed a new government composed of hard-liners. The Kulyab militia continued the battle for control of the south.

By mid-1992, as the crisis deepened in Tajikistan, the opposition became more willing to initiate violence itself. One dramatic example of this was the assassination of the republic's prosecutor general, Nurullo Huvaidulloev, in August 1992. He was despised by the opposition as an embodiment of the old guard's intransigence; he was associated with such unpopular moves as the arrest of Dushanbe's former mayor, Ikromov, and with unwillingness to compromise with the opposition during the spring 1992 confrontation.[80] The exact motives of his accused assassin, an army general, remained unclear.

The situation in Tajikistan during its first year of independence was bleak. The fighting continued even after the old guard captured Dushanbe at the end of 1992. Agricultural production decreased sharply. Both factors combined to threaten thousands of people with hunger as well as violence as winter approached. Desperate people tend to look for desperate solutions. The failure of the hard-liners to abide by any of the proposed compromises may undermine public support for the advocates of change who repeatedly showed a willingness to try compromise and conciliation. By a cruel irony, the old guard's obstinacy and double dealing had the greatest potential to strengthen the hitherto small camp of Islamicizing radicals, against whom the old guard claimed to be the best defense.

N·O·T·E·S

1. M. Dobbs, "Rebels Seize Most of Tajikistan's Capital," *Washington Post*, May 7, 1992, p. A33.

2. S. LeVine, "Tajikistan Slides Deeper into Political Abyss," *Washington Post*, September 7, 1992, pp. A18, A20; J. Krauze, "La Russie menace d'intervenir au Tadjikistan," *Le Monde*, September 7, 1992, p. 3.

3. M. Dobbs, "Tajik President Resigns in Opposition Custody," *Washington Post*, September 8, 1992, p. A14.

4. O. Blotskii, "Tajikistan: zelenoe—krasnoe," *Literaturnaia gazeta*, November 4, 1992, p. 11.

5. Ibid.

6. "Murojiati Raisi Jumhur Rahmon Nabiev ba mardumi Tojikiston," *Jumhuriyat*, April 4, 1992, p. 1

7. Ibid.

8. "Novyi shag na puti k sotrudnichestvu," *Narodnaia gazeta*, July 7, 1992, p. 1.

9. Radio Dushanbe (in Russian), September 27, 1991, in Foreign Broadcast Information Service (FBIS), *Daily Report. Soviet Union*, September 30, 1991, p. 93.

10. M. Khudoiev, "Gotovnost' k dialogu, no na printsipal'noi osnove," *Kommunist Tadzhikistana*, July 3, 1990, p. 1.

11. F. Karimov, "Muloqoti namoyandagoni quvvahoi demokrati," *Tojikistoni soveti*, May 15, 1991, p. 2.

12. "Az rui aqli solim," *Adabiyot va san"at*, August 16, 1990, p. 1.

13. "Ustav i programma organizatsii 'Rastokhez' (Vozrozhdenie) Tadzhikskoi SSR," *Rastokhez*, no. 5, 1990, p. 2.

14. "Navtarin Khabarhoi Ruz," *Tojikistoni shuravi*, September 4, 1991, p. 1.

15. U. Babakhanov and A. Mursaliev, "Pust' govoriat ob islamskom Tadzhikistane. A kazi protiv," *Komsomolskaia pravda*, October 4, 1991, p. 1; A. Istad, "Davlati milli chi guna boyad?" *Adabiyot va sanat*, June 4, 1992, p. 6; *Moscow News* (in English), September 6-13, 1992), in FBIS, *Report. Central Eurasia*, October 7, 1992, p. 117.

16. U. Babakhanov and A. Ganelin, "Budet li v Dushanbe ploshchad' pobedivshei oppozitii?" *Komsomolskaia pravda*, May 22, 1992, p. 1; S. Erlanger, "Politics in Central Asia Being Shaped by Islam," *New York Times*, June 9, 1992, p. A16; R. Wright, "Report from Turkestan," *The New Yorker*, April 6, 1992, p. 74.

17. *Report on the Helsinki Commission Visit to Armenia, Azerbaijan, Tajikistan, Uzbekistan, Kazakhstan, and Ukraine* (Washington, DC: Commission on Security and Cooperation in Europe, 1992), p. 25.

18. "Priem v posol'stve," *Narodnaia gazeta*, July 7, 1992, p. 1.

19. "Girdihamoi dar maidoni ba nomi Lenin," *Tojikistoni shuravi*, August 30, 1991, p. 2.

20. V. Zhukov, "A. Sobchak va E. Velikhov dar Tojikiston," *Jumhuriyat*, October 5, 1991, p. 1.

21. M. Egamzod, "Dushanbe, Maidoni Ozodi, 2-3 oktiabr," *Jumhuriyat*, October 4, 1991, p. 3; comments made in the author's presence.

22. *Moscow News* (in English), September 6-13, 1992, in FBIS, *Report. Central Eurasia*, October 7, 1992, p. 117.

23. "Soobshchenie komissii prezidiuma Verkhovnogo Soveta Tadzhikskoi SSR po proverke sobytii 12-14 Fevralia 1990 g. v Dushanbe," *Sogdiana*, no. 3 (October 1990): 2, 3, 4; Helsinki Watch, *Conflict in the Soviet Union. Tadzhikistan* (New York: Human Rights Watch, 1991), pp. 25-26, 40-42.

24. TASS (in English), April 11, 1991, in FBIS, *Daily Report. Soviet Union*, April 12, 1991, p. 75; *Moscow News* (in English), December 30, 1990, in ibid., January 4, 1991, p. 57; "Soobshchenie," pp. 2, 4, 7; Helsinki Watch, *Conflict*, pp. 30, 48, appendix C.

25. "Soobshchenie," pp. 2, 3, 6.

26. Helsinki Watch, *Conflict*, p. 49.

27. "Soobshchenie," p. 2; Helsinki Watch, *Conflict*, pp. 19, 20, 28.

28 TASS (in English), January 30, 1991, in FBIS, *Daily Report. Soviet Union*, February 4, 1991, p. 86.

29. V. Abdullo, "Roh kujost?" *Javononi Tojikiston*, October 12, 1991, p. 1.

30. A. Lukin and A. Ganelin, "Podpol'nyi obkim deistvuet," *Komsomol'skaia pravda*, March 23, 1991, p. 2.

31. Interfax, October 21, 1991, in FBIS *Daily Report. Soviet Union*, October 22, 1991, p. 74.

32. Maiak Radio (Moscow) (in Russian), November 25, 1991, in FBIS *Daily Report. Soviet Union*, November 26, 1991, p. 89; Dushanbe Radio (in Tajik), November 26, 1991, ibid., November 27, 1991, p. 72; comments made in the author's presence.

33. F. Karimzoda, "Rahmon Nabievro tarafdorem!" *Tojikistoni shuravi*, September 14, 1991, p. 1.

34. Comment made in the author's presence.

35. T. Abdulloev et al. , "Murojiatnoma," *Jumhuriyat*, October 4, 1991, p. 1.

36. Ibid.

37. H. Yorov, "Avvalin konfronsi matbuot dar huzuri R. Nabiev," *Jumhuriyat*, September 28, 1991, p. 1.

38. Gulrukhsor et al. , "Murojiatnomai adiboni Tojik ba mardumi sharifi Tojikiston," *Jumhuriyat*, September 28, 1991, p. 1.

39. Yorov, "Avvalin konfronsi matbuot."

40. M. Egamzod, "Ruzi boron, zeri khaima, man gurusna . . ." *Jumhuriyat*, September 28, 1991, p. 1.

41. "Qarori Shuroi Olii Jumhurii Tojikiston," *Jumhuriyat*, October 5, 1991, p. 1.

42. "Qonuni jumhurii Tojikiston," *Jumhuriyat*, April 3, 1992, p. 1.

43. Babakhanov and Mursaliev, "Pust' govoriat."

44. Interfax, October 8, 1991, in FBIS, *Daily Report. Soviet Union*, October 9, 1991, p. 74; *Report on the Helsinki Commission Visit*, p. 24.

45. *Report on the Helsinki Commission Visit*, p. 24.

46. S. Shihab, "Fausse sortie au Tadjikistan," *Le Monde*, May 10-11, 1992, p. 3.

47. *RFE/RL Daily Report*, no. 84, May 4, 1992, p. 3; ibid., no. 112, June 15, 1992, p. 3.

48. I Rotar', "Ob osvobozhdenii Dushanbe my podumaem pozzhe," *Nezavisimaia gazeta*, November 14, 1992, p. 3.

49. Ibid.

50. Ibid.

51. *RFE/RL Daily Report*, no. 165, August 28, 1992, p. 3.

52. Krauze, "La Russie menace."

53. Dobbs, "Tajik President Resigns"; *RFE/RL Daily Report*, no. 17, September 29, 1992, p. 1.

54. Rotar', "Ob osvobozhdenii Dushanbe"; *Komsomolskaia pravda*, September 22, 1992, in FBIS, *Report. Central Eurasia*, October 16, 1992, p. 99.

55. *RFE/RL Daily Report*, no. 211, November 2, 1992, p. 3.

56. I Rotar' and S. Ayubzod, "Stolknovenie v Shaartuze," *Nezavisimaia gazeta*, November 24, 1992, p. 1.

57. Cable News Network, *Headline News*, October 27, 1992.

58. Postfactum (Moscow) (in English), December 23, 1991, in FBIS, *Daily Report. Soviet Union*, December 27, 1991, p. 69.

59. J. Rupert, "Rival Factions Reach Accord in Tajikistan," *Washington Post*, May 8, 1992, p. A19; *RFE/RL Daily Report*, no. 77, April 22, 1992, p. 3.

60. Rotar' and Ayubzod, "Stolknovenie."

61. "Tajiks Agree to Form Coalition," *Financial Times,* May 12, 1992, p. 3; Rupert, "Rival Factions," p. A19.

62. *RFE/RL Daily Report,* no. 140, July 24, 1992, p. 3.

63. "Vsegda stoiu na strazhe zakona," *Naroдnaia gazeta,* July 3, 1992, p. 3.

64. *RFE/RL Daily Report,* no. 165, August 28, 1992, p. 3.

65. *RFE/RL Daily Report,* no. 140, July 24, 1992, p. 3.

66. TIA Khovar, "Za ukreplenie mezhdunarodnykh pozitsii Tadzhikistan," *Naroдnaia gazeta,* July 18, 1992, p. 2

67. The much more limited outbursts of violence of 1989 were different from the civil war being waged in 1992, not only in exxtent but also in character. The earlier incidents were uncoordinated expressions of grass-roots economic grievances and were directed at members of other historically Muslim nationalities.

68. J. Said, "Mevae nest beh zi ozodi," *Javononi Tojikiston,* October 12, 1991, p. 2; *RFE/RL Daily Report,* no. 82, April 30, 1992, p. 3.

69. Dushanbe Radio (in Tajik), September 26, 1991, in FBIS, *Soviet Union. Daily Report,* September 30, 1991, p. 94.

70. "Girdihamoi dar maidoni ba nomi Lenin," p. 2.

71. *RFE/RL Daily Report,* no. 65, April 2, 1992, p. 8.

72. Dobbs, "Rebels," pp. A33, A39; *RFE/RL Daily Report,* no. 84, May 4, 1992, p. 3.

73. S. Shihab, "Asie centrale: l'Iran se pose en médiateur," *Le Monde,* May 12, 1992, p. 3; S. Erlanger, "Tajik Police Fire on Demonstrators, Shaking Hope for Coalition," *New York Times,* May 11, 1992, p. A9.

74. Erlanger, "Tajik Police"; F. Hiatt, "Ukraine's Leader Won't Attend Summit," *Washington Post,* May 13, 1992, p. A28.

75. *RFE/RL Daily Report,* no. 91, May 13, 1992, p. 1.

76. "Protesters Seize Leader's Office in Tajikistan," *Washington Post,* September 1, 1992, p. A14; Associated Press, "Officials in Tajikistan Freed by Protesters," *New York Times,* September 2, 1992, p. A6; Associated Press, "Hostages Released in Tajikistan," *Washington Post,* September 2, 1992, p. A26.

77. M.I.T. Khovar, "Dar Devoni Vazironi Jumhurii Tojikiston," *Jumhuriyat,* September 8, 1992, p. 2.

78. "Ariza," *Jumhuriyat,* September 8, 1992, p. 1; "Qarori devoni vazironi jumhurii Tojikiston," ibid.

79. "Sozishnoma," *Jumhuriyat*, September 8, 1992, p. 1.

80. Huvaidulloev made prescient public comments about his unpopularity and assassination almost two months before he was killed. He blamed the mass media for waging a smear campaign against him, especially after Ikromov's arrest and the political confrontation in April and May 1992. By the time he voiced this complaint, rumors were already circulating that he had been assassinated. ("Vsegda stoiu na strazhe zakona.")

▲ ▽ ▲

13

Nationalism and Islamic Resurgence in Uzbekistan

◆

James Critchlow

The period since the breakup of the Soviet Union has been one of profound change for Uzbekistan. On August 31, 1991 within days of the collapse of the coup attempt in Moscow, the republic declared its independence. Although it adhered to the Commonwealth of Independent States (CIS) after creation of that entity in December 1991, its policies and actions demonstrated that the concept of independence was taken seriously. Indeed, despite the misperceptions of outside observers, Uzbekistan had as early as November 1990 been unwilling to relinquish any of its sovereignty to a federal structure. That fact emerged clearly from criticism by then party first secretary (later President) Islam A. Karimov and others prominent in the republic of a "union treaty draft" proposed by Mikhail Gorbachev. In the view of the Uzbek spokesmen it was unacceptable because, as Karimov put it, it infringed on Uzbekistan's sovereignty.[1]

Uzbekistan's declaration of independence was in fact the culmination of a long struggle conducted by the republic's elites, spearheaded by the cultural intelligentsia, against the strictures of central rule from Moscow. The elites of Uzbekistan were a peculiarly Soviet phenomenon. When Uzbekistan was established in the 1920s where no nation of that name had previously existed, Soviet planners in Moscow gave their new creation all the trappings of nationhood: boundaries, a flag, a national language, and national institutions. They also provided for the birth of a new national professional class to breathe life into the institutions, partly by co-opting members of the old Islamic intelligentsia, suitably transmuted, and partly through a massive campaign of recruitment and education of new native cadres. This intelligentsia was intended to serve, as in other Soviet republics, as the "transmission belt" of communism.

Throughout the period of Soviet rule, the new elites exhibited a perverse tendency, while feigning loyalty to Moscow, to engage in a subterranean struggle to defend Uzbek national interests. The struggle had early roots in the Stalinist era, but did not achieve fully overt form until the latter stage of the period of *perestroika* and *glasnost* introduced by Gorbachev. In the course of that struggle, the intelligentsia exploited popular dissatisfaction with Moscow's policies, especially in two areas: the economy and ethnicity. In the first, Uzbek disgruntlement was expressed most vividly in objection to hardships imposed on rank-and-file Uzbeks by the policy of making the republic a raw-materials base, above all for cotton-raising, to the detriment of development in other sectors of the economy and with severe environmental damage resulting in such public health problems as an increase in infant mortality. In the second area, Uzbek national feelings were aroused by Moscow's campaign to extirpate Uzbek ethnic differences in the name of efforts to create a homogeneous "Soviet man." In Uzbek eyes, an important ethnic difference was Islamic tradition; even Uzbeks who did not identify closely with Muslim belief and practice were resentful of Moscow's persecution of those who did.[2]

By 1991, the year of independence, objections to the abuses of central rule were being voiced openly and with increasing stridency in the public media, especially in those in the Uzbek language. At the same time, in Uzbekistan, as in other former Soviet republics, the suddenness of the transition to full autonomy caught both officials and the general public unprepared to exercise the prerogatives of independence. The declaration itself was couched in generalities, without a clear program for the future.

THE EUPHORIA OF THE SOVIET COLLAPSE

Visible signs of Uzbekistan's new status were not long in coming, however. Billboards proliferated proclaiming *mustaqillik* (independence). The new national flag, with a subtly Islamic motif, was flown everywhere. In Tashkent, the capital city, some Russian street signs were taken down and replaced with English ones, and at an institute of economics in Tashkent lectures began to be given in English (even by Uzbek instructors) instead of Russian. Following some initial hesitation, the massive statue of Lenin that dominated a central area of Tashkent was removed from its pedestal.

Uzbek historians set about, with renewed vigor, the task begun under *glasnost* of restoring their country's past from the Stalinist version of it as a primitive land able to progress thanks only to a helping hand from the Russian "elder brother." The glory days of the Great Silk Road and the Islamic Renaissance, when "Uzbek" regions like Bukhara, Samarkand, and Khorezm were at the pinnacle of world trade and civilization, replaced Marxist-Leninist ideology as a source of inspiration.

Such largely ceremonial changes were supplemented at the practical level by Uzbekistan's becoming a member of the United Nations Organization and a signatory to the Conference on Security and Co-operation in Europe (the Helsinki Pact). Its independence was generally recognized by foreign countries and diplomatic relations were established. A number of countries, including the United States, hastily set up embassies in Tashkent. There were visits from high-ranking foreign emissaries, including the Iranian foreign minister, the Saudi foreign minister, the Turkish prime minister, and the American secretary of state. In Tashkent, Samarkand, and Bukhara, new hotels were being constructed by an Indian firm to help accommodate the influx of visitors from abroad. Uzbekistan's ties with Muslim countries of the Middle East and South Asia were strengthened in February 1992 when the republic, together with other Central Asian republics, joined the Economic Co-operation Organization formed by Iran, Turkey, and Pakistan.

Freedom of travel was no longer controlled by Moscow. President Karimov and other Uzbek representatives began a schedule of visits to foreign countries, especially those that could be viewed as likely trading partners. Uzbekistan's new freedom to manage its own resources and to conclude direct bilateral trade agreements, without having to have them ratified in Moscow, gave new point to such exchanges. This was symbolized soon after independence, in February 1992, when Uzbekistan signed the protocol of an agreement to collaborate with an international mining company headquartered in Denver, Colorado (Newmont Mining Corporation) in processing a large stock of low-grade gold ore at deposits in Muruntau that had previously been worked in secret by Moscow under the control of the KGB.

Prior to independence, even Communist officials in Uzbekistan had been left in the dark about the extent of the republic's gold holdings. At a more prosaic level "Sovplastital," a firm established jointly with Italian interests, has been cited as a success story and an opportunity for Uzbeks to learn western business practices; it manufactures plastic dishware and other items. Also symbolic of new, direct ties with foreign countries was the rapid creation of a new company, Uzbekistan Airlines, which, using aircraft pre-empted from Aeroflot, the former Soviet airline, inaugurated regular service to Istanbul. To facilitate overland access to and from Uzbekistan, talks were held jointly with Pakistan and Afghanistan about improving land routes, especially those damaged by wartime fighting in Afghanistan.

Internally, there were certain economic reforms. Peasants' private plots, which in the 1960s and afterward had been all but eliminated to make room for growth of cotton acreage, were allowed to increase in size, although there were reports of resistance by local farm managers. To make this possible, there was a cutback in land sown to cotton. Moreover, in 1991, farms that fulfilled economic plans (now set by Tashkent, not Moscow) were given the right to dispose as they saw fit of 5 percent of planned production and all of whatever they could produce above the plan goal. In 1992, this was raised to 15 percent of planned production and, as before, all of surplus production. The result was a claimed increase in availability of foodstuffs. (In some cases, it was reported that farm managers were abusing their new freedom to sell production for foreign currency by using the proceeds to obtain Japanese automobiles for their own use.)

After decades of official persecution of Islam, the newly independent government of Uzbekistan reversed direction by turning over to worshippers mosques that had been seized as state property and by fostering the construction of new mosques. At his inauguration on January 4, President Karimov, a longtime Communist, swore an oath on the Quran. Religious observance became quite open, some Muslim holidays were made official, and Islamic publications circulated freely. The mufti of Tashkent and other members of the official clergy came to occupy a prominent place in the same media that had once regularly attacked Islam.

PROBLEMS OF INDEPENDENCE

If the blessings of independence created an initial atmosphere of euphoria in the minds of many people, a sober realization soon set in of attendant problems that in the long term could jeopardize not only independence but Uzbekistan's very survival as a nation. Above all, it became clear to Uzbeks that the solution of their problems was now up to them alone.

Prior to independence there had been hopes that Moscow, whose economic directives were responsible for the deterioration of Uzbekistan's economy and ecology, would help to right the wrong. As Russia now faced staggering problems of its own, those hopes faded. Moreover, Moscow was no longer around as a scapegoat, although Uzbek media continued to recite, and amplify, the record of Soviet-era abuses.

The new nation, wracked by crippling problems, most notably by massive unemployment and consumer shortages, now lacked a common external enemy to serve as a unifying force. Nationalism turned inward, accompanied by the fragmentation of society along clannic/tribal, local, and ethnic lines. There were haunting fears of a recurrence of the bloody ethnic violence of 1989 and 1990 that had broken out among Muslim nationalities in the Ferghana Valley. The panicky outmigration from Uzbekistan of other nationalities, especially Russians, that had been accelerated by the Ferghana disturbances, continued, despite efforts by the government to induce non-Uzbeks to remain. The rallying cry of "*miras*" (heritage) that had served the elites so well in their struggle against Moscow continued to be used by the government, but in the absence of foreign hegemony and with a dwindling foreign population it lost much of its cogency. The elites, having prevailed against Moscow, now began to display disillusionment with their own government.

Faced with these challenges, the government has at times responded with weakness and inertia where initiative and imaginative leadership are badly needed. At other times it has resorted to repression. The media of Uzbekistan, compared with those of neighboring Kazakhstan and Kyrgyzstan, cower in the shadow of dictatorship. Citizens of the republic fear surveillance by the security police; the Uzbek branch of the KGB has been taken over by the Karimov government, with little visible change in its style of operation. Critics of the regime have been savagely beaten. In June 1992, U.S. Senator Larry Pressler, during a visit to Tashkent, visited Abdurrahim Pulatov, leader of the Birlik movement, in the Tashkent hospital where he was recovering from wounds. Pulatov later left Uzbekistan to seek treatment for brain damage.

As for Islam, even many of those Muslims who have rejoiced at the lifting of official persecution are concerned about what they perceive as the danger of "fundamentalism" advancing from the south, whether from Afghanistan, Iran, or Saudi Arabia. By "fundamentalism" they mean a radical form of Islam, which would intrude on their social freedom by becoming the arbiter in civil matters. Exemplary of their outlook is the fact that, despite the new climate of religious tolerance, one seldom sees a woman wearing a veil in Uzbekistan. The fear that the veil or the *chador* might someday become compulsory, as in Iran, distresses many Uzbeks.

In fact, there are reasons to discount the likelihood of an Iranian "takeover" of Central Asia.

First, the Shi'ite variant of Islam, which is dominant in Iran, is uncongenial to Central Asia's Sunni Muslims. The two branches of the faith may unite in the face of encroachment by infidels, as was at times the case under Soviet rule, but it appears extremely doubtful that Central Asians would embrace Shi'ism freely, despite recent indications that Shi'ites are making some inroads among Uzbekistan's Iranian neighbors to the south, the Tajiks. Moreover, the looser structure of Sunni Islam, in which the clergy play a less salient role, is not adapted to imposition of religious norms on the society.

Second, in Iran itself the fervor of the Islamic revolution appears to be running its course. Recent visitors to the country have found a general relaxation accompanied by a new concentration on secular, material values.

Finally, although Iran is quite naturally interested in the future of its Central Asian neighbors, which may affect its own stability and well-being, most evidence suggests that as a nation it is driven more by economic than by political or theological motives. The theory that Iran and Turkey are locked in rivalry for the allegiance of the Central Asians is overshadowed by a lack of proof and by other factors, such as joint cooperation of the two powers with the Central Asian republics in the Economic Cooperation Organization.

To the extent that militant Islam may be a real threat to Central Asia, it would seem that Afghanistan would be a more plausible source. Contacts between the two regions have been continuous through most of history; the Central Asians are represented in Afghanistan by large numbers of co-ethnics (Tajiks, Uzbeks, Turkmens), and Afghanistan also espouses Sunni Islam. Such speculation is fueled by recent reports of the shipment of people and arms across the border into the Central Asian republics, presumably by such former radical mujahidin elements as those led by Gulbuddin Hekmatyar. This may introduce local destabilizing influences, but the present chaotic state of Afghanistan would seem to weaken the ability of such forces to intervene effectively in Central Asia.

Although fear of Iranian-style "fundamentalism" may be exaggerated, it has led the Central Asian elites to look hopefully toward Turkey as a model of a secular Islamic state. Turkey has reciprocated with aid, including a promise to send a Turkish "Peace Corps" to the region. In Uzbekistan, plans are under way to bring Uzbek and Turkish, related Turkic languages, more closely together by introducing a form of the Latin alphabet used in Turkey.

AN AUTHORITARIAN PRESIDENT

Central to Uzbekistan's problems is the personality of its first independent president, Islam Karimov. In the Soviet period, Karimov served at a relatively young age (he was born in 1937) in various posts, among them the chairmanship of the Republican Planning Commission (Gosplan) and the first secretaryship of the Communist Party in Kashka-Darya Oblast. When he was elevated to become first secretary of the Uzbek Communist Party in June 1989, his supporters proclaimed that this was a positive step for the republic, maintaining that Karimov, more than just an *apparatchik*, was a competent professional economist.

Indeed, Karimov deserves much credit for his early actions. Where his predecessors in office had been little more than toadies to Moscow, he provided energetic leadership in the struggle to weaken the central grip on Uzbekistan. He succeeded in obtaining a reduction in the cotton-delivery quota, the *goszakaz*, imposed on Uzbekistan. This enabled him to increase the amount of land allocated for peasants' private plots. He also managed to bargain with the Soviet military for some concessions relative to use of recruits from Uzbekistan, who had been complaining of mistreatment by Russians and other non-Uzbek nationalities with whom they were required to serve in other parts of the Soviet Union. Both before and after independence, he was energetic in promoting direct trading links between Uzbekistan and other countries. (Karimov has a personal tie with the United States, where his daughter lives as the wife of an Uzbek-American whose father owns an electronics store on New York's Fifth Avenue.)

In presidential elections held on December 29, 1991, Karimov won 86 percent of the popular vote against his sole opponent, the respected poet Muhammad Salih, who ran on behalf of the small Erk (Free) Party. His victory was somewhat sullied by the fact that media coverage of the electoral campaign was heavily slanted in his favor and that the two parties with the largest popular followings, the Birlik (Unity) movement and the Islamic Renaissance Party, were prevented by the authorities from fielding candidates.

Since independence, Karimov has headed the National Democratic Party, a renamed version of the Uzbek Communist Party, which apparently differs little in style and composition from its predecessor. In this he differs from his colleague in neighboring Kazakhstan, President Nursultan Nazarbaev, who has steadfastly refused to associate with the renamed Communist Party in his republic, now known as the Socialist Party.

Karimov's victory was further tarnished less than two weeks after his inauguration by an outbreak of student rioting, apparently caused by price increases. In dealing with the disturbance, the government received support from both Birlik and Erk, an indication that the general fear of street violence in Uzbekistan was able to cut across party lines.

In the months following his inauguration, there were signs that the burdens of office were becoming too great for Karimov. Even those who had been his supporters claimed that he was increasingly isolated from reality. In Tashkent he ruled through the Presidential Council, a body of some 150 staff members each of whom is said to report directly him. Regionally, presidential power in each *vilayat* (corresponding to the *oblasts* of the Soviet period) was wielded by a *hakim*, who also reported directly to Karimov.

This rigid system of many spokes radiating from a single hub called into question Karimov's ability to deal effectively with the many issues that he had taken into his own hands. It also provided little opportunity for political participation by lower echelons. In particular, it seems to have paralyzed efforts to deal with the economic crisis. Preferring to be "his own economist," Karimov refused to appoint an economic council or to delegate problems to advisors.

ECONOMIC AND ENVIRONMENTAL CHALLENGES

Today's economic problems are rooted in the history of Russian and Soviet rule. Not long after the tsarist conquest of the region in the last century, cotton raising was sharply increased by Russian entrepreneurs. To make this possible, the irrigation network was hastily expanded, often—due to the Russians' ignorance of the terrain and local conditions—with flooding and the creation of swampy wastelands. Institution of a credit system of financing crops resulted, in bad years, in peasants becoming impoverished and losing their land.

The Soviet period saw the creation of Uzbekistan for the first time as a discrete geographic and political entity, when the former tsarist province of Turkestan was carved into separate Soviet republics. The new republic of Uzbekistan soon bore the brunt of Stalin's drive to make the Soviet Union self-sufficient in cotton. As a result, its development in other areas was stunted. To be sure, its industrial base grew during World War II when whole factories were evacuated from European parts of the Soviet Union, but these brought with them their own personnel and existed throughout the Soviet period largely as foreign enclaves. Indigenous industrial labor was essentially limited to use for primary processing of cotton and other raw materials. Moscow resisted allocation of investment funds for development of local industry. All of this impeded creation of a skilled Asian labor force in the republic, for which it is today paying the price, exacerbated by the brain drain created by the outmigration of non-Uzbeks.

The 1960s saw the beginning of a further acute expansion of cotton production, as central planners, led after 1964 by Leonid Brezhnev, attempted not only to satisfy growing industrial and military demand for that crop by the Soviet economy but also to use cotton exports to other countries as a source of hard-currency reserves for Moscow. For Uzbekistan, the results of this policy of "monoculture," the epithet applied by Uzbek nationalists, were disastrous.

First, there was severe environmental damage. Indiscriminate use of toxic chemicals (fertilizers, herbicides, pesticides) polluted land and water resources over large areas. It is reported that today less than half the population of Uzbekistan has access to safe drinking water. As a result, there has been a sharp increase in mortality in some areas, particularly among infants, to the point where mothers have been urged not to nurse their babies so as not to pass on the toxicity of their own bodies.

In addition, diversion of water to irrigation has reduced the flow of mighty rivers to little more than a trickle. The most spectacular consequence has been drying of the Aral Sea, once the world's fourth largest inland body of water. This has created a new desert on the former seabed whose salt-laden dust is carried by wind erosion to points as far distant as the Arctic Circle, threatening arable land with contamination. Perhaps even more serious is the impact on climate: Reduction of the sea's moderating effect has led to colder winters and a shorter growing season, as well as a reported decrease in rain- and snowfall in the Pamir Mountains to the east, which feed the river system, further contributing to the loss of flow.

The direct economic impact of the cotton monoculture was no less disastrous. Production of other crops, such as fruits and vegetables that once grew abundantly in the region, was curtailed to make way for cotton. Trees were cut down for the same purpose, depriving the land of windbreaks and rural workers of shady refuges from the hot Central Asian sun at the edge of fields.

The stinginess of Moscow's investment policies was based on the principle of "socialist division of labor," a mask for a classic colonial cycle of ruthless exploitation of one nation by another. Uzbekistan and other Central Asian republics were required to deliver quotas of raw materials set by central planners at prices set by the same planners. In the absence of their own industry, the republics were forced to buy manufactures from other parts of the Soviet Union, mainly Russia, also at prices set by the central planners. In the case of cotton, this meant that bales were shipped to Russian textile centers such as Ivanovo, converted into shirts and other products, and then sold back to the Central Asians at state prices. The "subsidies" granted by the center to the republics, supposedly to alleviate the deficits of their economies, tempered but fell far short of offsetting such manipulations. Now that the central economy's stranglehold on the former Soviet republics has been broken, they are able to offer their raw materials at realistic world prices. In some cases, as with petroleum products from Turkmenistan, this has meant diversion of output from former Soviet buyers to foreign customers who pay world prices. Following independence, Uzbekistan withheld cotton from Russia at the old ruble prices until the latter, driven by unemployment in its textile mills, agreed to barter fuel in return. Cotton exports are controlled by the government.

Karimov has offered a new approach to economic problems by promising to lead Uzbekistan in the transition to a market economy. At the same time, he has opposed privatization of land and water resources for agriculture on largely practical grounds, citing the difficulty of insuring an equitable distribution. In many cases, larger agricultural and industrial enterprises are still in the hands of the same *nomenklatura* managers who controlled them in the Soviet era. On the other hand, smaller enterprises are responding energetically to improved incentives. In general, the recent influx of foreign businessmen and specialists is exposing the economy to new influences that are often critical of the existing way of doing things. A Swiss engineer assigned to install equipment at a textile enterprise with 15,000 employees in Bukhara told me: "Until they break up this plant and reorganize it with better supervision, even Swiss equipment won't help them."

Breakdown of trade with other Soviet republics has exacerbated shortages of manufactured goods and increased the need for Uzbekistan to develop its own industrial base, at least for those goods that cannot be obtained from new sources of supply. The most pressing reason for development, however, is to create jobs for Uzbekistan's millions of unemployed, most of them young and restless.

On the positive side, if one compares the economic situation today with the state of affairs under Soviet rule, it is possible to discern definite signs of progress. Yet, as Karimov himself has acknowledged, Uzbekistan is running out of time in the face of an increasingly impatient population that, with one of the highest birth rates in the world, is producing new mouths to feed and new bodies to house and clothe at the rate of half a million per year.

In the face of mounting unrest, the influence of Islam in this traditionally Muslim region may be crucial.

THE ROLE OF ISLAM

The Central Asian oases became an integral part of the Islamic religious and cultural world in the century of the Prophet Muhammad, the seventh of the Christian era, when Arab military forces overran the region. After that, Central Asian philosophers and scientists made lasting contributions to Islamic civilization. Sufi orders founded by Central Asians, the Yasawiya and the Naqshbandi, are of major importance today throughout Islam. Around the beginning of the sixteenth century, two developments combined to reduce the territory's contact with other Muslim countries. The great caravan routes fell into decline with the rise of sea travel around the Cape of Good Hope. At about the same time, the ruling dynasty of neighboring Iran adopted the Shia branch of Islam, erecting a religious and political barrier as Central Asia remained Sunni.

Until the second half of the nineteenth century, when Russia finally conquered the region, Central Asia was sheltered from the currents of European colonialism that affected much of the Muslim world. It was thus cut off from modern scientific and technical progress, but to many Muslims this enhanced the purity and sanctity of the Islamic doctrine preached in its mosques and madrasahs.

Russian rule and the building of railroads with their accompanying telegraph lines opened the region not only to Russia but to other parts of the Islamic world. Among young Muslim intellectuals of the Russian Empire, the influence of the Young Turks of the Ottoman Empire began to spread, giving birth to a modernizing movement, especially in education, that also took root in Central Asia.

After 1917, the new Soviet regime profoundly affected Central Asia. At first the Bolsheviks, who were intent on creating new elites to support them but lacked revolutionary adherents among the indigenous population, wooed local intellectuals, admitting large numbers to the Communist Party without careful screening of their views. As a result, the Turkistan Communist Party (as it was called before the 1925 breakup into individual republics) became infiltrated with Muslim believers who sought to use the new regime for their own nationalist agenda. In 1923, a Moscow-inspired campaign against religion had to be halted when it encountered protests from local party members. It was only after Stalin had consolidated his power five years later that he moved resolutely against Islam. Mullahs were arrested and killed, mosques were destroyed or converted to other purposes (many as "museums of atheism"), mass burnings of women's veils—often stripped violently from the head of the wearer—

were held, "atheist indoctrination" became compulsory in educational curricula, and religious observance was driven underground.

World War II brought a temporary abatement of the Soviet campaign
against religions, including Islam. The war brought about creation by the
Soviet authorities of a "Muslim spiritual directorate" headed by a mufti in
Tashkent with jurisdiction throughout Central Asia and Kazakhstan. If
this was a form of grudging recognition of the importance to people of
religion, it also represented an attempt to create a mechanism through
which the regime could channel and control religious activity, while providing a docile institution to advance Soviet interests in dealing with foreign Muslims. Succeeding decades saw an intricate four-partner dance
involving the Soviet authorities, the mufti and his official clergy, the mass
of Muslim believers, and foreign Muslim leaders who were often invited
to Central Asia in an attempt to improve the Soviet standing in Muslim
countries. This period was also characterized by periodic drives to perse-
cute believers who did not conform to the framework and strictures of
"official" Islam.

Through decades of Communist persecution, under Stalin and continuing after his death, Central Asians quietly defied the regime in order to
cling to Islamic observance. Sociological studies published in the relatively permissive climate of Brezhnev's later period, when the Soviet
leader was already in his dotage and the now-controversial Uzbek party
leader, the late Sharaf Rashidov, had succeeded in softening some of the
harsher aspects of Soviet rule, documented an astonishing persistence of
both belief and practice. This was especially true of Islamic lifestyle rituals
(*sunnat, nikah, janaza*). Fasting and feasting were also widespread.
Perestroika did not bring immediate relief to religious believers. As recently
as 1986, Gorbachev, in a speech in Tashkent, fulminated against local
Communist Party members who were taking part in religious services.
One of the strengths of Islam during this period was that, in the minds of
Uzbeks and other Central Asians, even nonbelievers, it had become associated with national identity and the struggle for ethnic survival against
assimilation and acculturation. Sayings such as "If you're not circumcised,
you're not an Uzbek" were commonplace.

Events of recent years have shown that, while Islam has been an effective
standard-bearer against rule by a foreign Communist regime, in other con-
texts there are limits to its integrative function for Muslim society in Central
Asia. In June 1989, Uzbek and Tajik youths went on the rampage against
fellow Muslims, Meskhetian Turks in the Ferghana Valley, with many
deaths and much destruction. The same lesson was brought home in the

summer of 1990 by bloody riots, also in the Ferghana Valley, between Uzbeks and Kyrgyz, both traditionally Muslim peoples. (The densely populated Ferghana Valley is the scene of severe unemployment and environmental problems; it is also said to be the heartland of Islamic "fundamentalism" in the republic. It was in the Ferghana city of Namangan that Islamic dissidents seized the regional headquarters of the former Communist Party.) Today the stability of Uzbekistan is threatened by tensions between the government and still another Muslim nationality, the large Tajik population centered in the ancient cities of Samarkand and Bukhara.

Islam in Uzbekistan is split along more than ethnic lines. The postindependence government, while more tolerant of religion than its Soviet predecessor, continues the attempt to use the official Islamic establishment as a means of controlling believers. The mufti of Tashkent, Muhammad Mama Yusuf, has regularly spoken out against organized political activity by Muslims, including efforts by the Islamic Renaissance Party to win recognition and participate in the political process. This may earn him the gratitude of Uzbeks who fear a "fundamentalist" Islamization of public life, but it has undermined his popularity with other Muslims. There have been at least two attempts to unseat him, once on the allegation that he had profited dishonestly from the sale of Qurans donated by Saudi Arabia. Each time he clung to his office, with the evident support of the civil authorities.

The split between Islamic factions provides fertile ground for further destabilization of a domestic situation already threatened by popular unrest over unsolved economic and social problems. This is obviously a major worry for the government: President Karimov has spoken openly of his fear that violence generated by a similar split in neighboring Tajikistan may spread to his republic. (In this, he may see a parallel between his own situation and the plight of Tajikistan's president Rahman Nabiev, another authoritarian former Communist leader.)

Should the potential of instability in Uzbekistan be of concern to the outside world?

TIES WITH AUTHORITARIAN ELEMENTS IN RUSSIA

Such attention as Uzbekistan and the other Central Asian republics have received from abroad since becoming independent has largely focused, echoing concerns of the local elites that tend to be played up and magnified in the Moscow press, on the perceived threat of vulnerability to a tide of Islamic "fundamentalism" advancing from the south. In the minds of some observers this has given birth to a new "domino theory" according to which the republics might, one by one, come under Iranian domination.

We have examined above the reasons why such theories appear to lack credibility for the near term.

In this writer's opinion, a more credible threat arises from the north. If authoritarian elements in Russia mount a successful challenge to the democratic, reformist elements in the leadership there, they may well seek to re-extend Moscow's domination over former parts of the Soviet Union. Such efforts could receive support in particular from Russian nationalists who have all along regarded Soviet territory as a legitimate extension of the Russian Empire, from "revanchist" elements of the former Soviet military who seek to restore past power and glory, and from members of the military-industrial complex, particularly those managers who have been chafing at the need to compete on the world market for raw materials from the former Soviet republics, without the artificial shelter afforded by the arbitrary and exploitative pricing structure of the old central planning system.

Regression by Moscow to something approaching the old system might actually be welcomed by those Central Asian leaders who began their careers as Communist *apparatchiki* and who have lacked the vision and courage to use independence to reform their economies and introduce greater democracy. Because of their inaction, they are faced with an accumulation of unsolved problems that are generating growing popular dissent, threatening their own status. A helping hand from authoritarians in Moscow may seem the lesser of two evils, easier to accept even with the attendant disadvantage of resubordination to the center than the alternative of political extinction at the hands of their own citizens. It would take the submission of only one of the major republics, perhaps Uzbekistan, to create a bandwagon effect in which even the more liberal leaders might feel constrained to go along.

Just as in the past preoccupation with Moscow and central Soviet politics diverted the attention of observers from the rising force of nationalism in the republics and its potential to break up the Soviet Union, one should not let today's fascination with Islamic fundamentalism cause blindness to the possibility of a reconstitution of a new Russian-led imperialism, with the acquiescence of embattled leaders of the new Central Asian republics.

FUTURE OUTLOOK

Is there hope that Uzbekistan will emerge from its early period of independence as a responsible democratic member of the world community?

Can ideas of political pluralism and social justice prevail against authoritarian currents at home and abroad? Clearly, the transition to democratic rule will have to be a slow and painful one, given the lack of democratic elements in the republic's present political life. To the extent that there is any hope at all of an eventual democratic evolution, it rests with Uzbekistan's native elites, the well-educated members of professions in the arts and sciences who in the Soviet period struggled successfully against great odds to advance the cause of Uzbek autonomy.

This class, while lacking practical experience with democratic ways, has at least the sophistication to understand the role of freedom in modern society. Its ability to exert a positive influence on the political evolution of Uzbekistan under present conditions will depend largely on internal factors, such as its own cohesiveness and ability to united around common goals. At the same time, it can derive strength from whatever practical and moral support may be available to it from well-wishers in other countries.

N·O·T·E·S

1. See James Critchlow, *Nationalism in Uzbekistan: A Soviet Republic's Road to Sovereignty* (Boulder, CO: Westview Press, 1991), pp. 191-97.

2. Ibid.

▲ ▽ ▲

14

New Relationships between Central and Southwest Asia and Pakistan's Regional Politics

◆

Hafeez Malik

During the crucial three years (1989-1991) that witnessed the unraveling of the Soviet Union, Pakistan was primarily preoccupied with internal political dynamics. After General Zia died in a plane crash in August 1988, elections were held in November and Benazir Bhutto, leader of the Pakistan's People's Party, became the prime minister. After nearly 20 chaotic months of her centrist government, she was dismissed by President Ghulam Ishaq Khan in the first week of August 1990. An interim government under Ghulam Mustafa Jatoi was installed, which organized new elections. The Islamic Democratic Alliance's (IDI) chief, Mian Muhammad Nawaz Sharif, was elected prime minister in November 1990.

On February 15, 1989, ten weeks after the Bhutto government's induction into office, the Soviet Union completed its withdrawal from Afghanistan, according to the Geneva Accords, which had been negotiated by the Zia regime and were signed in April 1988. However, Bhutto had retained Zia's minister of foreign affairs as a watchdog of Pakistan's policy toward Afghanistan. Maintenance of close ties with the United States was the primary focus of Bhutto's foreign policy. Actually, during Zia's 11-year rule, Pakistan's foreign policy toward the Soviet Union was devoted exclusively to achieving a rollback of Soviet power from Afghanistan with the support of the United States, China, and Saudi Arabia. Consequently, Pakistan lost touch with the internal dynamics of Soviet politics, especially in the former Soviet Central Asia.

Within Pakistan's Ministry of Foreign Affairs, no more than one or two diplomats know the Russian language or can claim to have a credible level of expertise on the former Soviet Union. Until 1991 Pakistan did not maintain even a single consulate general in Central Asia. No Pakistani diplomat has been meaningfully exposed to the cultural, religious, and political environments of the Central Asian republics; not a single Pakistani diplomat has any proficiency in any variety of the Turkic languages spoken in five out of six Muslim republics. The lack of knowledge and absence of touch with Central Asia in Pakistan's Foreign Office is appalling. Consequently, during the crucial three years from 1989 to 1991, there was no planning or even constructive thinking about the disintegration of the Soviet Union or the rise of independent and sovereign states in Central Asia. In the Foreign Office, a mere suspicion of having interest or a positive attitude toward the Soviet Union or a suspicion of being less pro-American could have spelled disaster for Pakistani diplomats' careers.

In November 1990, when the Nawaz Sharif government came to power, it immediately confronted the Gulf crisis and the U.S.-led war against Iraqi aggression in Kuwait. After the start of hostilities on January 15, 1991, the public opinion split three ways: (1) the Pakistan Peoples Party (PPP) and Jamat'-i Islami, which has been traditionally close to Saudi Arabia, led protest marches against the United States and the Nawaz Sharif government; (2) Pakistan's military distanced itself from the prime minister because the United States had suspended aid in October over the issue of Pakistan's nuclear program; (3) Prime Minister Sharif then undertook an unsuccessful tour of several states in the Middle East in order to demonstrate that his government, while retaining loyalty to the United States, was also interested in preventing war between Iraq and the United States.

Once the cease-fire took place in Iraq, Pakistan, as usual, became engrossed with the issues of the Afghan conflict: how to achieve military or negotiated victory for the Mujahideen over the Moscow-installed government in Kabul and the repatriation of Afghan refugees. U.S. pressures on Pakistan also increased on the nuclear issue, and fears began to grow in Pakistan that the United States, now the only superpower of the contemporary state system, might undertake destructive and punitive actions against its nuclear installations. Against this background, on June 6, 1991, Sharif finally gave a fairly extensive address on foreign policy to the National Defense College in Rawalpindi. He professed Pakistan's friendship with China, Japan, the Arab states, Iran and Turkey, and states in the Asia-Pacific Region. Finally, he discussed relations with the United

States, with which Pakistan has "a history of friendship going back to the 1950s." Sharif then revealed the heart of his foreign policy initiative—a proposal to the United States, the Soviet Union, and China, to help broker a nuclear nonproliferation pact between Pakistan and neighboring India.[1]

In this speech, Sharif mentioned the Soviet Union only this one time. From June 6 to August 19, 1991, when the coup attempt was aborted in Moscow, the Nawaz Sharif government did not seem overtly concerned about the Soviet Union. The Foreign Office was led by a competent secretary general, who was assigned the status of minister of state. Moreover, on September 11, a member of the National Assembly, Mohammad Siddiq Khan Kanju, was also designated minister of state, while Nawaz Sharif retained the ministry of Foreign Affairs under his personal control. However, no foreign policy initiative, especially in regard to the highly destabilized and fast-splintering Soviet Union, surfaced. Critics began to make uncharitable comments about Sharif's "lack of interest" in foreign affairs and absence of "understanding of anything outside of Model Town, Lahore."[2]

While the Sharif government was slow to comprehend the political dynamics in the Soviet Union and the consequences of its disintegration to Pakistan's security, informed public opinion and the print media reflected profound sensitivity to the developments in Central Asia. Also, Pakistan's general headquarters (GHQ), under chief of the Army General Staff General Aslam Beg, established a "cell" to watch closely the developments in Central Asia. General Beg retired on August 17, 1991, but some of the geopolitical ideas that he had inspired in Islamabad percolated gradually into the press and the informed segments of Pakistani society.

During the last 45 years, both the United States and the Soviet Union attached a great deal of importance to Pakistan's geostrategic location. It adjoins the Xinjiang province of China, is separated from the former Soviet Tajikistan by a portion of the Wakhan Corridor 11 miles wide and 31 miles long, and shares common borders with Afghanistan, Iran, and India. Also, Pakistan's Karachi and Gawader ports provide a maritime outlet to the Arabian/Persian Gulf states. However, the Gulf war and the collapse of the Soviet Union have convinced Pakistani policymakers that its geostrategic importance has been diminished in American eyes. Concomitantly, however, this sense of loss is made up by the realization that Pakistan's significance for the Central Asian republics has increased very greatly. Pakistanis started to speculate that their natural habitat includes Turkey, Iran, Afghanistan, and the Central Asian republics.

PROJECTION OF FUTURE RELATIONSHIPS

Three views, spotlighting the future of Pakistan's place in the complex of Southwest and Central Asian states, have emerged: (1) the so-called Beg doctrine; (2) an exceptionally imaginative paradigm of commonwealth consisting of the countries of Southwest and Central Asia; and (3) the Nawaz Sharif government's reluctant and hesitant pragmatic policy, which has followed informed public opinion rather than offering a resourceful and cohesive foreign policy endeavoring to mold new dynamics in this region.

The Beg Doctrine

General Beg's perception of the U.S. security policy and its war to disgorge Kuwait from Iraq's jaw was less than benign. Also, he miscalculated U.S. military capability in fighting a short war to victory against Saddam Hussein. He saw another Vietnam for America developing on the arid lands of Iraq. On January 24, 1991, he presented an anti-American thesis to senior army officers, condemning the allied invasion of Iraq; General Aslam's position conflicted with Prime Minister Sharif's essentially pro-American policy and earned him the charge of a new scheming Bonaparte.

The media embellished General Beg's anti-American pronouncements and added several strands to it, popularizing it as the Beg doctrine. This so-called doctrine postulated rampant anti-Americanism, the revival of a regional cold war necessitating a strategic consensus with "Iran, Afghanistan, China, and even the Central Asian state."[3] When the August 19, 1991, coup in Moscow was aborted, the Beg doctrine was discredited. Gorbachev lost his grip on the Soviet Union, which began to unravel swiftly, and the United States emerged as the only superpower on the horizon.

However, the positive side of the Moscow coup for Pakistan was the crippling of the KGB, the Communist Party of the Soviet Union (CPSU), the Soviet military, the three pillars of support to India, and the Moscow-installed government in Kabul. These collateral benefits are not insignificant for Pakistan's security. Also, in September 1991 the United States and Russia agreed to cut off arms supplies to the Kabul government and the Mujahideen as of January 1, 1992.[4] Subsequently, the Russians withdrew their demand for a role for President Najibullah and also admitted culpability for their illegal, as well as immoral, invasion of Afghanistan. The conflict in Afghanistan, however, still continues.

The decline of the Soviet Union is a serious blow to India's industrial development, international trade with the former Soviet Union on exceptionally favorable terms, and military preparedness. The Soviet Union was India's enthusiastic partner in dominating the Indian Ocean to the detriment of Pakistan's security. For nearly 35 years, India had anchored its foreign and security policy in Moscow; now it finds itself groping for a new sense of direction. India also looked in the direction of Central Asia, hoping to emerge as a major trading partner with these Muslim republics.

A Paradigm of Commonwealth of Southwest and Central Asian States

This paradigm is projected by the Pakistan Central Asia Friendship Society, which draws to its forum some outstanding academics, retired military officers, and businessmen. This society has conducted several workshops at Peshawar and Islamabad in cooperation with the Center of Central Asian Civilizations of the Quaid-i-Azam University at Islamabad and the Area Study Center of Peshawar University.

The society's futuristic planning is based on certain reasonable assumptions and builds a political structure on the basis of hard economic realities confronting Pakistan, Iran, and the Central Asian states: (1) the world economy is visualized as multipolar, and each pole is perceived to be "protective and exclusionary"; (2) one of the poles is "fortress Europe" or the European Economic Community (EEC), which like a magnet is drawing the East European countries. In Gorbachev's political language this is the European space to which Russia would want to belong, after shedding its Eurasian character; (3) another economic pole, more likely to be exclusionary, is the collection of 12 Pacific Rim states, which by the end of the twentieth century is "expected to control half of all international trade"; and finally, (4) the Gulf Cooperative Council (GCC) under the "protective" wings of Saudi Arabia, lacking in military capability, but devoted to developing a sub-Arab space in the Gulf region. The GCC countries have abolished visa requirements for each others' citizens and recognize diverse licensing practices. This mini-Arab world is not expected to "accept Pakistan—in the basic essential of free movement of peoples, money and goods."

What are Pakistan's options? The society's answer is to carve out a new regional market similar to the European Economic Community (EEC) or Commonwealth, consisting of six Central Asian states: Iran, Afghanistan, Kashmir, Pakistan, and China's province of Xinjiang. The concept is difficult to implement, but not outlandish. It calls for rereading of history. Before the British and Russian imperialisms erected iron curtains around these states in the nineteenth century, trade among them flourished, exchange of scholars and literary accomplishments was extensive, and the transfer of technical know-how was not restrained.

Evidently, the society's strategic planners are aware of the "dangers" of this non-Arab Pan-Islamic orientation. The West might equate it with militant Islam or Islamic fundamentalism. Extremism in the name of religion might lead the West, including Russia, to replace the old containment of communism with the policy of "the containment of Islam." The emphasis, therefore, in the society's formulations is on the Islamic modernism of Sir Sayyid Ahmad Khan (1817-1898) and poet-philosopher Dr. Muhammad Iqbal (1877-1938). This commonwealth is to be "a tolerant modern alliance of ethnic brotherly Muslim peoples." Moreover, the society perceives the current Islamic resurgence in Central Asia not as the revival of Islamic fundamentalism, but clearly as "ethnocultural movements" spawned by "economic self-interest." Quite accurately, the society also recognizes the Islamic resurgence among former autonomous socialist republics of Tatarstan, Chechen-Ingushtia, Daghestan, and Kabardino-Balkar, which are located in the Russian Federation.

Why is Turkey left out of this paradigm, despite its ethnic and linguistic affinity with Central Asia and territorial contiguity, like Iran with the Republic of Azerbaijan? The society assesses Turkey's admission to the EEC as "imminent." Historically, this has been the Republic of Turkey's secular ambition, while its Turkic heritage should have drawn it toward Central Asia. Turkey's model of a secular "Muslim polity" has an attraction for some of the Communist-turned-nationalist leaders of Central Asian republics, and Turkey has begun to respond to them positively. Turkey is a powerful regional state and cannot be so lightly read out.

The inclusion of Xinjiang in the proposed commonwealth is not only an intriguing idea but a practical necessity, if the transportation arteries are to remain open between Central Asia and Pakistan. A network of railroads must be established from the Caspian Sea to Xinjiang, and from there to Karachi; Baluchistan and Afghanistan must be connected with Central Asia. In view of Pakistan's cooperative relations with China, Xinjiang may remain under Chinese sovereignty, yet Beijing, to further its own national interest, may allow it to be an active member of the proposed commonwealth. Kashgar in Xinjiang would then become a hub, where trade routes from Gilgit and Hunza in Pakistan, from the Wakhan Corridor in Afghanistan, and from Central Asia converge.[5]

Needless to say, Afghanistan and Xinjiang are essential links in the proposed commonwealth. Afghanistan's ethnic, historical and political relations with Pakistan are too well known, although from 1947 to 1979 successive Afghan governments under the influence of the Soviet Union and India pursued antagonistic irredentist policies that came to be known as the demand for Pashtunistan. Thanks to the Soviet invasion of Afghanistan and India's support for the Soviet-installed regimes in Kabul, the Pashtunistan problem has been set aside. A new Afghan government, which would emerge as a consequence of settlement with the Mujahideen, is expected to maintain fraternal and cooperative relations with Pakistan, which would be in harmony with the Mujahideen's Islamic ethos.

However, Xinjiang's Islamic-national aspirations need to be appreciated. The Muslim-Turkic peoples of Xinjiang (called until recently Sinkiang, the new province) have more in common ethnically and linguistically with the Turkic Central Asians than with the Han Chinese. Table 14.1 presents their current demographic picture.

TABLE 14.1

1990 Location	Turkic-Muslim Census	Geographic Ethnic Group
1. Uighur	7,214,431	Xinjiang (1-5)
2. Kazakh	1,111,718	2-5 of column one have their
3. Kirghis	141,549	republics in Central Asia. Uigurs
4. Uzbek	14,502	are also scattered in Central
5. Tatar	4,873	Asian Republics.
TOTAL	**8,487,073**	

Source: State Statistical Bureau, Beijing Review 52 (1990): 30.

Although made a province of China in 1884, Xinjiang had been penetrated by China since the 1750s, much like the Russian expansion in Central Asia. Finally, the two imperial powers stabilized their conquests by virtue of the Treaty of Torbagatai (1864), and the Treaty of St. Petersburg (1881). Since the Chinese annexation of Xinjiang, several Muslim uprisings erupted against the Chinese overlordship. The Khanate of Kokand (now in Uzbekistan) was the main source of support for the rebels.[6]

In the mid-nineteenth century, the rebellion of Muhammad Yaqub Beg, who proclaimed himself Khan of Eastern Turkistan in 1869, had succeeded in "winning some degree of British and Turkish recognition of his position as an independent ruler during 1873-4."[7] However, the latest rebellion erupted in November 1944 near the Sino-Soviet border in the Ili Valley. The Muslims declared the establishment of Eastern Turkistan Republic (ETR) to oust all Chinese from Turkistan, which the Chinese then called Sinkiang. The ERT's government proclaimed its foreign policy program on July 15, 1946; it aimed to "improve relations with all Muslim nations (including the Central Asian Republics) on the basis of commonly shared religious belief and culture."[8] Finally, when the Chinese Red Army entered Urumqi, the capital of Xinjiang, in October 1949, the ERT ceased to exist.

However, Xinjiang has not been completely pacified or reconciled to the Chinese overlordship. In April 1990 unrest erupted again "around the legendary Silk Road city of Kashgar, not far from the border with Afghanistan and the [former] Soviet Union"[9]—that is, along the border with Tajikistan. This is precisely the area where the Eastern Turkistan Republic had originated and had the most grass-roots support from 1944 to 1949. This time the Chinese government banned all tourists and foreign correspondents from Xinjiang for several months in 1990. In mid-September 1990, China's Xinjiang Administration promulgated draconian regulations forbidding Muslim *ulama* (religious teachers) to meet foreigners or teach in the mosques the history of *jihad* (holy war). The administration blamed the Islamic Party of East Turkistan for inciting "counter-revolutionary armed rebellion" in Xinjiang. The ban included any chance encounter that a Xinjiang *alim* might have with Afghans, Pakistanis, or Muslim natives of the Central Asian Republics, who frequently visit Xinjiang.

The Turkic-Muslim population in Xinjiang not only suffered religious persecution under the Mao Zedong regime, but had to adopt Latin script, discarding historically established Arabic script for their language, while the Han Chinese retained their own traditional Chinese script.[11] Chinese religious and cultural policy has not been better than the Soviet repression in Central Asia, and the consequences of these policies have been very similar: Both led to Islamic resurgence and rousing aspirations for political independence.

However, Sino-Pakistani relations since the Communist takeover in Beijing have progressed into strategic collaboration, especially after the Sino-Indian border war of 1962. This is symbolized by the 774 km-long Kara Kuram Highway, which links Xinjiang with Islamabad through Hunza and Gilgit. Jointly conceived and funded by China and Pakistan in 1968, its construction was completed in 1982. Pakistan's strategic artery of transportation has thus been connected to Kashgar and Urumgi, and through this route to Tajikistan, Kirghistan, and Kazakhstan.

The Pakistan Central Asian Friendship Society's proposal to connect Xinjiang to Peshawar with a railroad system is practically impossible to achieve in view of the mountainous terrain of Gilgit and Hunza through which the railroad must pass. A much more feasible and alternative link would be an all-weather highway linking Chitral in Pakistan to Tajikistan through the border area of the Wakhan Corridor. This, however, must await the positive decision of the new Islamic-national government in Kabul.

The society has offered several proposals to the proposed commonwealth countries; they can be implemented if Turkey, Iran, Afghanistan,

Xinjiang, Pakistan, and the Central Asian republics can coordinate their diplomacy and economic policy. These proposals include: (1) rail and air links; (2) tourism; (3) free movement of goods; (4) joint programs in health, narcotics control, and environmental protection; (5) exchange of scholars and university students; (6) exchange of technologies; (7) mutual investment and banking; (8) cooperation in television and radio programming; (9) establishment of telecommunications; (10) joint exploration of gas and oil; (11) joint development of power grids; and, last but not least, (12) eliminating of visas to facilitate mobility.[12]

HISTORICAL LANDSCAPE OF REGIONAL PLANNING

The Pakistan Central Asia Friendship Society's proposed commonwealth did not grow out of intellectual vacuum; its importance, however, lies in its grass-roots origin and its attention to the emerging problems of Central Asia along with those of Iran, Afghanistan, and Pakistan. Clearly, this proposal is free from the Cold War syndrome. However, India has loomed very large in its formulations. In the 1950s and the 1970s, the United States and Iran toyed with the proposals of Afghanistan-Pakistan (Con)Federation, and the Shah of Iran's scheme for a common market.

Afghanistan-Pakistan (Con)Federation

From 1953 to 1954, the strong proponents of confederation or federation between the two countries were the former U.S. Vice President Richard Nixon and Chairman of the Joint Chiefs of Staff Admiral Radford. After visiting Pakistan and Afghanistan in December 1953, Nixon was firmly convinced of Pakistan's geostrategic significance in Southwest Asia and was determined, like President Eisenhower and Secretary of State John Foster Dulles, to keep Afghanistan out of the Soviet orbit. Primacy, however, was attached to Pakistan as a linchpin state in the containment of the Soviet Union. India's firmly aligned foreign policy was rightly perceived as nonsupportive of the U.S. strategy. Dulles was a fervent supporter of Pakistan, but was less enthusiastic about the prospects of Afghanistan-Pakistan federation. Moreover, Washington believed that if the Soviet Union invaded Iran, Pakistan would be drawn into general war. Ostensibly neutral, Pakistan's neutralism lacked "the doctrinaire quality of India."

However, Afghanistan's antagonistic policy toward Pakistan, encouraged by India, was problematic for the U.S. policy of containment. The

U.S. National Security Council proposed in February 1954 that the United States must make it quite clear to Afghanistan that it discouraged Afghanistan's Pashtunistan claims against Pakistan and that it must not expect U.S. military assistance. Finally, in order to find a stable solution to the Afghan-Pakistan tensions, the National Security Council at its 228th meeting on December 9, 1954, thoroughly discussed the possibility of a federation or confederation between Afghanistan and Pakistan.

Taking the lead in these discussions, the chairman of the Joint Chiefs of Staff, Admiral Radford, emphasized the prospects of a federation between Afghanistan and Pakistan. There was a real chance that "such federation would come about, and it would be a great stroke from the U.S. point of view." Radford saw two major obstacles: the Afghan royal family's opposition and Indian propaganda. Otherwise, he believed, the Afghan people "would be inclined to favor confederation." Enthusiastically supporting Radford, Vice President Nixon saw "the opposition to federation concentrated in the small oligarchy which ran Afghanistan." In Nixon's judgment "there were many more considerations that brought Afghanistan and Pakistan together than divided them." To Nixon, Islam was "a potential bond" in addition to other geostratic considerations. Known for his brinkmanship, Dulles was cautiously restrained in his support of (con)federation or aid to Afghanistan. "The Soviets were inclined to look on Afghanistan much as the United States did on Guatemala." The statement summed up the limitations of U.S.-Soviet confrontation in the Cold War.

With these confabulations in the background, firm policy guidelines were established: the United States should (1) if the Afghan and Pakistan governments demonstrated "a convincing mutual desire for confederation," encourage and assist its realization; (2) help to create favorable conditions for the settlement of the Pashtunistan dispute; (3) provide assistance for Afghanistan for those projects that would tend to strengthen its ties with Pakistan; (4) give military assistance to Afghanistan "through Pakistan if expedient"; and finally, (5) if the Soviet Union attacked Afghanistan overtly, attempt "to obtain prompt withdrawal of Soviet forces" and further action through the United Nations."[13]

Needless to say, neither Afghanistan nor Pakistan reflected any genuine desire for a (con)federation between the two neighboring states, and the plan was abandoned.

Common Market

After the Arab-Israeli War of 1973, when petro-dollars began to flow abundantly into Iran's treasury, the Shah became not only the gendarme for the Gulf, but also extended his interest for the security of the Indian Ocean right up to Australia. By 1977-78, the Shah projected his common market scheme, which included Afghanistan, Pakistan, and India. In 1972, India had won a Soviet-supported war against Pakistan, and this humiliation still rankled deeply in Pakistan's psyche. This loss had further shaken Pakistan's self-confidence when in July 1977 popularly elected Prime Minister Zulfiqar Bhutto was overthrown in a coup d'etat by General Zia-ul Haq. The Shah of Iran had consequently developed a paternalistic attitude toward Pakistan. The common market, including India, the Shah had reasoned, would encourage greater economic cooperation in the region and indirectly strengthen Pakistan's security.

In pursuit of this policy, the Shah extended several hundred million dollars of project aid to India in 1978. For Pakistan, the Shah offered guarantees to Citibank of New York for a $300 million loan and agreed to a two-year delay in start of the repayment for a $580 million Iranian loan. However, the Shah bluntly told General Zia that if Pakistan expected additional economic assistance, its economic performance had to improve. To wean Afghanistan away from the Soviet Union, the Shah committed almost $2 billion in project aid. While this economic generosity was not unwelcome in Pakistan, the Shah's political approach was most galling. In order to facilitate Iran's import and export trade with India, the Shah wanted both Iran and India to utilize Pakistan's transit facilities. When Pakistan pleaded that its transportation system was inadequate, the Shah offered further financial assistance to upgrade Pakistan's highways and railroads.

In 1978, the military regime of General Zia was quite fearful that at some point in the future "Iran and India might see it in their interest to cooperate to Pakistan's detriment." This assessment was reflected by Ambassador Arthur Hummel of the U.S. Embassy in Islamabad in a confidential telegram (control number 2182) sent to the State Department on February 10, 1978, after the Shah's visit to Pakistan on February 5.[14]

In 1979 when the Pahlavi regime was toppled by the Ayatollah Khomeini's Islamic Republic of Iran, Pakistan's ambassador in Tehran rushed to offer Pakistan's recognition of the government of provisional Prime Minister Mahdi Bazargan. The ambassador stated: "Pakistan viewed its relationship with Iran as fundamentally one of two peoples rather than just one of one government to another."[15] However, the quest for the common market or regional cooperation was postponed for another decade because of the Iran-Iraq War of 1980 to 1988, which was initiated by Saddam Hussein. When in the wake of the aborted coup of August 19, 1991, the Central Asian republics became independent and sovereign, and started to reorient their relations toward Turkey, Iran, Afghanistan, Xinjiang, and Pakistan, political and economic imperatives in these states became the catalyst for new cooperative thinking in this vast region.

FUSIONIST TRENDS IN CENTRAL AND WEST ASIA

Among the Muslim states of Central Asia, the Russian Federation and Southwest Asia fissional forces, as well as fusionist tendencies, are visible in three concentric circles. Probably these dialectical tensions would resolve themselves into a stable pattern of state formations within three to five years. At present only these tendencies can be highlighted, and some efforts can be made to discern their directions.

In Central Asia and within the Russian Federation, two cultural traditions have penetrated deeply: the Turkic and Iranian cultures. The latter is thoroughly reflected in Tajikistan. The third element of Islam provides a thread of religious unity, not only within the former Soviet states, but also with Southwest Asia. The resurgent Islam is put to use for both national self-determination and for regional cooperation. The exclusive and sectarian interpretation of Islam being offered in these states also leads to inter-Muslim and Muslim–non-Muslim conflicts, earning this process the less salutary description of "Islamic fundamentalism." Clearly, the historical forces that have operated within these states, especially the colonial rules that splintered these populations into various ethnic states, cannot be ignored. Ethnic identities are now very much intertwined with territorial identities.

Within the former Soviet Union, two tendencies are visible: Volga-Ural and Caucasian federative planning and Central Asian regional cooperative planning. In Southwest Asia, Turkey, Iran, and Pakistan are endeavoring to revive cooperative, economic, and political programs of the past, while the three states have not coordinated their policies in order to deal with the states of the former Soviet Union.

Saudi Arabia has stepped into this fluid political situation to extend its influence with plentiful dollars and the Wahabi brand of Islam.

However, at the analytical level, an attempt must be made to determine the extent to which the three regional states' cooperative planning is similar, which might lead to the development of a commonwealth of non-Arab Islamic states or lead more closely to the model of the European Economic

Community. Nevertheless, the possibility remains that after some initial enthusiasm for regional cooperation is worn out, these states may follow their own narrow national interests and fall under the sway of powerful and resourceful exogenous states.

Volga-Ural and Caucasian Federative Planning

Twelve autonomous Muslim-Turkic republics are located in these two regions. Unlike the 14 Soviet republics, they were constitutionally barred to exercise the right to secede from the Soviet Union. Five of these autonomous republics (Tatarstan, Bashkirtastan, Udmurtia, Mariya, and Chuvashia) are in the Volga-Ural basin; the other eight autonomous republics, including Daghistan, Chechen-Ingushtia, Kabardino-Balkar, Abkhazia, Adzharia, Karachaya-Cherkessia, Nakhichevan, and Kalmykia are located in the Caucasus.

Nakhichevan is an enclave in Armenia but is under the jurisdiction of Azerbaijan. Abkhazia is under the jurisdiction of Georgia. Nakhichevan has a common 130-km border with Iran.

In 1989-90, when the conflict between Azerbaijan and Armenia over Nogorno-Karabagh was raging, its impact on Nakhichevan was explosive. The Popular Front organized the march on the border post with Iran, and barbed wire separating Nakhichevan from Iran was ripped out and scattered. People demanded that the contact between them and Azerbaijanis in Iran must be restored. Azerbaijan's Popular Front demanded 600 million rubles from the Soviet government as compensation for the land in the frontier region that Azerbaijan could not cultivate for a period of 40 years.[16] Like Nagorno-Karabagh, Nakhichevan was gerrymandered into an autonomous republic, while it was separated from Azerbaijan by interposing the Armenian territory between the two kindred populations. In the future, this territorial juggling would be not only a threat to Armenian boundaries but a constant source of conflict among the three states. For help, both Azerbaijan and Nakhichevan would look to Turkey or Iran.

Another conflict erupted in 1991 in the autonomous Chechen-Ingush Republic (CIR). Conquered by the Russians in the mid-1800s, the area was given autonomous status in 1936 by Stalin, who combined the Chechen with the Ingush population, both Ibero-Caucasians, who professed Sunni-Hanafi Islam. Currently, together they number 1.3 million. On November 2 the CIR declared itself independent.

The events leading to the proclamation of independence reflected profound national grievances against Moscow. The Chechens, who are a majority in the CIR, had been deported to Siberia from the Caucasus by

Stalin during World War II. They were allowed to return only in 1957. After the deportation of the Ingush, their territories were transferred to North Ossetia. The movement for freedom from Moscow was launched by Dzhokhar Dudayev, a former Soviet Air Force general and commander of its unit in Estonia. He was born in 1944 in the mountains of Glanchezhsky District just before his people were evicted from their homes. Clearly, the precedent of the Baltic states' independence and his national persecution were the motivations for his commitment to self-determination.

Economic exploitation of the CIR is an additional negative incentive to separatism. Large quantities of oil are extracted and refined in the CIR, but are consumed elsewhere with no oil royalty accruing to the CIR. Among the CIR's 1.3 million population, more than 200,000 people are unemployed. In some localities the unemployment rate is 80 to 90 percent.[17] An appeal to Islam under these conditions becomes a rallying cry and an urge to reach out to the larger world of Islam; the Russians call this Islamic fundamentalism, Muslim fanaticism, and intolerance of others. The public movements in the CIR, including the Vainakh Democratic Party, the Islamic Path, the Green Movement, and the People's Front have supported CIR nationalism.

Right in character, Russian president Boris Yeltsin attempted to follow Moscow's historical role of suppression and the traditional but well-known policy of dividing Chechen from the Ingush. After the Russian vice president A. Rutskoi's visit to the CIR, the Presidium of the RSFSR Supreme Soviet decided on October 9, 1991, to authorize a Moscow loyalist, B. D. Bakhmadov (chairman of the Provisional Supreme Council), to take necessary steps to "stabilize the situation in the Republic." The Chechen National Congress (CNC) called this act "provocational" and Bakhmadov's appointment "a coup d'état, laying the groundwork for an armed incursion into the Republic."[18]

Defying Moscow, Dzhokar Dudayev held elections in the CIR on October 27, 1991, and was elected president with 85 percent of the vote. Yeltsin responded on November 10 by imposing emergency rule in the CIR and dispatched 600 troops to Grozny, the CIR's capital; but these troops were blocked by nationalist forces at a military airport near Grozny. However, on November 11 the Russian parliament refused to endorse Yeltsin's order imposing emergency rule.

The developments within the CIR from October to November 11 reveal the ethnic contradictions between the Turkic-Muslim populations and their relations with Moscow.

The Ingush movement openly expressed dissatisfaction with Dudayev's tough policy and favored the preservation of the CIR as part of the

Russian Federation. In tandem with this position, the Ingush demanded the return of the territories that were transferred to North Ossetia after their deportation to Siberia in 1944. In order to conduct negotiations with the Yeltsin government, an Ingush delegation was sent to Moscow on October 13. Eight days later the Ingush delegation returned from Moscow, where the territorial question was discussed with a delegation from North Ossetia and a commission of the Russian Federation's Supreme Soviet. The issue was resolved to Ingush satisfaction, except for the city of Vladikavkaz, a part of which the Ingush had demanded. In light of this development a referendum among the Ingush people was held in the first week of December 1991: "73.7 percent of the 132,000 registered voters cast their ballots, and 92.5 percent of them voted for a sovereign Ingushetia within the Russian Federation."[19] To further contain Dudyev's nationalism, the Terek Cossacks demanded a referendum on the question of shifting Naurskaya District of the CIR into Stavrapol Territory, and the Cossacks of Shelkovskaya District took a similar position.[20] Thus a wedge was drawn between the Chechen and the Ingush, while the transplanted Russian Cossacks played Moscow's game. The Russian parliament had acted wisely, while Yeltsin's actions might have started interminable strife in the Caucasus.

Fired by the example of the CIR, the Balkars in the Kabardino-Balkar autonomous state proclaimed the Republic of Balkaria as a sovereign state within the framework of the Russian Federation. The Balkars, like the Chechen and Ingush peoples, were deported in 1944 to Kazakhstan and other Central Asian states. They lost half of their population in the process. Not until 34 years later, after their return to their homeland, did the Soviet government take any steps toward their rehabilitation. The Balkars made no territorial claims on the Kabardinos since their territory was not transferred to another ethnic group, and no Kabardin village or town was built on Balkar land. Nevertheless, a problem may develop when they decide to redraw the borders of 1922, when the Balkars and Kabardins were united into one autonomous republic.[21]

By November 1991 political turmoil temporarily simmered down in the Caucasus, because the Russian Federation conceded independence to the republics of the former Soviet Union and has found it practically impossible to enforce its writ in the autonomous republics.

This situation, however, has not thwarted the onward march of nationalism in the Volga-Ural region's autonomous republics, especially in Tatarstan. The spillover impact of the Tatar national movement on Bashkirtastan, Udmurtia, Mari, and the Chuvash is unavoidable.

Among the Turkic-Muslim nationalities, Tatars historically have played a very significant leading role in Russian history. Muslim-Tatars conquered Russia in 1237-1240 and maintained their sovereignty over Russia for almost 250 years. Finally they were defeated in 1480. Nevertheless, the Tatars retained parts of Russia and the khanates of Kazan and Astrakhan. Kazan was conquered by the armies of Ivan IV in 1552. However, the Crimean Tatar Khanate survived until 1783. Under the Communists, the autonomous republic of Tatarstan as a part of the Russian Federation was created with Kazan as its capital. Stalin deported the Crimean Tatars in 1944 to Uzbekistan; 46.2 percent of them died during the deportation. The Soviet government had falsely accused all of them of helping the German enemy during the war. The real reasons for their deportation, western scholars have since judged, was that "Russia coveted the semitropical lands of the Crimea occupied by the Tatars. Also, Russians harbored a deep, irrational distrust of them that stemmed from early history."[22]

Steadily since 1989, Tatarstan has attempted to break out of the Russian Federation. By December 1991 the Tatar national movement was in full swing with "passionate" adherents and "rational" opponents of complete independence from the Russian Federation. Among the supporters are the Tatar Public Center (TPC), the Ittifak [alliance] National Independence Party, the Suverenitet [sovereignty] Committee, and the Tatarstan Group of Deputies in the State's Supreme Soviet. Among the opponents are the Democrats, who are positively oriented toward the democratic Russian Federation, and the People's Rule Faction in the Tatar Supreme Soviet. The current political dynamics are very similar to that of the Ukraine and the Baltic states.

In Tatarstan, the Russian-Tatar population is supposed to be almost even, with a small numerical edge in the Tatars' favor. Alarmed by the Tatar rising nationalism, local Russians have started repeating the slogan of "the Kremlin under the Crescent" and demanding the Tatars' expulsion to Mongolia. Among the Tatars, on the other hand, slogans about Turkic unity became increasingly popular. Tatarstan is also concluding treaties with former autonomous and union republics to form a Volga-Urals federation. However, Tatarstan's incumbent president, Mintimer Shaimiyev, has taken a centrist position, emphasizing full "sovereign autonomy" within the framework of the Russian Federation. This moderate policy exposed him to the opposing sides' scathing criticism.

The thesis of the Volga-Urals Federation is being articulated by the leadership of the Ittifak National Independence Party led by Fauzia Bairamova, a Tatarstan People's Deputy, elected to the Tatar Supreme

Soviet in 1990. She has already acquired an international reputation in the Islamic world. Like the Islamists in other Muslim countries, "her argument is that Islam is a religion which cannot be confined to private morality. It has a strong political component." However, like Islamic modernists elsewhere, she has argued that "women, even more than men, should be engaged in public activity, provided that their family lives are in order," and enjoy what she calls "inner harmony." To cleanse the combined impact of Russification and Sovietization, Bairamova founded the first unofficial Tatar journal in 1989. Called *Iman* (faith), the journal has argued for a regeneration of Tatar culture and Islamic practice. In her home village, there are 600 schoolchildren, of whom six are Russian. Yet, she revealed, all school lessons are taught in Russian. Why is this so? She lamented: "The Baltic Republics have only had 50 years within the Russian empire. We have had 440 years. We are deformed!"[23]

In 1989 Bashkirs and Tatars celebrated for ten days in Bashkirtostan's capital, Ufa, the 1,110th anniversary of the adoption of Islam in the Volga and Ural areas, and the 200th anniversary of the inception of the spiritual administration of Muslims of the European part of Russia and Siberia. This administration was established in Ufa by a decree of Catherine II (1762-1796). To participate in these celebrations, representatives of the Muslim communities in the Soviet Union and other countries, including Pakistan, South Yemen, United Arab Emirates, Australia, and the United States, came to Ufa. Tatarstan's government handed over the Azimov mosque in Kazan to the local Muslim community and allocated 450,000 rubles for its restoration. New mosques were authorized to be built in Naberezhniuye Chelny, Nizhnekamsk, and Bugulma in Tataristan; Salavat and Ishimbai in Bashkiria; and also in Ulyanov province.[24]

To Bairamova, these salutory developments were not enough. In her eyes, the Tatar tragedy is that "the nation has lost its pride"; otherwise would the Tatars "sell the Russians their language, customs and religion?" What is the Russian state? She has asserted, rightly, that "half of Russia's territory is Tatar lands." Consequently, she has openly raised the question of annexing to Tataristan the lands that belonged to the Tatars of old—the lands of Simbirsk, Saratov, Samara, Astrakhan, and Orenburg, the expanses of the Ufa Plateau, and all of the Urals' western slope. The Siberian Tatars and the Sergach Mishars, in her eyes, are a special question: "Their lands are also Tatar lands."[25]

These aspirations are indeed very high. Should they be realized, then the Volga-Ural region would become contiguous to the North Caucasus republics, raising the possibility of a larger Turkic-Islamic federation on a grand scale. Recently developments have taken place in the former Soviet Union that no one anywhere in the world could have predicted. Who can, in light of recent history, call the possibility of a Volga-Ural-Caucasian federation a pipe dream? However, the chairman of the Russian Republic Parliament, Ruslan Imranovich Khasbulatov, a Chechen Muslim whose family was deported in 1944 by Stalin, has contemptuously described the idea of Tataristan's independence from the Russian Federation as rubbish. Khasbulatov suggested that two referendums should be held in order to settle the issue of an autonomous republic's secession from the Russian Federation: the first referendum in Tataristan, to be followed up by a similar referendum in Russia. Only positive results in both can grant freedom to Tataristan. Accepting the challenge of this prescription, the Tataristan Supreme Soviet adopted in November 1991 a resolution proposing that a popular referendum will be held on the question of the "state status of the republic."[26] Its outcome, positive or negative, will have a profound impact on the future history of the Tatars and the Russians.

CENTRAL ASIAN REGIONAL PLANNING: RESPONSES FROM TURKEY, IRAN, AND PAKISTAN

Despite claims of the Communists and even of some western scholars that the Soviet Union had modernized and industrialized Central Asia, and had eliminated feudalism and ushered in prosperity, recently Russian observers openly admitted that "half the families in Central Asia live in poverty. The average income per working person fluctuates between 40 and 60 rubles [a month]. The number of people living below the official poverty line is more than 46 percent in Uzbekistan, 40 per cent in Kirgizia and Turkmenia and 60 percent in Tajikistan."[27]

In addition to widespread poverty, which has fueled nationalism in the Central Asian republics, additional factors of Islamic repression, Russian political domination, cultural Russification, and enforced isolation from the Islamic world may be added to complete the picture. Communists turned nationalists almost overnight, the current Central Asian leaders certainly bring the legacy of Soviet authoritarianism to their rule. During 1990-91 the presidents of six republics were elected unopposed with 95 to 98 percent of the votes. Failure of the Moscow-imposed command economy, the popular yearnings for self-determination, and more important, the dissolution of the Soviet Union in December 1991 made these leaders nationalists. In Tajikistan, the former Communists recaptured power in September 1991 through elections and began to grope for new national policies. With Russia, Ukraine, and Belarus looking to the United States and the West, the Central Asian leadership had no option left other than seeking aid and trade relations with Iran, Turkey, and Pakistan. However, Azerbaijan's conflict with Armenia over the enclave of Nogorno-Karabagh had encouraged it to seek closer political and economic ties with Iran starting in 1990. In November, the two sides had explored the possibility of establishing power plants, constructing a subway in Tabriz, and using the Aras river waters for power generation. These modest steps reflected Iran's cautious approach in the wake of Hashmi Rafsanjani's visit to Baku, the Azerbaijani capital, in 1989 as a part of Tehran's normalization of relations with Moscow, a process that began just before the death of Ayatollah Khomeini.

Even in January 1991, when Azerbaijan's deputy prime minister, accompanied by Nakhichevan Autonomous Republic's president, visited Tehran to seek closer cooperation with Iran, he was forthrightly informed that Tehran would reciprocate within the framework of existing cooperation between Tehran and Moscow.[28] Within this established framework Iran also signed agreements with Turkmenistan for border exchanges, agriculture, water resources and irrigation, the environment, solar energy, and protection of cultural heritage, linguistics, literature, and the humanities.[29]

In sensing a weakness of the Soviet center and recognizing the need for economic self-reliance, the Central Asian leaders congregated at Alma-Ata on June 23, 1990, and signed an intergovernmental agreement on scientific, economic, technical, and cultural cooperation between Kazakhstan, Uzbekistan, Kirghistan, Tajikistan, and Turkmenistan. This was probably the first major step collectively taken to initiate the process of regional planning in Central Asia. The agreement is to last until January 1, 1996, and included provisions to: (1) establish a functioning business coordinating council with a group based in Alma-Ata; (2) establish an interrepublican commission to coordinate efforts to restore ecological balance in the Aral area; (3) establish a fund to aid the population of the ecological disaster zone; (4) form the interrepublican scientific and production association; and (5) remove the existing restrictions on the exportation of consumer goods. These practical measures were underlined by a statement, which exuded an element of new Central Asian solidarity: "The peoples of Central Asia and Kazakhstan are united not only by their geographical neighborhood, but also by common historical destiny, by a kinship of cultures, traditions and habits."[30]

At Alma-Ata these Central Asian leaders made another declaration, in which the inviolability of the existing territories of the republics was reaffirmed and the ecological tragedy caused by the disappearance of the Aral Sea was made the Soviet Union's responsibility. They asked President Gorbachev to establish an All-Union Ecological Fund in order to restore balance in the Aral Sea region. Also, they recommended the transfer of a part of the Siberian rivers' flow to Central Asia.[31] To strengthen multilateral cooperation the republican leaders agreed to meet annually.

Despite this big fusionist step, fissional tendencies are also visible in Central Asia. Dreadful interethnic riots occurred in 1990 along the Kirghis-Uzbekistan border. The violence left 200 people dead and embittered relations between the two neighbors. Uzbekistan, the most heavily populated Central Asian republic, began to be feared by other republics for its so-called expansionist tendencies and historically rooted imperial tradition. Other presidents started to dismiss the idea of Central Asia unifying in a greater Turkistan as unreal. Moreover, the prospect of unified Turkistan and the resurgence of Islam is most frightening to the local Russian and other European nationalities. Table 14.2 presents the current demographic picture of Central Asia.

TABLE 14.2
Muslim Central Asian Republics' Population 1990

Republic	Population in Millions	Russians within the Republics (percent)	Other Nationalities within the Republics
Azerbaijan	7.1	6	6% Armenians
Turkenistan	3.6	10	9% Uzbeks; 3% Kazakhs; 1% Ukrainians
Uzbekistan	20.3	8	5% Tajiks; 4% Kazakhs
Tajikistan	5.3	8	24% Uzbeks; 1% Tatars; 1% Kirghiz; 1% Ukrainians
Kirghistan	4.4	22	13% Uzbeks; 3% Ukrainians; 2% Germans
Kazakhstan	16.7	38	6% Germans; 5% Ukrainians; Kazakhs (40%) are a minority in their own historical homeland
TOTAL	**57.4**		

Sources: "The Soviet Union's Unequal Parts: Diverse and Restless," *New York Times,* September 11, 1990; *Time,* September 9, 1991; *Statesman's Yearbook, 1990* (New York: St. Martin's Press, 1990).

Interethnic riots involving Russians have not taken place yet; however, Russian and other European nationalities have started to stream out of the republics. From Kirghizistan alone 74,000 left in the first six months of 1991.

At the present time, the emphasis is by no means on political unification of Central Asia but on regional cooperation. The president of Kazakhstan, Nursultan A. Nazarbayev, has been most energetic and imaginative in extending the fold of cooperation even to the Xinjiang Uighur Autonomous Region of China, where more than a million Kazakhs live, while a substantial number of Uighurs live in Kazakhstan. In the summer of 1991 Nazarbeyev visited Xinjiang and offered two proposals for China's approval: extending the Alma-Ata Urumaqi air route, which opened two years ago, to Beijing, and even further to South Korea and Japan; and making more effective use of the railroad that links Russia and China and passes through Kazakhstan. In 1990 an international main line was linked at the Druzhba (Russia)-Alashankou (China) junction. For China, the railroad shortened the route from the Pacific to Europe by almost 5,000 km and also shortened the Beijing-Moscow route. In this cooperative spirit, Kazakhstan's trade with Xinjiang increased fivefold, and joint enterprises have begun to develop.

Nazarbayev has presented to Iran a similar proposal for railroad construction, linking Iran with Kazakhstan. The railroad stretch would cover 320 km, which will provide Kazakhstan access to the Middle East and the Mediterranean.[32]

However, by December 1991 the Central Asian republics' relations began to develop very rapidly with Turkey, Iran, and Pakistan. Since the 1950s, these latter three countries have become very closely linked. They have recently formed the Economic Cooperation Organization (ECO), which superceded the Regional Cooperation for Development (RCD). The RCD was established in 1964. In June 1990 the first tripartite ministerial session of Turkey, Iran, and Pakistan signed a protocol to extend cooperative endeavors in the fields of economy, agriculture, industry and technology, science and culture, energy, transportation and communication, and related infrastructural projects. The three powers called this protocol the revitalization of the ECO to extend regional cooperation to a higher level of cooperation.[33] The ECO thus is a model of cooperation and regional planning to which the Central Asian republics can be drawn.

At this point in their history, the Central Asians are also constrained by certain objective conditions, including their mixed demographic composition, erosion of Islamic cultural values, and the current leadership, which is steeped in the ethos of national communism. Also, their economic needs and geopolitical imperatives are most compelling in the formulation of their regional approaches.

Turkey, Iran, and Pakistan present three different ideological orientations, while their economies, though roughly comparable, are at different levels of development: Turkey is a secular Muslim state with a population of 56.5 million, while its economy is growing at an annual rate of 5.3 percent. Militarily, Turkey is the strongest among the three partners. The western powers encourage the Central Asian republics to draw closer to Turkey for aid and trade. With a population of 54.6 million, Iran is an orthodox Shiite Islamic republic. While its foreign policy is national in orientation, Islam as an ideology is a major component of its foreign policy. Rich in oil, Iran has substantial resources to develop economically and maintain a credible military force that is already battle-tested. Overpopulated with 110 million citizens, Pakistan is a conservative Islamic state, constantly struggling to maintain a balance between the application of Islamic principles in its state system and the imperatives of modernity emphasizing democracy, scientific-industrial development, and human rights.

Based on geography, economic needs, and the type of Islamic forces that emerge in the Central Asian republics, they will selectively develop relations with Turkey, Iran, and Pakistan. Some trends are at present noticeable. Even before the official dissolution of the Soviet Union was declared on December 8, 1991, Kazakhstan's President Nazarbeyev, Turkmenistan's President Saparmurat Niyazov, and Nakhichevan Autonomous Republic's Prime Minister Beycan Ibrahimoglu visited Ankara and declared that they were looking at Turkey's economic and social examples to follow and "needed Turkey to show the way."

Azerbaijan's Prime Minister Hasan Hasanov declared that Azerbaijan would welcome Turkey's mediation in its conflict with Armenia over the disputed region of Nogorno-Karabagh.[34] In response, President Turgut Ozal of Turkey advised his government that "three important areas, the Balkans, the Caucasus and the Middle East, have opened in front of Turkey."[35] Clearly, at present, the Caucasus is an area of geopolitical significance for Turkey, while it has extended diplomatic recognition to all Central Asian republics and Kazakhstan.

Iran has already developed extensive relations with Azerbaijan, Turkmenistan, and Kazakhstan and extended recognition to all Central Asian republics. However, Iran's skillful diplomacy sprang into action at the sixth summit meeting of the Organization of the Islamic Conference (OIC), which ended on December 11, 1991, at Dakar, the capital of Senegal. There Iran determinedly set itself up as an alternative to Saudi Arabia as the world leader of Islam. Iran's President Hashami Rafsanjani not only sponsored a proposal for admitting Azerbaijan to the OIC, but also presented Azerbaijan's delegates, Sheik ul-Islam Allah Shakur Pasha-Zade (chairman of the Spiritual Administration of Caucasian Muslims) and Kazakhstan's deputy foreign minister, Sailau Batyrshaurly. Incidentally, both Azerbaijani and Kazakh delegates flew into Dakar in an Iranian plane as members of Iranian delegations. Azerbaijan was accepted as a full member of the OIC.[36]

Not to be left behind by the diplomatic initiatives of Turkey and Iran, Pakistan also moved to establish relations with the Central Asian republics, and especially with Azerbaijan. Azerbaijan sent a delegation in November 1991 to Pakistan, consisting of Sheik ul-Islam Allah Shuker Pasha-Zade and Fazal Murad Ali, members of the Azerbaijani Supreme Soviet. The delegation visited Prime Minister Nawaz Sharif on November 20 and urged him to extend diplomatic recognition to Azerbaijan. These Azerbaijanis also were able to mobilize Pakistani public opinion in favor of Azerbaijan over Nogorno-Karabagh and Nakhichavan, an Azerbaijani enclave separated by the Armenian territory. They also sought Pakistan's help to build up Azerbaijan's armed forces. "We do not possess nuclear weapons," stated Ali, "but we are rich in natural resources, including oil, natural gas, and trained technical personnel. An excellent institute of technology, specializing in oil extraction, is maintained at Baku, which attracts students from 54 countries. We are prepared to help and to receive help from advanced Islamic states."[37] Pakistan recognized Azerbaijan on December 11 at the OIC meeting and on December 20 extended diplomatic recognition to all Central Asian states.

Also in December, Pakistan sent a 26-man delegation to the Central Asian republics to lay down the foundations for cooperative relations. The delegation was led by Sardar Asaf Ali, the minister of state for economic affairs. With each Central Asian republic except Uzbekistan, he signed a memorandum of understanding to establish economic and cultural relations. Each republic was offered "a long-term revolving credit for the import of light engineering products of Pakistan"; Uzbekistan received a revolving credit line of $30 million. Moreover, Pakistan announced that it would in the very near future establish a direct Islamabad-Tashkent route for Pakistan International Airlines, the first step in starting air routes with other Central Asian republics.

The Pakistani delegation also established a working group with Kirghizistan and Kazakhstan to explore the possibility of linking these republics' highways with Pakistan through Xinjiang to the Karakoram Highway, and eventually to Karachi. This connection would provide these landlocked republics with an outlet to the sea. However, some proposed projects cannot be implemented until normal relations are restored in Afghanistan: (1) Pakistan promised to link Uzbekistan and Tajikistan with Karachi through Afghanistan and Peshawar; (2) with Tajikistan, Pakistan explored the possibility of importing electricity through the

Wakhan Corridor, especially for consumption in Pakistan's northern areas; (3) Pakistan offered to purchase Turkmen natural gas and pipe it to Pakistan via Afghanistan.

However, Pakistan's entrepreneurs and businessmen made the most impact on the Central Asian leaders, especially in Kazakhstan. On December 9 Kazakh prime minister Sergei Tereshchenko asked visiting Pakistani businessmen to raise $200 million on the international money market. Without this amount, Tereshchenko reasoned that Kazakhstan risked bankruptcy. Using his telephones and fax machines, Pakistani businessmen raised $100 million in three days! Pakistani businessmen on their own concluded several agreements in the Central Asian republics: (1) a Pakistani hotel chain signed letters of intent to build five-star hotels in four capitals; (2) a group signed a protocol to train Central Asian officials in business management and the English language; (3) four Pakistani banks agreed to open branches in the Central Asian capitals; (4) a Pakistani company, Istaphone, agreed to establish an international cellular telephone network in three republics; (5) the Tabbani Corporation, which had traded for 20 years with the former Soviet Union, signed a $200 million contract with Uzbekistan for consumer goods and agreed to establish a new airline — Asia Air — in collaboration with the government of Uzbekistan.

Pakistani industrialists, on the other hand, have been less bold in committing their capital to the textile industry in Uzbekistan. While the principle of profit-sharing and its repatriation is accepted, the Central Asians have not yet worked out a pricing system. Also, political instability and the absence of financial guarantees have discouraged industrialists from investing their resources in Central Asia, at least for the time being. Banking facilities, insurance, management training, and tourism are badly needed in Central Asia. In these areas, Pakistan can be helpful. However, in order to encourage foreign investment the republics have to decide how best to price electricity, water, and raw materials for jointly operated industrial enterprises, and determine the labor costs and how to facilitate the repatriation of profits in hard currency. The technical problems are very complex and need time to be resolved.[38]

Despite Pakistan's preoccupation with its internal political dynamics from 1989 to 1991 and despite Pakistani prime minister Nawaz Sharif's government's initially tepid approach to Central Asia, it finally sprang into action once Pakistani public opinion showed the way. Wisely, Pakistan's first initiatives have remained in the realm of economics and culture, while some military assistance program with Azerbaijan might be in the offing. The opening up of Central Asia presented Pakistan with a new security environment, especially after the Mujahideen's triumphal return to Afghanistan. Finally, Pakistan would be freed from the nutcracker squeeze, which the former Soviet Union had created through an "alliance" between Afghanistan and India. With the cooperation of a friendly Afghanistan, Pakistan would have the opportunity to take initiatives for building what the Pakistan Central Asia Friendship Society has called a commonwealth of Central and Southwest Asian Islamic states.

What are its prospects, especially in light of this analysis?

SOME TENTATIVE CONCLUDING COMMENTS

There are indeed three concentric circles of regional planning, which have begun to spin in Turkey-Iran-Pakistan, the six Central Asian republics, and the Volga-Ural-Caucasian regions. Some developments within these regions are conducive to regional interaction, and some certainly militate against this process.

Motivated by geographic imperatives, perceptions of security, economic opportunity, and a sense of future prospects, Turkey, Iran, and Pakistan have moved fairly rapidly to establish cooperative relations with the Central Asian states. The three neighboring states have had the advantage of regional economic and military cooperation during the last 40 years and can extend this know-how to the Central Asian states, including Xinjiang. Pakistan counts on its traditional strategic cooperation with China and does not question Chinese sovereignty over the Turkic-Islamic region of Xinjiang. It remains to be seen whether Beijing will let Xinjiang be extensively involved in the vortex of Central and Southwest Asian politics and run the risk of confronting nationalists' demands for self-determination in there.

Turkey, Iran, and Pakistan's movements in Central Asia have been unilateral. No evidence has surfaced indicating any coordination among these three states. On the contrary, much greater coordination between the United States and Turkey seems to be developing to counter expanding Iranian influence in the Central Asian republics. The United States seems to be determined to project Turkey as the role model—a secular Muslim state integrated into the community of western states. Comparatively speaking, Turkey and Iran have the advantages of geographic contiguity and ethnic affinity with Central Asia over Pakistan. This situation would be diminished to some degree when normalcy is restored to war-torn Afghanistan. Through Afghanistan and with its fraternal cooperation, and through Xinjiang, Pakistan should be able to establish close relations with Tajikistan, Kirghizistan, and Uzbekistan, because these states are geographically closer and the Karakuram highway linking Pakistan to

Xinjiang can be connected to the roads with Gorno-Badakhshan in Tajikistan and Kirghizistan. Similarly, Afghanistan and Pakistan, through the pooling of national resources, can build the extensions of Afghanistan's ring road to link up with Turkmenistan, Uzbekistan, and Tajikistan. However, the shortest route between Pakistan and Tajikistan will be a link road of approximately 11 miles, which may be constructed through the Wakhan Corridor from the region of Yasin in Chitral. Physically and financially, these projects are feasible.

Pakistan, for the foreseeable future, will be well advised to concentrate on its relations with Tajikistan, Kirghizistan, and Uzbekistan and avoid getting involved in the Nogorno-Karabagh conflict. The Caucasian area would remain beyond Pakistan's reach, while cultural and economic relations can be established at a rather comfortable level. The problems of the Caucasian states are very likely to involve Turkey and Iran, and they are already fostering relations not only with Azerbaijan, but also with autonomous republics of Nakhichevan and Adjaristan (former Adzhar Assr).

Azerbaijan has a split personality. Ethnically and linguistically most closely related to the Republic of Turkey, Azerbaijan (being 60 percent Shia) is denominationally related to the Iranian Azerbaijan. Within Iran, Azerbaijan has been very assertive of its ethnic personality and has at times verged on secession. Tajikistan, though widely separated from Iran by Turkmen and Uzbek territories, is an extension of Iranian culture. Recently the Azerbaijan Republic decided to adopt the Roman script, like Turkey, while Tajikistan decided to reintroduce the Persian-Arabic script and gradually drop the Cyrillic alphabet, which it was forced to adopt in 1940. In January 1992 Iran signed a cultural agreement with Tajikistan under which Iran will publish thousands of academic textbooks using the Persian script. These texts would also introduce Islamic concepts and vignettes from Islamic history.

Several Iranian poets recently organized a series of cultural evenings in Tajikistan to honor the noted Persian poets Ferdowsi, Rudeki, and Hafiz. According to the Iranian press, such events are also being requested in Uzbekistan, where the philosopher and physician Aricenna was born. Iran also plans to provide linguistic assistance to Afghanistan.[39] In other words, both Iran and Turkey are likely to be engaged in the struggle for cultural and linguistic extension in Central Asia, and there is a danger that this struggle may spawn a low-grade cold war, unless the two states coordinate their policies bilaterally or within the framework of ECO in order not to leave Pakistan out. Moreover, Saudi Arabia has also extended its cultural influence through Islam, but its might will be felt through petrodollars, which are likely to be made available by the Mecca-based Islamic Development Bank. An extension of the Shia-Sunni conflict into Central Asia by Saudi-Iran struggles would prove to be most counter-productive for all Islamic states. Already Turkish secularism is being pro-jected as an alternative to Iran's Shia fundamentalism and Saudi Arabia's Wahabi Islam. After the death of Marxism, Islam is perceived to be the last surviving example of a totalitarian ideology "that claims universal rel-evance." This makes Islam, in the West's perception, "an uncomfortable neighbor"[40] in the community of nations.

Counting on the support of its western allies, Turkey is carving out a distinctively national foreign policy in regard to the Central Asian states. Turkey has advised them to stay secular and to switch to the Latin script, like it. Also, Turkey is attempting to revitalize the Black Sea Economic Union to include both the Balkans and the Turkic republics. In order to strengthen secularism in Central Asia, the 38-state Conference on Security and Cooperation in Europe (CSCE) admitted the European and Asian successor states of the former Soviet Union to full membership on January 30, 1992.[41] Turkey also played a catalytic role in this develop-ment. To Iran, this was the West's determined attempt to "lure Central Asian Republics from Islamic roots."[42] Watching these developments from the sidelines, Pakistan announced that same month that it would open embassies in the Central Asian republics within two weeks.

While cooperating with each other within the framework of the ECO, Turkey, Iran, and Pakistan are interacting with the Central Asian republics independently, and even in contradiction of each others' policies.

The Central Asian republics recognize the need to create a mini common-wealth of states justified by geography, religion, common culture, language, and history. However, the long Russian domination and Soviet oppression has left a deep imprint on the personality of the Central Asians, on their political systems and their economies. The demographic composition in each republic has become heterogenous. Russian and other European nationali-ties range from 10 to 22 percent in five of the republics, and in Kazakhstan the indigenous Kazakh population is no more than 40 percent of the total population. During 1990-91, a large number of these exogenous nationalities left the Central Asian republics in droves; nevertheless, Kazakhstan still remains a binational Eurasian state. These European nationals would exer-cise a substantial influence on the outcome of any future election, and the state policy consequently would be considerably oriented toward Moscow. It is precisely for this reason that Kazakh president Nazarbeyev views him-self as a bridge between the East and the West.

In each Central Asian republic, an Islamic resurgence is noticeable. New mosques are being built and religious schools for children are multiplying. Islam-oriented political parties have appeared, even though they are supposed to be illegal since the constitutions of every republic bans religious-based political parties. Such parties are particularly active in Tajikistan and Uzbekistan. Moreover, national languages have been made official along with Russian. Russian names for towns and cities have been replaced by their native names.

Uzbekistan, the most populous of the Central Asian states, was the heart of Turkistan, which the Bolsheviks sliced up into several republics. Also in Uzbekistan, the history of the imperial tradition is exceptionally strong. There the Timurid Empire flourished, and from its Farghana Valley hailed Emperor Zahir-ud-Din Babur, who founded the Mughal Empire in India in 1526.

In Uzbekistan, the longing for the vast Central Asian state, a revival of the old idea of grand Turkistan, has come alive, inspired partly by Islam. Despite the pull of Islam, dreadful interethnic riots between the Uzbeks and Kirghiz and between Uzbek and Maskitian Turks took place in 1990-91. Clearly, the Islamic solidarity has not overcome narrow but deep ethnic cleavages. The ethnic identity will remain a major obstacle in the way of any national movement that would seek to unify the Central Asian states.

If the ethnic cleavage is a big divide in Central Asia, it is a formidable barrier in the Volga-Ural region, and its improbable unification with the slices of Caucasian autonomous republics. There the old imperial policy of divide and rule applies with full force. Russia will attempt to justify it in the name of the unity of the Russian Federation. The fact that Russia conquered Tatar territories and the ancestral lands of other Turkic nationalities in the Volga-Ural region is now a "forgotten" story, except for the Tatar Muslim nationalists, who want to unify the autonomous republics of this region with that of Caucasia and perhaps with Azerbaijan. Despite the Tatar aspirations, there is not substantial groundswell for independence and secession from the Russian Federation. But who really can predict what might take place during the next three to five years?

Azerbaijan's conflicts with Armenia over Nagorno-Karabagh and the eventual settlement of the Nakhichevan is likely to linger for many years, like the Arab-Israeli conflict or India-Pakistan dispute over Kashmir. Azerbaijan is not likely to surrender the Nagorno-Karabagh territory to Armenia, despite the Armenian majority in the enclave.

TABLE 14.3
Ethnic Composition of Nagorno-Karabagh

	1979	1989	Growth Percent	1989 Percentage of Total
Total	162,181	189,029	16.6	
Armenians	123,076	145,450	18.2	76.9
Azeri	37,264	40,632	9.0	21.5
Russians	1,265	1,922	51.9	1.0
Ukrainians	140	416	197.1	0.2
Belorussians	37	79	113.5	
All Slavs	1,442	2,417	67.6	1.3

Ethnic Composition of Nakhichevan

	1979	1989	Growth Percent	1989 Percentage of Total
Total	240,459	293,875	22.2	
Azeri	229,968	281,807	22.5	95.9
Armenians	3,406	1,858	-45.4	0.6
Kurds	1,696	3,127	84.4	1.1
Russians	3,807	3,782	-0.7	1.3
Ukrainians	942	1,906	102.3	0.6
Belorussians	94	450	378.7	0.2
All Slavs	4,843	6,138	26.7	2.1

Sources: Published by the State Committee on Statistics, *Natsional'ny Sostav Nasdeniia, Chast'II, Informatsionno-izdatel'ski Tsentr* (Moscow, 1989); Paul B. Henze, "The Demography of the Census, According to 1989 48 Soviet Census Data," *Central Asian Survey* 10, no. 1/2 (1992): 154-155.

Since the 1989 census, major population shifts have occurred in Nogorno-Karabagh, Nakhichevan, Armenia, and Azerbaijan. It is generally believed that hardly any Armenian population has remained in Nakhichevan, while the Armenian population in Karabagh has been greatly reduced. Since Azerbaijan has imposed an intermittent blockade of Karabagh, causing a reduction in the supply of fuel and food, a large number of Armenians have fled to Armenia.

To Azerbaijan, both enclaves historically belong to it. The Azaris contend that in the past, when Armenians were pushed out of Iranian and Turkish territories, they settled in Nagorno-Karabagh. This long sojourn in Nagorno-Karabagh does not entitle them to claim ownership. However, in addition to calling Karabagh authentically Armenian, the Armenian Republic has added other problems to Karabagh's claims: language, pollution, and democratization. Finally, the Armenian authorities supported the claims of Karabagh to unification with the Armenian Republic on February 20, 1990. Also, they called the Soviet decision of July 5, 1921, which placed Karabagh in Azerbaijan, null and void. While Nakhichevan is supposed to be an autonomous area as a part of Azerbaijan, it is separated from Azerbaijan by the intervening Armenian territory. How can this anomaly be resolved?

In a speech in December 1991 U.S. Secretary of State James Baker criticized Azerbaijan for its "aggressive policy," meaning its actions in Nagorno-Karabagh. While Armenia was recognized as an independent state, Azerbaijan was not because of its "record on human rights." Evidently, the United States has recently set aside this position in favor of a new policy that led Baker to Azerbaijan in February 1992 to establish diplomatic relations. The U.S. objective is to prevent the growth of trade, aid, and cultural relations between the Central Asian states and Iran. This new U.S. policy might start off another mini-cold war, which is unnecessary. At the present time, no threat to U.S. interests emanates from any pan-Islamic or pan-Turkic movement.

Finally, there is no good reason for the United States not to be able to cooperate with resurgent Islam in Central Asia. Relations between Iran and the United States will not be antagonistic indefinitely. In Central Asia, Turkey, Iran, Afghanistan, and Pakistan are likely to play a natural political role, which is determined by their geography, history, economy, religion, and culture. This process does not necessarily militate against the United States' national interests. In fact, a congruence of mutually complementary interests are in the offing.

N·O·T·E·S

1. Prime Minister Nawaz Sharif, *Address to the National Defense College* (Rawalpindi), June 16, 1991 (personal copy), p. 11.

2. Ahmad Rashid, "All Dressed Up and Nowhere to Go," *The Herald* (Karachi), (November 1991): p. 75.

3. Ahmad Rashid, "After the Fall," *The Herald* (September 1991).

4. *New York Times*, September 14, 1991.

5. For an exposition of this paradigm of commonwealth, see: Khalid Waheed, *Pakistan and the International Economic Order* (Peshawar), March 21, 1990 (personal copy), and his *Commonwealth of Peace and Prosperity* (Islamabad), September 3, 1990 (typescript).

6. Brian Hooks, ed., *The Cambridge Encyclopedia of China* (Cambridge: Cambridge University Press, 1991), p. 222.

7. Andrew D. W. Forbes, *Warlords and Muslims in Chinese Central Asia* (Cambridge: Cambridge University Press, 1986), p. 10.

8. Linda Benson, *The Ili Rebellion: The Moslem Challenge to Chinese Authority in Xinjiang, 1944-49* (New York: M. E. Sharpe, Inc.), p. 189.

9. Nicholas D. Kristof, "Unrest Reported in Muslim Areas of China; Foreigners are Barred," *New York Times*, April 13, 1990.

10. "Xinjiang Clampdown on Muslim Dialogue with Foreigners," *Tehran Times*, October 30, 1990.

11. Gunner Jarring, *Return to Kashgar*, trans. Eva Glaeson (Durham, NC: Duke University Press, 1986). Jarring has suggested that in the 1970s "books are once again printed in the old Arabic script. The Latin script seems to be used mainly in official publications" (p. 239).

12. For these proposals and analyses of other prospects, see a collection by Khalid Waheed, Khalid Aziz, Abdul Majid Khan, Tariq Rahim and Najam Abbas, *Selected Papers from Workshops for the Study of Central Asia*, ed. Khalid Waheed (Rawalpindi, 1990), pp. 7-10 ff.

13. "Memorandum of Discussion at the 228th Meeting of the National Security Council on December 9, 1954" and "U.S. Policy Toward South Asia, Memorandum by the Executive Secretary (Lay) to the National Security Council, December 14, 1954," *Foreign Relations of the United States, 1952-1954* (Washington, DC: Superintendent of Documents, 1983), vol. 11, pp. 1095, 1097, 1148-1150.

14. *Documents from the U.S. Espionage Den [U.S. Embassy in Tehran] (45: U.S. Intervention in Islamic Countries*, vol. 1 (Tehran, n.d.), pp. 13-14.

15. Ibid., p. 45.

16. Dmitry Sidorov, "Nakhichevan: Disturbances on the Border," *Moscow News*, January 14, 1990.

17. Irina Dementyeva, "The Emblem of the New Chechen Republic: A Lone Wolf Under the Moon," *Izvestia*, November 1, 1991; *CDSP*, vol. 43, no. 44, 1991.

18. "From Hot Spots: Only from the Standpoint of the Law," *Pravda*, October 10, 1991; A. Kazikhanov, *Izvestia*, October 10, 1991; *CDSP*, vol. 43, no. 42, 1991.

19. Ali Kazikhanov, "News Hotline: 92.5 Percent Cast Their Votes for a Sovereign Ingushetia," *Izvestia*, December 4, 1991; *CDSP*, vol. 43, no. 49, 1991.

20. Timur Muzayev, "Checheno-Ingushetic: Dzhokhar Dudayev Agrees to a Dialogue," *Nezavisimaya Gazeta*, October 15, 1991; V. Kharlamov, "Interview: Chechens Are Tired of Waiting," *Pravda*, October 21, 1991; A. Kazikhanov, "Preparations to Fight Are Under Way in Grozny," *Izvestia*, October 21, 1991; *CDSP*, vol. 43, no. 42, 1991.

21. A. Kazikhanov, "A New Republic Is Proclaimed—Balkaria," *Izvestia*, November 18, 1991; *CDSP*, vol. 43, no. 46, 1991.

22. Edward Allworth, ed., *Tatars of the Crimea* (Durham, NC: Duke University Press, 1988), p. 3. After the conquest of Kazan in 1552, "the Russian state pursued the policy of national integration that meant conversion to Christianity and cultural assimilation." Azade- Ayse Rorlich, *The Volga Tatars: A Profile in National Resilience* (Stanford, CA: Hoover Institution Press, 1986), p. 38.

23. "Muslim Woman Leader of Tatar Party Aims for Islamic Rejuvenation," *Tehran Times*, May 22, 1991.

24. A. Zinovyev, "Muslim Celebration," *Izvestia*, August 16, 1989; A. Sabirov, "In Republic Governments: Houses of Worship Are Being Turned Over to Believers," *Izvestia*, August 17, 1989: *CDSP*, vol. 41, no. 33, 1989.

25. A. Putko, "How It Is Being Proposed That the Tatars Free Themselves from the Russian Yoke," *Izvestia*, November 25, 1991; *CDSP*, vol. 43, no. 47, 1991.

26. "Ruslan Khasbulatov: I Don't Intend to Change My Views," *Nezavisimaya Gazeta*, November 27, 1991; Yevgeny Skukin, "Ordinary Ittifak Fascism," *Rossiiskaya Gazeta*, November 28, 1991; *CDSP*, vol. 43, no. 47, 1991.

27. Valery Vyzhutovich, "Uncoupled Train Car—Uzbekistan After the Proclamation of Independence," *Izvestia*, September 13, 1991; *CDSP*, vol. 43, no. 37, 1991.

28. *Tehran Times*, January 12, 1991.

29. Ibid., January 14, 1991.

30. Khalid Waheed, ed., *Central Asia Selected Papers* (Islamabad: Pakistan Central Asia Friendship Society, September 1990), p. 47.

31. For further details on these issues, see "Standing for Neighborliness," *Soviet Uzbekistan* (Tashkent) (August 1990), p. 2.

32. Yu. Savenkov, "Nursultan Nazarbeyev: I Believe in the Prospects for Cooperation with China," *Izvestia*, July 16, 1991; *CDSP*, vol. 43, no. 28, 1991.

33. "Iran, Pakistan, Turkey Sign Major Protocol, Revitalize ECO," *Tehran Times*, June 20, 1990.

34. Ibrahim Holozoglu, "Ozal: Turkey Should Capitalize on Situations in the Balkans and Caucasus," *Turkish Times*, January 1, 1992.

35. Ibid.

36. V. Lashkul and V. Skosyrev, "Iraq Completely Isolated," *Izvestia*, December 10, 1991; *CDSP*, vol. 43, no. 49, 1991.

37. Idrees Siddiqi, "Azerbaijan Key Adhan-i Hurriyat: Azerbaijan Kay Sheikh-ul-Islam Allah Shuker Pasha-Zadi Awr Rukan Parliament Janab Fazal Murad Ali Kay Sath Char Ghantay Key Inkashafat Say M'amur Guft-Gu," *Urdu Digest* (Lahore), (December 1991): 138.

38. For an excellent coverage of Pakistani delegation's visit to the Central Asian republics, see: Rashid Ahmad, "Coming Out Of Cold" and "Trade Winds," *The Herald* (Karachi) (January 1972), pp. 86-91.

39. "Efforts Underway to Revive Persian Language in Central Asia," *Tehran Times*, January 29, 1992.

40. For the fear of Islam and the projection of Turkish secularism, see: Brian Beedham, "Turkey, Star of Islam: Look Eastward, Europe, and See Why You Need a Successful Turkey," *The Economist*, December 14, 1991, pp. 1-18.

41. Thomas L. Friedman, "Ten Ex-Soviet Republics Gain Wider Recognition," *New York Times*, January 31, 1992.

42. "CSCE Seeks to Lure Central Asian Republics from Islamic Root," *Tehran Times*, January 29, 1992.

▲ ▽ ▲

15

Turkish and Iranian Policies in Central Asia

◆

Oleś M. Smolansky

INTRODUCTION

After the collapse of the Soviet Union, Iran and Turkey offered themselves as role models for the socioeconomic and political development
in the newly independent Muslim republics. Generally speaking,
Turkish and Iranian officials did not refer to their countries' interaction in southern Caucasus and Central Asia as "rivalry." Instead, as
Foreign Minister Hikmet Cetin put it, it was "natural" for Turkey to seek
close cooperation with the Muslim republics because of "shared history,
religion, ethnic ties, and language." (In order not to arouse old fears, Cetin
added that his government had no intention of pursuing the policy of Pan-
Turkism.[1]) On another occasion, he explicitly denied that Turkey was
involved in a rivalry with Iran. Rather, Ankara was simply accommodat-
ing the Muslim republics: They "view Turkey as a window to the Western
world and we do all we can to open this window for them."[2] Similar sentiments were expressed by Prime Minister Suleyman Demirel: "The
achievement of independence by these countries is an embodiment of the
age-old Turkish dream and . . . [Turkey] is prepared to do everything possible to help them implement political and economic reforms." However,
in an important admission, Demirel disclosed that by spring 1992, Ankara
was also entertaining more ambitious plans: Turkey, he said, "is prepared
to take upon itself the responsibility for the state of affairs in the region

stretching from the Adriatic Sea to the borders of China."[3] Even for the politically stable, economically sound, militarily strong, and western-backed Turkey, this was a rather tall order. However, its importance lay in the open challenge that Demirel's statement represented to the Islamic Republic (and, coincidentally, to Russia as well). Words were followed by action. As will be shown later, Ankara mounted a major effort to establish itself as a leading outside power in the newly independent Muslim republics.

By and large, Iran reacted negatively to the sentiments expressed by the Turkish officials. In December 1991, Mohammed Larijani, member of the Supreme Defense Council, accused Turkey of "trying to isolate Iran and to hinder the spread of Islamic ideas" in the Muslim republics of the Soviet Union. Other representatives of the Iranian government, including Foreign Minister Ali Akbar Velayati and speaker of the Majlis Mehdi Karrubi, made it clear that the disintegration of the Soviet Union and the emergence of independent Muslim republics provided opportunities that the Islamic Republic intended to pursue, thus implying that Tehran was determined to compete with Ankara for their allegiance.[4] Velayati, in particular, saw Iran as a "bridge linking the republics of Central Asia and Transcaucasus with the rest of the world" and called on Iranian investors to help their "brethren in the newly independent Muslim countries."[5]

Occasionally, Iran and Turkey attempted to maintain appearances and to present a common approach, as, for example, at the Economic Cooperation Organization (ECO) meeting, held in Tehran in February 1992. Thus, according to Velayati, there was "more cooperation than rivalry" between Tehran and Ankara in their dealings with the Muslim republics. Turkish President Turgut Ozal echoed these sentiments, insisting that there was no competition between the two states and no attempt to establish spheres of influence.[6] But these lofty pronouncements could not conceal the major differences that divided Ankara and Tehran. On another occasion, when Ozal argued that all of ECO's new members (the former Soviet Muslim republics, except Kazakhstan) should adopt a free market system, his Iranian counterpart, Ali Akbar Hashemi Rafsanjani, accused Turkey of efforts to "impose a western system to the detriment of traditional Islamic culture." He was supported by the Tehran press, which called Ankara a "pawn in service of U.S. interests."[7] Moreover, Iran's initiative to form an organization of the Caspian Sea states and Turkey's desire for a similar arrangement in the Black Sea area were criticized in Ankara and Tehran, respectively. In short, occasional conciliatory statements notwithstanding, in late 1991 and early 1992, it was obvious that

Iran and Turkey were engaged in serious competition in the Muslim republics of the former Soviet Union. Their respective policies in Central Asia are examined next.

IRAN AND CENTRAL ASIA

As alluded to earlier, the dissolution of the Soviet Union resulted in a marked upswing of Iranian activity in southern Caucasus and Central Asia. One of the newly independent Muslim states that demonstrated an early interest in securing Tehran's goodwill and support was Turkmenistan. Situated along the southeastern shore of the Caspian Sea, it shares a long border with the Islamic Republic. Cooperation between them began well in advance of the collapse of the Soviet Union. In September 1991, Ashkabat sent truckloads of building materials to assist the victims of a major Iranian earthquake. A short while later, President Saparmurad Niyazov opened a border checkpoint with simplified crossing procedures between Turkmenistan and Iran.[8] In October, Niyazov visited Tehran at the invitation of the Iranian government. During official ceremonies, he and Rafsanjani expressed an interest in expanding bilateral relations.[9]

Velayati Visit

In November 1991, with the Soviet Union still nominally intact, the Islamic Republic made a major move designed to establish Iranian presence in southern Caucasus and Central Asia: Foreign Minister Velayati traveled to Moscow and secured Soviet approval for the opening of Iranian consulates in the capitals of the six Muslim republics.[10] From Moscow, Velayati proceeded to Central Asia and Azerbaijan. His visits followed a uniform pattern—everywhere the minister emphasized the need for regional stability and expressed the hope that the republics' relations with Tehran would continue to expand. Similar sentiments were invariably voiced by his hosts as well. On a substantive level, Velayati opened Iranian consulates in all the capitals he visited, "signed memoranda and communiqués on the basic principles and objectives of cooperation, and discussed the creation of specific mechanisms for bilateral cooperation."[11]

In retrospect, there can be no doubt that Velayati's journey to the rapidly disintegrating Soviet Union was an important foreign policy initiative. Though very tactful in his dealings with Moscow—Iran had no intention of interfering in the internal affairs of the Soviet Union but

would respect any decision taken by it and its constituent republics[12] —
Velayati made it clear that Tehran had judged the Muslim republics'
march to independence to be irreversible. Under these circumstances, the
Islamic Republic had no choice but to throw its hat into the Central Asian
ring. There can be no doubt that Velayati's visit was highly successful.
Representatives of all the Central Asian republics recognized Iran as a
major regional power and assured Velayati that they wished to establish
close relations with it. According to Velayati, there were many reasons for
their attitude. Among them were the "common ties we share with those
republics; common religion, history, culture, customs, and traditions."[13] In
any event, Velayati's journey and the reception accorded to him gave a
clear indication that the Islamic Republic was determined to play an
important role in the former Soviet Muslim republics and that its decision
to do so was received favorably in their respective capitals. Soon afterward, Tehran recommended the admission of the six republics to the
Organization of Islamic Conference (OIC).[14]

One of Velayati's pet projects, which he discussed in all the Central
Asian capitals, was what he himself described as the "revival of the silk
route." What Velayati had in mind, and succeeded in inserting in all the
memoranda of understanding signed during his trip, was "to connect the
railway lines and land routes of these republics to the Islamic Republic."
He went on to explain that, through Iran, the Central Asian republics
would be connected not only to Europe but also to the Far East. More
specifically, supported by some Central Asian leaders, including
Kazakhstan's President Nursultan Nazarbayev, Velayati proposed to link
Iran with China "along the old silk route." With this in mind, Tehran
undertook to construct a railroad line from Mashhad to Sarakhs, a distance of some 200 kilometers. This would connect with another 200-kilo-
meter line running from Sarakhs to Tajan in Turkmenistan. Completion of
this system would link Iran with the railways of five Central Asian
republics. If, then, an additional 300-kilometer line would be built in
Kazakhstan, Iran's link to China and the Pacific would be completed.[15] In
short, Turkmenistan and Kazakhstan, in particular, were central to Iran's
geostrategic planning. Among other things, their importance was reflected
in the attention that Tehran paid after the dissolution of the Soviet Union
and Iran's recognition of the independence of the former Soviet republics
(except Moldova) in late 1991.[16]

Turkmenistan

In January 1992, with President Niyazov and Velayati in attendance, Iran and Turkmenistan officially opened another border crossing between them. The two officials signed a memorandum of cooperation that provided for work to begin on the construction of a railway line to link Turkmenistan to Iran as well as to the railroad network connecting Iran to Turkey and the Mediterranean Sea. Tehran also undertook to export crude oil to Turkmenistan and to buy natural gas from it.[17] In February, Vice-President Atta Charyev, who represented Ashkabat at the ECO summit in Tehran, requested Iran's assistance in conducting oil exploration projects in Turkmenistan and in constructing a refinery as well as a motor oil plant. The Iranians promised to study the requests.[18]

In March 1992, the two states entered into an economic agreement. Valued at over $80 million, it provided for barter of Turkmen "goods and raw materials" for use in the Iranian industry for some 250,000 tons of foodstuffs. In addition, "seven agreements and two memoranda of understanding in the fields of commerce, industry and transportation" were signed between Turkmenistan and the adjacent Iranian province of Khorasan.[19] In April, Tehran and Ashkabat signed an important accord on the construction of a gas pipeline between Turkmenistan and Turkey. It was to pass through Iranian territory and was to be built by Iranian firms.[20] The sides agreed also to expand "scientific and cultural relations" and to facilitate the "traffic of passengers and goods" across their border.[21]

In early May, Rafsanjani and Velayati received Charyev, who delivered a written message from Niyazov inviting the Iranian president to attend the forthcoming Central Asian summit conference in Ashkabat. Charyev used the occasion to express his government's satisfaction with the state of bilateral relations and particularly with "the fruitful cooperation . . . in oil and gas affairs, commercial road, air, and sea links, agricultural exchanges, consular affairs, and the facilitating of the transit of goods." He also called for an expansion of trade between the two states. The Iranian officials reciprocated Charyev's sentiments and expressed themselves in favor of broadening Iran's relations with the Central Asian republics. Velayati, in particular, noted that Tehran would "employ all its resources to that end."[22]

During the Ashkabat summit, Rafsanjani and Niyazov discussed the state of bilateral relations and signed "a memorandum on friendship and cooperation," as well as "agreements on customs and banking." The former provided for "cooperation in the areas of culture, technology, the economy, trade and politics" and called for periodic consultations on the foreign minister level. It is noteworthy that in his evaluation of the new accords, Charyev pointed to "the groundlessness of the widespread opinion about Iran's desire to export fundamentalism to Turkmenistan."[23]

A few days later, with Rafsanjani and Charyev present, work was begun on the Mashhad-Sarakhs railway. The president noted that the railroad would "play a significant role in strengthening economic and cultural ties between . . . [Iran] and the neighboring Muslim-inhabited republics." According to Radio Tehran, when completed, the railroad would carry 3 million tons of goods and 500,000 passengers. In time, these numbers were expected to increase to 10 million and 2 million, respectively.[24]

Kazakhstan

As noted, Kazakhstan was another Muslim republic whose territory figured prominently in Tehran's strategic vision for Central Asia. As in the case of Turkmenistan, relations between Tehran and Alma Ata, too, developed rapidly after the establishment of diplomatic relations in early 1992. In February, at the ECO summit in Tehran, Kazakh deputy premier discussed with Rafsanjani "expansion of economic and diplomatic relations." He called, in particular, for "economic cooperation, especially in the field of oil," and went on to say that "an advanced transportation system will boost economic cooperation among the neighboring states and the newly independent republics."[25] Later in the month, the Kazakh minister of transportation and his Iranian counterpart signed a memorandum of understanding that provided for continuous shipment of goods between the Caspian ports of Anzali and Now Shahr in Iran and the Kazakh port of Ekta'o (Aktau). It was also agreed to increase road transport and to inaugurate air service between Tehran and Alma Ata. In addition, the Kazakh government undertook to conduct a joint study of the feasibility of a rail network, connecting Beijing and Istanbul and passing through Alma Ata, Taskhent, and Tehran.[26] Finally, at the Caspian Sea conference, Kazakhstan expressed its desire to expand "economic and commercial ties" with Iran and offered the Caspian port of Shevchenko for the transport of goods between Iran and the Far East. In return, Alma Ata expected to gain access to Tehran's transportation system and the Persian Gulf ports.[27]

Of the other Central Asian republics, Tajikistan, Kyrgyzstan, and Uzbekistan also expressed an interest in broadening relations with Iran and Turkey. However, Uzbekistan from the very beginning leaned toward

Ankara, while Tajikistan and Kyrgyzstan appeared to be mainly interested in establishing cultural relations with the Islamic Republic. In the case of the Tajiks, this was not surprising, because they are closely related to the Persians in terms of ethnicity, language, culture, and history.

Tajikistan

In February 1992, Foreign Minister Hakim Kayumov met Rafsanjani and expressed Dushanbe's desire for "cultural, political, and economic cooperation" between the two states. Shortly afterward, the state television companies of Tajikistan and Iran signed an agreement that provided for "regular exchanges for journalists, information, and joint film projects."[28] In April, a "goodwill mission," led by the Tajik minister of economic affairs, visited Tehran and was received by Velayati. The guests delivered a message from President Rahman Nabiyev. In it, the Tajik head of state acknowledged "the shared historical and cultural features of the two countries," praised the economic, political, and cultural relations that had been established since Tajikistan's independence, and expressed a desire to expand them. Velayati responded favorably to the sentiments expressed by Nabiyev and, among other things, promised to grant Tajikistan export credits and to print its currency.[29]

In May, at a meeting between the Tajik and Iranian ministers of culture, the former noted that Farsi was now being taught throughout Tajikistan and "called for cooperation in publishing Farsi books and periodicals." His Iranian counterpart expressed himself in favor of cultural and ideological exchanges and went on to say that Tehran was in favor of expanding ties between the two states. It is not entirely clear what the reference to "ideological exchanges" meant, but it must have put the Tajik official on guard. His response was both cautious and nebulous: "Iran, Afghanistan, and Tajikistan," related as they were by ethnic and cultural ties, "could remain alongside one another and continue their actions through the means of culture."[30] It would appear that Dushanbe preferred to distance itself from Tehran's Islamic ideology while cooperating with Iran in the cultural and economic spheres.

Kyrgyzstan and Uzbekistan

During the Ashkabat summit meeting in May 1992, Iran established diplomatic relations with Kyrgyzstan and Uzbekistan. A short while later, Bishkek and Tehran signed two memoranda of understanding on cultural affairs. They dealt with "establishing news links and holding fairs." A third agreement provided for organizing "cultural institutes and libraries as well as . . . cultural weeks and exhibitions." According to Iranian Minister of Culture and Islamic Guidance Mohammed Khatami, Tehran was prepared to assist the Muslim republics in "eras[ing] the vestiges of colonial culture and . . . [in] find[ing] their Islamic roots." He noted that Iran would also render help in promoting the "revival of the Persian language and its instruction."[31]

Finally, Uzbekistan, as noted, was interested mainly in economic cooperation. In early February 1992, an Uzbek trade delegation visited Iran, Turkey, and other Middle Eastern countries. Soon thereafter, at the ECO summit in Tehran, the head of the Uzbek delegation, chairman of the Supreme Soviet Shokat Yuldashev, met with presidents Rafsanjani and Ozal to discuss bilateral relations. Various agreements were reportedly reached during the conference, and members of the Uzbek delegation met with ECO government officials and business representatives to discuss their implementation.[32] In his meetings with the Iranian leaders, Yuldashev expressed a particular interest in technical cooperation and in the conduct of "extensive preliminary studies" for establishing air service and land transportation between the two states.[33]

Regional Initiatives

In addition to bilateral relations, the Islamic Republic also embarked upon a number of regional initiatives designed to promote its image as the leader of the Muslim world and as a major outside player on the former Soviet Muslim scene. In mid-February 1992, as noted, Tehran played host to the Economic Cooperation Organization summit. Founded in 1964 as the Regional Cooperation for Development, the organization was intended to foster economic, technical, and cultural cooperation among Turkey, Iran, and Pakistan—America's "northern tier" allies in the Middle East.[34] It became inactive after the Islamic revolution in Iran (1979) but was revived in 1985 as the Economic Cooperation Organization. Tehran's change of heart was prompted by efforts to shore up the country's economy during the war against Iraq. In 1992, the original founders of the ECO recognized its potential for expanding their political and economic presence in the newly independent states of southern Caucasus and Central Asia. These considerations help explain the decision to hold an ECO summit and to invite the former Soviet Muslim republics to attend. They obliged. The presidents of Azerbaijan and Turkmenistan, the deputy premiers of Kazakhstan and Kyrgyzstan, the foreign minister of Tajikistan, and the chairman of the Uzbek parliament participated in the work of the summit. Of the republics, Azerbaijan, Turkmenistan, and Uzbekistan had been admitted to ECO membership shortly before the meeting; Tajikistan and Kyrgyzstan joined the ECO at Tehran; and Kazakhstan had requested and obtained the status of an observer. According to Velayati, all of them "expressed . . . full desire to further strengthen ECO."[35]

Addressing the conference, President Rafsanjani spoke of "momentous global changes" that had occurred in the recent past. Among them were "the collapse of communism and upheavals besetting the political, economic, and social infrastructures of most countries with centralized economies, the end of the bipolar era, . . . the independence of the former Soviet republics." He went on to say that, in view of these developments, "viable stability and peace are of great importance to our strategic and sensitive region." To secure them, "extensive collaboration of all regional countries" was required, and the ECO provided the framework through which these goals could be achieved. Similar sentiments were expressed by all the participants, including the representatives of Azerbaijan and the Central Asian republics.[36] In any event, the conference proved to be a considerable success for the Islamic Republic, reinforcing its claim to a leadership position in the Muslim world and its aspiration to become an important participant in the affairs of southern Caucasus and Central Asia.

In another regional initiative, Tehran attempted to organize the states bordering on the Caspian Sea. In addition to Iran, they included Azerbaijan, Turkmenistan, Kazakhstan, and Russia. An early indication of Tehran's interest in another regional organization in which it, because of its geographic location, was bound to play a dominant role was provided at the ECO summit. On that occasion, Rafsanjani urged the states adjacent to the Caspian Sea to "establish cooperation in various fields, including utilization of marine resources." His proposal was adopted by the littoral states, which agreed to set up a Caspian Cooperation Organization with headquarters in Tehran.[37] An international conference on Caspian "maritime cooperation" was held in April. In his opening statement, the Iranian representative reminded all concerned that his country's location enabled it "to transfer its exportable goods to international waters in the south, to Caspian Sea littoral states in the north, to the Middle East in the southwest and to Turkey and Europe in the west." In any event, the participants signed a protocol "on protection of the Caspian environment, navigation, passenger traffic between their respective ports, and related issues."[38] This meant, in part, that Iran had agreed to the transit of goods from the other Caspian Sea states through its territory to the Persian Gulf.[39]

Another major regional event in which Tehran played an important role was the first ECO summit to be convened in a Central Asian republic. Called by President Niyazov, it met at Ashkabat (Turkmenistan) in May 1992 and was attended by the leaders of Iran, Turkey, Pakistan, Turkmenistan, Uzbekistan, Kyrgyzstan, and Kazakhstan. Tajikistan and Azerbaijan did not participate because of internal political crises. In a joint statement, the attendees reiterated their determination "to expand economic and political cooperation" but went on to point out that they had "no intention of creating any blocs that would threaten the interests of other states."[40] Otherwise, the signatories agreed to grant each other most favored trade status and to investigate the possibility of free movement of people and goods across their respective borders. A published accord spelled out plans to complete the construction of the Mashhad-Sarakhs-Tajan railroad by 1995; to construct a gas pipeline from Turkmenistan to Iran, Turkey, and, from there, to Europe; and to complete a highway linking Istanbul, Tehran, Islamabad, Tashkent, Bishkek, and Alma Ata.[41]

Iran was pleased with the summit's accomplishments. Commenting on the conference, Rafsanjani said that the Islamic Republic was rapidly emerging as the "economic trade center of the region"—the participants came to the conclusion that "the main outlet of the Central Asian republics to the world market" passes through Iranian territory.[42] And Foreign Minister Velayati described Iran's "unique geopolitical status in Central Asia" in the following fashion: "If the Central Asian republics with gas and. oil resources seek to export them to the world through the Persian Gulf, they must either use [our] pipelines or our roads and rail links." He added that Tehran was also "ready to provide the republics with telecommunication facilities."[43]

TURKEY AND CENTRAL ASIA

As already mentioned, Turkey, too, endeavored to establish itself as a major outside participant in the affairs of the Muslim republics of the former Soviet Union. In the developing competition with Tehran, Ankara had valuable assets of its own. In addition to geographic proximity and its historic, ethnic, religious, cultural, and linguistic affinity with the Turkic-speaking republics (only Tajiks speak a language that is related to Farsi), Turkey possesses a well-developed and stable economy, close ties with the industrial West, and a secular form of government. The latter model appealed to the former Communist *apparatchiks* in Azerbaijan and Central Asia much more than the fundamentalist Islamic propensities of the Iranian government.

In any event, Turkey moved to establish its presence in the Muslim republics even prior to the dissolution of the Soviet Union. For example, in 1990, Ankara reacted favorably to Azeri and Kazakh requests for cooperation in telecommunications and signed an economic and cultural cooperation agreement with Turkmenistan.[44] In late 1991, Ankara moved decisively to establish its position in the newly independent Muslim states. In November, Turkey was the first foreign country to recognize the independence of Azerbaijan and, in December, it extended recognition to and expressed an interest in developing closer relations with all the other republics of the former Soviet Union.[45] In addition, the presidents of Turkmenistan, Uzbekistan, and Kyrgyzstan visited Ankara and emphasized the ethnic ties binding their people to Turkey. The latter responded by offering various types of political, economic, and cultural assistance. In February 1992, Prime Minister Demirel met with the presidents of Azerbaijan, Kazakhstan, and Uzbekistan, who were attending the meeting of the World Economic Forum, held in Switzerland, while Foreign Minister Cetin visited all six Muslim republics. His journey was widely interpreted as another attempt to counteract the spread of Iranian influence.[46] Finally, in May, Demirel visited the Muslim republics. According to diplomatic sources in Ankara, his trip was intended to "demonstrate . . . [Turkey's] commitment to the real independence of the Turkic republics and to help them overcome the difficulties in the transition to a market economy."[47] Ankara's overtures were particularly well received in Uzbekistan.

Uzbekistan

Former Communist party leader Islam Karimov traveled to Ankara in mid-December 1991 and held talks with Ozal and Demirel. Even at this relatively early point, Karimov announced that Tashkent intended to follow Turkey's path to a market economy.[48] Commenting on the visit, *Pravda Vostoka* said that relations between Uzbekistan and Turkey had entered "a qualitatively new stage." In addition to opening consulates, the sides had signed agreements on cooperation in the spheres of "economy, trade, transport, communications, culture, education, science, the media, tourism, and sports." A separate "Agreement on the Foundations and Goals of the Ties between Uzbekistan and Turkey" noted the "common Turkic elements" shared by the peoples of the two countries.[49]

A veritable flurry of activity followed Karimov's visit. In January 1992, Turkish businessmen explored the possibility of establishing joint enterprises with their Uzbek counterparts; a Turkish cultural center opened in

Tashkent; and in his telegram congratulating Karimov on his election as president, Demirel assured him that the agreements reached in Ankara were being resolutely implemented by Turkey.[50] In February, as already mentioned, an Uzbek trade delegation visited several Middle Eastern countries, including Turkey, while Supreme Soviet Chairman Yuldashev met with Ozal at the ECO summit at Tehran to review the development of bilateral relations.[51] In addition, Turkish and Uzbek ministries of education agreed to exchange teachers and students and to hold joint academic conferences.[52] During his March 1992 visit to Tashkent, Foreign Minister Cetin reportedly offered Ankara's assistance in representing Uzbekistan's interests abroad. According to Russian sources, Karimov was intrigued by the proposal because of Tashkent's reluctance to allow Moscow too big a role in Uzbek affairs. At about the same time, Radio Tashkent began to transmit broadcasts in Turkish.[53]

In late April 1992, Prime Minister Demirel visited Uzbekistan and *Izvestiia* noted that Tashkent had not witnessed "such a reception" for a very long time. At a joint press conference, Karimov reiterated his intention to adhere to the Turkish model of economic development, while Demirel promised continuous assistance to Uzbekistan in its quest for political and economic independence and cultural development. The two leaders also participated in the opening of the Turkish embassy.[54] During Demirel's visit, Uzbekistan and Turkey signed nine additional accords expanding cooperation in the areas agreed upon in December 1991. Ankara also reportedly made available to Tashkent $500 million in credit—by far the most generous offer made to a Muslim republic—while Karimov expressed his support for the Turkish project of establishing a "Central Asia and Caucasus Development Bank."[55] Prior to Demirel's visit, a high-level Turkish government delegation arrived in Tashkent and negotiated agreements on cooperation in the spheres of public health and education. The latter provided for 2,000 scholarships, enabling Uzbek students to enroll in Turkish universities.[56] These developments left no doubt that Uzbekistan had emerged as Turkey's number-one ally in Central Asia. The other country in which Ankara had shown a great deal of interest was Kazakhstan, the largest, potentially the richest, and industrially the most developed Central Asian state.

Kazakhstan

Relations between the two states were off to a slow start. In January 1992, a Turkish-language school opened in Alma Ata and the Turkish newspaper *Zaman* appeared in a bimonthly edition. Its first issue contained messages from presidents Nazarbayev and Ozal "expressing hope for close contacts between [their] peoples."[57] In February, a group of Turkish businessmen arrived in Alma Ata to explore the opportunities for "international export-import operations, joint enterprises, and the opening of offices of Turkish companies in Kazakhstan." In March, the latter began to intensify its "foreign policy activity" and endeavored to develop what a Russian publication described as "special relations" with Turkey. In fact, during Foreign Minister Cetin's visit to Alma Ata, the sides concluded five agreements. Nevertheless, especially in comparison with Uzbekistan, the scale of Turkish involvement in Kazakhstan was much more modest.[58] In addition, as noted earlier, Alma Ata also attempted to maintain close relations with Tehran.

Some light on the Kazakh thinking was provided by Alma Ata's Association of Central Asian Research, which, in mid-March, published a report on the state of Turkish-Kazakh relations. It found that the prospects for economic cooperation between the two states remained limited because Ankara proved reluctant to invest money in the Kazakh economy. Nor was Turkey seen as Alma Ata's principal foreign policy partner, even though, in the ideological-cultural sphere, it was expected to have more success in Kazakhstan than Iran, provided Ankara refrained from pursuing the "obsolete . . . idea of a single pan-Turkic state." What made Turkey attractive was "its experience in entering the Western market," which the report described as "useful" to Kazakhstan. Similarly, Turkey could serve as a model for the modernization of the armed forces. In sum, the report concluded that Ankara's experience was worth studying—it demonstrated that "chaos can be averted in the transition to democracy and a market economy by relying on a regime of enlightened, secular authoritarianism."[59] Otherwise, prior to Demirel's visit, the two countries signed a protocol on cooperation in education and initiated weekly charter flights between Alma Ata and Istanbul. In addition, more Turkish businessmen came to explore economic opportunities in Kazakhstan.[60]

Prime Minister Demirel arrived in Alma Ata on April 29. In his discussions with Nazarbayev, the latter thanked Turkey for its early recognition of Kazakhstan's independence and for its willingness to cooperate with Alma Ata. But, unlike Uzbek President Karimov, Nazarbayev made no mention of the Turkish model of development. Instead, he emphasized the importance of the "experience of transforming the Turkish economy through the encouragement of [private] enterprise and attraction of foreign investment." Demirel offered $200 million in credit as well as help in a number of major projects. On May 1, the two sides signed a "joint document" and a joint communiqué that expressed satisfaction with the development of bilateral relations, particularly in the spheres of "business, banking, education, science, culture, sports, media cooperation, civil aviation and other transport, and the restoration of historic monuments." Turkish firms were to assist Kazakhstan in oil exploration, as well as in the construction of oil refineries and of an electric power station, the laying of a pipeline to Turkey (to be extended later to the Persian Gulf), the reconstruction of the port of Aktau, the transport of Kazakh goods from the Caspian to the Black and Baltic seas (thus bypassing Iran), and the distribution of Kazakh goods in Turkey. Ankara also undertook to train 2,000 Kazakh specialists and generally assist Alma Ata in the shift to "new economic relations."[61]

It is thus clear that Demirel's visit and negotiations with Nazarbayev provided an important stimulus to the development of Kazakh-Turkish relations. Some reservations probably remained but the offer of economic and technical assistance proved sufficiently attractive to persuade Alma Ata to step up significantly its cooperation with Ankara.

In addition to Uzbekistan and Kazakhstan, Turkmenistan and Kyrgyzstan were the other Central Asian republics with which Turkey attempted to establish close relations.

Turkmenistan

In spite of extensive cooperation with Iran, President Niyazov visited Turkey in December 1991 and declared that Ashkabat was counting on "the fraternal aid of the Turkish people" to assist it in its economic development. Ankara reportedly assured him that help would be forthcoming.[62] During the visit, the sides signed a Treaty of Friendship and Cooperation and concluded a number of agreements designed "to develop [Turkmenistan's] material-technological basis."[63] In March 1992, Foreign Minister Cetin arrived in Alma Ata and signed a protocol establishing diplomatic relations between the two states. Cetin announced that Turkey was prepared to assist Turkmenistan in "training personnel in business, management, and banking" and in shifting from the Cyrillic to the Latin alphabet. In addition, the sides discussed the opening of a Turkish-language school, a library, and a branch of a Turkish bank in Ashkabat, as well as the transmission of Turkish television programs to Turkmenistan.[64]

Demirel arrived in Ashkabat in early May 1992. It is noteworthy that, a few days earlier, *Turkmenskaia iskra* praised Turkey's success in becoming a "democratic and secular state." But the lead article, entitled "How the Turkish Example Is Instructive," pointed out that, in some cases, the government had made "concessions to religious circles." To be sure, it did so "without subverting the secular nature of the political regime." In any event, during Demirel's visit, the sides concluded a number of cooperation agreements and Ankara offered Ashkabat $75 million in credit (compared with $500 million made available to Uzbekistan and $200 million to Kazakhstan).[65] The joint communiqué noted the "great potential for expanding [bilateral] relations, particularly in areas of health care, the media, telephone communication, banking, air and ground transportation, tourism, and business." Specific agreements were reached, among other things, on the sale on credit of Turkish grain and sugar and on the delivery of Turkmen gas to Turkey. Soon afterward, *Turkmenskaia iskra* reported that a joint bank, devoted to "the development of the agro-industrial complex," would be set up in the near future. Ankara also agreed to assist Ashkabat in obtaining access to the international telecommunications network and to provide access to space satellites for relaying Turkish television programs.[66]

The gas deal was of particular importance to Turkmenistan and its southern neighbors, and the politics of the accord shed some light on the development of their respective relations. For one thing, natural gas constituted Turkmenistan's main export item, and Ashkabat went out of its way to indicate that it had no intention of squandering its "main wealth." Rather, the purpose of the Iranian-Turkish pipeline (and of the Turkmen-Turkish deal) was to enable Ashkabat "to integrate itself into the world economy through the planned transcontinental gas pipeline." To build it, according to a high Turkmen official, an "international consortium" would be set up in the near future.[67] Since one of the purposes of the proposed pipeline was to make it unnecessary for Turkmenistan to use the existing gas export network—that is, the pipelines running through Russia and Ukraine (with whom Ashkabat was then engaged in a heated price argument)—and thus to render the Central Asian republic more independent of its Slavic neighbors and customers, both Iran and Turkey assumed supportive roles. They did, as noted, endorse the project at the Ashkabat ECO summit of May 1992. However, since getting gas to Turkey required the use of Iranian territory, Tehran held an important trump card. It proceeded to play it in securing Ankara's approval for Iranian firms to engage in the construction of the pipeline.

Kyrgyzstan

President Askar Akayev, another early Central Asian visitor to Ankara, used the occasion to express his satisfaction with the resumption of "fraternal ties" between the two peoples and received Turkish assurances of help "in the form of shipments of medicine and food products."[68] Because of its relative remoteness, Kyrgyzstan was clearly less important to Turkey than the other Turkic republics. Still, Demiel visited Bishkek during his Central Asian visit, opened the Turkish embassy, and offered $75 million in export credits and preferential loans for the purchase of Turkish goods.[69]

Tajikistan

Tajikistan was the Central Asian republic in which Turkey showed least interest. Geographically remote like Kyrgyzstan, and Farsi-speaking, Dushanbe, as noted, publicly preferred to cooperate with its southern neighbors, Iran and Afghanistan. There was some economic interaction between Tajikistan and Turkey,[70] but it remained very limited even in comparison with Kyrgyzstan, let alone the other Turkic-speaking republics. In addition, domestic political turmoil precluded Tajikistan's participation in the Ashkabat ECO summit and made it impossible for Prime Minister Demirel to visit Dushanbe.

CENTRAL ASIAN REACTIONS

Before turning to the evaluation of the Iranian-Turkish competition, it might be appropriate to examine how some of the leaders of the newly independent Muslim states reacted to Tehran's and Ankara's pronouncements and actions. Thus, on the subject of religion, so dear to the hearts of the Iranian establishment, the views expressed in Central Asia clearly favored the Turkish model. Mufti Mohammed Yusuf Mohammed Sadiq, head of the Spiritual Board of the Muslims of Central Asia, categorically denied that Uzbekistan could emerge as a prototype of the fundamentalist Islamic state: "The Turkish course of development is close to us, with secular authority, economic reforms, the Muslim revolution." Similar sentiments were expressed by Tajikistan's religious leader, Akbar Turajanzadeh, who urged his countrymen to follow the Turkish, and not the Iranian, example.[71] And President Niyazov, who, as has been shown, cooperated closely with the Islamic Republic, insisted that Turkmenistan had no intention of becoming a "Muslim state."[72] There is little doubt that these sentiments are shared by the leaders of all the former Soviet Muslim republics.

The same conclusion applies to the issue of the role of the state in the political and socioeconomic development in the newly independent countries. The leading spokesman has been President Karimov of Uzbekistan, Turkey's main ally in Central Asia. He went on record early[73] and has maintained his position since. In a May 1992 interview, Karimov noted that the Uzbeks were engaged in working out their own developmental scheme. But they were also relying on the Turkish experience because it represented a "secular civilized path of societal development" and was therefore "more acceptable to us." In contrast, the "Iranian model is not acceptable to us." This, Karimov concluded, was the "opinion of Central Asia as a whole."[74] Additional light on Uzbekistan's position was shed by an important article that appeared in *Pravda Vostoka*. It discussed the stages of Turkey's economic and political development since the 1960s and noted that Ankara's experience could be viewed as a "useful model for Uzbekistan." For one thing, Turkey's "transition to the market" was accompanied by "intensification of authoritarianism in state management and the formation of political structures." Moreover, Turkey could serve as a useful model because of "similar starting conditions and the shared language, history, culture, and the Sunni Muslim orientation."[75]

Most of the other Central Asian leaders were more diplomatic than Karimov but did not try to conceal their preferences. Kyrgyzstan's Akayev noted that his government was "waging a struggle against all kinds of extremism" and felt "closest to Turkey," which he poetically described as "the morning star that shows the Turkic republics the way." According to Nazarbayev, Kazakhstan was determined "to implement a free-market economy [and] for this our only model is Turkey."[76] And only Nabiyev of Tajikistan, the sole ethnically Persian and Farsi-speaking Central Asian republic, told visiting U.S. Secretary of State James Baker that, although the Tajik authorities were not in favor of following Tehran's example, he "could not guarantee that his people shared the leadership's attitude toward Islam and the Iranian option." Asked at a press conference which model of development he preferred, Nabiyev answered: "Tajikistan is an independent state which will develop along its own independent path on the basis of the values of an open, civilized society." In any event, according to a Russian source, Baker had been privately assured in all the Central Asian capitals that the leaders of the newly independent Muslim republics disliked Islamic fundamentalism and did not view Iran as a "model for economic development."[77]

EVALUATION

In a perceptive analysis of the situation developing in the southern regions of the former Soviet Union, Abdulla Nurullaev wrote that the disintegration of the Soviet Union and the concomitant rupture of economic ties between the republics, accompanied by the cessation of financial aid from the central government, left the newly independent Central Asian states no choice but to seek assistance from Iran and Turkey.[78] As demonstrated earlier, these two Middle Eastern powers responded favorably to the requests for help, and one may legitimately wonder about their motives. Since the latter have been conditioned by their respective interests, as defined by Ankara and Tehran, it is to this subject that we turn next. For analytical purposes, Turkish and Iranian interests may be divided into the following categories: military-strategic, economic, and politico-religious.

Military-Strategic Interests

Their respective geographic position as well as their legitimate preoccupation with national security leave Turkey and the Islamic Republic no choice but to be highly concerned about the volatile and dangerous situation that has developed along their northern border. This is, of course, particularly true of the southern Caucasus or, more precisely, of the conflict between Armenia and Azerbaijan over Nagorno-Karabakh (a subject outside the scope of this chapter). Suffice it to say that both Ankara and Tehran are apprehensive that this regional imbroglio will degenerate into a general war between Erevan and Baku. Should this occur, Turkey and Iran as well as Russia would be under considerable pressure to join it. None of them wishes to become entangled in such a confrontation; all explain their genuine efforts to resolve that regional conflict by peaceful means. The situation in Central Asia is not as critical. However, the region's manifold economic and political problems, as well as its ethnic differences, coupled with Iran's geographic proximity and with Ankara's and Tehran's commitment to assist the newly independent republics, have raised the outsiders' apprehension about regional instability and about the effect it may have on Turkey's and, particularly, Iran's security. In sum, in this particular respect, Ankara's and Tehran's interests have converged, as both of them have sought to stabilize the political situation in southern Caucasus and Central Asia.

However, the shared, and genuine, concern for regional stability has not obscured the differences that have emerged between Turkey and Iran in connection with their respective ambitions in Central Asia. Thus, even a semblance of Pan-Turkic aspirations, vehemently denied by Ankara, has caused apprehension in Tehran, which is worried about the security of its northern border. Similarly, loose talk about unified Turkistan (embracing the Central Asian republics, minus Kazakhstan, under Uzbek leadership) or Demirel's notion of Turkish leadership in the regions situated between the Adriatic and the Chinese border have been perceived as threats to Iran's security, leaving Tehran no choice but to become actively involved in Central Asian affairs.[79] Genuine and legitimate though Iran's concerns may have been, however, it should be borne in mind that Velayati's late 1991 visit to Central Asia and the repeatedly stated intention to play a major role in that region predate the expressions of troublesome sentiments from Ankara and from some Central Asian capitals.

Before turning to other factors, it should be noted that, according to some U.S. officials, one of the major Iranian interests in the military-strategic category has been the determination to secure Soviet arms and, possibly, nuclear technology. Tehran's acquisition of Soviet conventional weapons, both before and after the collapse of the Soviet Union, is well documented and requires little elaboration. Suffice it to say that a major effort to rebuild Iran's armed forces after the end of the war against Iraq (1980-1988) had been under way since before the dissolution of the Soviet Union. T-72 tanks, MIG-29 fighters, and SU-24 bombers have by now been incorporated into the Iranian army and air force. Efforts to expand them have continued in 1992. Although most of this equipment, plus two or three submarines, have come from the Soviet Union/Russia, it stands to reason that interest in acquiring additional quantities of advanced weapon systems has been communicated to the other former Soviet republics as well. Some of them, including those in Central Asia, may well be tempted to sell or to barter military equipment stationed in their respective territories.[80] In contrast, Turkey's arsenal, well stocked by the United States, has had no such restraints.

In addition to conventional weapons, Iran was also reported to be interested in acquiring from the Central Asian republics enriched uranium as well as technology for the production of an atomic bomb.[81] Statements by officials from the International Atomic Energy Commission to the effect that "based on their findings, Iran's nuclear activity and ability were entirely for peaceful purposes" did not lessen Washington's apprehension. Hence, during his visit to Central Asia, Secretary of State Baker secured from some of the republics agreements not to sell uranium and relevant technology to countries that could use them to build atomic bombs.[82] Tehran was also said to have attempted to get former Soviet nuclear scientists (particularly those from the Muslim republics) to work in Iran. "Headhunters" from the Iranian Organization of Atomic Energy were reportedly offering $20,000 in monthly salary and $100,000 in various benefits to relocate to the Islamic Republic. They were after what some U.S. official described as close to 2,000 "loose brains" looking for work after the collapse of the Soviet Union.[83] Whether such allegations had any substance cannot be ascertained. However, it stands to reason that various opportunities that had become available after the demise of the Soviet Union were in fact explored by the Iranian authorities. In any event, military-strategic considerations aside, Turkish and Iranian interests in Central Asia clashed head on in a number of other respects.

Economic Interests

A vast, economically underdeveloped territory, Central Asia is rich in some mineral resources, among them coal, oil, natural gas, uranium, gold, and diamonds. It is also a major cotton-growing area. However, in addition to the fact that these resources are unevenly distributed among them, the newly independent republics face two major economic problems. Both are a direct consequence of the control exercised by the imperial and, subsequently, Communist center. For one thing, St. Petersburg/Moscow traditionally saw Central Asia as a producer of raw materials. For example, during the U.S. civil war, Russia was deprived of American cotton and St. Petersburg decided to grow its own. Because of climatic conditions, Central Asia was regarded as an ideal region for the task at hand. The Communist revolution changed nothing in this respect, and Central Asia remained the Soviet Union's main cotton-producing area. In addition, as noted, gold and diamonds were mined as well. More recently, oil, natural gas, and uranium were also mined. The problem, as the newly independent Muslim republics themselves see it, is that heavy emphasis on extraction and processing of raw materials precluded the establishment of a well-rounded economic and industrial base. The end result is that efforts to redress the economic imbalance created under Russian/Soviet control must be undertaken now. It is equally plain that enormous financial resources must be allocated to this task, resources that the new Muslim republics do not possess.

The other major problem concerns Central Asia's transportation system and particularly its railroad network. Since, prior to 1992, "most [Central Asian] roads led to Moscow," and since, after independence, the Muslim republics have decided to open up major transportation routes to their south and west, additional capital will have to be allocated to building new railway links and improving river and Caspian Sea navigation facilities, to mention but the most obvious projects. As noted earlier, Tehran has been anxious to help in exporting Central Asian products. Turkey, too, has expressed willingness to make its territory available for such purposes. However, the major difficulty faced by the Central Asian republics, as well as Iran and Turkey, is that all of these projects require the infusion of tens of billions of dollars, amounts simply nowhere to be had.

Otherwise, Ankara and Tehran see Central Asia as a large and potentially profitable market. Turkey, in particular, has been on a lookout for markets for its surplus industrial production. Ordinarily, the European Economic Community might have served as an ideal market for low-priced Turkish goods. However, since the EEC's antidumping legislation has effectively shut Ankara out, Eastern Europe and the former Soviet Union offer a potential alternative market. These considerations help explain Turkey's interest in such regional organizations as the Black Sea Economic Cooperation Organization as well as in cultivation of relations with all the members of the Commonwealth of Independent States (CIS) and not just the Muslim republics. Since Iran, too, has aspired to a share of the former Soviet market and has developed some regional cooperative plans of its own (the Caspian Sea Economic Cooperation Organization), Ankara's and Tehran's interests have clashed. As noted, there were occasional attempts to present a "united front." But such collaborative efforts as the February 1992 ECO conference in Tehran have been overshadowed by the competitive drive for economic advantages that has marked Turkish and Iranian activity in Central Asia.

As demonstrated earlier, both governments have taken an active part in encouraging their respective business communities to expand their dealings with the CIS and particularly its Muslim republics. They have also opened credit lines for the Central Asian states to purchase Turkish and Iranian products, though, in this respect, Ankara, with western backing, has been much more active than Tehran. For example, during his visit to Kyrgyzstan, Prime Minister Demirel argued that, although the Soviet Union had collapsed, the Central Asian republics were left "under the domination of the ruble." To help them leave the ruble zone, Demirel suggested the creation of a new international financial organization, The Central Asia and Caucasus Development Bank, with headquarters in Ankara.[84] The projected bank was designed gradually to wean the economies of Central Asia away from Russia and the CIS and to keep Turkey ahead in its competition with the Islamic Republic. However, given the financial constraints under which Ankara was operating, the Demirel plan did not offer chances for an early success.

In short, in Iran's and Turkey's economic competition in Central Asia, Turkey seems to have come out ahead — it has allocated more money in credits for the purchase of Turkish goods than Iran (more than $1 billion as against some $200 million) and it has offered more numerous and extensive programs to Central Asians in business, banking, and other related activities. However, it must be borne in mind that neither Turkey nor Iran, nor the two of them combined, possess sufficient resources to develop Central Asian economies. Even with Ankara's and Tehran's assistance, the new Muslim states face an uncertain economic future, a condition they share with all the other republics of the former Soviet Union.

Politico-Religious Interests

But it was in the realm of Central Asian politics and religious affairs that the competition between Turkey and Iran has manifested itself more clearly than in any other respect. Thus, as is well known, Tehran and Ankara differ fundamentally on the role of religion in shaping the political and socioeconomic structures and policies of an Islamic state. While Turkey introduced and continues to adhere to the Kemalist principle that the state system should remain secular and that religion should not determine the country's politics, economics, or foreign relations, the Islamic Republic has proclaimed the exact opposite. Generally speaking, Tehran has regarded itself as the champion of Muslim causes and has provided material assistance to the fundamentalist groups in Lebanon, Sudan, and Algeria. It is true that Iranian policy in Central Asia, in contrast, has been much more restrained and circumspect. Aware of the atheist upbringing and secular outlook of many of the region's leaders, Tehran has toned down its appeals and has refrained from advocating the spread of a militant form of Islam. As stated by Velayati: "Iran's improving relations with . . . Central Asian countries does not mean we force them to accept our standards. We advise them on the methods we prefer."[85] Nevertheless, playing for the long haul, Tehran, unlike Ankara, has devoted resources to proselytizing Islam in the mosques and in religious schools, whose numbers have increased dramatically over the past few years. Interestingly, its main competition has come from fundamentalist, but Sunni, Saudi Arabia.

In any event, the clash of world outlooks has remained an integral part of the Iranian-Turkish competition in Central Asia. And since Tehran is widely assumed to be intent on spreading militant Islam, Ankara's secular and democratic tendencies have created a commonality of Turkish-western (and, for that matter, Turkish-western-Russian) interests. Ankara has also gained Moscow's approval and western material support. (The Kremlin, for reasons of its own, is also opposed to the spread of fundamentalist Islam.) Little wonder, therefore, that Iran has reacted coolly to Turkey's efforts to embrace the Muslim republics and that Tehran and Ankara have become engaged in a spirited competition in Central Asia and southern Caucasus.

CONCLUSION

Based on the material just presented, there can be no doubt that, in Central Asia, Turkey is considerably ahead in its competition with Iran. Several factors are usually cited to explain the advantages that Ankara enjoys over Tehran in dealing with the region's newly independent states.

First, there is the common Turkic heritage, including history, ethnicity, and language, shared by all Central Asians with the exception of the Tajiks.

Second, there is the adherence to the Sunni branch of Islam, which the Central Asians, including the Tajiks, share with their Turkish co-religionists. Moreover, most Central Asian leaders and elites prefer Ankara's low-key brand of state-controlled Islam to the radical, fundamentalist brand of Shii Islam propagated by Tehran.

Third, by and large, the Turkish model of political and socioeconomic development is found more attractive in the Muslim republics than its Iranian counterpart. More specifically, it is the secularism of Kemalism, combined with free market economy and extended political and commercial relations with the West, that makes Ankara's example worthy of Central Asian emulation. The Turkish attachment to a democratic form of government, in contrast, is a feature that, lip-service apart, has not attracted too many followers. On the contrary, most leaders of the former Soviet republics, including the Muslim ones, prefer an authoritarian form of government that, the currently perfunctory bows to nationalism aside, is mainly concerned with maintaining in power the old and corrupt Communist Party machines. As President Niyazov told reporters in May 1992, "time is not ripe in Turkmenistan for multi-party democracy."[86]

Fourth, given the state of their economies, the Central Asian republics desperately need assistance and Turkey, with western help, is in a position to offer more than does Iran. Thus, Prime Minister Demirel, during his spring 1992 visit to the region, "pledged $1.2 billion in credits, export guarantees and soft loans" and promised aid with other projects.[87]

Fifth, in addition to the preceding factors, it should also be reiterated that the Ankara-Tehran competition in Central Asia and Caucasus is not merely a local or regional rivalry between two Middle Eastern powers. For obvious reasons, Russia has remained a major player. Moreover, the West—and particularly the United States—have injected themselves into the regional picture. Like Turkey, these outsiders have opposed the spread of Islamic radicalism, usually associated with Iran. And so has also Saudi Arabia, which has played a relatively modest but not insignificant part in the effort to curtail Iranian influence in the Muslim republics. Hence, Tehran has found itself confronting an informal, but politically and economically powerful, coalition in the competition for allegiance of the new Central Asian states.

In sum, in contrast with Iran, which has been advocating its own, indigenous "Islamic model of society," Turkey is offering the Muslim republics what one Russian commentator described as an "Eurasian version of Western democracy and market economy."[88] As already noted, in this competition, Ankara is more likely to succeed than Tehran. Nevertheless, it is obvious that the Islamic Republic, because of its central geographic location and of the economic opportunities that it offers to the newly independent Muslim states, will remain a significant regional player. However, when all is said and done, it should be clear to Turkey and Iran as well as to Russia and the West that the Central Asian republics will first and above all pursue their own interests, as defined by their respective leaders. In this endeavor, the local actors will try to extract maximum benefits from all the outsiders and will not compromise their national interests in the name of ethnicity, religion, or anything else.

N·O·T·E·S

1. As quoted in *Pravda* (Moscow), January 22, 1992.

2. As quoted in *Bakinskii rabochii* (Baku), February 29, 1992.

3. See ibid., April 1, 1992; and V. Volodin, *Izvestiia* (Moscow), April 27, 1992.

4. See M. Iusin, *Izvestiia*, December 3, 1991; and V. Lashkul, *Izvestiia*, January 3, 1992.

5. As quoted in *Bakinskii rabochii*, January 9 and 28, 1992.

6. As quoted in A. Portanskii, *Izvestiia*, February 17, and *Pravda Vostoka* (Tashkent), February 21, 1992.

7. See A. Portanskii, *Izvestiia*, February 17 and 18, 1992.

8. *Bakinskii rabochii*, September 3, 1991, and *Trud* (Moscow), September 24, 1991.

9. *Izvestiia*, October 9, 1991.

10. Radio Tehran, November 26, 1991, in FBIS-NES, November 26, 1991, p. 57.

11. Radio Moscow, December 4, 1991, in FBIS-SOV, December 6, 1991, p. 10.

12. Radio Tehran, December 6, 1991, in FBIS-NES, December 9, 1991, p. 20.

13. Radio Tehran, December 8, 1991, in FBIS-NES, December 9, 1991, pp. 65-66.

14. See note 12.

15. See note 13.

16. Radio Tehran, December 25, 1991, in FBIS-NES, December 27, 1991, p. 27.

17. For more details, see *Pravda Vostoka*, January 17, 1992; and Radio Tehran, January 17 and 24, 1992, in FBIS-NES, January 23, 1992, p. 55, and January 28, 1992, p. 50.

18. Ibid., February 17, 1992, in FBIS-NES, February 18, 1992, p. 50.

19. Ibid., March 5, 1992, in FBIS-NES, March 10, 1992, p. 39.

20. See *Izvestiia*, April 18, 1992.

21. Radio Tehran, April 15, 1992, in FBIS-NES, April 16, 1992, pp. 55 and 56, respectively.

22. Ibid., May 3, 1992, in FBIS-NES, May 4, 1992, pp. 57-58.

23. *Turkmenskaia iskra* (Ashkabat), May 12 and 13, 1992.

24. Radio Tehran, May 15, 1992, in FBIS-NES, May 20, 1992, p. 51.

25. Radio Tehran, February 17, 1992, in FBIS-NES, February 18, 1992, p. 48.

26. Radio Tehran, February 29 and March 2, 1992, in FBIS-NES, March 5, 1992, pp. 42 and 43.

27. Radio Tehran, April 27, 1992, in FBIS-NES, May 5, 1992, p. 52.

28. Radio Tehran, February 17, 1992, in FBIS-NES, February 18, 1992, p. 49; and *Pravda Vostoka*, February 25, 1992.

29. Radio Tehran, April 20, 1992, in FBIS-NES, April 21, 1992, p. 54.

30. Radio Tehran, May 9, 1992, in FBIS-NES, May 12, 1992, p. 4.

31. Radio Tehran, May 11 and 15, 1992, in FBIS-NES, May 12, 1992, p. 44, and May 20, 1992, p. 51.

32. See *Pravda Vostoka*, February 7 and 22, 1992, respectively.

33. Radio Tehran, February 17, 1992, in FBIS-NES, February 18, 1992, pp. 48 and 50.

34. For some details, see Radio Tehran, February 16, 1992, in FBIS-NES, February 18, 1992, p. 47.

35. Radio Tehran, February 17 and 16, 1992, in FBIS-NES, February 18, 1992, pp. 48 and 47.

36. Radio Tehran, February 16 and 17, 1992, in FBIS-NES, February 18, 1992, pp. 46 and 47-48.

37. Radio Tehran, February 17, 1992, in FBIS-NES, February 18, 1992, pp. 47 and 48.

38. Radio Tehran, April 26 and 29, 1992, in FBIS-NES, April 27 and 30, 1992, pp. 55 and 39.

39. *Bakinskii rabochii*, April 30, 1992.

40. *Turkmenskaia iskra*, May 11 and 13, 1992. Reference was made to Russia, which was not invited to attend the Ashkabat conference.

41. Ibid., May 13; and *Pravda Vostoka*, May 14, 1992.

42. *Kazakhstanskaia pravda* (Alma Ata), May 14, 1992.

43. *Radio Tehran*, May 16, 1992, in FBIS-NES, May 20, 1992, p. 52.

44. See *Bakinskii rabochii*, November 3, 1990, and *Izvestiia*, November 15, 1990.

45. *Pravda*, December 18, 1991.

46. *Bakinskii rabochii*, February 4 and 29, 1992.

47. Ibid., April 9, 1992.

48. A. Kaipbergenov, *Pravda,* December 21, 1991.

49. *Pravda Vostoka,* January 1, 1992, and A. Kasymov and V. Gulin, *Pravda Vostoka,* January 16, 1992.

50. *Pravda Vostoka,* January 15 and 21; January 28; and January 24, 1992.

51. Ibid., February 7 and 22, 1992, respectively.

52. Ibid., February 7, 1992.

53. A. Sychev, *Izvestiia,* March 5, 1992, and *Pravda Vostoka,* March 4, 1992.

54. V. Volodin, *Izvestiia,* April 28, 1992; and *Pravda Vostoka,* April 30, 1992.

55. A. Kamorin, *Izvestiia,* April 29, 1992.

56. *Pravda Vostoka,* April 18 and 23, 1992.

57. *Kazakhstanskaia pravda,* January 22 and 23, 1992.

58. See *Pravda Vostoka,* February 28, 1992, and V. Kiianitsa, *Moskovskie novosti* (Moscow), March 15, 1992.

59. As quoted by Sh. Baibolova, *Kazakhstanskaia pravda,* March 14, 1992.

60. Ibid., March 24 and 19, 1992. By mid-April, some 20 Turkish firms were reported doing business in Kazakhstan. Ibid., April 15, 1992.

61. Ibid., April 30, May 5, and May 1, 1992.

62. As quoted by M. Iusin, *Izvestiia,* December 3, 1991; and *Trud,* December 5, 1991.

63. See Niyazov's interview with V. Kuleshov, *Izvestiia,* January 6, 1992.

64. *Turkmenskaia iskra,* March 3 and 2, 1992.

65. Ibid., May 1 and 4, 1992.

66. Ibid., May 5 and 7, 1992.

67. Nazar Suyunov, member of the Turkmenistan Presidential Council, in an interview with *Izvestiia,* April 18, 1992.

68. See *Komsomol'skaia pravda* (Moscow), December 26, 1991, and *Izvestiia,* December 25, 1991.

69. See *Pravda Vostoka,* May 1, 1992, and *Izvestiia,* April 29, 1992.

70. See *Narodnaia gazeta* (Dushanbe), May 12, 1992.

71. See *Izvestiia,* January 8, 1992, and *The Economist* (London), April 25, 1992.

72. Interview with *Nezavisimaia gazeta* (Moscow), February 14, 1992.

73. See, for example, A. Kaipbergenov, *Pravda,* December 21, 1991; and *Pravda Vostoka,* January 15 and February 5, 1992.

74. *Nezavisimaia gazeta,* May 15, 1992.

75. Anvar Kasymov, *Pravda Vostoka,* March 26, 1992.

76. As quoted by Francis X. Clines, *New York Times,* February 9, 1992, and *The Economist,* April 25, 1992, p. 34.

77. A. Karpov, *Izvestiia,* February 14, and *Moskovskie novosti,* February 23, 1992.

78. Ibid., April 12, 1992.

79. This point is developed by Shireen Hunter, *Christian Science Monitor,* March 2, 1992.

80. Some weapon systems, including missiles, have reportedly also been provided by China and North Korea. For some details of Iran's arms acquisition, see David Hoffman, *Washington Post,* February 2, 1992, and Peter Grier, *Christian Science Monitor,* February 10, 1992.

81. Turkey, too, was suspected of the same ambition. This was categorically denied by the Turkish Ministry of Foreign Affairs (*Izvestiia,* January 11, 1992) and all the other concerned parties.

82. See, for example, reference to an agreement with Tajikistan in Thomas L. Friedman, *New York Times,* February 14, 1992. Uranium ore is also produced in Turkmenistan and Uzbekistan in addition to Tajikistan. Tajikistan officially denied that it had any intention of selling enriched uranium abroad. *Radio Moscow,* January 7, 1992, as quoted in FBIS-SOV, January 8, 1992, p. 70.

83. See Safa Haeri, *Sunday Times* (London), January 26, 1992.

84. A. Kamorin, *Izvestiia,* April 29, 1992.

85. As quoted in *New York Times,* March 22, 1992.

86. As quoted in *The Economist,* May 16, 1992, p. 44.

87. Ibid.

88. V. Volodin, *Izvestiia,* April 27, 1992.

▲ ▽ ▲

16

Central Asia: Emerging Relations with the Arab States and Israel

◆

Carol R. Saivetz

The unexpected independence of the Muslim states of Central Asia[1] forced each one to deal with the problems of nation-building and to carve out for itself a role in the international arena. In the words of Kazakh President Nursultan Nazarbayev: ". . . it has become clear that it is time for the republic to *determine its geopolitical place* and the strategy of its own development."[2] In reality, independent foreign policies began to emerge in the late Gorbachev period, 1990-91, as Kazakhstan, Kyrgyzstan, Tajikistan, Turkmenistan, and Uzbekistan initiated tentative contacts with the outside world. Following the collapse of the Soviet Union in December 1991, this effort became more determined.

After nearly a year of independence, it seems clear that the foreign policy priorities of the new Central Asian states will include the search for full independence, international legitimacy, military security, and economic and technical assistance. Security is, of course, related to geography, and none of the Central Asian states could fashion a foreign policy without considering its geostrategic location—more or less bordering Russia, China, and the Middle East. In many respects, the last, ties with the states of the Middle East, appears to be especially significant.

It seems to be assumed that, as Muslim states, Kazakhstan, Kyrgyzstan, Tajikistan, Turkmenistan, and Uzbekistan will become Middle East actors or, at the least, a bridge to the Middle East. Given this context, most of the world's attention has focused on the rivalry between Iran and Turkey for influence in the former Soviet republics of Central Asia. Yet other Middle East states have also sought relations with the five Central Asian Muslim states on the same assumption. Oman, Saudi Arabia, Egypt, and Israel, among others, have been actively proffering various kinds of assistance to Central Asia in the hopes of influencing the future role these Soviet successor states will play in the Middle East state system.

The focus of this chapter is emerging Central Asian relations with the Arab states and Israel. The first section looks at the context in which these early links are being forged—the collapse of the Soviet Union and the evolving competition between Iran and Turkey for influence in Central Asia. The second section examines the trends that have become visible in the first year of independence. The intent is not to offer a catalogue of visiting delegations and individual agreements, but to highlight the most significant bilateral and multilateral accords and to characterize the nature of Central Asia's emerging relations with the Arab states and Israel. Finally, the last section offers a tentative assessment of the benefits to both the Arabs and Israel, on the one hand, and Central Asia, on the other, of these new ties. The section also speculates on future foreign policy trends for the Central Asians.

COLLAPSE OF THE SOVIET UNION
AND IRANIAN-TURKISH COMPETITION IN CENTRAL ASIA

The attempted hard-line coup of August 1991 left the leaderships of the Central Asian republics in precarious positions: They were Communists forced to react to the coup attempt, and, when the coup failed, they were Communists who had to dissociate themselves from the old regime in order to prove their nationalist credentials. Thus, following the coup, they were ambivalent toward Mikhail S. Gorbachev's efforts to conclude a new union treaty and enthusiastic about forging links with the outside world. Between August and December, contacts were made with Turkey, Iran, the United States, Pakistan, Korea, Cyprus, in addition to Russia. As these states worked to establish their independence, relations with the non-Soviet world served to enhance their standing vis-à-vis Moscow.

A brief survey of the policies of the five Central Asian states in this period reveals no single pattern; however, several themes do emerge. First, the Central Asian states—and particularly Kazakhstan—resented their exclusion from the Minsk meeting at which Russia, Belarus, and Ukraine created the Commonwealth of Independent States (CIS) and decided upon a joint approach to what was at first a Slavic confederation. Second, the United States seemed most interested in Kazakhstan, obviously because of the strategic nuclear weapons deployed on Kazakh territory. Finally, of the outside states, Iran and Turkey were decidedly the most active in establishing a presence in Central Asia.[3]

Even prior to the August 1991 abortive coup, the Central Asian states met in Tashkent to decide a joint approach to the pressing economic problems facing the country and to the then ongoing negotiations for a union treaty. In the fall, as the Soviet Union disintegrated, the Central Asian leaders advocated—to varying degrees—a single economic space, but were careful not to relinquish too much authority to Moscow. Following the Minsk meeting, the presidents of the Central Asian republics convened in Ashkhabad, Turkmenistan, on December 12 to decide their response to the establishment of the new commonwealth. They agreed to join the CIS, but only if they would be listed as coequal founders of the new commonwealth. Their declaration said in part:

> There must be a guarantee of equal participation by the subjects of the former Union in the process of elaborating decisions and documents of the Commonwealth of Independent States. . . .
>
> One should take into account in these documents, decisions, and agreements, the historic and socioeconomic realities of the republics of Central Asia and Kazakhstan, who were not considered, unfortunately, during the preparation of the agreement on a commonwealth.[4]

During this same period, Kazakhstan and only very secondarily Kyrgyzstan merited western attention. On September 15, 1991, U.S. Secretary of State James Baker visited Alma Ata. According to press accounts, Baker offered vague promises of economic assistance; however, it was clear that the fate of the strategic nuclear weapons deployed in Kazakhstan, was of primary importance. In mid-October, former German Foreign Minister Hans Dietrich Genscher traveled to Kazakhstan and later that month President Nursultan Nazarbayev visited London. With each bilateral meeting, Nazarbayev was pressured to commit his country to become a nonnuclear power. Baker returned to Kazakhstan in December, just prior to the Alma Ata summit at which the Central Asian states joined the CIS. For Nazarbayev the message was clear: Kazakhstan's prestige was derived primarily from the weapons deployed there. Kyrgyzstan stands out as somewhat of an anomaly. Its president, Askar Akaev, traveled to the United States in late October to speak at the United Nations and to meet with Bush administration officials in Washington. As president of the most democratic of the Central Asian states, Akaev hoped to garner much needed economic assistance from the United States. Washington responded with a return visit from Baker in mid-December.

As the old "center" collapsed during the fall, the Central Asian states looked to Turkey and Iran for economic assistance and for international recognition. President Nazarbayev was the first president to visit Ankara in the postcoup period, and he returned to Alma Ata with several bilateral agreements on economic cooperation, transportation, and television and telephone links.[5] Turkmen President Saparmurad Niyazov followed in December. He, too, garnered numerous agreements on trade, economic cooperation, and culture.

Ties to Iran also proliferated in this period, although Iranian activities especially in Tajikistan began much earlier.[6] Tehran proceeded carefully out of concern for stability on its border; however, caution was matched by the worry that Turkey was getting a head start in the influence battle in Central Asia.[7] After the coup, President Niyazov of Turkmenistan traveled to Tehran and returned with several cooperation accords, as well as the promise of more long-term and wider-ranging agreements in the future. Kyrgyzstan followed when the chairman of the Supreme Soviet, Medetkan Sherimkulov, visited Tehran in early November. On December 25, Iran recognized the independence of all five Central Asian states.

In late 1991, contacts with the rest of the Middle East were minimal, at best; nonetheless, even prior to the final collapse of the Soviet Union, several Arab states did make overtures to the Muslim states of Central Asia.[8] During the crisis and war in the Gulf in 1990-91, Saudi Arabia offered credits to the Soviet Union as repayment for support for the anti-Iraq coalition: Among the Saudi investments was $175 million contributed to a joint Soviet-Saudi bank to be established in Alma Ata. Other contacts included transporting Central Asian pilgrims to Mecca and providing a million copies of the Quran. In an interview with the London *Sawt al-Kuwait al-Duwali*, Nazarbayev indicated his interest in economic agreements with Riyadh and in accepting an invitation to visit Saudi Arabia.[9] Kazakhstan also established early contact with Oman when Deputy Prime Minister Kalyk Abdullayev traveled to the sultanate. Oman agreed to provide assistance to the Kazakh oil industry and to participate in an international oil pipeline. In addition, the two countries also discussed a $200 million loan.

It should also be noted that in this preindependence period, questions of linking the Central Asians with Islamic and Middle Eastern international organizations arose. The Muslim successor states were all invited to the

December 1991 meeting of the Islamic Conference Organization (ICO) held in Senegal. According to several reports, Tajikistan, Turkmenistan, and Kazakhstan considered joining the organization, while Kyrgyzstan claimed that it was not interested in ICO membership. All claimed that they were interested in the economic contacts that membership would facilitate, not in religious identification. Additionally, media reports indicated that Kazakhstan was studying the possibility of joining the Arab League.[10]

Since our focus is on Central Asian relations with the Middle East, two other items should be noted. First, Israel moved quickly to recognize the official independence of Uzbekistan and to establish formal diplomatic relations. Within a short period of time, as will be seen later, Tel Aviv expanded its diplomatic presence in the region. Second, Palestine Liberation Organization (PLO) chairman Yasir Arafat visited Alma Ata in late December. In a meeting with Nazarbayev, Arafat sought Kazakh recognition of the Palestinian state and allegedly urged the Kazakh president to include the Palestinian question on the CIS agenda.

Thus by December 25, 1991, when Mikhail S. Gorbachev resigned as general secretary of the Communist Party and the Soviet Union ceased to exist, the Central Asian states were the scene of a developing contest for influence between secular but Muslim Turkey and Islamic Iran. Other Middle Eastern states seemed to be operating at the periphery of this core Turkish-Iranian bidding war. With the new year and independence for Kazakhstan, Kyrgyzstan, Tajikistan, Turkmenistan, and Uzbekistan, all of these trends accelerated.

AFTER INDEPENDENCE

Precipitous independence altered the parameters of both the foreign and domestic policy debates within Central Asia. The now-national leaderships were confronted with achieving legitimacy for themselves at the same time as they were faced with acquiring international recognition for their new countries. This meant serious and responsible approaches to the sharply deteriorating economic conditions they were all experiencing and steering a balanced course among all their "international" neighbors. These goals were combined in the search for foreign economic and technical assistance.

Before examining Central Asia's emerging ties with the Arabs and Israel in the postindependence period, several other trends must be noted. In the search for international recognition, all of the Central Asian states established relations with a broad spectrum of countries, including Cuba,

Mongolia, the European powers, and the United States; moreover, they sought admission to several multilateral organizations, for example, the Conference on Security and Cooperation in Europe, the United Nations, and the Economic Cooperation Organization (ECO) founded by Turkey, Iran, and Pakistan. Simultaneously, in the first few months of 1992, Russia was preoccupied with its own position in the world and with its quest for economic assistance. Andrei Kozyrev, the Russian foreign minister, devoted most of his attention to links with Western Europe and the United States and was soundly criticized by conservatives and by Russian nationalists for abandoning what had been Russia's historic preserve in Central Asia.[11] This ostensible neglect of the "near abroad" left the field relatively open to Iran, Turkey, and other Middle Eastern actors.

With the formal independence of the former republics of the Soviet Union, Iran and Turkey intensified their rivalry for influence in Central Asia. Both offered economic assistance and in effect different models of society and politics. Would the Central Asian states follow the model of secular Turkey or Islamic Iran? According to longtime Middle East hand Dmitry Volsky, the Central Asian states have three choices: to follow a path toward democracy in conjunction with Russia and the West; to gravitate towards the Turkish model of secular Islam; or to follow Islamic fundamentalism.[12]

Thus far, none of the states is slavishly following any particular model, although there is strong interest in Iran and Turkey because of their proximity and shared cultural and linguistic heritages.

As the competition between Iran and Turkey intensified and in the absence—at least initially—of a strong Russian presence, several other Middle East actors enhanced efforts to establish a presence in Central Asia. Among those who were active in the early part of 1992 were Saudi Arabia, Egypt, Kuwait, Oman, and Israel. Some moved because of the economic opportunities that appeared, while others reacted out of fear that Tehran could succeed in creating some sort of pro-Iranian alliance in the region. In either case, all seemed to be positioning themselves for Central Asia's entry into the Middle East state system. By the end of January, Kuwait had recognized all the republics of the former Soviet Union, and Israel had established diplomatic relations with Uzbekistan. In the economic sphere, Saudi Arabia began some early business ventures, such as a plan to import marble, and Israel established direct communications links with Kazakhstan.

In mid-February, Saudi Foreign Minister Prince Saud al Faysal Bin Abd al Aziz al Saud made a much-publicized tour through Central Asia. He not only established diplomatic relations with the Muslim republics, but also brought with him promises of humanitarian and economic assistance and a million Qurans. The prince, while in Ashkhabad, said that Saudi Arabia "has focused its attention on cooperation with brothers in the Islamic world. . . . We express to [the peoples of Central Asia] our desire and hope to cooperate with them and to establish ties of amity in order for the future of this region to be as prosperous as its past was."[13] Saudi Arabia began to play an even more active role when King Fahad hosted the presidents of Turkmenistan and Uzbekistan in separate visits in April.

In both instances, economic cooperation agreements were initialed and, it was hoped, Saudi businessmen could be attracted to invest in Central Asia. In one such deal, Saudi investors reached an agreement for oil and gas exploration and development with Uzbekneft.[14] Earlier Oman promised Kazakhstan $100 million credit to assist Alma Ata in supplying oil to other countries, and almost simultaneously with the Saudi visit, a Kuwaiti delegation toured the CIS and was rumored to be willing to underwrite a $1 billion credit for the successor states.[15] All told, the Gulf states have decided to channel some $3 billion to the Central Asian states.[16]

Nor has Israel missed the opportunity to establish relations with all of the Central Asian states except Turkmenistan. Israel's motivation is clearly political: a strong desire to prevent these new Muslim states from siding with anti-Israel Iran. By the same token, the Israeli business community views Central Asia as a potentially vast export market and has projected up to $100-million-a-year business in the future.[17] Israeli firms have already established direct-dial links with Kazakhstan and helped Uzbekistan with irrigation techniques. For the most part, trade contacts seem to be with Kazakhstan: In April alone the Kazakh agricultural minister traveled to Israel, and Nazarbayev received Israeli ambassador to Moscow Arye Levin, who went to Alma Ata to open formal diplomatic relations between the two countries.

The Gulf states, given their oil wealth, are probably in the best positions to aid the new countries of Central Asia. Nevertheless, they are not the only Arab states to seek opportunities, especially in purchasing arms. During March a Libyan delegation visited Kazakhstan and the Syrian foreign minister traveled to Alma Ata, Dushanbe, Ashkhabad, and Tashkent. One can presume that they were in search of nuclear technology and/or conventional arms transfers. All of the Central Asian states possessed tactical nuclear weapons, but there seems to be some question as to whether or not all of them have been dismantled; moreover, there remains the possibility that fissionable materials taken from these weapons might be sold to countries in the Middle East.

Any of the Central Asian states might also sell surplus Soviet equipment for hard currency. For example, Kazakhstan, having privatized some weapons production facilities, has allowed these factories to negotiate private international sales—the recipients most often named are Syria and Iran. Furthermore, several of the Central Asian states possess uranium that could be sold to generate hard currency. In the words of a Moscow Radio announcer:

> Tajikistan intends to export enriched uranium in the near future. Representatives of Saudi Arabia, Iran, Turkey, Iraq, and Pakistan have already visited Dushanbe. Experts believe that these countries are the potential purchasers of enriched uranium manufactured in this former Soviet republic.[18]

The context in which these diplomatic, economic, and military contacts were made began to change in April for several reasons. First, the Yeltsin government, under pressure from Russian nationalists, initiated new links with the Central Asian states. Kozyrev signaled a renewed interest in the "near abroad" when he proposed creating a commonwealth office within the Russian Foreign Ministry. Then, in April, he traveled to Tajikistan and Turkmenistan on his way to the Gulf. Throughout the summer, Russia signed a series of bilateral treaties with the Central Asian states guaranteeing economic and military cooperation.

Kozyrev's trip to the Gulf deserves some examination. According to Russian press accounts, the foreign minister was there to further economic and diplomatic relations and to sell military equipment. Yet, at each stop—in Saudi Arabia, Qatar, Bahrain, Oman, the United Arab Emirates, and Kuwait—he discussed Islamic radicalism and the problems both within Russia and in the CIS. One could question whether it was coincidental that within a month Bahrain, Oman, and Kuwait moved to further their business contacts with the Muslim states of Central Asia. Certainly it could be argued that the Gulf Cooperation Council (GCC) had its own geostrategic reasons for wanting to thwart any growth in Iran's influence throughout the region.

Second, Kazakhstan, Kyrgyzstan, Tajikistan, Turkmenistan, and Uzbekistan convened two summits—one in Bishkek in April and a second in Ashkhabad in May. At their April meeting, delegations from the five states discussed the creation of a common economic space, banking issues, and transportation proposals. They were also careful to assure outsiders that the meeting did not signify the failure of the CIS or Central Asian withdrawal from the CIS. The final resolutions of the conference called for the mutual renunciation of force among them, the pursuit of a joint regional security policy, and support for continuing cooperation with neighboring Asian states, given their "deep-rooted traditional links going back to ancient times."[19] Nazarbayev, commenting on the work of the summit, noted that the participants looked to further develop contacts with India, Pakistan, and the Arab countries.[20]

The heads of the Central Asian states (minus Tajikistan, which was in the midst of civil war) met again in May in Ashkhabad. This time the president of Iran and the prime ministers of Turkey and Pakistan participated as well. Focusing on economic cooperation and development, the participants pledged to expand trade and cultural exchanges. Additionally, they discussed joint transportation networks and the construction of specific oil and natural gas pipelines.

In addition to the attention given to the renewal of Russian interest in the "near abroad" and the attempts at cooperation both among the former Soviet republics and between them and Iran, Turkey, and Pakistan, the Central Asian states continued to pursue contacts with the Arabs and Israel. In May, Oman established relations with Kyrgyzstan and Kazakhstan, and a Bahraini delegation traveled to Kazakhstan and Uzbekistan, also to initiate diplomatic links. Morocco, too, moved to establish diplomatic relations with Kyrgyzstan. Throughout the summer, the pattern of bilateral economic and diplomatic contacts continued. For example, Israeli businessmen and government officials continued their economic and diplomatic contacts in the region. In August, Ambassador Arye Levin was welcomed in Dushanbe by President Nabiyev who indicated a strong interest in Israeli investment. In light of the Tajik civil war, one might also speculate that Levin was in Dushanbe to establish contact with the small local Jewish community. In September, an Israeli agricultural delegation arrived in Kyrgyzstan and Kazakh Prime Minister Sergei Tereshchenko traveled to Israel to discuss more joint ventures.

Egypt continued to pursue economic and political ties as well. Earlier, Egyptian investors began negotiations for a $200 million countertrade agreement with Kazakhstan.[21] Closer relations with Kazakhstan were further enhanced by the appointment of an Egyptian-born economist and legal scholar as an economic advisor to Nazarbayev. Additionally, the Egyptian education minister traveled to Alma Ata in August to establish a program to train economic managers, and the minister of religion visited Ashkhabad in September.

In the economics sphere, the largest deals concluded were between Oman and Kazakhstan. Oman agreed to explore and develop the Atyrau area and further develop the known reserves in the Dunga field. In an even more far-reaching deal, the two agreed in mid-June to form an oil consortium to build a pipeline to enable Kazakhstan to export oil from the Tengiz oilfield. Other former Soviet republics may join the consortium, as may Turkey and Iran. The estimated cost of the accord ranges from $700 million to $1.6 billion. The consortium may also be involved in the construction of a Turkmen pipeline as well.[22]

A PRELIMINARY ASSESSMENT

This brief survey of the first year of Central Asia's emerging relations with the Arab states and Israel indicates that the demands of nation-building—the creation of a new national identity; establishing a functioning, growing economy; and assuring military security—are paramount for the new Muslim states of the region. Islam and ethnic factors are clearly part of the new non-Soviet identities that Kazakhstan, Kyrgyzstan, Tajikistan, Turkmenistan, and Uzbekistan are striving to establish. This drive enhances the interest in both Turkey and Iran among the Central Asian states: As noted, Turkey represents a secular model of development and is linked with western interests; Iran, in contrast, represents a radical Islamic model of society, antiwesternism, and anti-Israel positions. In general, with the exception of Tajikistan, the consensus seems to be that Islamic symbols—such as the pilgrimage—are valuable to a former Communist leadership trying to assert its nationalist credentials; nonetheless, as pragmatists and ex-Communists, they have rejected full Islamicization as an option.

The search for economic assistance means that almost all offers of help are welcomed by the struggling Central Asian leaderships. Iran and Turkey, as described by Oles M. Smolansky in Chapter 15, have proffered cultural, economic, and technical assistance; yet they may not be in the best positions to contribute the large sums of development assistance needed by the Central Asian states. Saudi Arabia, Kuwait, and Oman would seem to be better able to provide the kind of long-term economic assistance required by Kazakhstan, Kyrgyzstan, Tajikistan, Turkmenistan, and Uzbekistan. Israel, too, possesses technical and agricultural skills vitally needed by the Central Asians.

Finally, of course, security concerns will continue to predominate in the foreign policy calculations of these ex-Soviet republics. By the end of the period under discussion here, another shift in the international context for emerging Central Asian foreign policies had occurred. Even though economic ties with the Arabs and Israel continued to proliferate, the focus of the Central Asian leaderships shifted to immediate security concerns. The final collapse of the Najib government in Afghan and the ensuing civil war there, coupled with the civil war in Tajikistan and the ouster of Tajik President Rahman Nabiyev, made the remaining Central Asian states increasingly leery of Islamic forces and fearful of an actual spillover of the two civil wars.

The unrest in Afghanistan and especially Tajikistan has also made the other Central Asian leaderships wary of possible Iranian involvement. Indeed, Interfax reported that the Uzbek foreign minister warned Iranian diplomats in Tashkent against "endeavors to advocate Iranian fundamentalism locally."[23] Much more attention was, therefore, paid to cultivating ties with Russia, to the north. Geopolitics clearly predominated, as each in turn signed bilateral agreements — including military cooperation treaties — with Russia. In the words of the new Turkmen foreign minister: "[Russians] can be counted on in troubled days. . . .

> It's becoming a geographic reality that we are defending Russia's southern border, henceforth our mutual interest in military cooperation. . . . the Russian factor will continue to dominate in Turkmenistan's foreign policy."[24]

As for the outside powers, for the time being, the competition between Iran and Turkey will remain central to Central Asia's emerging relations with the Middle East. Moreover, Kazakhstan, Kyrgyzstan, Turkmenistan, and Uzbekistan for their parts will continue to balance ties with these two outside rivals. By the same token, this ongoing bidding war will also trigger the involvement of other Middle Eastern states. From this perspective, it is in the interests of those who oppose Iranian policies in the Middle East and who fear Iranian-style Islamic forces to work in Central Asia to counter Iranian influence. This goes a long way toward explaining Saudi Arabian and GCC interest in Central Asia as well as Israeli involvement. For example, in analyzing the February tour of Central Asia by the Saudi foreign minister, *Izvestiia* claimed that Riyadh was clearly concerned about Iranian influence in Central Asia and offered the assessment that Saudi Arabia and the GCC states "have every chance to counter Iranian influence in the Muslim republics of the CIS."[25]

The concerns of the Saudis and the other Arabs are religious as well as geopolitical. The partially religious thrust of Prince Saud al Faysal Bin Abd al Aziz al Saud's visit may be understood as an attempt to counter influences that are seen as detrimental to mainstream Sunni Islam.[26] When Russian Foreign Minister Kozyrev was in Saudi Arabia, it was reported that King Fahd said that he (the king) was well aware of those who were trying to exploit the religious factor to achieve power.[27] Some western observers second this assessment. They note that Egypt, along with the Gulf states, is determined to promote Sunni Islam in Central Asia by sending Egyptian *ulema* to preach there.[28]

If the Saudis (and others) are concerned about Iranian-style Shi'i Islam, Russians seem to view all this activity from a slightly different perspective. According to *Komsomolskaia Pravda,* Egyptian goods purchased by monies from the Gulf states began to arrive in March and April.[29] Moreover, Arab activity, when seen in conjunction with U.S. fears of Iranian influence, is a means to "attract these new young countries to the Turkish model of development."[30] In the words of Russia's ambassador to the United States, Vladimir Lukin: "a resurgence of Islamic fundamentalism (both anti-Western and anti-Russian) combined with a persistent economic crisis in Transcaucasia and Central Asia would endanger not only Russia's interests, but also the stability of the Islamic and Asian worlds."[31]

Thus, even Russian conservatives, who tend to view all this outside activity with suspicion, must be more comfortable with the combined opposition to the spread of Iranian-inspired Islamic radicalism than with the Iranian presence. Russians also seem aware that the cultural and linguistic ties between Turkey and the Central Asian states will reinforce the Turkish position. For example, in commenting on Turkish television broadcasts to Central Asia, an Ostankino narrator said: "While Iran and the Arabic countries are trying to consolidate their positions via the mosques, the Turks are unstinting when it comes to expanding their TV presence."[32]

Israeli concerns mirror, to a large extent, those of the Arabs and Turkey. The Israeli government has worked to open embassies in the Central Asian capitals, while Israeli entrepreneurs seek to invest and put together joint ventures there. The businessmen readily acknowledge the risks entailed in investing in Central Asia, but they also recognize the political advantages accruing to their investments. Israel will gain more than profits from these endeavors. First, an Israeli presence could well protect local Jewish communities—as in Dushanbe. And second, Israel hopes to encourage or gain neutrality from the states with regard to the Arab-Israeli dispute. For example, in an interview with the Israeli newspaper *Yedi'ot Aharonot,* Nazarbayev claimed that Kazakhstan's "approach to the rival sides in the Middle East is even-handed."[33]

In the final analysis, Central Asia remains a scene of tremendous potential instability, as events in Tajikistan illustrate. The foreign policy tendencies discussed are dependent, in large measure, on the current leaders; Islamicization could well portend significant shifts in foreign policies.

Whether intended or not, there seems to be a community of interests among Russia, Turkey, the Arabs, Israel, and the current secular Central Asian leaders. As one conservative commentator wrote in *New Times*: "The menace from the South will impel local rulers to preserve the alliance with Moscow, whose stabilizing role in the region is of great interest not only to the West, but also to Israel and the wealthy Arabs, especially Saudi Arabia."[34] Although each has its own policy agenda with regard to Central Asia, preventing Islamicization and radicalization appears to be in all their interests. Moreover, if Turkey, the oil-rich Gulf states, and Israel can assist in the economic stabilization of the region, that would also be to Russia's advantage.

In the short run, foreign policy trends will probably continue as they have for the now almost completed first year of independence. Military security dictates ties to Moscow—which still has troops stationed in all of the successor states—while economic needs mandate continuing ties to Iran, Turkey, Israel, and the Arab states. (Of course, the United States and Western Europe are still vitally important as sources of international legitimacy and economic assistance.) In the specifically Middle Eastern context, Iran and Turkey are certain to continue their competition for influence over Central Asia, and their bidding war will be the central focus for Kazakhstan, Kyrgyzstan, Turkmenistan, Tajikistan, and Uzbekistan. Nonetheless, as has been discussed, there is room for the Arab states and Israel in the picture, and they, for their own reasons, are likely to persist in expanding their ties to the new Muslim states of Central Asia. For the current leaders, then, the pursuit of true independence and economic assistance requires balance—among Russia, Iran and Turkey, and the Arabs and Israel.

N·O·T·E·S

1. In Soviet parlance, the term Central Asia referred only to Kirghizia (now Kyrgyzstan), Tajikistan, Turkmenistan, and Uzbekistan. Western usage has varied, sometimes to include Kazakhstan. Since Kazakhstan has participated in the post-Soviet Central Asian summits, I shall use the more inclusive definition of Central Asia.

2. Interview with Nazarbayev, *Nezavisimaia gazeta,* May 6, 1992, p. 5.

3. Iranian and Turkish relations with the new states of Central Asia are discussed by Oles M. Smolansky in Chapter 15.

4. TASS, December 13, 1992, in FBIS-SOV 91 240, December 13, 1992, pp. 84-85.

5. See summary: Moscow Radio Rossii Network, September 30, 1991, in FBIS-SOV 91 191, October 2, 1991, p. 85.

6. Contacts with Iran intensified following the passage of a new language law that directed that Tajik should be written in Arabic script. Iran has provided teachers and printing materials. Thereafter multiple economic and cultural links were established.

7. *Jomhuri Islami,* September 6, 1991, as cited in *Middle East Economic Digest* (hereafter *MEED*), September 20, 1991, p. 14.

8. During the Soviet period, of course, the Arab states enjoyed diplomatic relations with Moscow. Under Gorbachev, these formal links expanded to include Oman, the United Arab Emirates, and Saudi Arabia.

9. London, *Sawt al-Kuwait al-Duwali* (in Arabic), November 7, 1991, p. 10, in FBIS-SOV 91 217, November 8, 1991, p. 75.

10. See for example, Moscow Radio, December 9, 1991, in FBIS-SOV 91 242, December 17, 1991, p. 74.

11. There has been all spring 1992 an intense debate within the Russian Foreign Ministry about the goals of Russian foreign policy. This debate included Andrei Kozyrev and those who supported his pro-western policies, those who argued that Russia was relinquishing its "traditional" role in Central Asia, and those who championed the cause of ethnic Russians living in Central Asia.

12. Dmitry Volsky, "After Bishkek — What?" *New Times,* no. 19 (May 1992), p. 7.

13. Riyadh, SPA, February 22, 1992, in FBIS-SOV 92 039, February 27, 1992, p. 72.

14. *MEED,* May 1, 1992, p. 21.

15. Reports were unclear as to who would receive the credits. See, for example, *Izvestiia,* February 18, 1992, p. 4, in FBIS-SOV 92 034, February 20, 1992, p. 19.

16. *MEED,* February 14, 1992, p. 5.

17. Hugh Carnegy, "Israel Extends Its Arm to Tie Up Central Asian Links," *Financial Times,* May 6, 1992, p. 6.

18. Moscow Radio, Rossii Network, August 9, 1992, in FBIS-SOV 92 155, August 11, 1992, p. 2.

19. Transcript of joint resolution: Postfactum, April 23, 1992, in FBIS-SOV 92 080, April 24, 1992, pp. 7-8.

20. Interfax, April 23, 1992, in FBIS-SOV 92 080, April 24, 1992, p. 9.

21. *MEED,* April 17, 1992, p. 13.

22. For more discussion of the deals and the costs see: *MEED,* June 26, 1992, p. 28; *MEED,* July 3, 1992, p. 19; and *MEED,* July 17, 1992, p. 24.

23. Interfax, August 30, 1992, in FBIS-SOV 92 169, August 31, 1992, p. 42.

24. Interfax, August 7, 1992, in FBIS-SOV 92 154, August 10, 1992, p. 64.

25. *Izvestiia,* February 21, 1992, p. 7, in FBIS-USR 92 023, March 5, 1992, p. 29.

26. See, for example, Tony Walker, "Battle for Hearts and Minds in Central Asia," *Financial Times,* January 24, 1992, p. 4.

27. See, for example, *Krasnaia zvezda,* May 6, 1992, p. 3, or *Izvestiia,* May 6, 1992, p. 7.

28. Walker, "Battle for Hearts and Minds."

29. *Komsomolskaia Pravda,* February 18, 1992, p. 3, in FBIS-SOV 92 034, February 20, 1992, p. 19.

30. See, for example, Ostankino broadcast, February 8, 1992, in FBIS-SOV 92 029, February 12, 1992, pp. 6-7.

31. Vladimir Lukin, "Our Security Predicament," *Foreign Policy,* no. 88 (Fall 1992): 62.

32. Moscow, Ostankino, June 8, 1992, in FBIS-SOV 92 114, June 12, 1992, p. 80.

33. *Yedi'ot Aharonot,* April 13, 1992, p. 18, in FBIS-SOV 072, April 14, 1992, p. 56.

34. Vladimir Kulistikov, "Afghan Volcano Threatens Tranquility in ex-Soviet Central Asia and Binds Local Rulers Still More Firmly to Moscow," *New Times,* no. 17 (April 1992): 3.

N·O·T·E·S O·N T·H·E
C·O·N·T·R·I·B·U·T·O·R·S

HAFEEZ MALIK is Professor of Political Science at Villanova University in Pennsylvania. From 1961 to 1963, and from 1966 to 1984, he was Visiting Lecturer at the Foreign Service Institute of the U.S. Department of State. An author/editor of several books and numerous articles, he was from 1971 to 1974 president of the Pakistan Council of the Asia Society, New York. Also, he is President of the Pakistan-American Foundation; founding Director (1973-88) of the American Institute of Pakistan Studies, and since 1977 editor of the *Journal of South Asian and Middle Eastern Studies*, and Executive Director of the American Council for the Study of Islamic Societies since 1983.

SEYMOUR BECKER is Professor of History at Rutgers University and is the author of several books and numerous articles on Russia.

STEPHEN BLANK is Associate Research Professor of Soviet Studies at the U.S. Army War College, Carlisle, Pennsylvania.

ABDUJABBAR A. ABDUVAKHITOV was a Senior Scientific Secretary at the Institute of Oriental Studies in Tashkent, Uzbekistan. Currently, he is president of the Miros Foundation in Tashkent.

MELVIN A. GOODMAN is Professor of International Studies in the Department of National Security Policy at the National War College, Ft. McNair, Washington, D.C. An author of numerous articles, he specializes in Soviet foreign policy toward the states in the Middle East.

VICTOR SPOLNIKOV is a former Major General of the KGB of the former Soviet Union. Currently, he is Senior Research Scholar at the Institute of Oriental Studies in Moscow.

YURI V. GANKOVSKY is Professor in the Near and Middle East Department of the Institute of Oriental Studies, USSR Academy of Sciences, Moscow. He is the author of several books and numerous articles on Pakistan and Afghanistan.

GRAHAM E. FULLER is a Senior Political Scientist at RAND Corporation. He is the former vice chairman of the National Intelligence Council at the CIA, where he was responsible for long-range forecasting. He is author of *Democracy Trap: Perils of the Post-Cold War World*.

TADEUSZ SWIETOCHOWSKI is Professor of History at Monmouth College, New Jersey, and Adjunct Professor at Columbia University's Institute of Slavic Studies.

MICHAEL H. GLANTZ is the director of the National Center for Atmospheric Research in Boulder, Colorado.

ALVIN Z. RUBINSTEIN is Professor of Political Science and Senior Fellow of the Foreign Policy Research Institute, University of Pennsylvania. An author of several books, Rubinstein received several fellowships from the Ford Foundation, the Rockefeller Foundation, and the John Simon Guggenheim Memorial Foundation.

IGOR ZONN is associated with Soyuzvodproyect, Moscow, Russian Federation.

MAVLON MAKHAMOV, a Tajik scholar specializing in Central Asia, is Senior Research Associate at the Institute of Oriental Studies, Moscow.

MURIEL ATKIN is an Associate Professor in the Department of History at George Washington University. She is the author of *Russia and Iran, 1780-1828*, and *The Subtlest Battle: Islam in Soviet Tajikistan*, as well as numerous articles on Islam in the Soviet Union.

JAMES CRITCHLOW, a specialist on Central Asia, is associated with Harvard University's Russian Research Center, Cambridge, Massachusetts.

OLES M. SMOLANSKY is Professor of International Relations, specializing in Russian foreign policy, at Lehigh University, Bethlehem, Pennsylvania.

CAROL R. SAIVETZ is associated with Harvard University's Russian Research Center, Cambridge, Massachusetts.

I·N·D·E·X